IN THEIR PLACE: WHITE AMERICA
DEFINES HER MINORITIES, 1850–1950

"The Bootleggers" *The Independent* March 14, 1925

In Their Place: White America Defines Her Minorities, 1850-1950

Lewis H. Carlson
Associate Professor of History
Western Michigan University

George A. Colburn
Instructor, American Thought and Language
Michigan State University

Introduction by **Senator George McGovern**

John Wiley & Sons, Inc. New York · London · Sydney · Toronto

For today's youth who would understand the problems
of their America and to their parents and grandparents who
never knew such problems existed.

Introduction

We occasionally look back several decades in American history and lament the passing of "the good old days." Life was more tranquil, our values seemed safe, and we were spared the violent upheaval which may result today from the unrestrained presentation of the demands of various groups in our society.

But if we take a closer look at "the good old days," we find that tranquility resulted from a state of affairs in which every man and woman "knew his place." In the case of the white majority, this meant a place of unchallenged dominance. To other groups, it meant a subordinate and submissive place where they were supposed to give thanks simply for the opportunity of living in the United States.

It did not matter that life for these groups failed consistently to live up to the promise of the Founding Fathers. Somehow it was to be understood that the offer of America was intended to be interpreted differently depending on your race, your religion, or the color of your skin.

Now we have sacrificed this tranquility and have seen national values subjected to unrelenting challenge. No longer does any man or woman accept to be put "in his place." More and more the members of minority groups have grown restless with that classification and have demanded to be accepted for what they are—whatever that may be.

In the struggle to vindicate not only their rights but their own personality and character, they have occasionally been forced to break the mold into which American society has placed them. The shock has not been pleasant and it has often been misinterpreted. Yet we should be proud that this struggle is taking place. It may make this period the most enlightened period that we have yet seen in our history.

The struggle to achieve a true equality is an effort to realize the ideals of the Declaration of Independence and the Constitution. We have not yet succeeded in the great experiment that we began almost 200 years ago. And we shall not succeed unless we can eradicate from our consciousness the kind of racism documented in this book. It should be clear that it is far from certain that we will succeed, although we can gain encouragement from the progress we have, in fact, made toward a society unlike any other in the world.

We can draw strength from the passionate efforts of Indians, blacks, and Mexican-Americans to assert their own identities. Asian-Americans and other groups are beginning to experience the same fever for freedom. And many groups who had striven in the past for the ideal of the "melting pot" are now rediscovering themselves.

These groups provide not only ferment to our country; they provide the very life blood of variety of experience and culture which can make our mass democracy succeed. We should not seek to stifle the efforts of these groups. Instead we should nourish them.

This book shows us where we have been. By doing so, it helps show us where we must go. The greatness of the American nation is its ability to grow. If we fail to understand the errors of the past as well as the successes, we risk losing that ability and, with it, our greatness.

Senator George McGovern

Preface

This book is a historical perspective on white racism that examines the roots of current racial views in America. However, it is neither a definition nor a summary of contemporary racism in American society, and it is not designed to serve the ethnic needs of America's various minority groups. Instead, it attempts to document the pervasiveness of white racism in the United States from the post-Reconstruction era to the years immediately following World War II. Therefore, this anthology is directed to white America, because until whites understand why this country put its minorities "in their place," there will be no escape from that "place" by those still outside society's mainstream.

In recent years, a great many books have been written on American minorities in an attempt to recover and correct their lost or distorted past. The reasons for this outpouring, however, have been infrequently explored. Underlying these reasons is the fact that the minorities themselves almost always have been viewed as the problem; indeed, social reformers continually have tried to solve the "Negro problem" or the "Indian problem" or the "Mexican problem." Thus, well-meaning whites, living within society's mainstream, never mounted a serious attack on white racism itself. The oppressing majority never has endured a searching examination of the white problem.

The term "white racism" only recently has been added to the basic American vocabulary. Previously, Americans had admitted that "prejudice" and "discrimination" existed, but these terms generally implied shortcomings on the part of individuals. But times have changed. Those involved in the post-World War II civil rights movement, urban disorders, confrontation politics, and the young people's revolt speak of a national responsibility from which no white American escapes. Our examination of the century prior to these events of the past few years leads us to the same conclusion. It is not individuals alone, nor a specific region, that bears responsibility for the treatment of America's minorities; our entire society must shoulder the blame.

We did not have to search far to find convincing evidence of racism in the most influential sectors of mainstream American society during the

1850-to-1950 period. The sources utilized here illustrate this fact very well. We have included addresses by American Presidents, speeches by Congressmen and Senators, decisions by the U.S. Supreme Court, and articles in prestigious scholarly journals, popular fiction, mass-circulation magazines, and major newspapers. Therefore, this book focuses on popular and scholarly ideas that make possible the continued flourishing of mainstream and institutional racism. In our treatment of racism we have ignored society's extremist fringe, where strong racist attitudes normally are expected.

From the end of Reconstruction until sometime after World War II, popular and scholarly conclusions about the inferiority of ethnic minorities nicely merged, producing an overwhelming climate of opinion that greatly influenced the average American. To illustrate this, only the most widely read publications and books (both popular and scholarly), the leading public officials, and the outstanding scientists are quoted in our collection. In selecting each document, we attempted to determine the prestige or popular following of the author or publication.

Finally, we must admit that the selections in this book are only a start in resurrecting a deplorable aspect of America's past that has been obscured by inspirational stories of the melting pot and liberty under a democratic government. It is not pleasant or satisfying to find that our Presidents, Supreme Court Justices, leading scholars, respected scientists, and literary luminaries actually contributed to the "white problem" with their racist thoughts and actions. We feel that this unfortunate chapter in American history has been hidden from view too long. Removal of this veil is painful because, underneath, we find overt racism practiced by our leaders and generations of American citizens accepting this racism. But not only America's minorities demand removal of the veil; so do increasing numbers of white youths in America's mainstream.

As teachers at two large public universities we know that these young people are greatly disturbed by the racism they see about them. Yet, we have seen that only when they examine the source material itself are they ready to accept the historical fact that racism has been rampant in all sectors of American society for the past century and that it was directed at all nonwhite or otherwise "foreign" people within the society. Hopefully, this book of historical documents will create a greater understanding of the dimensions of our present-day racial problems.

As awareness grows, our past never again can be the serene success story our historians often have made it. Yet, perhaps the past still will serve a positive purpose in the nation's history by making Americans aware of the roots of a social problem that we only recently have begun to acknowledge.

Many people inspired and helped this study. We specifically thank

Steve Bensko, Gary Ciadella, Barbara Colburn, Neal Colburn, Opal Ellis, Dorothy Gamel, Becky Greenman, Wendie Karpinski, Tim Peters, Michael Phelan, Mark Roberts, Janet Scieszka, Myrna Yabs, the library staffs at our respective schools, and our students, whose research brought much of this information to light.

Lewis H. Carlson
George A. Colburn

Table of Contents

VII THE ANGLO-SAXON AND THE NEW IMMIGRANT

I
NATIVE AMERICANS

I suppose I should be ashamed to say that I take the Western view of the Indian. I don't go so far as to think that the only good Indians are the dead Indians, but I believe nine out of every ten are, and I shouldn't inquire too closely into the case of the tenth. The most vicious cowboy has more moral principle than the average Indian.

Theodore Roosevelt, 1889

INTRODUCTION

"It is the fate of the American Indians that they exist in the national consciousness mainly as figures in a myth of the American past," claims Professor John R. Howard. The question is, of course, how did this myth develop? The evidence shows that not only are the frontiersmen and early governmental officials to blame for our distorted image of the Indian, but that historians, scientists, novelists, and journalists must also share in the responsibility; and their views reached a far greater audience.

For most Americans, Indians served to fulfill a historical function: they provided the challenge that whites successfully overcame in their march across the continent. Thus, in the words of Professor Daniel Boorstin, the Indian was considered little more than "sand in the smoothly oiled gear of American progress."

As early as the mid-1600's, the pattern of America's treatment of the Indian was being established by English colonists. Indians were either forced off coveted land or placed on reservations. When the reservation land was later desired, treaties were ignored and threats or force were used to convince the Indians to move on. By the time of the American Revolution, white attitudes toward Indians had been well formed. The Constitution of the United States ignored the Indians other than to classify the tribes as autonomous foreign nations. Few of the nation's leaders believed that the Indians had a right or a title to the land they had in-

1

habited for so many centuries. It was felt that title to the land could only belong to those who cultivated it. In effect, it was the beginning of a constant and unwavering policy that sought to transform the Indian from hunter to farmer. Nevertheless, even if the Indians understood and wanted to comply, they could not. The Northwest Ordinance of 1787, which stated that "the utmost good faith shall always be observed toward the Indians, their lands and property shall never be taken from them without their consent," was typical of the promises made but not kept.

In 1825, this pledge was revoked when the Federal Government decided that Indian land was far too valuable to leave under Indian control. Thus, a policy of forcing the movement of all Indians to new reservations across the Mississippi River was begun. The general belief at the time was that the Plains of the West were unsuitable for human life; a "final solution" had apparently been reached. The new policy even applied to 17,000 Cherokees of Georgia who had decided years before to adopt the ways of their white conquerors. They farmed their land, sent their children to school, edited a newspaper, and elected officials as called for in a written constitution. Any hope the Cherokees or any tribe had of remaining on their land was dashed in 1830 when Congress passed the Indian Removal Act, authorizing the President to resettle any Eastern tribe regardless of existing treaties.

It was not long before the Indian realized that his new home was also in jeopardy. The Mexican War and the discovery of gold in California promoted interest in the lands beyond the Mississippi. One quick result was that California Indians lost most of their land, which had been guaranteed under treaties made with the Bureau of Indian Affairs in 1851.

Within a decade, the Indians were being referred to as the "vanishing race." They were disappearing for many reasons: killing of Indians was never considered a crime, the barren land often could not support a family, and disease and the lack of proper medical care devastated some tribes. The usual rationalization for the declining numbers was that the Indian could not adjust to civilization.

As white settlers moved relentlessly westward, the Indians were forced onto more barren and confining reservations. Their alternatives were few: they could either accept their treatment peacefully, or fight the settlers and the U. S. Army. As the second half of the nineteenth century progressed, more and more Indians chose to fight. The majority of whites denounced these Indians as incorrigible savages, and the wars served to reinforce their prevailing notions of superiority. Inflamed by tales of massacres in the popular press, the public encouraged the conquering of the West through the destruction of its native inhabitants.

By the end of the century, the virulent hostility of the white man toward the Indian was diminishing. Racism had not disappeared; Americans no longer considered the Indians a threat or their land to be valuable. Many Americans, therefore, felt it was time to take up the "white man's burden" and care for this vanquished foe.

As early as 1887, Congress had acted to provide the Indians with the apparent means to become "worthy" residents of the nation. With the passage of the Dawes Severalty Act in 1887, the Indian tribes were dissolved as legal entities, and tribal land was divided up among individual members. The liberal reformer who still believed in the civilizing magic of private property and the Indian-hater who wanted the surplus Indian land both favored the measure. In the end, however, it was the whites, not the Indians, who profited. As Indian authority William T. Hagan pointed out, "Severalty may not have civilized the Indian, but it definitely corrupted most of the white men who had any contact with it."

Attempts to plug the loopholes in the Dawes Act produced few discernible changes in the end result; Indian life remained much the same. It was not until the New Deal era that the Government's basic attitude toward the Indian changed. Between the Dawes Act of 1887 and the Wheeler-Howard Act of 1934, approximately 90 of the 138 million acres held by Indians passed into white ownership. By the mid-1920's, when the government finally granted citizenship to Indians, the Indians' death rate was exceeding their birth rate. Moreover, it was clear that they were not being assimilated. Under the leadership of John Collier, Commissioner of Indian Affairs, the New Deal government repudiated the severalty policy and called for the allotted lands to be consolidated for tribal use. With significant Federal aid, the death rate gradually declined, but even in the 1960's the life expectancy of an Indian was only 47 years.

Government policy toward the Indian, including the ill-conceived "termination" of Federal control over Indians that was suggested during the 1950's, could not have been carried out without the acquiescence of the American people, who either ignored the Native Americans or were conditioned to dismiss them as an inferior people. In the mid-nineteenth century the American Government had virtually practiced genocide, but there was barely a murmur of protest from the public. Sharing the blame must be the schools, the newspapers, the publishing companies, and the missionaries; for, in the end, it was they who first prepared and dispensed the information received by the American people about the continent's original inhabitants. These impressions, more than anything else, enabled the government utterly to disregard basic human rights in America's brutalizing march to the Pacific Coast. As Grover Cleveland facetiously noted in 1887, "The hunger and thirst of the white man for the Indian's land is almost equal to his hunger and thirst after righteousness." The white man, however, was conditioned to believe that he had a right to that land.

1
The Government and the Native American

Today, the Indians are America's most impoverished minority. The reason for their tragic circumstances is directly traceable to the policies of the Federal Government beginning in the early nineteenth century. The brutal physical elimination of the Indian came to an end with the close of the century, and a more patronizing attitude toward him was adopted. Much of the sympathy for the Indian's plight was inspired by the publication in 1881 of Helen Hunt Jackson's *A Century of Dishonor* and a few years later by her more widely read novel, *Ramona*.

When Indian reservations were discovered to rest on valuable lands, Congress still did not hesitate to appropriate them, but the possibility of such land being in Indian possession after 1880 appeared remote; thus the government could afford to pay heed to the reformers and humanitarians. As it developed, this new attitude resulted in new programs with the well-being of the Indians in mind, but the Indians themselves were rarely consulted, and once a program was instituted, the Indians were forced to comply. In spite of the well-meaning reforms of the period between 1890 and 1930, the Indians lost almost two thirds of their land. This statistic—along with the abject poverty and declining population—stood in testimony of the bankruptcy of the Government's Indian policies. The Indians were never considered in terms of their own culture. Reformers who sought to end the brutal practices of the past were, nevertheless, convinced that the Indian could be saved only if he adopted the white man's style of living. The policy of "termination," introduced during the Eisenhower years and still being debated, is the logical conclusion of such policies. By closing the Bureau of Indian Affairs and ending Governmental programs, the Indians would once and for all be forced to join the system that for over three centuries has rejected them.

A. INDIANS FORCED OFF THEIR LAND BY "THE ADVANCING TIDE OF CIVILIZATION," 1880

When Congress discovered in 1880 that the Ute reservation in Colorado was the site of a rich mineral field, it moved quickly to buy the land "at a very small price" but "a very good price for the Indians." It was to be an oft-repeated tactic. The alternative, said Representative Dudley C. Haskell of Kansas, was the extermination of the Indians by those in the "on-rushing tide of civilization." In the same congressional debate, Colorado's James B. Belford endorsed the efforts to oust "an idle and thriftless race of savages" from the "treasure vaults of the nation."[1]

REP. HASKELL. Mr. Speaker, if there is no other member of the House who desires to speak against this bill, I wish to present to the House as briefly as I am able the causes that have led to this Ute agreement, and the main features of the bill.

It will not be necesary for me to enter into any description of the Ute outbreak, and the conflict between the Indians and the troops out of which this agreement grew. It is a well-known fact that our policy of maintaining large Indian reservations immediately in front of the advancing tide of civilization has been found to be a poor policy, and one which we cannot sustain. It has been found thus with this Ute reservation. A large territory embracing over twelve millions of acres of the richest mineral lands of Colorado has been allowed to be occupied exclusively by less than four thousand Utes. Within twenty miles of the eastern boundary of this reservation is a city of forty thousand inhabitants. Looking longingly across the borderline of that reservation are hundreds and thousands of venturous miners who desire to secure possession of the immense mineral wealth that it contains, and this is what led to the conflict originally between the United States and the Indians. The Interior Department became well advised that it would be utterly impossible to prevent a conflict between the Indians and the miners desiring to enter upon these lands for the sake of prospecting for minerals, and in view of the fact that an outbreak had occurred they sent for and brought on here the head chiefs of the Ute Nation, in order that a peaceful conference could be

[1]*Congressional Record*, 46th Cong., 2nd Sess., June 7, 1880, pp. 4260–4262.

had which might avert the impending danger of an Indian war and bring about a peaceful settlement of the difficulty. . . .

The bill is made up essentially of two parts: one an agreement between the Indians and the Government to sell their lands, and the other the simple legislation necessary to carry into effect the terms of that agreement. The amount of money appropriated in the bill is $422,000. That is to provide for the payment of the first annuity, to provide for the expenses of the commission, to provide for the survey of the lands, to provide for the payment to the Indians of the improvements they have made, and to provide further that schools shall be established and school-houses built, and also to furnish more or less of subsistence, as may be needed. . . .

There are, Mr. Speaker, before this Congress of the United States, in my judgment, but two roads open. One is to accept this bill . . . or we are to abandon this bill and undertake to maintain in that rich mineral district of Colorado a great Indian reservation of twelve millions of acres, against the on-rushing tide of civilization and of adventurous miners. . . . There is no other course open. Already the miners are clustered on the borders of the reservation ready to enter. It is a mountainous country that would require three times the force the United States has at its disposal to protect and defend. It is a mountainous country, in which if we went to war there would be simply a reproduction on a larger scale of those terrible scenes in the lava-beds when we captured the Modocs. In other words, it means the absolute extermination of the Indian at a great cost of blood and treasure to the United States, or it means the peaceable solution of the question by which the Government buy their land, pay them year by year a fair stipend, care for their little ones in school, protect them under the laws of the land, put whites and Indians side by side, under the same law, and teach the red men the arts of civilization by actual contact with the civilized man himself. . . .

MR. BELFORD. If you pass this bill you at once open up a tract of country almost as large as New England; a country abounding in great material wealth, and fitted to become the home of a million active and enterprising citizens. You give the sanction of the Government to the act of the miner in taking up a claim; you open a way by which he can acquire title to land; and you apprise the Indian that he can no longer stand as a breakwater against the constantly swelling tide of civilization. The passage of this bill is the reclamation of eleven millions of acres of land from the domain of barbarism. It enlarges the possible achievements of the white man by enlarging the field in which he can labor. It settles for all time the doctrine which has received illustrations in the past that an idle and thriftless race of savages cannot be permitted to guard the treasure vaults of the nation which hold our gold and silver, but that they shall always be open, to the end that the prospector and miner may enter in and by enriching himself enrich the nation and bless the world by the results of his toil.

B. THE DAWES SEVERALTY ACT: SAVING THE UNCIVILIZED, 1887

For a number of reasons, Federal officials had been attracted by the concept of "severalty" long before it was implemented in 1887. For one thing, scholars seemed to agree that private property is the basis of civilization. For another, turning the land over to individuals would break up the reservations and reduce the power of the chiefs. Critics of the policy were few; on this issue, both the sympathetic reformers and the most rabid Indian-hater could agree, with the latter usually being interested in the sale of the "surplus" Indian land. Senator Henry L. Dawes of Massachusetts, a Yale graduate, lawyer, and sponsor of the severalty act, explained in the following article the need to transform the "lawless savage" to a "civilized" American.[1]

Have We Failed the Indian?

The present Indian policy of the government is of comparatively recent date. It is hardly yet twenty-five years since the first step was taken. The beginning was small and tentative, but the policy has steadily grown in the public confidence and in the enlargement of effort, until, judged by results, it now stands justified. Before its adoption the attitude of the government toward the different tribes was in general that of kind, patient care. There were exceptional cases in this treatment—instances of hardship, injustice, and wrong—not to be defended; traceable, however, almost always to unfit stewards and unfaithful public servants, and not to the deliberate act of the government itself. The prevailing idea was that of guardianship of an uncivilized race among us, incapable of self-support or self-restraint, over which public safety as well as the dictates of humanity required the exercise of a constant, restraining care, until it should fade out of existence in the irresistible march of civilization. It very soon became apparent that under this treatment the race did not diminish, but, by reason of protection from the slaughter of one another in wars among themselves and from diseases inseparable from savage life, it increased in number. . . .

What was to become of the untutored, defenseless Indian, when he

[1]Henry L. Dawes, "Have We Failed the Indian?" *Atlantic Monthly*, LXXXIV, August 1899, pp. 280–284.

found himself thus pushed out of the life and home of the reservation, and cut off from the hunting and fishing which furnished the only and scanty supply of his daily wants? It was plain that if he were left alone he must of necessity become a tramp and beggar with all the evil passions of a savage, a homeless and lawless poacher upon civilization, and a terror to the peaceful citizen.

It was this condition which forced on the nation its present Indian policy. It was born of sheer necessity. Inasmuch as the Indian refused to fade out, but multiplied under the sheltering care of reservation life, and the reservation itself was slipping away from him, there was but one alternative: either he must be endured as a lawless savage, a constant menace to civilized life, or he must be fitted to become a part of that life and be absorbed into it. To permit him to be a roving savage was unendurable, and therefore the task of fitting him for civilized life was undertaken.

This, then, is the present Indian policy of the nation—to fit the Indian for civilization and to absorb him into it. It is a national work. It is less than twenty-five years since the government turned from the policy of keeping him on reservations, as quiet as possible, out of the way of civilization, waiting, with no excess of patience, for the race to fade out of existence and to cease from troubling. . . .

This recognition of the home and family as a force in Indian civilization became a part of the present policy of dealing with the race only twelve years ago. . . .

We are at peace with the Indian all along the border, and the line between the Indian and the white settlements is fast fading out. The pioneer goes forth to trade and barter with the red man as safely as he does with his white neighbor, and returns at night to his defenseless home with less apprehension of peril to those within than when scouts and sentinels mounted guard over it. This change has come quite as much from causes at work among the Indians themselves as from the influence of those who have the shaping of our policy. During these twelve years, families and adult Indians without families, in all more than 30,000, have found homes of their own on Indian lands, and are maintaining themselves by farming, stock-raising, and other pursuits to which peace is essential, and have themselves become peacemakers. . . .

But let it ever be kept in mind that, after all, the civilization of the Indian cannot be enacted. The function of the law in this work is little more than the clearing of the way, the removal of disabilities, the creation of opportunities, and the shelter and protection of agencies elsewhere vitalized. The one vitalizing force, without which all else will prove vain, is the Indian's own willingness to adopt civilized life. Until this is quickened into activity, everything else will wilt and perish like a plant without root. Every effort must recognize this cardinal principle. Much can be done to kindle in him a desire for a better life and to nurse its beginnings, building it up to an aggressive force; but until this exists, any attempt, through legislation or in any other way, to impose civilization upon the race will prove a failure. When that desire and hope for a better life shall begin to prevail over savage instincts, if the law shall then have made the way clear and the path plain, and, cooperating with outside efforts to strengthen and mature the new impulses, shall have made sure the rewards of civilization and the immunities of citizenship, it will have fulfilled its purpose. This is the endeavor of the Indian policy of today. Opening up so wide a field, and imposing an obligation for increased effort on every friend of the race, whatever may be his theory, it may calmly await the first stone from any of those who can claim Scriptural authority for casting it.

C.   THE SUPREME COURT DECIDES THAT RESERVATION INDIANS HAVE NO PROPERTY RIGHTS, 1902

On June 6, 1901, Lone Wolf, on behalf of members of the Kiowa, Comanche, and Apache tribes of Fort Hall (Idaho) Indian Reservation sued Ethan Allen Hitchcock, the Secretary of the Interior. Lone Wolf claimed than an 1892 treaty with the government fraudulently deprived the Indians of two million acres of reservation land granted them in 1867. The controversy, which had begun soon after the 1892 treaty signing, prompted Congress in 1900 to pass legislation designed to give legal effect to the treaty, even though the Secretary of the Interior confirmed Indian charges that less than the minimum number of adult males had signed the treaty. In the following selection, Justice Edward D. White explains why the U. S. Supreme Court believed that Congress was justified in ignoring its treaty obligations when dealing with Indians.[1]

The appellants base their right to relief on the proposition that by the effect of the article just quoted the confederated tribes of Kiowas, Comanches, and Apaches were vested with an interest in the lands held in common within the reservation, which interest could not be devested by Congress in any other mode than that specified in the said twelfth article, and that as a result of the said stipulation the interest of the Indians in

[1]"Lone Wolf v. Hitchcock," *U.S. Supreme Court Reports*, 187 U.S. 563, 1902, pp. 299–307.

the common lands fell within the protection of the 5th Amendment to the Constitution of the United States, and such interest—indirectly at least—came under the control of the judicial branch of the government. We are unable to yield our assent to this view.

The contention in effect ignores the status of the contracting Indians and the relation of dependency they bore and continue to bear towards the government of the United States. To uphold the claim would be to adjudge that the indirect operation of the treaty was to materially limit and qualify the controlling authority of Congress in respect to the care and protection of the Indians, and to deprive Congress, in a possible emergency, when the necessity might be urgent for a partition and disposal of the tribal lands, of all power to act, if the assent of the Indians could not be obtained. . . .

The power exists to abrogate the provisions of an Indian treaty, though presumably such power will be exercised only when circumstances arise which will not only justify the government in disregarding the stipulations of the treaty, but may demand, in the interest of the country and the Indians themselves, that it should do so. When, therefore, treaties were entered into between the United States and a tribe of Indians it was never doubted that the *power* to abrogate existed in Congress, and that in a contingency such power might be availed of from considerations of governmental policy, particularly if consistent with perfect good faith towards the Indians. . . .

The act of June 6, 1900, which is complained of in the bill, was enacted at a time when the tribal relations between the confederated tribes of Kiowas, Comanches, and Apaches still existed, and that statute and the statutes supplementary thereto dealt with the disposition of tribal property, and purported to give an adequate consideration for the surplus lands not allotted among the Indians or reserved for their benefit. Indeed, the controversy which this case presents is concluded by the decision in *Cherokee Nation v. Hitchcock* . . . decided at this term, where it was held that full administrative power was possessed by Congress over Indian tribal property. In effect, the action of Congress now complained of was but an exercise of such power, a mere change in the form of investment of Indian tribal property, the property of those who, as we have held, were in substantial effect the wards of the government. We must presume that Congress acted in perfect good faith in the dealings with the Indians of which complaint is made, and that the legislative branch of the government exercised its best judgment in the premises. In any event, as Congress possessed full power in the matter, the judiciary cannot question or inquire into the motives which prompted the enactment of this legislation. If injury was occasioned, which we do not wish to be understood as implying, by the use made by Congress of its power, relief must be sought by an appeal to that body for redress, and not to the courts. The legislation in question was constitutional, and the demurrer to the bill was therefore rightly sustained.

D.   INDIAN COMMISSION SEEKS TO END INDIANS' "PECULIAR RACE TRAITS," 1905

Although few in this country believed that the Native American could be assimilated, the Bureau of Indian Affairs always claimed that it was striving toward that goal. The following 1905 Report of the Board of Indian Commissioners is especially revealing because it typifies the prevailing attitude of the government for the half-century preceding the New Deal.[1]

We believe that the strength of our American life is due in no small part to the fact that various and different race elements have entered into the making of the American the citizen of the United States in the twentieth century. No one racial stock is exclusively in control in our land. The typical modern American is a fine "composite," with race elements drawn from many sources. We do not believe that the Government of the United States in dealing with its Indian wards would act righteously or wisely if it were to attempt to crush out from those who are of Indian descent all the racial traits which differentiate the North American Indian from the other race stocks of the world. Certain conceptions of physical courage, a certain heroic stoicism in enduring physical pain, an inherited tendency to respect one's self, even if that tendency shows itself at times in unwarrantable conceit, are race traits which have value, if the people who have them become civilized and subject themselves to the laws of social morality and to the obligation of industrial efficiency, which are essential if any race stock or any group of families is to hold its own in the modern civilized world.

But the facts seem to us to be that good results are to be hoped for not by keeping the North American Indians peculiar in dress or in customs. We think that the wisest friends of the Indian recognize with great delight and value highly the art impulse in certain Indian tribes, which has shown itself in Indian music, in Indian art forms—such as the birch-

[1]*Annual Reports of the Department of the Interior*, House Documents, Vol. 20, 59th Cong., 1st Sess., June 30, 1905, pp. 17–18.

bark canoe, in Indian basketry, and more rarely in Indian pottery. But we firmly believe that the way to preserve the best of what is distinctively characteristic in the North American Indians is to civilize and educate them, that they may be fit for the life of the twentieth century under our American system of self-government. Because we value the elements for good which may come into our American life through the stock of North American Indians, we wish to see children of Indian descent educated in the industrial and practical arts and trained to habits of personal cleanliness, social purity, and industrious family life. We do not believe that it is right to keep the Indians out of civilization in order that certain picturesque aspects of savagery and barbarism may continue to be within reach of the traveler and the curious, or even of the scientific observer. In the objectionable "Indian dances" which are breaking out afresh at many points we see not a desirable maintenance of racial traits, but a distinct reversion toward barbarism and superstition. We believe that while the effort should never be made to "make a white man out of an Indian," in the sense of seeking to do violence to respect to parents or a proper or intelligent regard for what is fine in the traits and the history of one's ancestors, it is still most desirable that all the Indians on our territory should come as speedily as possible to the white man's habits of home-making, industry, cleanliness, social purity, and family integrity.

Precisely as all intelligent American patriots have seen danger to our national life in the attempt, wherever it has been made, to perpetuate in the United States large groups of foreign-born immigrants who try to keep their children from learning English and seek to perpetuate upon our territory (at the cost of true Americanism for their children) what was characteristic in the life of their own people on other continents and in past generations, precisely as in such cases we feel that the hope of our American system lies in the public schools and such educational institutions as shall maintain standards of public living that inevitably bring the children of foreign-born immigrants into the great body of English-speaking, home-loving, industrious, and pure-minded Americans —precisely so does it seem to us that all the efforts of the Government, and far more of distinctive missionary effort on the part of the Christian people of this country than has ever yet been used with this end in view, should be steadily employed in the effort to make out of the Indian children of this country intelligent, English-speaking, industrious, law-abiding Americans. We believe that the breaking up of tribal funds as rapidly as practicable will help toward this end. Even if many of the Indians do for a time misuse money while they are learning how to use it properly, even if some of them squander it utterly, we believe that there is hope for the Indians in the future only as by education, faith in work, and obedience to Christian principles of morality and clean living, their children shall come to have the social standards and the social habits of our better American life throughout the land.

Our task is to hasten the slow work of race evolution. Inevitably, but often grimly and harshly by the outworking of natural forces, the national life of the stronger and more highly civilized race stock dominates in time the life of the less civilized, when races like the Anglo-Saxon and the Indian are brought into close contact. In our work for the Indians we want to discern clearly those influences and habits of life which are of the greatest advantage in leading races upward into Christian civilization; and these influences and habits we wish to make as strongly influential as possible, and as speedily as possible influential upon the life of all these American tribes. It is not unreasonable to hope that through governmental agencies and through the altruistic missionary spirit of one of the foremost Christian races and governments of the world much can be done to hasten that process of civilization which natural law, left to itself, works out too slowly and at too great a loss to the less-favored race. We want to make the conditions for our less-favored brethren of the red race so favorable that the social forces which have developed themselves slowly and at great expense of time and life in our American race and our American system of government shall be made to help in the uplifting of the Indians and to shorten that interval of time which of necessity must elapse between savagery and Christian civilization.

E.   PRESIDENT ROOSEVELT ADVISES INDIANS
TO WORK AND SAVE, 1905

When dealing with Indians, Theodore Roosevelt usually reflected the Western viewpoint. During his presidency, Roosevelt's "cowboy philosophy" was somewhat toned down, but there were no basic changes from his earlier attitude about the "weaker race," which he had expressed in his four-volume The Winning of the West. *In the following letter to Chief No Shirt, Roosevelt handled the complainant like a patient father would a "headstrong child" who does not know right from wrong. The "strong friend of the red people" in the Indian Office referred to by Roosevelt in the letter was Francis E. Leupp, a New York City journalist, who employed a paternalistic approach toward the Indians. Leupp's boss, however, Interior Secretary Ethan Allen Hitchcock, was no friend of the Indians. Hitchcock was a McKinley-appointed businessman who had served as president of several mining and railway companies before coming to Washington as Secretary of the Interior in 1897.*[1]

Washington, May 18, 1905

It is true, as you say, that the earth is occupied by the white people and the red people; that, if the red people would prosper, they must follow the mode of life which has made the white people so strong; and that it is only right that the white people should show the red people what to do and how to live right. It is for that reason, because I wish to be as much a father to the red people as to the white, that I have placed in charge of the Indian Office a Commissioner in whom I have confidence, knowing him to be a strong friend of the red people and anxious to help them in every way.

But I am sorry to learn that when you sent the Commissioner word that you wished to come to Washington and he sent you a message not to come then but to send your complaints in writing, you followed your own will, like a headstrong child, instead of doing what the Commissioner advised. That is not the way to get along nicely in your new mode of life, and is not a good example to set to your people. You see, also, what the result was: you traveled three thousand miles across the country, at considerable expense, to see me, and then had to go back without seeing me. If you had done what the Commissioner wished you to, you would have avoided all this. I hope that you and your people will lay this lesson to heart for the future. . . .

This brings me to another point in your letter, where you give your reason for wishing your leases to be so arranged that you will have two payments every year instead of one. You say: "I have to have money to make my living . . . and of course I want my money whenever I need it." I suppose you realize that you will get only the same amount of money, whether you get it in one payment or in two. In other words, if a white lessee is going to give you $100 a year for the use of a piece of land, he will either give you the whole $100 in one payment or only $50 if he makes two payments. Now, if your leesee pays you $100 all at one time, it is not necessary that you should spend it all at one time; you can just as well spend $50 of it and keep the other $50 for six months, if that is what you wish to do. If he pays you only $50 at one time, the other $50 remains in his pocket until the next payment; surely, it ought to be just as safe in your pocket as in his. Besides, the lesson in saving would be of great value to you. No matter how much the Government or the white people do for the Indian, he will always remain poor if he foolishly spends his money just as fast as he gets it. The white man grows rich by learning to spend only part of his money and lay the other part aside till it is absolutely necessary to use it. Then he finds that he can be just as happy and do without a great many things which formerly he supposed he absolutely must have. . . .

Indians . . . who wish to lease their own lands only for the purpose of shirking work, will not be permitted to do so. I wish you to tell this to your people very plainly, and say to them that the President intends to support the Commissioner in every way in insisting that able-bodied Indians shall earn their own living, just as able-bodied white men do. . . .

Now, my friend, I hope that you will lay what I have said to heart. Try to set your people a good example of upright and industrious life, patience under difficulties, and respect for the authority of the officers I have appointed to care for your affairs. If you try as hard to help them as you do to find something in their conduct to censure, you will be surprised to discover how much real satisfaction life holds in store for you.

F. THE AMERICAN INDIAN: "A CONTINENT LOST—A CIVILIZATION WON," 1937

J. P. Kinney, who labored for 25 years in the Bureau of Indian Affairs, in 1937 published a justification of the government's Indian policy entitled, A Continent Lost, a Civilization Won. *Kinney felt himself to be enlightened on matters concerning the Indian, but he placed much of the blame for the Bureau's failures on the Indians who lacked "certain qualities conducive to intellectual, moral and economic progress." Thus, concluded Kinney, "The future of the race as a whole is in the hands of the individuals of the race." The following selection is from the book's preface.[1]*

Those who are accustomed to condemn in unmeasured terms the conduct of the whites toward the Indians have failed to view the relationship between the races from a sufficiently detached viewpoint. If one considers only individual instances of misfortune and injustice in any society his sympathy may lead him to a distorted view of the wrongs

[1]Reprinted by permission of the publisher from J. P. Kinney, *A Continent Lost, A Civilization Won,* Johns Hopkins Press, Baltimore, 1937, pp. x–xv.

suffered by individuals; and the same is true as to groups of individuals. . . .

Passionate feelings must be accompanied by, or followed by, sustained and well-directed effort toward alleviation of the unfavorable conditions. In most instances it will be found that one of the difficulties encountered will be the awakening of the unfortunate as to the possibilities of a fuller life; and the zealous advocate of an enriched life for the poverty-stricken and suppressed members of society may experience many a disappointment because of the failure of the objects of his solicitude to react to the stimuli of improved economic and moral conditions. In an attempt to appraise the success attained, or the failure experienced, in efforts to improve the conditions of life among the Indians, either in the past or in the future, one must not overlook the fact that certain qualities conducive to intellectual, moral and economic progress are lacking or strangely dormant in many Indians; and that the best of intentions, carried into execution with zeal and intelligence, frequently produce mediocre results.

Furthermore, students of the Indian problem must not confine their view to the present. The people of the United States have been wrestling with this problem for nearly a century and a half. In that time there have been many changes in the economic and social order, changes that could not have been foreseen even one decade in advance in many instances. Those of previous generations should not be too harshly judged for the adoption of methods and plans that later developments have shown to be unwise or poorly suited for the accomplishment of the results desired. In preparing a schedule of the wrongs that the present generation of Indians have suffered at the hands of the whites, a double-entry system should be used and there should be entered upon the balance-sheet the advantages that such a generation has enjoyed. In listing the wrongs and misfortunes that their ancestors suffered, one should also set down on the opposite side of the sheet the wrongs and the sufferings that such ancestors inflicted upon the whites.

2
Popular Images of the Indian

Until the Red Power movement began to shatter America's illusions, the Native American had been neatly stereotyped through innumerable novels, films, and television scripts. Through these media he might appear as the courageous and noble savage who provided a worthy adversary for the early pioneers, but he also had the barbaric traits that contrasted nicely with the quiet strength and admirable character of the typical Western hero. In real life, the Indian did not exist for most Americans—or, if he did, it was in some kind of human zoo, where he painfully went through the motions of a lost past for the benefit of white onlookers.

The traditional image of the Indian began not long after the first white settlers confronted him. The Puritans were only anticipating future actions when they decided that the Indians could not be saved, and since they were "devils," one was only doing God's bidding by eliminating them. As America moved westward, this basic view was reinforced by returning frontiersmen and missionaries, and soon it was so popular that Eastern writers, who had never left home, could inform their readers on the travails of frontier life. Although such stories appeared early, it was not until the post-Civil War period and the emergence of the so-called "dime novel" that an increasingly literate public could be reached in great numbers.

Favorite tales were those concerning whites who had lived among the savages and who, presumably, could then describe them with accuracy. Also popular were the eye-witness accounts of battles with the Indians, usually written by military men, who convincingly contrasted the brutal cruelty of the Indian with the cool courage of their own troops. Even after the fighting stopped, the Indian did not fare much better in

18

the popular press. He was no longer the savage, albeit sometimes noble, adversary, who could bring out the best in our early settlers; now he became an inferior, downtrodden object who needed the help and leadership of a superior people. However, when the Indian did not always respond favorably to his patrons' attention, a kind of dismay, anger, cynicism, and, finally, silence resulted. Thus, in the popular mind the Indian evolved from a troublesome heathen to a mortal enemy to an unfortunate ward of the state to a nonperson.

A. DESCRIBING THE HORRORS OF INDIAN CAPTIVITY, 1859

Throughout the last half of the nineteenth century, the American public was treated to numerous personal accounts of Indian captivity. These spine-tingling adventures usually thrilled their readers, but they did little to foster understanding between whites and Indians. The stories were filled with vivid descriptions of strange rituals, shocking tortures, and unsavory living habits, all of which helped convince the reader of the Indian's innate barbarism.

One of the more significant books in this genre was Three Years Among the Comanches: the Narrative of Nelson Lee, the Texas Ranger. *First published in 1859, it was reissued by the Western Frontier Library of the University of Oklahoma Press in 1957. The selection that follows is a typical description of an Indian torture ritual.*[1]

Three Years Among the Comanches

There were Aikens, Martin, and Stewart, stripped entirely naked, and bound as follows: Strong, high posts, had been driven in the ground about three feet apart. Standing between them, their arms had been drawn up as far as they could reach, the right hand tied to the stake on the right side and the left hand to the stake opposite. Their feet, likewise, were tied to the posts near the ground. Martin and Stewart were thus strung up side by side. Directly in front of them, and within ten feet, was Aikens, in the same situation. A short time sufficed to divest me of my scanty Indian apparel and place me by the side of the latter, and in like condition. Thus we stood, or rather hung. Aikens and myself facing Stewart and Martin, all awaiting in tormenting suspense to learn what diabolical rite was now to be performed.

[1]From *Three Years Among the Comanches: The Narrative of Nelson Lee, The Texas Ranger,* with an introduction by Walter Prescott Webb. New edition copyright 1957 by the University of Oklahoma Press.

The Big Wolf and a number of his old men stationed themselves near us, when the war chief, at the head of the warriors, of whom there were probably two hundred, moved forward slowly, silently, and in single file. Their pace was peculiar and difficult to describe, half walk, half shuffle, a spasmodic, nervous motion, like the artificial motion of figures in a puppet show. Each carried in one hand his knife or tomahawk, and the other a flint stone, three inches or more in length and fashioned into the shape of a sharp pointed arrow. The head of the procession as it circled a long way round, first approached Stewart and Martin. As it passed them, two of the youngest warriors broke from the line, seized them by the hair, and scalped them, then resumed their places and moved on. This operation consists of cutting off only a portion of the skin which covers the skull, of the dimensions of a dollar, and does not necessarily destroy life, as is very generally supposed; on the contrary, I have seen men, resident on the borders of Texas, who had been scalped and yet were alive and well. In this instance, the wounds inflicted were by no means mortal; nevertheless, blood flowed from them in profusion, running down over the face, and trickling from their long beards.

They passed Aikens and myself without molestation, marching round again in the same order as before. Up to this time there had been entire silence, except a yell from the two young men when in the act of scalping, but now the whole party halted a half-minute, and slapping their hands upon their mouths, united in a general and energetic war whoop. Then in silence the circuitous march was continued. When they reached Stewart and Martin the second time, the sharp flint arrowheads were brought into requisition. Each man, as he passed, with a wild screech, would brandish his tomahawk in their faces an instant, and then draw the sharp point of the stone across their bodies, not cutting deep, but penetrating the flesh just far enough to cause the blood to ooze out in great crimson gouts. By the time the line had passed, our poor suffering companions presented an awful spectacle. Still they left Aikens and myself as yet unharmed; nevertheless, we regarded it as a matter of certainty that very soon we should be subjected to similar tortures. We would have been devoutly thankful at that terrible hour—would have hailed it as a grateful privilege—could we have been permitted to choose our own mode of being put to death. How many times they circled round, halting to sound the war whoop, and going through the same demoniac exercise, I cannot tell. Suffice it to say, they persisted in the hellish work until ever inch of the bodies of the unhappy men was haggled, and hacked and scarified, and covered with clotted blood. It would have been a relief to me, much more to them, could they have only died, but the object of the tormentors was to drain the fountain of their lives by slow degrees.

In the progress of their torture, there occurred an intermission of some quarter of an hour. During this period, some threw themselves on the ground and lighted their pipes, others collected in little groups, all, however, laughing and shouting, and pointing their fingers at the prisoners in derision, as if taunting them as cowards and miscreants. The prisoners bore themselves differently. Stewart uttered not a word, but his sobs and groans were such as only the intensest pain and agony can wring from the human heart. On the contrary, the pitiful cries and prayers of Martin were unceasing. Constantly he was exclaiming—"Oh! God have mercy on me!" "Oh, Father in heaven pity me!" "Oh! Lord Jesus, come and put me out of pain!" and many other expressions of like character.

I hung down my head and closed my eyes to shut out from sight the heart-sickening scene before me, but this poor comfort was not vouchsafed me. They would grasp myself, as well as Aikens, by the hair, drawing our heads back violently, compelling us, however unwillingly, to stare directly at the agonized and writhing sufferers.

At the end of, perhaps, two hours, came the last act of the fearful tragedy. The warriors halted on their last round in the form of a half-circle, when two of them moved out from the center, striking into the war dance, raising the war song, advancing, receding, now moving to the right, now to the left, occupying ten minutes in proceeding as many paces. Finally, they reached the victims, for some time danced before them, as it were, the hideous dance of hell, then drew their hatchets suddenly, and sent the bright blades crashing through their skulls.

B. CUSTER TELLS WHY CIVILIZATION WILL DESTROY THE INDIAN, 1874

As the white man moved across the Mississippi, he drove the Indian further West, or isolated him on remote reservations. Because not all the Indians peacefully submitted to the white man's encroachments, the U. S. Army was obligated to act as "peacemaker" for several decades. Prominent Army officers often became heroes to the public, and their views were solicited on the subject of the Indians. Many of those achieving success on the battlefield later wrote their memoirs, thereby supplying movie-makers of a later day with a vast, albeit one-sided, reservoir of information about life on the Indian frontier. One such military hero was General George A. Custer. Despite a limited career on the Plains, the flamboyant Custer published his recollections in 1874, two years before his demise in the Battle of the Little Big Horn. My Life on the Plains *provides the reader with an interesting example of a military man's thoughts on the Indian and his cause.*[1]

Stripped of the beautiful romance with which we have been so long willing to envelop him, transferred from the inviting pages of the novelist to the localities where we are compelled to meet with him, in his native village, on the war path, and when raiding upon our frontier settlements and lines of travel, the Indian forfeits his claim to the appellation of the "noble red man." We see him as he is, and, so far as all knowledge goes, as he ever has been, a savage in every sense of the word; not worse, perhaps, than his white brother would be similarly born and bred, but one whose cruel and ferocious nature far exceeds that of any wild beast of the desert. That this is true no one who has been brought into intimate contact with the wild tribes will deny. Perhaps there are some who, as members of peace commissions or as wandering agents of some benevolent society, may have visited these tribes or attended with them at councils held for some pacific purpose, and who, by passing through the villages of the Indian while at peace, may imagine their opportunities for judging of the Indian nature all that could be desired. But the Indian, while he can seldom be accused of indulging in a great variety of wardrobe, can be said to have a character capable of adapting itself to almost every occasion. He has one character, perhaps his most serviceable one, which he preserves carefully, and only airs it when making his appeal to the Government or its agents for arms, ammunition, and license to employ them. This character is invariably paraded, and often with telling effect, when the motive is a peaceful one. Prominent chiefs invited to visit Washington invariably don this character, and in their "talks" with the "Great Father" and other less prominent personages they successfully contrive to exhibit but this one phase. Seeing them under these or similar circumstances only, it is not surprising that by many the Indian is looked upon as a simple-minded "son of nature," desiring nothing beyond the privilege of roaming and hunting over the vast unsettled wilds of the West, inheriting and asserting but few native rights, and never trespassing upon the rights of others. This view is equally erroneous with that which regards the Indian as a creature possessing the human form but divested of all other attributes of humanity,

[1]George A. Custer, *My Life on the Plains, or Personal Experiences with Indians,* Sheldon and Co., New York, 1874, pp. 11–12, 17–18.

and whose traits of character, habits, modes of life, disposition and savage customs disqualify him from the exercise of all rights and privileges, even those pertaining to life itself. Taking him as we find him, at peace or at war, at home or abroad, waiving all prejudices, and laying aside all partiality, we will discover in the Indian a subject for thoughtful study and investigation. In him we will find the representative of a race whose origin is, and promises to be, a subject forever wrapped in mystery; a race incapable of being judged by the rules or laws applicable to any other known race of men; one between which and civilization there seems to have existed from time immemorial a determined and unceasing warfare—a hostility so deep-seated and inbred with the Indian character, that in the exceptional instances where the modes and habits of civilization have been reluctantly adopted, it has been at the sacrifice of power and influence as a tribe, and the more serious loss of health, vigor, and courage as individuals. . . .

Nature intended him for a savage state; every instinct, every impulse of his soul inclines him to it. The white race might fall into a barbarous state, and afterwards, subjected to the influence of civilization, be reclaimed and prosper. Not so the Indian. He cannot be himself and be civilized; he fades away and dies. Cultivation such as the white man would give him deprives him of his identity. Education, strange as it may appear, seems to weaken rather than strengthen his intellect. . . .

He can hunt, roam, and camp when and wheresoever he pleases, provided always that in so doing he does not run contrary to the requirements of civilization in its advancing tread. When the soil which he has claimed and hunted over for so long a time is demanded by this to him insatiable monster, there is no appeal; he must yield, or, like the car of Juggernaut, it will roll mercilessly over him, destroying as it advances. Destiny seems to have so willed it, and the world looks on and nods its approval.

C. SOLVING THE INDIAN PROBLEM WITH "REAL OLD-FASHIONED" INDIAN HUNTS, 1885.

In 1885, several Arizona and New Mexico counties paid a high price for Indian scalps. Significantly, a major Eastern newspaper that reported this news from the frontier was unperturbed, and willing to rationalize the policy. The following article on the legalized scalping of Indians appeared on page one of the New York Times. *Its tone leans heavily toward justification of scalping and tends to discredit "Northern and Eastern sentimentalists" who might decry murder-for-money.*

MONEY FOR INDIAN SCALPS

Arizona and New Mexico Settlers Propose to Destroy the Savages[1]

Deming, New-Mexico, Oct. 11—It has been recently telegraphed that the pioneer settlers in the border counties of Arizona have brought to light an old law in several counties offering a reward of $250 each for Indian scalps. Under this law, which is nothing more than an order made by the County Commissioners, the ranchmen and cowboys in Cochise, Pima, and Yavapai Counties are organizing in armed bodies for the purpose of going on a real old-fashioned Indian hunt, and they propose to bring back the scalps and obtain the reward. Word now comes from Tombstone, the county seat of Cochise County, that the reward in that county has been increased to $500 for a buck Indian's scalp. The authorities of Pima and Yavapai Counties have taken steps to increase the reward to $500, and it is said Yuma, Apache, and Maricopa Counties will follow suit.

This reward system, while it may seem savage and brutal to the Northern and Eastern sentimentalist, is looked upon in this section as the only means possible of ridding Arizona of the murderous Apaches. The settlers of New-Mexico and Arizona are aroused on this question, and propose to act henceforth independent of the military authorities. From time immemorial all border counties have offered rewards for bear and wolf scalps and other animals that destroyed the pioneer's stock or molested his family. Why, therefore, asks the Arizona settler, should not the authorities place a reward upon the head of the terrible Apache, who murders the white man's family and steals his stock like the wolves? "Extermination" is the battle cry now, and the coming Winter will witness bloody work in this section.

D.   CIVILIZING THE INDIAN WITH A GOOD AMERICAN EDUCATION, 1887

On the fast-vanishing frontier in the 1880's, a few young Indians were still resisting the advance of the paleface's civilization. Far more, however, were being introduced to the white man's values and principles in numerous government boarding schools. In the article that follows, the

[1]*New York Times*, October 12, 1885.

New York Times *indicated that such Indian schools might very well be successful in transforming the savage into someone who really understood that work and education were "civilizers."*

EDUCATED INDIANS

The Carlisle School's Way of Solving the Indian Problem[1]

Over 100 young Indians of various tribes, now being educated at the Carlisle Indian School, gave an extremely interesting entertainment in the Academy of Music last evening before a large audience. The boys wore a light blue military uniform, trimmed with red, and the girls wore dark blue flannel costumes, consisting of a plain skirt and a basque buttoned in front with brass buttons. Their long black hair was done up in single braids tied with neat bows of ribbon. Some of the girls were very bright-faced and pretty, while others had the Indian features too strongly marked to be handsome.

Probably the most interesting thing in the entertainment was the "first lessons," illustrated by half a dozen Chiricahua Apache boys who have been in the school three months. They were supplied with long slips of paper with which they performed simple operations in arithmetic, answering in halting but grammatical English. At the request of the instructor they named and described objects, and one of the lads put the others through a similar course. Another interesting feature was a recitation by half a dozen boys and three girls, under the direction of an Indian girl, on the Constitution of the United States. The boys and girls answered intelligently questions as to the powers of the three branches of the Government, the methods of election, terms of office, Presidential succession, and duties of citizens. An Arapahoe boy said a citizen's duty was to pay his taxes and to vote.

Joshua Given, a Kiowa, told the story of his life from wild Indian boyhood up to the status of theological student. He said he wanted to be a citizen of the United States, but was told he could not without a special act of Congress. Carlos Montezuma, an Apache, who is a college graduate, a drug clerk and a medical student, was presented by invitation and narrated his experience. He was taken captive by hostile Indians 15 years ago and sold for $30 to a gentleman who was collecting curiosities, as he humorously put it, and who educated him. Samuel Townsend, a Pawnee, delivered an original speech on "Work a Civilizer,"

[1]*New York Times*, February 5, 1887.

and Jemima Wheelock, an Oneida, spoke on "Education a Civilizer." There was singing by the school choir and music by the school brass band, and an interesting exhibition of boys working at type setting, cobbling, tailoring, blacksmithing, carpentering, and tinsmithing, and girls at sewing, washing, ironing, crocheting, and other feminine occupations.

The visitors during the day paid a visit to the Statue of Liberty and also crossed the Brooklyn Bridge. They were reviewed in front of the City Hall by Acting Mayor Beekman, Controller Loew, Deputy Controller Storrs, and President Coleman, of the Department of Taxes and Assessments.

E. AN UNFLATTERING PORTRAIT OF THE OIL-RICH OSAGE INDIANS, 1920

In 1915, oil was discovered on the barren reservation of the Osage Indians of Oklahoma, and overnight many Indians became wealthy. William G. Shepherd, the author of the following article, and later Professor of Economics at the University of Michigan, estimated that each family had an income of $25,000 four years after the first strike. The thought of Indians with money was evidently humerous to Shepherd, and he called his article "Lo, the Rich Indians," a parody on the time-honored phrase by which whites indicated their alleged concern for the plight of the country's original settlers. A similarly negative view of the Osage Indians and oil is found in Edna Ferber's Cimarron, *the number one best-selling novel for 1930. Shepherd makes it quite clear that the Indians were better off when they were attempting to cultivate the barren soil of the Oklahoma dustbowl than when squandering their money on material goods, since in those days, at least, they were not able to afford mescal, "the cocaine, the heroin, the alcohol, all rolled into one, of the American Indian!"[1]*

A huge car of expensive make comes up to the curb. An unshaven young man, coatless, wearing a greasy golf cap and no collar, is at the wheel. Before long you will see many of his type; he is a well-paid chauffeur for a rich Indian family. He brings the car to a stop with a suggestion of a flourish. He does not descend to open the rear door; instead he begins to roll a cigarette. From the back seat steps a huge Indian woman; she is blanketed, and her glistening hair is parted in the middle and brushed back above her ears. She has a bead necklace and a beaded

---

[1]William G. Shepherd, "Lo, the Rich Indians," *Harper's Magazine*, November 1920, pp. 723–734.

bag, but you catch a flash of a silk stocking and you see that instead of moccasins she is wearing heelless, patent-leather slippers, attached to her feet with an ankle strap. Marie Antoinette, in her empire gowns, was shod like this. Behind her descends a huge red man. His garb is Indian to the last observable stitch, except for his hat. His blue trousers are edged here and there with beads and are of a soft and glistening broadcloth. A gayly colored blanket is about his shoulders. His companion has not waited for him to alight. She strides off through the entrance of a store; he follows; fifteen feet behind her. They both "Toe in," she in her empire slippers and he in his soft, beaded moccasins. The chauffeur settles back in his seat to smoke, with one leg crossed high over his knee. In other cities men of his calling, with masters not so rich by far as his, have far more dignity than he. When in distant places you heard of these Indians with their chauffeurs, you expected to see liveried autocrats at the wheels of glistening limousines, but you soon discover, in Pawhuska, that a chauffeur does not even keep a car glistening, much less wear a livery. Mud and dust on a car's sides do not affect its speed. . . .

It will pay you well, after you have seen the picture in the streets, to exercise your right to become acquainted with the white citizens of Pawhuska and tell them that you wish to know something of their red neighbors. They will soon let you in behind the scenes of Pawhuska life. It will be nothing for you to be invited to sit in the offices of at least a dozen business and professional men within the next two days to hear what they know of Indians. Their stories of the disregard of the Indians for high prices make our silk-shirt buying citizens seem miserly.

When the cherries first appeared in market this year, for example, an old Indian drove up to a store in his car, pulled out a tin pail, and went over to the counter where there was a case of cherries in little boxes. He emptied one box after another into his pail, and when he had them all he turned to the storekeeper and said, "How much?"

"Dollar a box," said the storekeeper. "You took eighteen boxes."

"All right. Charge it," said the Indian.

Not all their spending is selfish indulgence; gentler emotions often come into play.

"I want to buy best baby-carriage," said a proud young Indian mother to a storekeeper.

"But your mother bought a carriage for the baby to-day," said the storekeeper. "She said she wanted him to ride in his grandmother's carriage."

"All right. But he's my baby and I want him to ride in his mother's carriage sometimes, too," said the mother, as she selected a carriage, twin of the one her mother had bought.

Planning in advance is not an Indian trait, and "wanting a thing when

you want it" is oftentimes the mother of invention, as when an Indian
sent word into town that he wanted a garage man to send a big car out
to his farm in a hurry. The cost was seven dollars.

When the car arrived the Indian gave the driver a bill and said:

"You go to Pawhuskee, buy me beefsteak."

"How much beefsteak?" asked the driver.

"Much as money you got left from the bill," said the Indian. "Me
hungry."

It worked out that the Indian got a $3 steak for a $10 bill, and he was
so satisfied with the arrangement that it became a habit with him to
have his meat delivered in this fashion. . . .

There is one other gift that Bacon Rind wishes to show you. He draws
forth a chamois-skin bag, of incredible softness, and empties its contents
onto the sofa. You see a heap of what look at first glance like dried apri-
cots, a double-handful. Bacon Rind's great brown fingers toy with the
small treasure.

"Mescal," he says, importantly.

The cocaine, the heroin, the alcohol, all rolled into one, of the American Indian!

"Do you drink it?" you ask.

"No, no, no!" says Bacon Rind. "Eat four, five! Then you come very
close to God!" He raises his gaze to the ceiling and lifts one huge hand.
"You put some in water; they get very large, like apple. Then eat,
slowly, like tobacco. Throw water away; never drink mescal; very bad."

Mr. McGuire explains. "Mescal is a drug, but the Indians don't know
it. They believe that it is a gift of God to bring them closer to Him. The
effect is very quick and very strong; it gives them a dreamy, happy feeling and they think it is religion."

Bacon Rind talks rapidly to your interpreter and then Mr. McGuire
tells you:

"Bacon Rind says that he is going to talk about God in the meeting-
house Sunday. It will be a mescal ceremony. Everyone will eat a little
mescal and then he will talk about the Great Spirit. It will make everyone there happy, Bacon Rind says."

"Yes, yes!" rumbles Bacon Rind, raising a hand above his head. "Me
talk God, Sunday. That very good."

Mescal is a luxury, you learn. Before the Osages became rich they
could not afford to send down into Mexico for the dried pods of the
mescal plant. The man who sends down there for a bag of mescal like
this of Bacon Rind's will spend a good $500 for the venture.

"Me go eat now," says Bacon Rind. "Good-by." . . .

There are 265,000 Indians in the United States; their race is not dying
out. But, of them all, it is not improbable that these Osage Indians, with

their wealth, are the unhappiest. You have that impression as you leave Pawhuska; it is not a happy town.

A blight of gold and oil and greed is on it, as heavy a curse as Indians have ever had from their wickedest medicine man.

F. THE "PAGANISM" OF THE NEW DEAL'S INDIAN POLICY, 1934

When Franklin D. Roosevelt came into office in 1933, the Native Americans were on the road to extinction, with a death rate that exceeded their birth rate. As with so many other problems, New Deal officials decided some changes had to be made. John Collier, unquestionably the most discerning Commissioner of Indian Affairs, brought to a close the Government's attempt to "civilize" and "assimilate" the Indian. Thus, Indians were allowed to freely resume old practices, including their particular religious ceremonies. For those who felt the Indian's salvation lay through Christianity, this "reversion" came as a profound shock. In the following selection from the Christian Century, *Elaine Goodale Eastman criticizes the Government's decision.*[1]

Does Uncle Sam Foster Paganism?

Sanctioning Ancient Religions

Not only are the elders of the tribe to be officially invited to resume their archaic rites, but in the most recent orders promulgated by the Indian office we read the following: "Any denomination or missionary, including any representative of a native Indian religion, may be granted . . . the use of rooms or other conveniences in boarding schools. . . . Any child at any Indian service day school, upon written request of his or her parents . . . shall be excused for religious instruction, including instruction in the native Indian religion, if any, for not more than one hour each week."

It is to be clearly understood that the native religions thus affirmatively sanctioned, certainly for the first time in our history, have no sacred books or formal theology which may be taught by word of mouth. Their priests, if any, are medicine-men or shamans, dispensing wisdom and healing through the medium of songs and incantations. We never went so far as to give them our blessing, but apparently we were

---

[1]Elaine Goodale Eastman, "Does Uncle Sam Foster Paganism?" Copyright 1934, Christian Century Foundation. Reprinted by permission from the August 8, 1934, issue of *Christian Century*.

wrong. At all events, Mr. Collier's new order definitely "supersedes any former regulation, instruction, or practice."

Now that two full generations of Sioux and other northwestern groups have grown up in the atmosphere of Christian teaching and more or less scientific medical and hospital care under government auspices, the official re-entry of the primitive medicine-man in all his glory, handsomely panoplied in paint, furs and feathers, armed with his sacred rattles, his skins of totemic beasts, his dried bodies of lizards or snakes, hair, entrails, and other bodily detritus, will be observed with profound interest—whether as an aid to religous meditation or as a sanitary precaution. Naturally, a strip of red flannel tied to a stick must hereafter be recognized by all Indian school superintendents as an official prayer, on an exact equality with the most eloquent invocation that may be pronounced by a bishop!

Will It Make a Bastard Religion?

It will perhaps be objected that no such reversion to primitive concepts is possible among a group already well advanced in transition, or, as worded by a supervisor of Congregational missions in the two Dakotas, "converted from paganism." All very well—but there are still isolated bodies of nearly full-blood Indians in the remoter parts of the southwest whose advancement may well be notably delayed by the new government policy. We should also give serious thought to the possibility of an undesired amalgamation, or the production of what might be termed a bastard religion, through the union of seemingly irreconcilable elements of pagan and Christian theologies.

The widespread "ghost dance craze" of 1890–91, with its tragic and desperate sequel, will be readily called to mind as a comparatively recent instance of such a revelation, spontaneously arising among a people in a critical stage of cultural disintegration. Its central motive was the adoration of a pretended Indian messiah, in expectation of the disappearance of the alien invader and a joyful return to the old "buffalo days." Worship was by nocturnal song and dance, without food or fire or light, around a "sacred tree" cut down by a virgin.

Far from promoting this pathetic illusion, both missionaries and government officials did their utmost to discourage it. When their efforts proved ineffectual, the United States army was called upon to suppress a threatened "outbreak." . . .

Religion for Revenue

To drop all speculation and return to the solid ground of contemporaneous fact, we find rain dances and alligator dances and other esoteric or curious rites still celebrated from time to time in village or pueblo, partly "for excitement and fun," as we are told, but principally, one gathers, as tourist attractions and commercial enterprises. This may be financially profitable, but is it spiritually edifying?

However, the "native religion" most in vogue today is obviously the so-called "Peyote church," introduced from Mexico about thirty years ago, of which I quote a brief account from the well-known report of the Institute for government research ("Problems of Indian Administration," 1928): "The Indians assemble for meetings in churches, so-called, where they fall into trance-like stupor from the use of peyote. The organization is of no practical value to the community, and peyote addiction is probably harmful physically as well as socially. The 'Shakers' and the Peyote church are both reported to be growing."

This drug is the dried button of a small cactus found along the Rio Grande and southward into Mexico. Mrs. Flora Warren Seymour, in her "Story of the Red Man," describes the Peyote addict thus: "In a house bestrewn with a disorderly litter of rubbish, a stalwart Ute sits cross-legged on the floor. His glazed eyes stare before him, unseeing. His right arm beats upon the skin drum, as a monotonous droning chant issues from his throat. Soon he will pass entirely into the Peyote dream he is wooing with his incantations, and will see beatific visions of ineffable delight."

Indians given to the practice of this "religion" strenuously uphold their sacred right under the constitution of the United States to continue and extend it. It is, however, forbidden by state law in South Dakota and elsewhere. Shall we soon see it introduced into tax-supported schools, under the present regime? If not, why not?

Attacks on the Missionaries

A Sioux is quoted in the bulletin issued bi-monthly by the Indian office as asserting that "our primitive Sioux had a true conception of revealed religion. The best our missionaries accomplished was to organize them into different denominations!"

"What a mockery," exclaims an educated Chippewa, aroused to indignation by the new order, "what a mockery of wholesome missionaries who gave their lives for the Indians' salvation!"

For such as he, one might as well seek to revive African voodooism in Harlem, or witchcraft in New England!

3
The Scientists and the Indian

No single group did more to legitimatize race stereotyping than did American scientists. Through their supposedly objective studies of craniology, physiogonomy, eugenics, ethnology, intelligence, and social behavior, these scholars, operating from a basically Anglo-Saxon norm, attempted to prove that popular images of minorities were scientifically correct. Their work on behalf of Anglo-Saxon superiority, however, only proved that their racial prejudice was stronger than their scientific dedication. J. A. Rogers, a long-ignored black anthropologist, once observed that "if the kind of science that is in ethnology went into engineering, no automobile would ever run, no air ship would ever leave the ground, in fact not even a clock would run." Unfortunately, Americans traditionally have worshipped at the shrine of scientific objectivity and few persons questioned the validity of the scientists' conclusions on race. In actuality, scientists, like novelists, historians, journalists, and politicians, reflect their personal biases and those of the society about them.

Although it was not too surprising to find frontiersmen and generals in agreement that Indians could best serve the nation in a deceased state, early scientists were scarcely less harsh. As early as 1839, Dr. Samuel George Morton, an authority on craniology, insisted that Indians were inherently savage and intractable. Two decades later, his student in anthropology, Josiah Clark Nott, concluded that there was no such thing as a "civilized full-blooded Indian." If such derogatory assessments lessened by the end of the nineteenth century, it was perhaps because the Indian had ceased to be a threat rather than because of any fundamental change on the part of the scientists. To be sure, many scholars were beginning to take a genuine interest in studying the Native American, but seldom did this interest result in conclusions that might gain him racial parity.

The scientific arguments used to assess the Indian were familiar ones. From his physiognomy to his inability to score well on intelligence tests, the Indian was clearly of a lesser race. One prominent Yale geographer went so far as to suggest that the Native American's mental weaknesses could be explained by "Siberian Hysteria," a disease he had contracted during his migration from Asia some 10,000 years before.

A. THE INDIAN ANATOMY: PROOF OF INFERIORITY, 1891

Scientists in the twentieth century could turn to Dr. Daniel G. Brinton's 1891 study, The American Race, *for evidence on the superiority of the white race. Brinton, a Yale graduate who served as medical director of the Eleventh Army during the Civil War and later taught at the University of Pennsylvania, made a careful study of the Indian's anatomy and came away convinced of his inferiority.*[1]

The American Race

A special feature in [Native] American skulls is the presence of the epactal bone, or *os Incae*, in the occiput. It is found in a complete or incomplete condition in 3.86 per cent of the skulls throughout the continent, and in particular localities much more frequently; among the ancient Peruvians for example in 6.08 per cent, and among the former inhabitants of the Gila valley in 6.81 per cent. This is far more frequently than in other races, the highest being the negro [sic], which offers 2.65 per cent, while the Europeans yield but 1.19. The presence of the bone is due to a persistence of the transverse occipital suture, which is usually closed in fetal life. Hence it is a sign of arrested development, and indicative of an inferior race.

The majority of the Americans have a tendency to meso- or brachycephaly, but in certain families, as the Eskimos in the extreme north and the Tapuyas in Brazil, the skulls are usually decidedly long. In other instances there is a remarkable difference in members of the same tribe and even of the same household. Thus among the Yumas there are some with as low an index as 68, while the majority are above 80, and among

[1]Daniel G. Brinton, *The American Race*, N. D. C. Hodges, New York 1891, pp. 38–43.

the dolichocephalic Eskimos we occasionally find an almost globular skull. So far as can be learned, these variations appear in persons of pure blood. Often the crania differ in no wise from those of the European. Dr. Hensell, for instance, says that the skulls of pure-blood Corcados of Brazil, which he examined, corresponded in all points to those of the average German.

The average cubical capacity of the American skull falls below that of the white, and rises above that of the black race. Taking both sexes, the Parisians of to-day have a cranial capacity of 1448 cubic centimeters; the Negroes 1344 c.c.; the American Indians 1376. But single examples of Indian skulls have yielded the extraordinary capacity of 1747, 1825, and even 1920 cub. cent., which are not exceeded in any other race. . . .

The stature and muscular force vary. The Patagonians have long been celebrated as giants, although in fact there are not many of them over six feet tall. The average throughout the continent would probably be less than that of the European. But there are no instances of dwarfish size to compare with the Lapps, the Bushmen, or the Andaman Islanders. The hands and feet are uniformly smaller than those of Europeans of the same height. The arms are longer in proportion to the other members than in the European, but not so much as in the African race. This is held to be one of the anatomical evidences of inferiority.

Beyond all other criteria of a race must rank its mental endowments. These are what decide irrevocably its place in history and its destiny in time. . . . But the final decision as to the abilities of a race or of an individual must be based on actual accomplished results, not on supposed endowments. Thus appraised, the American race certainly stands higher than the Australian, the Polynesian or the African, but does not equal the Asian. . . .

While these facts bear testimony to a good natural capacity, it is also true that the receptivty of the race for a foreign civilization is not great. Even individual instances of highly educated Indians are rare; and I do not recall any who have achieved distinction in art or science, or large wealth in the business world.

B.   INTELLIGENCE TESTS "PROVE" INDIANS TO BE
MENTALLY INFERIOR, 1931

Until his death in 1939, psychologist Thomas R. Garth stood at the top of his discipline as an expert on the American Indian. After completing his Ph.D. at Columbia, Garth directed numerous expeditions to study Indians, and as late as 1937, he served the Government as a spe-

cialist on Indian education. In his 1931 book, Race Psychology, *Garth set down his conclusions on racial differences in intelligence. Using various tests on intelligence and racial characteristics, Garth found the Indians to be intellectually inferior. In addition, he concluded that mixed-blood Indians were more intelligent than full-blood Indians, the intelligence "tending to increase with the degree of white blood."*[1]

Racial Differences in Intelligence

As we have said in the last chapter, the first use of the Binet Scale for the Measurement of Intelligence in race psychology was made by Alice C. Strong in Columbia, S. C., on a group of Negroes; and by Rowe in Michigan who studied a group of whites and Indians with the Binet. In all these studies the performance of the whites was superior to that of the Negroes and Indians. . . .

So far as we know the only use of the Binet with Indians was made by Helen M. and E. C. Rowe. They used the Goddard form on 268 Indians in an Indian school in comparison with 547 whites, all in Michigan, in grades running from kindergarten through the eighth grade. Their results were reported in 1914 by E. C. Rowe in terms of relative mental age. He says that 94 per cent of the Indian children were mentally below the whites. At that time the I. Q. was not in general use.

So, unfortunately, we are unable to give Binet I. Q.'s for Indians, since no study is available in which they are supplied. We shall have to make use of the group I. Q.'s obtained from such tests as the National Intelligence Test and the Otis Intelligence Test. The Indian subjects of these tests have been largely the students in the United States Indian schools and were tested in Oklahoma, Colorado, New Mexico, and South Dakota. They are fairly representative of all tribes of Indians, such as Sioux, Cherokee, Arapaho, Navajo, Ute, and Pueblo, and are the descendants of those who in early days before the advent of the white man, lurked in the forests, stalked the plains, or followed agricultural pursuits in the Southwest.

Much of the testing reported on Indians has been done by Garth and students under his direction. With the National Intelligence Test, Garth *et al.* obtained a median group I. Q. of 68.6 for 1,050 full-blood Indians of the fairly representative tribal population above mentioned. For a group of 1,000 full bloods with the Otis Intelligence Test they obtained a median group I. Q. of 70.4. This makes in all 2,650 full bloods with a group I. Q. of around 69. Another group I. Q. of 72.5 for full bloods

[1]Reprinted by permission of the publisher from Thomas R. Garth, *Race Psychology,* McGraw-Hill, New York, 1931, pp. 71, 75–76, 83–84.

not attending the United States Indian schools but attending the public schools along with white children was reported by Garth and Garrett.

As to the I. Q.'s of mixed blood Indians, they are found to be higher than those of full bloods, tending to increase with the degree of white blood. As we have said, Garth *et al.* found a positive correlation of 0.42 for degree of white blood and I. Q. as obtained by the National Intelligence Test with 765 subjects. The I. Q. of one-quarter bloods was 77, of half bloods, 75, and of three-quarter bloods 74. Hunter and Sommermeir found a positive correlation of 0.41 between degree of white blood and Otis intelligence score (holding age and school attendance constant) using a group of mixed bloods. . . .

Disregarding the I. Q.'s of the immigrant groups, which we do not believe are measures of the average of the groups in their home lands, the racial I. Q.'s as found are, by way of résumé: whites, 100; Chinese, 99; Japanese, 99; Mexicans, 78; southern Negroes, 75; northern Negroes, 85; American Indians, full blood, 70. If one says that what is fair for one is fair for another, then regardless of environmental difficulties, the Chinese and Japanese score so nearly like the white that the difference is negligible. Certainly they possess a quality which places them in a class beyond the Negro, the Mexican in the United States, and the American Indian, whatever that is. Perhaps it is temperament which makes the latter groups unable to cope with the white man's test. Again, it is barely possible they cannot take the white man's seriousness seriously. . . .

The number of superior individuals in these groups is small to be sure. Of 1,272 Negroes there are 96, to express it in numbers, who are as good as or better than the average white. There are 90 Mexicans out of 1,004 and 75 Indians out of 667 who are seen to do as well as or better than the white median performance. Regardless of race and though few in number, they make a small group which intelligent people must recognize, though it might be wished they were more numerous.

4
The Indian in American History

Although they were virtually exterminated by the white man in less than three centuries, the Native Americans rarely received sympathy from those who chronicled the American experience. In reviewing this country's past, the president of Harvard declared in 1896 that America's principal contribution to civilization was in the abandonment of war as the means of settling disputes. The Indians did not provide a contradiction for President Charles Eliot because these "Stone-Age" men had to be "resisted and quelled by force" because "they could not be assimilated . . . or even reasoned with." Thus, these wars were necessities.

Likewise, most writers of American history who touched on Indian relations believed that the related wars should be treated as unique experiences. Professor Walter Prescott Webb, in his classic history of *The Great Plains* (1931), concluded that "so far as the Indian goes, the historical problem comes down to the single issue of his ways in war," which forced "white men to save one bullet for themselves." Thus the brutal and implacable foe, the unassimilable aborigine and the inferior savage were all assumed to be acceptable synonyms for the Indian by most historians. James Truslow Adams in *The Epic of America* (1931) claimed that the Indians' nervous systems "were unstable and they were of a markedly hysterical make-up . . . cruel and revengeful. . . . They were childishly lacking in self-control." Obligated to comment on the Aztec civilization, Adams relied on reports "by early writers" to emphasize the Aztecs' "ghastly" cruel religion, which made use of human sacrifices. This emphasis on Indian cruelty—especially as manifested during the frontier wars—is one main thread running through virtually all American history books. Another is the failure to discuss thoroughly the impact of our policy on the Indian people. Settling the land with white pioneers is the main focus of these books, and the Indian danger is usually treated as one of the hazards on the frontier along with the other natural dangers of life in a wild, uncivilized, and unfriendly land.

A. FRANCIS PARKMAN EXPLAINS
THE INDIAN CHARACTER, 1851

Although Francis Parkman's epic history of Pontiac's conspiracy and the Indian War was first published in 1851, it retained its popularity for future generations. The Boston-born, Harvard-educated Parkman was convinced that the Indian was doomed to extinction by the advance of the white man's civilization, and while he willingly admitted certain noble qualities, it was the "dark, cold, and sinister" side of the Indians he chose to emphasize.[1]

Nature has stamped the Indian with a hard and stern physiognomy. Ambition, revenge, envy, jealousy, are his ruling passions; and his cold temperament is little exposed to those effeminate vices which are the bane of milder races. With him revenge is an overpowering instinct; nay, more, it is a point of honor and a duty. His pride sets all language at defiance. He loathes the thought of coercion; and few of his race have ever stooped to discharge a menial office. A wild love of liberty, an utter intolerance of control, lie at the basis of his character, and fire his whole existence. Yet, in spite of this haughty independence, he is a devout hero-worshipper; and high achievement in war or policy touches a chord to which his nature never fails to respond. He looks up with admiring reverence to the sages and heroes of his tribe; and it is this principle, joined to the respect for age springing from the patriarchal element in his social system, which, beyond all others, contributes union and harmony to the erratic members of an Indian community. With him the love of glory kindles into a burning passion; and to allay its cravings, he will dare cold and famine, fire, tempest, torture, and death itself.

These generous traits are overcast by much that is dark, cold, and sinister, by sleepless distrust, and rankling jealousy. Treacherous himself, he is always suspicious of treachery in others. Brave as he is—and few of mankind are braver—he will vent his passion by a secret stab rather than an open blow. His warfare is full of ambuscade and stratagem; and he never rushes into battle with that joyous self-abandonment, with

[1]Francis Parkman, *The Conspiracy of Pontiac and the Indian War After the Conquest of Canada, 1888* revised edition, Little, Brown & Co., Boston, pp. 39–44.

which the warriors of the Gothic races flung themselves into the ranks of their enemies. In his feasts and his drinking bouts we find none of that robust and full-toned mirth, which reigned at the rude carousals of our barbaric ancestry. He is never jovial in his cups, and maudlin sorrow or maniacal rage is the sole result of his potations.

Over all emotion he throws the veil of an iron self-control, originating in a peculiar form of pride, and fostered by rigorous discipline from childhood upward. He is trained to conceal passion, and not to subdue it. The inscrutable warrior is aptly imaged by the hackneyed figure of a volcano covered with snow; and no man can say when or where the wild-fire will burst forth. This shallow self-mastery serves to give dignity to public deliberation, and harmony to social life. Wrangling and quarrel are strangers to an Indian dwelling; and while an assembly of the ancient Gauls was garrulous as a convocation of magpies, a Roman senate might have taken a lesson from the grave solemnity of an Indian council. In the midst of his family and friends, he hides affections, by nature none of the most tender, under a mask of icy coldness; and in the torturing fires of his enemy, the haughty sufferer maintains to the last his look of grim defiance.

His intellect is as peculiar as his moral organization. Among all savages, the powers of perception preponderate over those of reason and analysis; but this is more especially the case with the Indian. An acute judge of character, at least of such parts of it as his experience enables him to comprehend; keen to a proverb in all exercises of war and the chase, he seldom traces effects to their causes, or follows out actions to their remote results. Though a close observer of external nature, he no sooner attempts to account for her phenomena than he involves himself in the most ridiculous absurdities; and quite content with these puerilities, he has not the least desire to push his inquiries further. His curiosity, abundantly active within its own narrow circle, is dead to all things else; and to attempt rousing it from its torpor is but a bootless task. He seldom takes cognizance of general or abstract ideas; and his language has scarcely the power to express them, except through the medium of figures drawn from the external world, and often highly picturesque and forcible. The absence of reflection makes him grossly improvident, and unfits him for pursuing any complicated scheme of war or policy.

Some races of men seem moulded in wax, soft and melting, at once plastic and feeble. Some races, like some metals, combine the greatest flexibility with the greatest strength. But the Indian is hewn out of a rock. You can rarely change the form without destruction of the substance. Races of inferior energy have possessed a power of expansion and assimilation to which he is a stranger; and it is this fixed and rigid quality which has proved his ruin. He will not learn the arts of civilization, and he and his forest must perish together.

B.   WHY AMERICA SHOULD BELONG TO ARYANS, NOT INDIANS, 1894

Geologist and Dean of Harvard's Lawrence Scientific School, Professor Nathaniel S. Shaler, in editing an 1894 two-volume history of the United States, explained in the first chapter why America was aptly suited to be the home of the great northern Aryan race. In the course of his discussion, he was forced to deal with the Native American who had lived in this country long before any white man appeared. Shaler concluded that the Indian's culture had been vastly exaggerated and that he had not advanced above the level of savagery. In fact, the inferior Indian was fortunate that the superior white race did not practice genocide or slavery as other conquering races had.[1]

The Continent and the Reasons For Its Fitness to be the Home of a Great People

We have now to consider the reason why our North American Indians, who have evidently been so long upon a continent well fitted for the uses of civilized men, have failed to advance beyond the primitive condition of men. We cannot fairly attribute this retardation in their social development to an original lack of intellectual capacity. On the whole, these people seem to have more than the usual measure of ability which is found among savages. . . .

The greatest difficulty which our people have encountered in dealing with the conditions presented by the central portion of the continent has arisen from the presence of the Indians in that field. Although the wars with the aborigines were often sanguinary and always harassing, the most serious obstacles were not those of a military sort. It has always proved easy to overcome the armed resistance of the savages, but always extremely difficult to make any satisfactory disposition of them. Although at no time has the population of these native folk north of the Rio Grande exceeded three hundred thousand souls, their habits were such as to require a great extend of land for their subsistence. In general, it may be said that the Indian needs from one to three square miles of land for the support of each of the members of his tribe. If confined

[1]Nathaniel S. Shaler, Ed., *The United States of America—A Study*, 2 vols., D. Appleton & Co., New York, 1894, pp. 32–49.

within a smaller area, at least until he has adopted the agricultural habit, he is sure to become restless and predatory. Thus it has come about that our people have adopted the rather curious plan of confining these savages within large reservations, around which the tide of civilization has soon closed. In time these great areas given over to savagery have proved to be exceedingly inconvenient, whereupon the tribes were forced to move westward on to lands which were by new treaties devoted to their use. . . .

Although much of the criticism which has been directed against our administration of Indian affairs is doubtless well founded, few of the critics perceive how almost insuperable are the difficulties of dealing with an indigenous people having the qualities of this native American race. Centuries of experience has taught us that these folk are, from the point of view of our civilization, essentially untamable. In general, they can not take up the burden of our Anglo-Saxon civilization, or even accommodate themselves to our ways of living. Here and there, though rarely, some of the tribes, particularly those of the more southern parts of the country, when the more desperate element of the population has been weeded out by war and the blood somewhat commingled with that of the whites, have become soil-tillers, and thereby ceased to be troublesome to the state. The choice before our people in dealing with this indomitable folk lay between a method of extermination, such as has been practiced in other lands, and something like the system which we have adopted. A cruel-minded race such as the Romans would have made short work of the Indian problem. Each war would have been one of extermination, and the primitive tribes would have been slain or enslaved, and thus removed from the field. The difficulties which we have encountered in dealing with the Indians have been in large measure due to the fact that even when exasperated by conflicts with them our frontier people have retained a large share of the just and humane motives which are characteristic of our race. They have recognized the fact that our own people were the invaders of the Indian's realm, and there has been an element of the apologetic in their treatment of the natives each time they came to make peace with them.

Although the foregoing sketch of the conditions which determined the fitness of this country to the uses of our race is inadequate, it may serve to show the reader how great and admirable was the fortune which gave this broad and fruitful land as the field for the development of our people. It is clear that it is better suited for the needs of the northern Aryans than any other extensive territory which has ever come into their possession. From their first scanty holding on its shores they have extended their empire with a swiftness and certainty which of itself shows how well suited the land was to their needs, and how well they were themselves suited to the inheritance.

C. A POPULAR HIGH SCHOOL HISTORY TEXT EXAMINES INDIAN PROBLEMS

Normally a considerable period of time elapses before minority images that first appear in scholarly monographs are incorporated into textbooks for young people; unfortunately, it often takes just as long to eliminate these same images from the elementary and secondary school text once they have been discredited by a new generation of scholars. For example, one still widely-used elementary social studies text informs its young readers that "a pioneer settles on land where only savages have lived before." The ethnocentrism of such a view is obvious, but still often the rule.

In the following passage, the authors' patronizing attitude is apparent in their attempt to explain the ineptness of the reservation Indians and the latter's need to take on the life style of the white majority. Syracuse University's Ralph Volney Harlow was a well-known textbook writer for both secondary and college students, and his Story of America, *co-authored with Herman Noyes, went through seven editions between 1937 and 1964.*[1]

In 1887, the government tried a new approach. Congress enacted the Dawes Act which provided for dividing up among individuals the reservation lands owned by the tribes in common. Any Indian who wished could get 160 acres for nothing. Many took advantage of the opportunity and became self-supporting. Civilized Indians were also granted citizenship.

The Indians who chose to remain on the reservations under the guardianship of the government made little progress. Poverty and disease continued to weaken the tribes. Education was made compulsory for Indian children in 1891; but since Congress appropriated only small amounts of money for Indian schools, many children still received little or no education. Many Indians seemed to lack both energy and the training necessary for success in the white man's world.

Nevertheless, there are encouraging signs that the Indian is at last gradually taking his proper place as an independent American. . . . In

[1]Ralph Volney Harlow and Herman Noyes, *Story of America*, © 1964, pp. 373–374. Reprinted by permission of Holt, Rinehart and Winston.

1924 full citizenship was granted to all Indians. More recently, Congress has taken important steps to encourage them to be self-reliant. Money is being provided for health, education, and vocational training, and some effort is being made to establish industries near Indian lands to provide jobs. Advice and financial assistance are also being given to individual Indians who want to seek better opportunities in some of our large cities. On the whole, the Indian's future looks brighter today than it has for many years. However, friends of the Indians are often critical of the haste with which govenrment supervision is being withdrawn.

5

The Indian in Literature

That a poem entitled "The Only Good Indian Is a Dead Indian" could still be published by a major American magazine in 1902 without any noticeable rebuttal from its readers, testifies to how insensitive white Americans could be to the so-called "Indian problem." Once the Indians had been defeated and left to wither away on the reservation, most Americans forgot the real Indian; however, his literary counterpart would live on, providing the ready victim for countless fictional heroes.

The sordid realities of life on the frontier for Indian and white alike became lost in the highly romanticized version of the West that emerged in the Beadle dime novels in the 1880's and lived on in pulp fiction for future Americans. The West served as a vicarious experience for author, publisher, and reader. Men like Edward S. Ellis, a New Jersey high school principal turned Western writer, could thrill their Eastern readers with tales of the Old West that had little basis in fact, and when competition for sales became fierce, one needed only to make his battle scenes more vivid and the corpses more numerous. It would be futile to try to estimate how many Indians have been killed through literature, movies, and television, but the number must be staggering. Indeed, this is precisely the impression one is left with after examining the popular literature on the Wild West—the Indian, who had been all but eliminated with real bullets, now had to be resurrected to be killed off again with printer's ink.

A. THE INDIAN'S BASIC VOCABULARY:
"TAKE SCALP . . . KILL . . . GIN," 1896

Edward Ellis was one of many Eastern writers who realized the tremendous potential of writing about the "Wild West." In 1876, at the age

44

of 35, he quit his post as principal of a Trenton, New Jersey high school and began to write juvenile stories. Later he expanded this interest to the writing of state, national, and world histories. In this 1896 novel entitled The Golden Rock, *Ellis described the eternal struggle on the frontier between the white man and the Indian.*[1]

Dick had just straightened up, with the heavy fish grasped one in each hand, when, as he confronted the frightful-looking redskin, he dropped both, and simply stared at the savage in terror.

The latter could not but know how great fear he inspired in an unarmed and helpless foe, especially one of such years as the youth that stood before him.

"Me kill," were the first cheerful words he uttered in his broken English, "little white papoose—take scalp—shoot—cut head off—kill—shoot—gin."

This was a terrible threat beyond all question, and, awe-inspiring as it was, it was hardly capable of adding to the apprehension of Dick, who supposed, as a matter of course, the redskin would put him to a sudden and shocking death.

He stood a minute gazing at him, and then he furtively turned his head, to learn whether Sam was anywhere in sight. . . .

There can be little doubt that the Indian intended from the first to destroy the boy before him; but, as the highest earthly enjoyment for one of his race is to witness the suffering of a fellow-mortal, it may have occurred to him, while keeping up his jerky conversation, that it would be a much wiser and more satisfactory proceeding to take the little fellow home with him as a prisoner. By this means he would earn the everlasting gratitude of all the warriors, squaws, and children, down to the toddling papooses in his tribe.

What a treat it would be to see the white prisoner writhe under the torture which they would be sure to apply!

Some such thoughts must have passed through the head of the warrior, to cause him to change his intention, as shown in the sudden stoppage when in the very act of advancing to carry out his purpose of putting him to death.

"White dog go with big Injin," said the redskin, once more striding toward the shrinking boy.

"Do you mean to kill me?" asked Dick, uncertain as to whether he should cry out and try to make his escape by starting on a run in the

[1]Edward Ellis, *The Golden Rock*, American Publishers Corp., New York, 1896, pp. 114–132.

direction of where he supposed Sam to be, or whether he should stand still a little while longer, in the hope of gaining a few more minutes, in which it was possible the trapper might come to his rescue.

"No; me no kill—me take home—make my son—grow big warrior." . . .

The Indian indicated that the boy should follow a course that led directly up the stream from which the fish were taken, and Dick had scarcely started, when he played a little trick that would have done credit to one of a great many more years than he.

Like the land all around them, the surface was much broken, and the boy had taken but a step or two when he stumbled on purpose.

At the instant of striking, he gave utterance to a sharp cry, loud enough to be heard a considerable distance.

The Indian jerked out his hunting-knife, and with his painted face aflame with passion, made a rush at him.

Dick dropped upon his knees, threw up his hands, and let out a scream louder than before, and which contained no notes that were not genuine.

The Indian was furious, and could not forgive such an exposure of the game, even though he believed it involuntary.

The hair of the boy was short, but his captor seemed determined to secure the scalp, and no doubt would have succeeded but for the reason that he was prevented.

He had not yet succeeded in getting a firm hold of the short locks, when a sharp, clear voice rang out:

"Hold thar!"

The Indian paused, with one hand in the hair of the cowering boy, and with the other resting on the handle of his hunting-knife.

He turned his head toward the point whence came the voice, and, as he did so, he was just in time to catch the flash of a gun not more than a dozen yards away.

That gun was held in the hands of Black Sam, the trapper, and the aim was as true as ever made by hunter. It may be truly said that the Sioux never knew what killed him. He had time scarcely to utter the single outcry, which all Indians are supposed to give as the breath leaves the body. . . .

During the brief period thus occupied, Sam related how it was that he came to reach the spot in time to save his young friend, in the hands of the Sioux Indian. . . .

"How was it the Indian didn't kill me as he said he meant to do when he first caught me?"

"Did he tell you that?" asked Sam, in surprise.

"Yes; and he told me that he had killed you, too."

"That's the way with all of them varmints you meet in this part of the world. They have 'nough of our style of talkin' to brag and blow of what they can do; I hope you didn't believe what he told you 'bout raisin' my hair."

"I was a little scared at first, but when I come to think, I knew he wasn't telling the truth."

"No, my boy, it will never do to think anything truth that you hear an Injin tell."

"It seems to me that if there is one Indian near here, there is apt to be more."

"Your head is level on that p'int, Dick; you couldn't very well go amiss on that, anyway. Injins are as nat'ral to this part of the country as rattlesnakes and all sorts of varmints."

B. "THE ONLY GOOD INDIAN IS A DEAD INDIAN," 1902

The Indian resisted not only the white man's physical assault on the continent but also his attempt at spiritual conquest. The missionaries were never far behind the explorers and settlers, but when their preachments had little effect on the Indians, they often concluded that the red man was incapable of salvation. Hartley Alexander put this feeling into verse with his "The Only Good Indian Is a Dead Indian," a poem that suggested that a violent end would be the only kind of redemption an Indian might understand.[1]

THE ONLY GOOD INDIAN IS A DEAD INDIAN

So there he lies, redeemed at last!
    His knees drawn tense, just as he fell
    And shrieked out his soul in a battle-yell;
One hand with the rifle still clutched fast;
One stretched straight out, the fingers clenched
    In the knotted roots of the sun-bleached grass;
    His head flung back on a tangled mass
Of raven mane, with war-plume wrenched
Awry and torn; the painted face
    Still foewards turned, the white teeth bare
    'Twixt the livid lips, the wide-eyed glare,

[1]Hartley Alexander, "The Only Good Indian Is a Dead Indian," *Atlantic Monthly*, November 1902, p. 656.

The bronze cheek gaped by battle-trace
In dying rage rent fresh apart:—
    A strange expression for one all good!—
    On his naked breast a splotch of blood
Where the lead Evangel cleft his heart.

So there he lies, and last made whole,
Regenerate! Christ rest his soul!

C. ZANE GREY'S DESCRIPTION OF
AN INDIAN MASSACRE, 1932

Zane Grey gave up his New York dental practice in 1904 and embarked on a career of writing Western novels. He had spectacular success. In all, he wrote fifty-four novels, many of which achieved individual sales in excess of a million copies. In 1918 and 1920 his novels topped the best-seller lists. For millions of American urbanites, Grey's stories offered an escape from their sedentary life through the excitement of frontier life. While these novels had little literary value, they were important in reinforcing long-standing stereotypes about cowboys and Indians. In the following selection from the 1932 novel, The Lost Wagon Train, *Grey's description of the white girl's fear of "a fate worse than death" is typical of much Western writing.*[1]

Cynthia Bowden crawled under her cot inside Bowden's big canvas-covered wagon. . . .

She knew what would happen to her if she were carried into captivity. Horrible! She would take her own life. There was a pistol somewhere in the wagon. But could she commit what her religion held a sin? Cynthia wavered and resorted to prayer and hope. . . .

And here she, Cynthia Bowden, heiress and beauty, a runaway from home and courtiers, lay wretched and terror-stricken in a wagon out on the wild plains, surrounded by blood-thirsty savages! It was inconceivable and insupportable. But the hands that dug into her breasts proclaimed the truth.

She thought that she must scream out to rend the unbearable silence. But as she bit her lips to hold back another shriek there rose out of the night stillness a cry so wild and weird, so ringing and sharp, swelling and sustaining its tremendous note of doom that it curdled her blood

---

[1]Reprinted by permission of Zane Grey Inc. from Zane Grey, *The Lost Wagon Train*, Grosset & Dunlap, New York, 1932, pp. 75–81.

and froze the marrow in her bones. It shocked Cynthia into a dazed state if not an actual faint. . . .

Then followed a hideous period of increasing terror. With no means of suicide she had no hope except that a merciful arrow or bullet would find her. Then suddenly a calmness of despair settled over her. What avail all this torture of spirit? She crawled from her covert and sat upon the cot, expecting surely a death-dealing missile would find her there. But not one of the hissing things touched her.

All at once the shots of guns were drowned in a sound so sudden, unexpected, and terrible that she fell flat, as if actually struck a blow. It was not like any sound she had ever conceived. But it issued from throats—from the throats of men, of human beings, of these wild savages. It was the concatenated, staccato mingling of hundreds of shrieks, all different, all pitched high to the limit of vocal power, all pealing forth the same note, a monstrous and appalling revenge. This must be the notorious war-cry of the Indians. . . .

Cynthia had the strength to peer out through the slit in the canvas door at the rear. The circle inclosed by the white-tented wagons appeared as light as day. Slim, nimble dark forms were darting here, there, everywhere. Savages! She clutched the flaps to keep from sliding out of the door. And for the time being she was so paralyzed with a new and mortal fright that she could only gaze with magnifying eyes.

Red bursts of flames and puffs of smoke blotted out a part of the silvered circle, and then, as they vanished there, they appeared at another part, at the far end, along the opposite line of wagons, and again in the center. Boom and crack of guns, no longer incessant, were emphasized by being segregated from a whole. She could see along the curve of the inner line of wagons where here and there the wild dark forms came into sight. Some ran out, others to and fro. Four or five dragged something heavy and struggling from under the second wagon next to Bowden's. Horrid cries pierced her ears. She saw a white man's face in the moonlight. The fiends dragged him, threw him, to stand over his prostrate body and hack with hatchets. Then they closed into a compact bunch, hiding the wretched victim, tore and fought over him, suddenly to leap up and run, waving arms aloft.

Cynthia saw everything at once, like a boy at a circus, only under a vastly different kind of emotion. She was witness to a massacre. She could not move, nor even close her eyes. Every instant the number of moving figures increased within the circle. Other white men were dragged out before her horror-stricken gaze, butchered and stripped and left stark in the moonlight. Fewer and fewer grew the red spurts of guns. The battle now had changed again. Bowden's men, those that were alive, were driven from their posts into the open, there to contend in a hand-to-hand struggle, a few against many.

From under the wagon next to hers, on the outside, had burst a continuous fire. Streaks of smoke kept shooting out from the wheels. Then through the narrow gap between the wagons, she saw out on the other side, where a giant leaped into sight, swinging a gleaming object upon savages that rose right out of the ground. Yells and shots did not drown sodden hollow cracks. Her distended sight and stunned faculties still retained power of recognition. That giant was Anderson beating at a pack of savages, like a stag bayed by wolves. Then he ceased his gigantic swings, swayed and fell, to disappear under a swarm of wriggling Indians.

Suddenly Cynthia's hands were rudely wrenched from the flaps of canvas. They were spread wide. In the aperture appeared lean dark arms, dark nude shoulders, dark small head. The moonlight fell upon them and upon a barbaric visage—bronze, cruel, sharp features of a savage. His eyes roved from upward glance to downward, then fixed upon her—eyes black as coal, yet burning with a terrific light.

Those hellish orbs and the dark face blurred and faded. Cynthia lost her senses.

D.   A BEST-SELLING WESTERN DESCRIBES
THE RACE STRUGGLE, 1943

Ernest Haycox is not as well known today as Zane Grey, but as a writer of both film scripts and best-selling novels he has probably reached as many Americans as did any Western writer. Between 1929 and 1946, there was rarely a year when he did not publish a Western novel; in addition, many of these stories were serialized in Collier's *and the* Saturday Evening Post, *and his long list of film credits includes such hits as "Stagecoach." The following selection is taken from* Bugles in the Afternoon *(1943), one of the all-time best-selling Westerns. In the encounter between the Indians and the U. S. Cavalry, the Indians exhibit all their expected characteristics, and the hero is able to define the battle in terms of perpetual race struggle.*[1]

[1]From Ernest Haycox, *Bugles in the Afternoon,* 1943, pp. 64–75. Reprinted by permission of Jill Marie Haycox, Owner under Last Will and Testament of Ernest Haycox, deceased, and Owner's agents, Scott Meredith Literary Agency, Inc., 580 Fifth Avenue, New York, New York 10036.

The column followed Bannack Bill downgrade toward a thin fringe of willows scattered along a creek. There was something scattered on the ground which, upon a steady inspection, had to Shafter a familiar attitude, he had seen many men thus, arms crooked carelessly, bodies lying in the disheveled posture of death. The guide waited near by and said nothing when Smith halted the column. There were three men stripped naked, two of them apparently beyond middle age and a young one. This was not entirely a matter of certainty, for they had all been scalped, their heads cracked in and their bodies mutilated. Each man had half a dozen arrows thrust into them. . . .

"It was that party we passed yesterday late," said Bannack Bill.

"How sure are you of it?" asked Smith.

"A party of bucks would of scalped these fellers and let it go like that. That knife work was done by squaws and the arrers prob'ly by kids practisin' up on their shootin'. You'll find them scalps with that party."

"We'll go see," said Smith. . . .

A line of warriors milled out from the rear of the long Indian column, racing forward, low-bent and weaving on their ponies. The older men in the forefront of the procession ranked themselves and sat still. Smith stopped in front of them and murmured to Bannack Bill:—

"Tell them I'm glad to see them and hope they have had a good summer. Tell them I presume they're going to the Agency for winter. Tell them we're pleased to have them come in, that the meat is fat at the Agency. Tell them any compliment you happen to think of for about two minutes. I want to watch these young bucks while you're talking." . . .

Shafter murmured: "There's a fresh scalp hanging to the arrow pouch of that pug-nosed lad out on the left."

"Very good, Sergeant," said Smith coolly. "That's what we're looking for."

"You'll probably find the blankets and the clothes among the squaws."

"Ever try to handle a squaw?" said Smith, dryly. "We'll leave those dusky beauties alone."

Bannack Bill finished his interpreting and sat idle in the saddle. All the old men remained silent, thereby lending dignity to the parley. A good deal later one of them straightened on his horse and spoke in the guttural, abrupt Sioux tongue.

Bill said: "He says he's very happy to see the government soldiers. They are his friends. He is their friend. All Sioux are friends of all whites. All whites should be friends of the Sioux, though sometimes they are not. He says he is on his way to the Agency and is glad to hear the beef is fat. Most years, he says, it is very poor and the Indians starve. Why is that, he asks." . . .

Shafter said: "The lad next to the lad with the scalp has got a gold watch and chain wrapped around his neck."

"Two out of three will do nicely," said Smith. "You've got a good eye, Sergeant." He eased himself in the saddle, rolling from side to side, which was his signal to Garnett a hundred feet behind him. The old Sioux men watched him in beady interest, their glances flicking back to the troopers now idly deploying into skirmish lines. The young bucks saw it as well and stirred uneasily, drifting their ponies back and forth.

"Bill," said Smith, "tell him we're happy over everything but the murder of the three white men. Ask him if he knows of that evil thing."

Bannack Bill murmured: "You sure you're ready to start the fireworks?"

"Let it start," said Smith. He waited until Bannack Bill began speaking; then he turned his head and gave Shafter the kind of glance which not only delved for toughness in another man, but mirrored his own essentially hard spirit. "We need a display of decision here, Sergeant. It has to be done quietly, but without any show of hesitation. When I give the word, ride over and bring out those two bucks. I shall back you up."

Shafter said, "Yes sir," and felt the continuing force of Smith's glance. The lieutenant was aware of the risk involved in so brisk a show of power, for the warriors in this band were all well-armed and they could muster as much strength as the detachment. Meanwhile Bannack Bill said his say and waited for reply. It was not long in coming. The old spokesman of the Sioux straightened himself, pointed to the earth, to the sky and to the four cardinal points, no doubt invoking all the gods he knew about to attest his sincerity, and launched into speech.

"Winding himself up," murmured Smith and impassively listened. When the old one had finished, Bannack Bill paused a moment to summarize what he had heard, and proceeded to translate it freehand.

"The old codger decorates his damned lie as follows: His heart is pure, his mouth is wide open to truth, his soul is hurt to think the lieutenant would think that Red Owl's band would hurt a white man. Not one of his people touched a hair on those three prospectors. He has seen many bad things done by the whites but he's ready to forgive and forget and would share his blanket with any white man to show he means it. He says likewise it is gettin' late and he's got forty miles more to go before reachin' the Agency. The nights are growin' chilly and some of his old ones are hungry. Which is a way of sayin' to us that it is time to quit the foolin' around."

Smith nodded, meeting the old warrior's eyes. They were eyes of black liquid, full of pride and complete confidence—and touched with shrewd scheming as they stared back at the lieutenant. Smith said. "Tell him I'm glad to hear of his peaceful intentions. Ask him this: If he knew that some of his young men had killed the prospectors, would he bring them to the fort as a sign of his good will?"

Bannack Bill asked it. Out on the wings of the crowd the young bucks grew increasingly restive and there was a murmuring among them. The old one placed a hand on his heart and briefly answered the question. Bannack Bill said: "He says he would bring in his own son if his son had done it."

"Go get them Sergeant," murmured Smith, not turning his head. He stared at the old one. "Tell him I believe his word to be true. Tell him he has no doubt been deceived by his own young men, for we see the scalp and we see the watch. Tell him we take him at his word and will carry the two young men back to the fort with us."

Bannack Bill hesitated, casting a bland stare at Smith. "I hope you got the best cards in this game, Lieutenant."

"Tell him," said Smith.

Shafter had meanwhile turned and now rode directly and unhurriedly to the left, passing along the ranks of the younger warriors. They sat still, staring back at him with their haughty faces, with the snake-twining of insolence in their eyes. He came to the warrior who had the fresh scalp hanging from his quiver and to the warrior with the watch wrapped by its chain around his neck. He stopped, looking at the scalp and at the watch. Suddenly other bucks crowded close to these two and grasped their carbines and lifted them suggestively and a steady, thick stream of Sioux words went back and forth along the line, growing sharper, growing more excited.

Shafter heard Bannack Bill say: "He says there must be a mistake. That is an old scalp, from many years ago. The watch was a present."

"Tell him we shall take the two warriors to Lincoln. If he speaks the truth we shall release them." . . .

One buck swung his arm toward his revolver. Shafter laid the gun on him at once and stopped him, and pulled the weapon back to his original target. He heard Smith coolly say: "Ask him if a chief swallows his words as soon as they are spoken." . . .

Bannack Bill repeated it to Red Owl and Red Owl sat still thoughtfully. Back in the column the women were beginning to lift their shrill voices, the savage intent of their words scraping Shafter's nerves and inciting the young warriors to greater violence. One brave flung his carbine around and took a steady aim on Shafter. Then Red Owl's voice came out quickly and spoke three words that settled the question, for the two wanted warriors moved out of the group, Shafter behind them.

They rode straight toward the waiting cavalry, never turning their heads.
. . .

Smith rode a long distance in silence. . . . Now and then his thoughts laid a temporary shadow across his face; now and then he shook his head as his thinking took him to impassable ground. Presently he shrugged his shoulders. "You're right," he said. "There will be a campaign. Well, it is one of those things over which a soldier has no control, and never will. We do what we are told to do, and presently we shall be told to subjugate the Indians. The fault is higher up." Then he corrected that. "Still, the men higher up are not free agents either. Something pushes them on, whether they like it or not. It goes back to one race against another race. The white man's idea against the red man's idea. If the situation were reversed, the Indians would be doing to us what we are now trying to do to them. White men have fought each other since the beginning of time. Red men have fought each other. Now the races fight. Well, we're in the hands of history, and history is a cruel thing."

SELECTED READINGS

Collier, John, *The Indians of the Americas*, W. W. Norton and Company, New York, 1947.
A sympathetic but not patronizing history of American Indians by Franklin D. Roosevelt's Commissioner of Indian Affairs.

Deloria, Vine, *Custer Died for Your Sins*, Macmillan, New York, 1969.
A delightful but incisive account of our Indian policy. Particularly noteworthy are his comments on the scholars and missionaries who found the Indian such a time-consuming object.

Deloria, Vine, *We Talk You Listen*, Macmillan, New York, 1970.
In this volume Deloria elaborates on several of the themes introduced in *Custer Died for Your Sins*.

Forbes, Jack, Ed., *The Indian in America's Past*, Prentice-Hall, Englewood Cliffs, New Jersey, 1964.
A series of short quotes that depict historical white attitudes toward Native Americans.

Pearce, Roy Harvey, *The Savages of America; A Study of the Indian and the Idea of Civilization*, Johns Hopkins Press, Baltimore, 1953, 1965.
Concerns itself mainly with the American image of the Indian prior to 1851.

Spicer, Edward, *A Short History of the Indians of the United States,* Van Nostrand Reinhold Company, New York, 1969.
   In addition to being a short history, Spicer's volume contains many valuable documents.

Steiner, Stan, *The New Indian,* Dell Publishing Company, New York, 1968.
   Primarily based on interviews with young activists of today.

II
AFRO-AMERICANS

I confess, if I were a missionary, I would prefer to try my hand in a country like China that has a history of two or three or four or five thousand years, than to go into Africa that hasn't any history at all except that which we trace to the apes.

> William Howard Taft
> Address to Methodist Missionary Society, 1909

INTRODUCTION

Recent years have seen the introduction and rapid expansion of black studies. Many of the educators and students who advocate such programs have stressed the need "to set the record straight" on black contributions and the necessity of developing a black awareness. Such reasons are self-evident and have served to attract white as well as black students into courses on black history and culture. These students, for the most part, sincerely believe that a historical knowledge of blacks will make it possible to better understand and improve our present society. But a requisite for this task is missing. Americans must find out how and why the Afro-American has been historically ignored and/or misrepresented. "It is not enough to put a few Black heroes into our texts," wrote one critic, "we must study why they've been left out." To do so means the recognition that America has always had a "white" rather than a "Negro" problem. It also necessitates the study of racism in a manner quite different from the mere inclusion of forgotten minorities in our textbooks. Stokely Carmichael illustrated this point when he insisted that the civil rights laws were not passed for black folks—who knew what rights were due them—but to explain to whites that blacks had such rights.

The following selections illustrate that "mainstream America" was fairly well united on the racial issue. The scientists, for example, forcefully and frequently stated their doubts as to the blacks' innate ability to improve their racial stock. Journalists described the comic antics and behavioral foibles of black stereotypes in a most degrading manner. In the creation and enforcement of laws our legislators mirrored their racist times. Historians reinforced race thinking by describing a more orderly slave past when both blacks and whites seemed happier. The Supreme Court concluded that while the Constitution guaranteed legal rights to all, these ought not be confused with the social customs that had always prevailed. The novelists, as well, used their artistry to draw together the various negative images of blacks for their expanding reading public. What emerged was a black man—a Negro—who deservedly bore the mark, "Made in America."

Most of the selections in this chapter are drawn from the half-century preceding World War II. Racism did not, of course, have its initial roots in the late nineteenth century. Winthrop Jordan's fine study *White over Black* (1968), concludes that negative racial attitudes existed in England well before any slaves were introduced into English settlements in the New World. Nor did racism in America die out after World War II, although it often manifested itself in more subtle forms. An analysis of today's racism, however, often ignores its recent historical roots. Today's attitudes, and the resultant problems, did not just happen; they are endemic to our society and their pervasive quality can be seen in this general period when for the first time white America was forced to deal with massive numbers of free blacks.

The formal end to Reconstruction came in 1877 when President Rutherford B. Hayes withdrew the remaining Federal troops from the South. Historian Rayford Logan calls this action and its aftermath "the nadir" for the Afro-American. Not even under slavery had anti-Negro feelings been so intense and widespread, since under "the peculiar institution" a Negro's place was well defined. But after the Civil War and the brief experiment of Reconstruction, free blacks had to be given a new place in a society that emphasized white supremacy. Jim Crow was introduced as the South's solution, and the rest of the country gave its approval in a variety of ways. "A comprehensive doctrine of race was essential," wrote Oscar Handlin, "to justify the developing patterns of segregation." Many of the resultant scholarly theories and legislative and judicial actions, therefore, simply reflected the contemporary realities of their day.

There were also historical forces at work in this period that exacerbated race feelings. For a long time social and economic Darwinism prevailed in America's domestic and foreign policies, with the terms "survival of the fittest" and "natural selection" finding their way into race theorizing. It was also a time of growing nationalism and overseas expansion. Historians and scientists enthusiastically explored the past in an attempt to explain the forceful present. Finally, a rising literacy rate meant a new kind of reading public. These avid readers not only enjoyed the sensational but also demanded simplistic explanations to contemporary problems. Race theorists, therefore, found an eager audience for their writings.

The following selections will be unfamiliar to most Americans; in fact, they were chosen for that reason and because there is no valid justification for this unfamiliarity. Represented in this chapter are Presidential addresses, Supreme Court decisions, popular novels, mass-circulation magazine and newspaper articles, scientific opinions, and historical treatises. The very fact that such documents, which so vividly demonstrate America's racial views, have so long been ignored not only suggests the dimension of the race problem but also stresses the fact that America has even failed to recognize its existence.

1
In Their Place

The South long insisted that she not only knew and understood her blacks, but that she deeply loved them as well. There seems to be little doubt that many Southerners were sincere in such allegations, but always overlooked was the fact that this affection was meant only for those who knew their place and met the stereotyped image the South held. This was Sambo, the childlike man who, although carefree, slow-witted, passive, and somewhat dishonest, was nevertheless capable of showing the greatest of affection and fidelity toward his benevolent white superiors. His infectious good humor and his ofttimes canny ability to get what he wanted made him the object of kind paternalistic attentions from the white community.

This view was simply the updating of the myth of the "contented slave." By the end of the nineteenth century many in the North were also willing to suggest that freedom had actually worked a hardship on blacks. The black thus became the "wretched freedman" who seemingly was incapable of competing in an open society.

Perhaps, then, this unhappy individual was not only better suited for the plantation life but would probably be much more at ease with the built-in security of such a system. In the first quarter of the twentieth century, U. B. Phillips published his scholarly histories that suggested that the plantation was actually the "best school" for those caught in limbo between barbarism and civilization. Many writers, composers, politicians, scholars, and clergymen had long agreed—and if they as whites reached such conclusions, it followed that blacks must be entertaining similar nostalgic thoughts. And for those blacks who refused to stay in their place, the white majority had a variety of responses: there was always the threat of lynching or journalistic ridicule, scholarly denunciation, Jim Crow legislation, economic ostracism, and Christian moralizing.

A. STEPHEN FOSTER

Stephen Foster has long stood as one of America's foremost composers. At an early age most Americans are exposed to "Old Black Joe" or the "Old Folks at Home." Surely there could be nothing offensive about such well-loved songs, and, to be sure, for whites there was only the beautiful melodies and the sadly nostalgic words. But the words that often brought tears to white eyes were recalling days that certainly held no joy for blacks. Perhaps there were some who missed the plantation or pined for "Massa" after he was gone, but for the most part this was what white folks expected of blacks. Stephen Foster was not a Southerner. He did most of his composing in Pennsylvania, Ohio, and New York and the bulk of his contacts with "blacks" seems to have come from observing the minstrel singers. Although Stephen Foster's songs were written over 100 years ago, they lost little of their popularity in the twentieth century.

OLD FOLKS AT HOME

Way down upon de Swanee ribber,
Far, far away,
Dere's wha my heart is thrning ebber,
Dere's wha de old folks stay.
All up and down de whole creation,
Sadly I roam,
Still longing for de old plantation,
And for de old folks at home.

All round de little farm I wandered
When I was young.
Den many happy days I squandered,
Many de songs I sung.
When I was playing wid my brudder
Happy was I.
Oh! take me to my kind old mudder,
Dere let me live and die.

One little hut among de bushes,
One dat I love,
Still sadly to my mem'ry rushes,
No matter where I rove.

When will I see de bees a humming
All round de comb?
When will I hear de banjo tumming
Down in my good old home?

CHORUS   All de world am sad and dreary,
Ebrywhere I roam,
Oh! Darkies how my heart grows weary,
Far from de old folks at home.

MASSA'S IN DE COLD GROUND

Round de meadows am a ringing
De darkeys' mournful song.
While de mocking bird am singing,
Happy as de day am long.
Where de ivy am a creeping
O'er de grassy mound,
Dare old massa am a sleeping,
Sleeping in de cold, cold ground.

When de autumn leaves were falling,
When de days were cold,
'Twas hard to hear old massa calling,
Cayse he was so weak and old.
Now de orange tree am blooming
On de sandy shore,
Now de summer days am coming,
Massa nebber calls no more.

Massa made de darkeys love him,
Cayse he was so kind,
Now dey sadly weep above him,
Mourning cayse he leave dem behind.
I cannot work before tomorrow,
Cayse de ter drop flow.
I try to drive away my sorrow
Pickin' on de old banjo.

CHORUS   Down in de cornfield
Hear dat mournful sound:
All de darkeys am a weeping,
Massa's in de cold cold ground.

B.   JOEL CHANDLER HARRIS AND UNCLE REMUS, 1881

If Stephen Foster's songs were often among the first contacts many white children had with blacks, so too did the Uncle Remus stories help mold their images. A few black writers have been critical of Joel Chandler Harris for his racial stereotyping, but for the most part whites have ignored the possibility that his writings might be offensive to blacks. After all, Uncle Remus was black and such a lovely old man was he who weaved those wonderous tales of Brer Fox and Brer Rabbit. Yet Uncle Remus with his Harris-inspired Negro dialect seldom deviated from his acceptable place in Southern society. Harris was more overt in his view of blacks in his unsigned editorials in the Atlantic Constitution, *but there is no missing his point in the brief story concerning Uncle Remus and Negro education.*[1]

As to Education

As Uncle Remus came up Whitehall Street recently, he met a little colored boy carrying a slate and a number of books. Some words passed between them, but their exact purport will probably never be known. They were unpleasant, for the attention of a wandering policeman was called to the matter by hearing the old man bawl out:

"Don't you come foolin' longer me, nigger. Youer flippin' you' sass at de wrong color. You k'n go roun' yer an' sass deze w'ite people, an' maybe dey'll stan' it, but w'en you come a slingin' you' jaw at a man w'at waz gray w'en de fahmin' days gin out, you better go an' get yo' hide greased."

"What's the matter, old man?" asked a sympathizing policeman.

"Nothin', boss, 'ceppin I ain't gwineter hav' no nigger chillun a hoopin' an' a hollerin' at me w'en I'm gwine 'long de streets."

"Oh, well, school-children—you know how they are."

"Dat's w'at make I say w'at I duz. Dey better be home pickin' up chips. W'at a nigger gwineter l'arn outen books? I kin take a bar'l stave an' fling mo' sense into a nigger in one minute dan all de school-houses be-twixt dis en de State er Midgigin. Don't talk, honey! Wid one bar'l stave I kin fa'rly lif' de vail er ignunce."

"Then you don't believe in education?"

"Hit's de ruinashun er dis country. Look at my gal. De ole 'oman sont 'er ter school las' year, an' now we dassent hardly ax 'er fer ter kyar

[1]Joel Chandler Harris, *Uncle Remus: His Songs and His Sayings,* 1881 edition, D. Appleton & Co., New York, pp. 255–256.

de washin' home. She done got beyant'er bizness. I ain't larnt nuthin' in books, 'en yit I kin count all de money I gits. No use talkin', boss. Put a spellin'-book in a nigger's han's, en right den en dar' you loozes a plow-hand. I done had de speunce un it."

C. TWO BEST-SELLING NOVELS OF THE PROGRESSIVE ERA

Thomas Dixon's The Clansman *rose to number five on the best-seller list for 1905, and Owen Wister's* Lady Baltimore *ranked number two during the following year. Over the years Dixon's* The Clansman *achieved longer-lasting fame, first as a popular play and then in 1915 as the movie,* Birth of a Nation. *The movie version became the greatest attraction of the silent picture era. Ironically enough, it finally lost its number-one box-office rating to* Gone With the Wind, *another picture that did its share of racial stereotyping.*

Both Dixon and Wister were writing in a time when historians and novelists were stressing sectional unity in their works: the Civil War should never have been fought—reconstruction and the behavior of the free blacks proved that. In both novels Northerners must be convinced of the "Southern way of life." The Clansman *takes place during Reconstruction and pits the aristocratic Camerons of South Carolina against the Stonemans of Pennsylvania. Standing between the two families is the black man, and it is not until his moral degeneracy is recognized that harmony reigns between the two families and, one presumes, the North and South as well.*

Lady Baltimore *takes place after the turn of the century. The scene is Charleston, South Carolina, and the Northern narrator has taken up residence there for his magnolia education. The story opens to find that the good people of "King's Port" have been duly offended by President Roosevelt's appointment of a Negro to the custom's post.*

1. *The Clansman,* 1905

Many historians have emphasized that the inability of blacks to rule contributed heavily to the failure of Reconstruction. These historians, while ignoring the positive results of the Reconstruction governments, attempted to support their conclusions by describing the abuse of privileges in the various State Houses of the South. In the following passage, Dixon reflects such a viewpoint in a scene from the South Carolina Legislature.[1]

[1]Thomas Dixon Jr., *The Clansman*, Grosset & Dunlap, New York, 1905, pp. 263–267.

As he passed inside the doors of the House of Representatives the rush of foul air staggered him. The reek of vile cigars and stale whiskey, mingled with the odour of perspiring negroes [sic], was overwhelming. He paused and gasped for breath.

The space behind the seats of the members was strewn with corks, broken glass, stale crusts, greasy pieces of paper, and picked bones. The hall was packed with negroes, smoking, chewing, jabbering, pushing, perspiring.

A carpet-bagger at his elbow was explaining to an old darkey from down east why his forty acres and a mule hadn't come.

On the other side of him a big negro bawled:

"Dat's all right! De cullud man on top!"

The doctor surveyed the hall in dismay. At first not a white member was visible. The galleries were packed with negroes. The Speaker presiding was a negro, the Clerk a negro, the doorkeepers negroes, the little pages all coal-black negroes, the Chaplain a negro. The negro party consisted of one hundred and one—ninety-four blacks and seven scallawags, who claimed to be white. The remains of Aryan civilization were represented by twenty-three white men from the Scotch-Irish hill counties.

The doctor had served three terms as the member from Ulster in this hall in the old days, and its appearance now was beyond any conceivable depth of degradation.

The ninety-four Africans, constituting almost its solid membership, were a motley crew. Every negro type was there, from the genteel butler to the clodhopper from the cotton and rice fields. Some had on second-hand seedy frock-coats their old master had given them before the war, glossy and threadbare. Old stovepipe hats, of every style in vogue since Noah came out of the ark, were placed conspicuously on the desks or cocked on the backs of the heads of the honourable members. Some wore the coarse clothes of the field, stained with red mud.

Old Aleck, he noted had a red woollen comforter wound round his neck in place of a shirt or collar. He had tried to go barefooted, but the Speaker had issued a rule members should come shod. He was easing his feet by placing his brogans under the desk, wearing only his red socks.

Each member had his name painted in enormous gold letters on his desk, and had placed beside it a sixty-dollar French imported spittoon. Even the Congress of the United States, under the inspiration of Oakes Ames and Speaker Colfax, could only afford one of domestic make, which cost a dollar.

The uproar was deafening. From four to six negroes were trying to speak at the same time. Aleck's majestic mouth with blue gums and projecting teeth led the chorus as he ambled down the aisle, his bow-legs flying their red-sock ensigns.

The speaker singled him out—his voice was something which simply could not be ignored—rapped and yelled:

"De genman from Ulster set down!"

Aleck turned crestfallen and resumed his seat, throwing his big flat feet in their red woollens up on his desk and hiding his face behind their enormous spread.

He had barely settled in his chair before a new idea flashed through his head and up he jumped again:

"Mistah Speaker!" be bawled.

"Orda da!" yelled another.

"Knock 'im in de head!"

"Seddown, nigger!"

The Speaker pointed his gavel at Aleck and threatened him laughingly:

"Ef de genman from Ulster doan set down I gwine call 'im ter orda!"

Uncle Aleck greeted this threat with a wild guffaw, which the whole House about him joined in heartily. They laughed like so many hens cackling—when one started the other would follow.

The most of them were munching peanuts, and the crush of hulls under heavy feet added a subnote to the confusion like the crackle of prairie fire.

The ambition of each negro seemed to be to speak at least a half-dozen times on each question, saying the same thing every time.

No man was allowed to talk five minutes without an interruption which brought on another and another until the speaker was drowned in a storm of contending yells. Their struggles to get the floor with bawl-ings, bellowings, and contortions, and the senseless rap of the Speaker's gavel, were something appalling.

On this scene, through fetid smoke and animal roar, looked down from the walls, in marble bas-relief, the still white faces of Robert Hayne and George McDuffie, through whose veins flowed the blood of Scottish kings, while over it brooded in solemn wonder the face of John Laurens, whose diplomatic genius at the court of France won millions of gold for our tottering cause, and sent a French fleet and army into the Chesa-peake to entrap Cornwallis at Yorktown.

The little group of twenty-three white men, the descendants of these spirits, to whom Dr. Cameron had brought his memorial, presented a pathetic spectacle. Most of them were old men, who sat in given silence with nothing to do or say as they watched the raging black tide, their dignity, reserve, and decorum at once the wonder and the shame of the modern world.

At least they knew that the minstrel farce being enacted on that floor was a tragedy as deep and dark as was ever woven of the blood and tears of a conquered people. Beneath those loud guffaws they could hear the death rattle in the throat of their beloved State, barbarism strangling civilization by brute force.

2. *Lady Baltimore*, 1906

The narrator in Lady Baltimore *proved to be an able student of Southern life. In the following section he not only has learned the difference between the "old" and the "new" Negro, but he gets a lesson in popular anthropology as well. Finally he is able to apply his newly acquired knowledge of anatomy when he strikes a Negro on his "weak spot."*[1]

If all the negroes [sic] in Kings Port were like Daddy Ben, Mrs. Gregory St. Michael would not have spoken of having them "to deal with," and the girl behind the counter would not have been thrown into such indignation when she alluded to their conceit and ignorance. Daddy Ben had, so far from being puffed up by the appointment in the Custom House, disapproved of this. I had heard enough about the difference between the old and new generations of the negro of Kings Port to believe it to be true, and I had come to discern how evidently it lay at the bottom of many things here: John Mayrant and his kind were a band united by a number of strong ties, but by nothing so much as by their hatred of the modern negro in their town. Yes, I was obliged to believe the young Kings Port African, left to freedom and the ballot, was a worse African than his slave parents; but this afternoon brought me a taste of it more pungent than all the assurances in the world.

I bought my kettle-supporter, and learned from the robber who sold it to me (Kings Port prices for "old things" are the most exorbitant that I know anywhere) that a carpenter lived not far from Mrs. Trevise's boarding-house, and that he would make for me the box in which I could pack my various purchases.

"That is, if he's working this week," added the robber.

"What else would he be doing?"

"It may be his week for getting drunk on what he earned the week before." And upon this he announced with as much bitterness as if he had been John Mayrant or any of his aunts, "That's what Boston philanthropy has done for him."

I flared up at this. "I suppose that's a Southern argument for reestablishing slavery."

[1]Owen Wister, *Lady Baltimore*, Macmillan Co., New York, 1906, pp. 172–183.

"I am not Southern; Breslau is my native town, and I came from New York here to live five years ago. I've seen what your emancipation has done for the black, and I say to you, my friend, honest I don't know a fool from a philanthropist any longer."

He had much right upon his side; and it can be seen daily that philanthropy does not always walk hand-in-hand with wisdom. Does anything or anybody always walk so? Moreover, I am a friend to not many superlatives, and have perceived no saying to be more true than the one that extremes meet: they meet indeed, and folly is their meetingplace. Nor could I say in the case of the negro which folly were the more ridiculous:—that which expects a race which has lived no one knows how many thousand years in mental nakedness while Confucius, Moses, and Napoleon were flowering upon adjacent human stems, should put on suddenly the white man's intelligence, or that other folly which declares we can do nothing for the African, as if Hampton had not already wrought excellent things for him. I had no mind to enter into all the inextricable error with this Teuton, and it was he who continued:—

"Oh, these Boston philanthropists; oh, these know-it-alls! Why don't they stay home? Why do they come down here to worry us with their ignorance? See here, my friend, let me show you!"

He rushed about his shop in a search of distraught eagerness, and with a multitude of small exclamations, until, screeching jubilantly once, he pounced upon a shabby and learned-looking volume. This he brought me, thrusting it with his trembling fingers between my own, and shuffling the open pages. But when the apparently right one was found, he exclaimed, "No, I have better!" and dashed away to a pile of pamphlets on the floor, where he began to plough and harrow. Wondering if I was closeted with a maniac, I looked at the book in my passive hand, and saw diagrams of various bones to me unknown, and men's names of which I was equally ignorant—Mivart, Topinard, and more,—but at last that of Huxley. But this agreeable sight was spoiled at once by the quite horrible words Nycticebida, olatyrrhine, catarrhine, from which I raised my eyes to see him coming at me with two pamphlets, and scolding as he came.

"Are you educated, yes? Have been to college, yes? Then perhaps you will understand."

Certainly I understood immediately that he and his pamphlets were as bad as the book, or worse, in their use of a vocabulary designed to cause almost any listener the gravest inconvenience. Common Eocene ancestors occurred at the beginning of his lecture; and I believed that if it got no stronger than this, I could at least preserve the appearance of comprehending him; but it got stronger, and at sacro-iliac notch I may say, without using any grossly exaggerated expression, that I became unconscious. At least, all intelligence left me. When it returned, he was saying:—

"but this is only the beginning. Come in here to my crania and jaws."

Evidently he held me hypnotized, for he now hurried me unresisting through a back door into a dark little room, where he turned up the gas, and I saw shelves as in a museum, to one of which he led me. I suppose that it was curiosity that rendered me thus sheep-like. Upon the shelf were a number of skulls and jaws in admirable condition and graded arrangement, beginning to the left with that flat kind of skull which one associates with gorillas. He resumed his scolding harangue, and for a few brief moments I understood him. Here, told by themselves, was as much of the story of the skulls as we know, from manlike apes through glacial man to the modern senator or railroad president. But my intelligence was destined soon to die away again.

"That is the Caucasian skull; your skull," he said, touching a specimen at the right.

"Interesting," I murmured. "I'm afraid I know nothing about skulls."

"But you shall know something before you leave," he retorted, wagging his head at me; and this time it was not the book, but a specimen, that he pushed into my grasp. He gave it a name, not as bad as platyrrhine, but I feared worse was coming; then he took it away from me, gave me another skull, and while I obediently held it, pronounced something quite beyond me.

"And what is the translation of that?" he demanded excitedly.

"Tell me," I feebly answered.

He shouted with overwhelming triumph: "The translation of that is South Carolina nigger! Notice well this so excellent specimen. Prognathous, megadont, platyrrhine."

"Ha! Platyrrhine!" I saluted the one word I recognized as I drowned.

"You have said it yourself! was his extraordinary answer;—for what had I said? Almost as if he were going to break into a dance for joy, he took the Caucasian skull and the other two, and set the three together by themselves, away from the rest of the collection. The picture which they thus made spoke more than all measurements and statistics which he now chartered out upon me, reading from his book as I contemplated the skulls. There was a similarity of shape, a kinship there between the three, which stared you in the face; but in the contours of vaulted skull, the projecting jaws, and the great molar teeth—what was to be seen? Why, in every respect that the African departed from the Caucasian, he departed in the direction of the ape! Here was zoology mutely but eloquently telling us why there had blossomed no Confucius, no Moses, no

Napoleon, upon that black stem; why no Iliad, no Parthenon, no Sistine Madonna, had ever risen from that tropic mud.

The collector touched my sleeve. "Have you now learned something about skulls, my friend? Will you invite those Boston philanthropists to stay home? They will get better results in civilization by giving votes to monkeys than teaching Henry Wadsworth Longfellow to niggers."

Twice, as I went, I broke into laughter over my interview in the shop, which I fear has lost its comical quality in the relating. To enter a door and come serenely in among dingy mahogany and glass objects, to bargain haughtily for a brass bauble with the shopkeeper, and to have a few exchanged remarks suddenly turn the whole place into a sort of bedlam with a gibbering scientist dashing skulls at me to prove his fixed idea, and myself quite furious—I laughed more than twice; but, by the time I had approached the neighborhood of the carpenter's shop, another side of it had brought reflection to my mind. Here was a foreigner to whom slavery and the Lost Cause were nothing, whose whole association with the South had begun but five years ago; and the race question had brought his feelings to this pitch! He had seen the Kings Port negro with the eyes of the flesh, and not with the eyes of theory, and as a result the reddest rag for him was pale beside a Boston philanthropist!

Nevertheless, I have said already that I am no lover of superlatives, and in doctrine especially is this true. We need not expect a Confucius from the negro, nor yet a Chesterfield; but I am an enemy also of that blind and base hate against him, which conducts nowhere save to the de-civilizing of white and black alike. Who brought him here? Did he invite himself? Then let us make the best of it and teach him, lead him, compel him to live self-respecting, not as statesman, poet, or financier, but by the honorable toil of his hand and sweat of his brow. Because "the door of hope" was once opened too suddenly for him is no reason for slamming it now forever in his face.

Thus mentally I lectured back at the Teuton as I went through the streets of Kings Port; and after a while I turned a corner which took me abruptly, as with one magic step, out of the white man's world into the blackest Congo. Even the well-inhabited quarter of Kings Port (and I had now come within this limited domain) holds narrow lanes and recesses which teem and swarm with negroes. As cracks will run through fine porcelain, so do these black rifts of Africa lurk almost invisible among the gardens and the houses. The picture that these places offered, tropic, squalid, and fecund, often caused me to walk through them and watch the basking population; the intricate, broken wooden galleries, the rickety outside staircases, the red and yellow splashes of color on the clotheslines, the agglomerate rags that stuffed holes in decaying roofs or hung nakedly on human frames, the small, choked dwellings, bursting open at doors and windows with black, round-eyed babies as an overripe melon bursts with seeds, the children playing marbles in the court, the parents playing cards in the room, the grandparents smoking pipes on the porch, and the great-grandparents upstairs gazing out at you like creatures from the Old Testament or the jungle. From the jungle we had stolen them, North and South had stolen them together, long ago, to be slaves, not to be citizens, and now here they were, the fruits of our theft; and for some reason (possibly the Teuton was the reason) that passage from the Book of Exodus came into my head: "For I the Lord thy God am a jealous God, visiting the iniquity of the fathers upon the children."

These thoughts were interrupted by sounds as of altercation. I had nearly reached the end of the lane, where I should again emerge into the white man's world, and where I was now walking the lane spread into a broader space with ells and angles and rotting steps, and habitations mostly too ruinous to be inhabited. It was from a sashless window in one of these that the angry voices came. The first words which were distinct aroused my interest quite beyond the scale of an ordinary altercation:—

"Calls you'self a reconstruckted niggah?"

This was said sharply and with prodigious scorn. The answer which it brought was lengthy and of such a general sullen incoherence that I could make out only a frequent repetition of "custom house," and that somebody was going to take care of somebody hereafter.

Into this the first voice broke with tones of highest contempt and rapidity:—

"President gwine to gib brekfus' an' dinnah an suppah to de likes ob you fo' de whole remaindah ob youh wuthless nat'ral life? Get out ob my sight, you reconstruckted niggah. I come out ob de St. Michael."

There came through the window immediately upon this sounds of scuffling and of a fall, and then cries for help which took me running into the dilapidated building. Daddy Ben lay on the floor, and a thick, young savage was kicking him. In some remarkable way I thought of the solidity of their heads, and before the assailant even knew that he had a witness, I sped forward, aiming my kettle-supporter and with its sharp brass edge I dealt him a crack over his shin with astonishing accuracy.

D. RACISM AND WARTIME

In every major American war, blacks have proven their support for the nation through their battlefield bravery; yet in every war they have

*had to battle almost as hard for the right to fight as they did against the
enemy. George Washington was hesitant to use black troops until forced
to by military expediency. Abraham Lincoln summed up a general feeling toward black soldiers when he initially opposed their use in the
Civil War because he feared whites could not be made to fight alongside them and because he doubted the ability and courage of blacks under fire. "To arm the negroes [sic] would turn 50,000 bayonets from
the loyal Border States against us that were for us," said Lincoln, and
a short time later he insisted that "if we were to arm [the Negroes], I
fear that in a few weeks the arms would be in the hands of the rebels."*

*During World War I the United States further insulted black troops
by warning the French about the dangers of treating black soldiers as
equals, and President Wilson sent Tuskegee President Robert Moton to
check on reports that American black troops were ravishing French
women. Nor had things changed much 23 years later when America
fought against Hitler's racism with its own segregated army. In 1949
President Harry Truman declared an end to segregation in the Armed
Forces, and his executive order was gradually implemented during the
Korean War.*

1. "Mobilizing 'Rastus,' " 1918

*In popular stereotyping black Americans were either too lazy, too
ignorant, or too scared to be trained for the serious business of fighting
for one's country. The fact that during World War I a lesser percentage
of blacks was rejected for induction than whites, that Northern blacks
scored generally higher than Southern whites on the army's intelligence
tests, and that blacks won the enthusiastic plaudits of the French nation
for their enviable war record, meant little to an America that got its
picture of blacks from the articles and cartoons of our national magazines and newspapers. The following excerpts from* Outlook's *"Mobilizing Rastus" cover many of the popular concepts concerning the
ineptness of America's Black citizens.*[1]

"Name?" asked the captain, as he glanced up at the denim-clad Negro
on the other side of the desk.

" 'Tass," the man replied, shifting uneasily from one foot to the other
as the officers in the registering line looked at him.

" 'Tass who?" queried the lieutenant at the service record desk.

"Po-Potassium Aceta' Smith, Cap'n."

[1]Lieutenant Charles C. Lynde, "Mobilizing Rastus," *Outlook*, March 13, 1918,
pp. 412–418.

At the full name the lieutenant laid down his pen with a hearty laugh.

" 'Postassium Acetate Smith,' " he repeated, slowly. "We ought to transfer that boy to the medical department, if only on account of his drugstore name."

The officers were a part of the force enrolling the draft quotas in the Negro division being formed as a portion of the National Army. All day they had been struggling with incomplete registration records, improperly filled out designations of beneficiaries, and slighted physical examination cards. . . .

Potassium Acetate, together with some fifty-odd of his fellows, was marched over to one of the outlying barracks, and his military training begun. Single file the men marched past the door of the supply room and clean underclothing, soap, towels, and a suit of blue denim overalls —fatigue uniforms, in the service nomenclature—were issued to them. The line entered one door of the barracks and was ushered out through the other to the bath-house. A shower-bath, with plenty of hot water, was required of each recruit. Most of the men welcomed the opportunity for bathing, though the cold shower ordered at the finish was slighted as far as possible under the deterrent eye of the watchful commanding officer. . . .

Many of the darkies evidently had never before met a shower-bath, and after the ablutions were finished one of them approached the lieutenant in charge to ask if he might take "one of them there shower pipes" every day. In the course of the conversation which followed the man admitted that he never before had been wet all over at once, except the time he fell off a gangplank into the Mississippi River. . . .

At sick call [the next] morning one recruit reported severe pains all over his back—"misery," he called it. On the theory that sick-call malingering could be checked only by examining personally each case up for medical attention, the lieutenant ordered the man to take off his shirt. It was removed, revealing a back crisscrossed at regular intervals by ridges and furrows.

"How long have you been this way?" asked the commanding officer.

"All night, suh lieutenant," was the reply; "didn't get no rest 'tall, mah back was a-hurtin' me so. Anyways I try to sleep 'pear to me like dat misery 'd get worse. I ain't used to dese here army beds nohow!"

The last remark, about the army bed, solved the puzzle. The man had filled his bed sack properly, and then had spread a blanket over the wire springs of his cot and crawled under the tick to sleep. Naturally the springs left their imprint on his body, with some two hundred and twenty pounds of avoirdupois to counteract the slight padding effect of one blanket. . . .

New songs for group singing were taught by taking advantage of the imitative nature of the Negro. A small talking machine was secured, and the song to be learned was played over a time or two. If the music was catchy, it was only a little while before the men would begin to join in on the words, and the first thing they knew the song would be learned. After the men acquired confidence the machine would be stopped suddenly, leaving the group to carry the song.

An example of the unifying effect of song occurred early in the life of the organization. The company was engaged in clearing the ground around the barracks, and it was necessary to move some heavy timbers. Ten or twelve men would cluster around a stick and try to move it, the acting sergeant in charge strutting along ahead and counting "One, two, three, four-r-r!" for the step. Some would start on the right foot instead of the left, and then would throw the entire squad off when they attempted to change cadence. Finally Potassium Acetate, in one of the intervals while the sergeant was calling down one of the clumsy ones, began to chant:

"Left, Ah left, Ah had a good home an' left,
Ah left my wife an' a big fat baby.
Hayfoot, strawfoot, a belly full o' bean soup,
Left, Ah left, Ah had a good home an' left—
Kill dat nigger ef he don' keep step!"

and in less than the time it took the sergeant to count fours the men were all in step and carrying the timber with half their previous effort.
. . .

All the instruction was founded on the natural imitative tendencies of the Negro. He learns from example quickly, and it was but a short time before the men had mastered the simpler movements of the manual of arms, and could go through them without a single pause. From the manual to evolutions on the drill field was but a step, each new formation being drilled into a picked squad first, and this squad used to lead the others until the entire company had picked up the movement. . . .

The semaphore system of signaling—taught to troops in all branches of the service for communication over short distances—was difficult to master. The average Negro has no conception of angles, and since a variation of over twenty degrees in the position of one arm may make either a poor "l," or an equally incorrect "m," or a weak "r," or a slipshod "s," the first attempts at transmission were almost hopeless. If the sender stopped to look at the hand he was holding over his head, he invariably shifted the other arm to such an extent that when he was satisfied as to his upper arm the position of the lower had changed the letter to something entirely different. This was gradually overcome, as in the facing drill, by careful practice with men in front to set the proper example.

Reading messages given to the sender verbally was more a matter of mindreading than a signaling. The Negro's spelling is usually phonetic with variations. The first time the lieutenant attempted to read what was being sent he failed so miserably that he spent two hours that night brushing up on his semaphore work, thinking that he must have grown rusty in reading the positions.

The next day showed no improvement, and it was not until the C.O. attempting to receive wrote down each letter as it was formed that he was able to decipher the message. Such spelling as "b-a-r-a-x," "M-i-s-u-r-i," and "F-en-n-i-x" were noted in the morning's sending. Phonetically, each word approximates the one intended, but coming a letter at a time, with many shifts of the arm positions, it was easy to see why the men progressed comparatively rapidly as senders and so slowly as receivers. . . .

The first pay day, long and anxiously awaited, finally came and the men were mustered and inspected before being marched to the paymaster. The quartermaster in charge, to facilitate quick payment, had arranged before him piles of bills in large denominations and heaps of silver dollars six to eight inches high in the centers. Scarcely any of the men even so much as glanced at the bills, but the mountains of silver fascinated them. One man, after receiving a twenty-dollar and ten-dollar bill as his pay, stood around, hat in hand, until the entire company had been paid off. He approached the pay desk timidly, one eye on the pile of silver and the other on the service automatic ostentatiously worn by the paymaster.

"Cap'n boss," began the darky, laying down his two bills "cain't you-all gimme dis in money 'stead of paper?"

And when the paymaster explained that he had just dollars enough to make the proper change for each man, he asked "Den could you stack me up what this comes to in dollars, so's I can see how much I'se got?"

How much he had didn't matter much, as by next morning a luckier —or more skillful—member of another company had taken away the twenty, as well as considerable money from others of the organization. The lure of the "bones" with a month's pay in hand was too strong to be resisted; though there were many men who took most or all of their pay to the lieutenant asking that he dole it out to them in little bits during the month.

2. "The Clash of Color," 1919

The Afro-American has never suffered from a lack of advice from his white counterpart. Although traditionally this might take many forms, it invariably counsels patience and self-improvement while often ignoring the need for fundamental changes in white society. During times of racial crisis this advice is more freely and vigorously given, and sometimes the good advice sounds a bit like a threat.

After World War I, the black soldiers returned hoping to find that the world "made safe for democracy" included the United States. They were doomed to disappointment. Race relations reached the nadir during the "Red Summer" of 1919 when city after city erupted in racial rioting. Something was wrong and America wanted an answer. In the following article, Glenn Frank, then an assistant editor of Century *and soon to be President of the University of Wisconsin, analyzed why the "clash of color" had occurred and what might be done to avert its repetition in the future. Among other things, he cited the adverse effect the "French experience" had had on the black soldiers. For an amiable future he stressed the need for the Negro to follow the right kind of leader.[1]*

Tasting the Wine of Equality

Another matter to be taken into account is the fact that our negro [sic] soldiers tasted social equality in France. To them it was no doubt an exhilarating wine, and many of them have returned still flushed with its intoxication. In Europe they found a white attitude toward the negro different from the attitude they had known at home. There he was a white man with a black skin. Certain bitter partisans are using, with the demagogue's disregard of accuracy, the phrase "French-women-ruined" to describe the mass of returned negro soldiers. This wholesale charge is manifestly unfair both to the French women and to the American negro, but it rests upon the clear fact that the American negro's social adventures in France have further complicated our race problem.

An interesting side-light on the French attitude toward the negro has just come to my attention through the translation by Theodore Stanton of an incident from pages 3730-2 of the "Journal Officiel" of the French Chamber of Deputies for the sitting of July 25, 1919. M. Rene Boisneuf, one of the negro deputies of the Chamber, read an official communication, dated last August, which Colonel Linard, chief of the French military mission with the American Army in France, addressed to French officers. The communication attempted to interpret to French officers the attitude of the white American officers toward the American negro officers, and to prescribe how French officers should act in their relations with American colored soldiers in general in order to conserve French-

[1]Glenn Frank, "The Clash of Color," *Century*, November 1919, pp. 86–98.

American harmony in the matter. The communication contained a long and explicit set of recommendations. The tone of the communication is illustrated by this quotation:

> American opinion is unanimous on this "negro question" and permits no discussion of the matter. . . . The kindly spirit which exists in France for the negro profoundly wounds Americans, who consider it an infringement on one of their national dogmas, and if observed by us will greatly indispose American opinion toward us. . . . If French officers treat American negroes as they treat French negro officers, white American officers will warmly resent it. We should not sit at table with them and should avoid shaking hands with them. . . . The merits of the American negro troops should not be too much praised, especially in the presence of Americans.

M. Boisneuf paid a glowing tribute to the American colored troops, and declared amidst enthusiastic applause that "in France no distinction is made between her sons, no one asks whence they come or who they may chance to be." The interpellation ended with the unanimous passage of the resolution:

> The Chamber of Deputies, faithful to the immortal principles of the Rights of Man and the Citizen, reproving and condemning every prejudice of faith, caste, and race, affirms and proclaims the absolute equality of all men without distinction of origin or color in the enjoyment of the benefits and protection of all the laws of the land.

The subtle psychological influence of this French attitude on the minds of many of our returning negro soldiers is being played upon and appealed to by that element in negro leadership which has a hankering after social equality.

Three Kinds of Negro Leadership

Much will depend upon the type of leadership the mass of American negroes choose to follow. Speaking in the broad, there are three types of negro leadership to-day bidding for the allegiance of the race. These are:

First, the ultra-radical or revolutionary type of leadership to which reference has already been made. . . .

It will be unfortunate if the American negro to any marked extent follows these leaders. It would inevitably bring down upon the negro the wrath of the conservative white world and make more difficult his fight for even the most elementary justice. And it appeals to me as very short-sighted policy upon the part of ultra-radicals to attempt the winning of the negro to their side. They will succeed only in confusing their social and economic issues with the unreasoning hatreds, prejudices, and passions that cluster around the race question.

Second, there is the Du Bois school of leadership, which urges the negro to wage an uncompromising fight for the full and unqualified rights of American citizenship. This school would transplant in America the European conception of the negro as a white man with an accidental blackness of skin. This school, in the main, is no more averse to aggressive methods than the first sort of leadership mentioned, but is more concerned with the dogma of equality than with radical social revolution as an economic consideration. Du Bois, in the earlier days of his public career as scholar and writer, wrote in a style of liquid beauty his protests against the color line in American life. . . .

But in these later days hate has rusted his pen. He speaks more bluntly. He snarls as a wolf at bay. The poet has abdicated in favor of the propagandist. He tells the negro soldier that he went to Europe as a fighting man and that he must return fighting, fighting, fighting for the unqualified rights of an American citizen. He is an apostle of impatience.

Third, is what may best be called the Booker Washington school of leadership. This type of leadership covets the best for the race no less than do the two schools just mentioned, but frankly recognizes the existence of race prejudice and puts its faith in evolution rather than in edicts. . . .

Statesman that he was, Booker Washington accepted the fact of race prejudice and shaped his policies around that central fact. The color line saddened Washington just as it saddened Du Bois, but he felt that his mission was to achieve all possible progress, and he knew that battering his brains against a stone wall would help very little. So he accepted exclusion as inevitable, and worked out his Tuskegee program of making useful men who would, as skilled engineers and farmers, as trained artisans, make it more and more difficult to launch the charge of incompetence, ignorance, slovenly farming, and careless house management against his race. . . .

When all is said and done nothing since his death has invalidated the essential soundness of Booker Washington's policy. In this time of universal unrest and fresh aspirations it will not be easy for the negro to accept the full implications of the policy, but it is the most statesmanlike program that the race has yet evolved, simply because it reckons with facts and looks toward possible progress rather than theoretical perfection.

The poorest friend the negro has is the sentimental philanthropist who, sweeping all of the biological facts in the case aside, thinks to lift the race by according to black men smatterings of classical education and social equality. Some one has suggested that to these well-meaning, but blind, guides the negro might address the words of Andres to Don Quixote: "For the love of God, Signor Knight Errant, if ever you meet me again, though you see me beaten to pieces, do not come to my help, but leave me to my fate, which cannot be so bad but that it will be made worse by your worship." The negro is not a white man with a black skin; he is a different race at a different stage in racial evolution. It is not fair to judge him by the standards of the white race. It is folly to expect him to respond with white alacrity to the opportunities that white men enjoy. We must remember that the Anglo-Saxon did not leap to his present supremacy at one bound; he has walked over the slow road of racial evolution. That fact should counsel the negro to patience under certain discriminations that may off-hand appear unjust, and should also throw light upon the white man's program for the negro.

E.   THE BLACK MAMMY'S MONUMENT, 1923

Nowhere is covert racism more evident than when white Americans talk patronizingly about Negroes whom they have deeply loved, and the "black mammy" has long produced such nostalgic reminiscences. "Why, I loved her as much as my own mother," comes the grateful acknowledgement from those thus served. When such praise is not met with reassuring acceptance by black people in general, a note of disbelief, if not anger, is the general response from those same whites who felt they so well knew their Negroes.

In 1923 a bill that met with favorable response in the Senate would have empowered the Army engineers to select a suitable site in the capital on which they would erect a statue to "The Black Mammy of the South." The response from blacks was quick and generally negative. The Literary Digest *of March 31, 1923 (p. 56) and April 28, 1923 (pp. 48–52) carried the comments of several newspapers on the subject. The following article from the* Baltimore Sun *well summed up the attitude of those whites who felt the project was a meaningful tribute to the Negro.*[1]

[1]Reprinted by permission of the *Baltimore Sun.*

The Black Mammy of the South

The board of directors of Phyllis Wheatley Y.W.C.A. of Washington, representing two thousand colored women of the District of Columbia, have [sic] adopted resolutions protesting against the erection of a statue to the "Black Mammy of the South," either in Washington or anywhere else. And they consider the matter of so much importance that they have appealed to Vice-President Coolidge and to Speaker Gillett of the House to use their influence against the approval by Congress of such a project. The resolutions declare that "the colored women of the city of Washington do not like to be vividly reminded of the unfortunate condition of some of our ancestors, as were the helots of Greece or the serfs of Russia." They add: "The old mammy as a slave, however well she may have performed her part as a foster mother to many of the progeny of the South, represents the shadows of the past. Such irritants are not conducive to the harmony of citizenship."

The suggestion of the Southern Mammy statue was inspired by affectionate recollections of a type worthy, it seemed to those with whom the idea originated, of an enduring eulogy and memorial. It never occurred to them that the present generation of colored people would be ashamed of her. And the last thing in their minds was to wound sensitive feelings or to remind her descendants that they came from a race of slaves. What they proposed was a tribute to the noblest of human qualities, loyalty, fidelity and love. They felt they owed a debt to her and sought to pay it in this way.

None of these sentimentalists, it may safely be assumed, will attempt to force this honor upon her against the wishes of those who now affect to speak of her with condescending pity and patronage. We have a notion that, could she speak to these resolutions, she would give her learned and superior grandchildren a sharp piece of her very sharp mind. She did not have much book learning, but she could be as scornful as the most scornful to persons who "put on airs" in her vicinity, and she wouldn't stand any nonsense from any person of color, free or slave. She never put herself in the latter class. She considered herself a member of the family in which she found herself, and in refinement, good breeding and good manners was a model whom few of her descendants of to-day can approach. She will not suffer by being excluded from colored circles in Washington. Statues to her may be erected in the South without the permission of the Federal Government. She has been immortalized already in Southern literature in such tender sketches as those of Thomas Nelson Page; and it is she rather than the college graduate of the present who makes for the "harmony of citizenship" in the South to-day.

F.   JIM CROW, 1949

The 1950's witnessed the first concerted legal attack on discrimination since Reconstruction. The Supreme Court initiated action and Congress followed with a series of civil rights acts. It was a time of great optimism for blacks and liberal whites, who hoped that legal equality would soon lead to economic and social equality as well. The following 1949 chart does show the need for Federal guarantees of human rights.[1]

		ALA.	ARIZ.	ARK.	CAL.	COLO.	CONN.	DEL.	D.C.	FLA.	GA.	IDAHO	ILL.	IND.	IOWA	KANS.	KY.	LA.	ME.	MD.	MASS.	MICH.	MINN.	MISS.	MO.
AMUSEMENTS	BILLIARD & POOL ROOMS									✔															
PUBLIC HALLS	PARKS, PLAYGROUNDS, BEACHES, BOATING ③																								✔
	PUBLIC HALLS, THEATRES																								
	RACETRACKS				✔												✔								
	CIRCUSES																								
EDUCATION ①	CONSTITUTIONAL PROVISION	✔					✔		✔	✔						✔	✔							✔	✔
	STATUTORY PROVISION—PUBLIC SCHOOLS	✔	✔	✔			✔	✔	✔	✔				✔		✔	✔			✔				✔	✔
	PRIVATE SCHOOLS								✔																
	SCHOOLS FOR DEAF		✔					✔	✔								✔	✔						✔	
	SCHOOLS FOR DUMB																								
	SCHOOLS FOR BLIND		✔						✔					✔	✔									✔	
	JUVENILE DELINQUENT & REFORM SCHOOLS	✔	✔			✔	✔	✔	✔					✔	✔		✔					✔	✔		
	AGRICULTURE & TRADE SCHOOLS	✔	✔					✔	✔					✔	✔							✔	✔		
	COLLEGES & UNIVERSITIES	✔	✔			✔		✔	✔					✔②	✔	✔						✔	✔		
	TEACHERS' TRAINING SCHOOLS	✔	✔			✔		✔	✔					✔	✔	✔						✔	✔		
	SEPARATE SCHOOLS FOR INDIANS							✔														✔			
	SEPARATE TEXTBOOKS FOR NEGRO & WHITE								✔																
	SEPARATE LIBRARIES																								✔
EMPLOYMENT	SEPARATE WASHROOMS IN MINES		✔																						
	SEPARATE TOILETS IN MFG. BUSINESS																								
	SEGREGATION IN COTTON TEXTILE FACTORIES																							✔	
HOSPITALS	SEGREGATION GENERALLY	✔							✔							✔	✔	✔		✔				✔	✔
	MENTAL PATIENTS	✔			✔												✔	✔		✔					
	TUBERCULAR PATIENTS	✔																						✔	
	NURSING	✔																						✔	
PENAL	SEGREGATION GENERALLY	✔	✔					✔	✔								✔								
INSTITUTIONS	WHITES & NEGROES NOT TO BE CHAINED TOGETHER	✔	✔					✔	✔																
WELFARE	HOMES FOR AGED & ORPHANS ④					✔										✔	✔								
INSTITUTIONS	PAUPERS	✔																							
TRANSPORTATION⑤	BUSSES	✔						✔⑥	✔							✔				✔				✔	
	RAILROADS	✔	✔					✔	✔							✔	✔	✔		✔				✔	
	STREET CARS, STREET RAILWAYS, ELECTRIC CARS		✔					✔									✔	✔		✔					
	STEAMBOATS, FERRIES																	✔							
	WAITING ROOMS	✔	✔					✔								✔				✔					
	SLEEPING COMPARTMENTS		✔					✔																✔⑦	
MISCELLANEOUS	MIXED MARRIAGES PROHIBITED ⑧																								
RESTRICTIONS	WHITE & NEGRO OR MULATTO	✔	✔	✔	✔⑦	✔		✔		✔	✔⑧	✔		✔		✔	✔	✔		✔				✔	✔
	WHITE & AMERICAN INDIAN																								
	WHITE & MONGOLIAN, ORIENTAL	✔		✔⑦						✔	✔					✔							✔	✔	
	COHABITATION BETWEEN RACES PROHIBITED	✔	✔					✔								✔	✔	✔							
	ADOPTION BY PERSONS OF SAME RACE ONLY												✔												
	ARMY—SEPARATE BATALLIONS																								
	BOXING—NEGRO & WHITE PROHIBITED																								
	FRATERNAL ASSOC.—NEGRO & WHITE PROHIBITED																							✔	
	SOCIAL EQUALITY, CRIME TO PUBLISH ADVOCATING																								
	TELEPHONE BOOTHS																								
	VOTING LISTS, POLL TAX LISTS, TAX LISTS ⑩	✔	✔					✔		✔															
	VOTING PLACES																								
	INDIANS—FURNISHING LIQUOR TO, FORBIDDEN	✔	✔					✔				✔								✔					
	INDIANS—FURNISHING FIREARMS TO FORBIDDEN	✔								✔															
	HOUSING—SEGREGATION ⑨																✔								

[1]Reprinted by permission of The Board of Missions of the United Methodist Church from Pauli Murray, *States' Laws on Race and Color*, Woman's Division of Christian Services, Board of Missions and Church Extension, the Methodist Church, Cincinnati, 1949, p. 705.

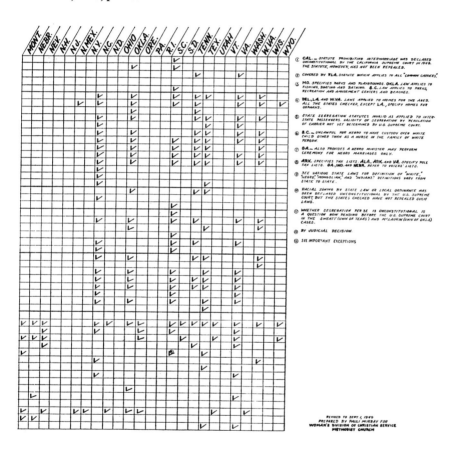

G. BILLY GRAHAM'S SOLUTION FOR SEGREGATION

*Motivated by "the crisis brought about by the school segregation de-
cision of the Supreme Court," the editors of Life, on September 3, 1956,
began a five-part series on the historical and current problems created
by segregation. The concluding installment dealt with the basic moral
and religous questions raised by segregation in the Southern United
States. To examine these questions, Life published an article by the Rev.
Billy Graham written especially for the series. Accompanying the Graham
article was a summary of a special "round table" discussion on the subject by a group of seven "eminent southern churchmen and leading
church laymen." All the participants were white. In an editorial commenting on these articles, Life concluded that "even in Christian ethics,
racial segregation is a complicated problem." The Rev. Graham's personal reflections support Life's contention.*

*Historically the church has been one of America's most segregated in-
stitutions. This was still true in 1956. To explain this would be to examine
the very tenets of American Christianity, and neither Rev. Graham nor
the panel proved willing to do this. For Billy Graham it was largely a
problem of sin—man's "soul sickness," as he called it—and the solution
was spiritual salvation. Unfortunately, to equate the problem with personal sin was to ignore the institutional nature of segregation. Nor did
Rev. Graham escape the past when he warned the Negroes not to be
resentful and to continue to practice their well-known "patience and
faith as a people."[1]*

Billy Graham Makes A Plea
For An End To Intolerance

Last April when I returned from a tour of India and the Far East, I
was invited to the White House. I thought that the President wanted a
report of my impressions of India. I was wrong. The main topic of our
conversation was the racial problem in the United States. The President
was deeply concerned about it, and he felt strongly that the church
could make a contribution toward the bettering of race relations.

Upon leaving the White House, I want back to my hotel room and
knelt in prayer, asking God to help me make any contribution I could
toward the easing of racial tensions. Since then I have talked about the

[1]"Billy Graham Makes A Plea For An End To Intolerance," *Life* Magazine,
October 1, 1956. © 1956, Time Inc. Reprinted by permission.

problem with leaders of all denominations and both colors. And I have come to the conclusion that the vast majority of the ministers of the South are not extremists on either side. Most of them feel that segregation should be ended now on buses, in railroad and bus stations, hotels and in restaurants. However, most of them feel that it is far too early to implement school integration in some sections of the deep South. They seem to feel that the day will come when both races will be psychologically and spiritually ready for it, but that the time has not come yet. Another conclusion I have come to is that most ministers of the South agree that race relations are worse now than they were two years ago. Then, with an uneasy conscience, most of them have confessed that the church is doing far too little about it. . . .

The guilt and the problems are by no means limited to America. The slaves were captured and sold largely by Africans. However, it must be remembered that they did not have the Christian concept of the Golden Rule. To the everlasting shame of the Dutch, the English and the northern Americans, it was their traders who took an active part, by and large, in slavery. I say this not to ease the conscience of southern American readers, but so that no one may feel unchallenged by the high demands of Christian love.

I have observed discrimination in almost every country I have visited. . . . And in the United States we have discriminated against Mexicans, Japanese, Indians, and Jews. Nor is prejudice confined to whites.

In a southern city this summer I talked with a Negro leader who understood, but could not conquer his own feelings. "I have as much prejudice in my heart against a man because his skin is white as any man had against a Negro because his skin is black," he told me. "I know that is sinful," he said, "and I'm working on it, but it's still there. . . ."

We must keep in mind that the race problem has two sides. The definition of what is right and the dynamic for doing the right. The Christian minister must be on guard in both respects lest he conform his message to the climate of the times. Is Christianity against segregation and for integration? These terms are often "loaded" today but they need to be clarified. There are times when men think they are being discriminated against when actually they are not. The Bible speaks against any kind of discrimination. But, there can be voluntary alignments on the basis of social and other preferences, where personal choice alone is involved and where the Christian ethic is not at stake.

The Bible requires neighbor-love alongside the love for God, and neighbor-love strikes far deeper than what usually passes today as "an end to segregation," and "community integration." The Christian layman must speak out against the social ills of our times, but he must be careful to speak with the voice of the biblical prophets and apostles and not in the spirit of secular and socializing views. This warning is even more necessary in the sphere of action. The pulpit does only half its job when it tells men what they ought to do and neglects the "power" for social reconstruction peculiar to the Christian religion.

It would be folly, of course, to argue that Christians (and I use the term more narrowly than church members), taken as a whole, are exemplary in their racial attitudes. . . . But one thing is sure. True neighbor-love flows from a regenerate life alone. "Absence of prejudice" doubtless belongs to neighbor-love, but it is far from the whole of it. Christian missionaries going to the perilous wastes of Africa and Asia in self-denial to bring a worthwhile life to the neglected natives are a commentary on it, and Jesus is its true exemplar. The church, if its aims be the true church, dares not segregate the message of good racial relations from the message of regeneration, for the human race is sinful—and man as sinner is prone to desert God and neighbor alike. . . .

Although the church is the strongest unifying force in the South, its voice is partly hushed. However, the responsibility for discrimination is not all one-sided. The Negroes, too, must share the responsibility. When we were in Jackson, Mississippi, four years ago, we still had segregation in our meetings. The average attendance of Negroes was between two and three thousand. When they came forward to receive Christ they mingled with whites at the altar. However, when we went to Richmond, Nashville and Oklahoma City, where there was no segregation in our meetings, we averaged only about two or three hundred Negroes a night. I asked many Negroes about it. They said they felt much more comfortable sitting by themselves.

Most Negro leaders have told me that they really do not want to intermingle with whites, but that they rebel at laws and ropes that bar them. As someone has said, "Take the dare out of it, and 90% of the problem is solved." I think probably one of the United States' finest examples of race relations is found in Honolulu. There is little discrimination and segregation there, and many races are living together. Yet when it comes to the church, there is the Chinese church, the Korean church, the white churches, the Negro churches, etc. Why? The reason is that the church is probably the most voluntary of all organizations. There is nothing sinful in races wanting to stay together. The sin comes when a church puts up its color bar at the Cross of Christ. . . .

Racial discrimination, like other social sins, is a product of man's sinfulness. (Though in the foregoing words I have tried to diagnose the illness, I am keenly aware that I have been dealing with symptoms rather than causes.) Many voices more capable than mine are analyzing our social ills, but the work of the diagnostician is useless without the skill of the physician. This problem cannot be solved without the aid of him who said, "The Spirit of the Lord is upon me. . . . He has sent me to proclaim release to the captives and recovering of sight to the blind and to set at liberty those who are oppressed." The Bible says of man's soul sickness, "The whole head is sick, and the whole heart faint." Too long now we have tried to cope with our social ills in our own strength. Self-treatment only leads to deeper entrenchment in our social infirmities. Christ stands ready, willing, and able to redeem all who call upon him. Until we confront the Redeemer with our problem of lostness we cannot find a satisfactory answer to our social problems.

Christ said, "You must be born anew. . . ." Force, legislation, persuasion and preachments will avail nothing if hearts are not filled with the love of God. . . .

For the Negro today the Bible has many words of comfort and also a word of warning: "If when you do right and suffer for it you take it patiently, you have God's approval . . . because Christ also suffered for you, leaving you an example, that you should follow in his steps."

Do not let yourself be drawn into retaliation or hatred. Resentment always damages the subject more than the object. You have been known for your patience and faith as a people. Continue to grow in faith, hope and love.

2

The Supreme Court and Three Presidents Consider "The Negro Problem"

In the last quarter of the nineteenth century the Supreme Court declared unconstitutional most of the civil rights laws that had been carefully passed by the Radical Republicans during Reconstruction. These decisions encouraged the South to continue relegating blacks to second-class citizenship. Americans have often castigated the South for her Jim Crow tactics, but this is to ignore the fact that she could not have done so without at least the tacit approval of the rest of the country. The Supreme Court during this period, for example, was dominated by Northern Republicans.

Likewise, with the exception of Woodrow Wilson, the presidents in the decades following the Reconstruction came from outside the South; and although they avoided giving formal recognition to the South's segregation policies, several did differentiate between civil and social rights while adopting a patronizing attitude toward the overall role of blacks in America.

A.   THE CIVIL RIGHTS CASES OF 1883

Of the nine members of the Court in 1883 there were only two Southerners and one Democrat. It was thus not a Southern decision that declared the Civil Rights Act of 1875 unconstitutional. The 1875 Act had deemed it essential that the government "recognize the equality of all men before the law, and . . . to mete out equal and exact justice to all, of whatever nativity, race, color, or persuasion." The act further provided that all persons within the jurisdiction of the United States should be entitled to "the full and equal enjoyment of the accommodations, facilities, and privileges of inns, public conveyances on land or water, theatres, and other places of public amusement." In short, this act brought together several Federal laws that had been passed to countermand the South's post-Civil War Black Codes.

Of the five cases decided, three originated in the North and concerned the denial of admittance or full enjoyment in various public places and on railroad carriers. Justice Andrew C. Bradley's majority decision concluded that the first section of the Fourteenth Amendment was prohibitory upon the states only and not upon individuals. He also maintained that Congress was authorized by the amendment to adopt only "corrective rather than general legislation." Thus individuals could discriminate in public places, although presumably the states could not; however, 13 years later, in Plessy v. Ferguson, the Supreme Court upheld a Louisiana segregation law. This became the famous "separate but equal" decision that was not revoked until 1954.

The following editorial appeared in the New York Times and was generally typical of those applauding the decision in the North.[1]

The Rights of Negroes

It is more than ten years since the late lamented Mr. Sumner conceived the idea that the fourteenth amendment and sundry scattered passages of the Constitution gave to Congress authority to enforce the right of negroes [sic] to the same treatment as whites on public conveyances and in inns and places of entertainment. He passed away before he succeeded in convincing or persuading the majority of Republicans . . . that his view was correct. But after his death, a bill, the result of the combined efforts of those eminent jurists, Senator Howe and Gen. Ben Butler, was passed. While these various measures were under discussion, *The Times* took occasion frequently to point out that they were each and all impracticable, unwise, and, above all, without authority in the Constitution. As early as December, 1873, we remarked:

> Law has done all that it can for the negroes, and the sooner they set about securing their future for themselves the better it will be for them and their descendants.

[1]*New York Times*, October 18, 1883.

In the following May, pointing out the legal effect of the measure then before Congress as well as the political consequences which must follow its passage, we said:

> This bill is in fact a distinction against all classes except the negroes, and as such it is sure to meet with very general opposition. If it is accepted as a Republican measure the party is sure to suffer from it.

Again, in December, 1874, we called attention to the fact that the granting of the suffrage to the negro had been urged and had been justified by the argument that "with the ballot in his hand the negro would be enabled to defend himself, and that the Federal Government would from that time be less and less called upon to intervene in the affairs of the individual States to protect him in those liberties which it had guaranteed to him." We maintained that this argument had been accepted in good faith, and that the country would not consent that it should be ignored, and that the general Government should attempt to do for the negro by forced construction of the Constitution that which the ballot, properly used, should enable him to do for himself. Of the bill which had then passed under the wing of General Butler we declared:

> It is clear to us that the Republican Party cannot do better with it than to kill it or to let it die.

The bill was passed. In April 1875, commenting on a decision of the Supreme Court to the effect that the fourteenth amendment did not confer the right of suffrage upon women, we indicated the error of trying to stretch the amendment to cover much, including "civil rights," which could not be fairly brought under it. . . .

Finally, after eight years, in which the law has been practically a dead letter, the Supreme Court has decided, as it was evident that it must decide, that the act was unconstitutional. But while the law has, in one sense, been inoperative, in another it has been of great influence, and that mischievous. It has kept alive a prejudice against the negroes and against the Republican Party in the South, which without it would have gradually died out. It has furnished demagogues like Butler with the means of misleading the colored race, arousing hostility among the Southern whites, and rendering the Republican Party ridiculous. Unhappily, the decision which kills the law comes too late to remedy the ills which it produced. The principle which it involves is no longer an issue in national politics and can never again be made one. The judgment of the court is but a final chapter in a history full of wretched blunders, made possible by the sincerest and noblest sentiment of humanity, but in which the cunning and conscienceless schemers of the Butler school have played the larger part.

Some four decades later, the decision still appeared admirable to Harvard-educated Charles Warren, one of the five young Boston patricians who founded the Immigration Restriction League. In view of his anti-immigration activities, it was not surprising that Warren, an Assistant U.S. Attorney General during World War I, would term the decision "most fortunate" in his widely used three-volume legal text, The Supreme Court in U.S. History.[1]

Viewed in historical perspective now, however, there can be no question that the decisions in these cases were most fortunate. They largely eliminated from National politics the negro [sic] question which had so long embittered Congressional debates; they relegated the burden and the duty of protecting the negro to the States, to whom they properly belonged; and they served to restore confidence in the National Court in the Southern States. As an eminent Southern lawyer has said: "When the decision was reached and the prisoners were released, the utmost joy succeeded [in Louisiana], and with it a return of confidence which gave best hopes for the future. . . . What gave satisfaction to the South and strength to bear the affliction in which they found themselves was the determination of the Court to maintain the true character of the Government, and to hold, notwithstanding the excited feeling growing out of the war, that the existence of the States, with powers for domestic and local government including regulation of civil rights, the rights of persons and property, was essential to the perfect working of our complex form of government."

B. PRESIDENTIAL LEADERSHIP AND RACIAL EQUALITY

After 1877 U.S. Presidents often stressed the theme of national unity. President Hayes did so when he relegated the "Negro Problem" to the South with the assurance that Negroes could expect fair treatment from their white neighbors. When it became apparent that fair treatment was not forthcoming, succeeding Presidents were caught in their own rhetoric. Both parties continued to stress civil rights in their platforms but neither made any real attempt to implement them. It was thus a grateful Republic that received Booker T. Washington's 1895 Atlanta Exposition speech which, among other things, counseled the black man to be patient and to build up his manual skills. These were excellent suggestions

[1]Reprinted by permission of the President and Fellows of Harvard College from Charles Warren, *The Supreme Court in U.S. History*, Vol. III, Little Brown & Co., Boston, 1924, p. 330.

*for those who wanted to avoid the contradiction of their liberal political
statements and the ugly realities of an expanding Jim Crow and increased
lynching.*

1. William Howard Taft, 1909

*President Taft was typical of many Americans when he insisted that
he had absolutely no prejudices. This belief made it virtually impossible
for Taft, as well as other whites, to see any race problem in America.
The following is taken from his 1909 Inaugural Address and is particularly noteworthy for his patronizing attitude and the kinds of vocations
he saw blacks as capable of performing.*[1]

The colored men must base their hope on the results of their own
industry, self-restraint, thrift, and business success, as well as upon the
aid and comfort and sympathy which they may receive from their white
neighbors of the South. . . .

There is in the South a stronger feeling than ever among the intelligent, well-to-do, and influential element in favor of the industrial education of the Negro and the encouragement of the race to make themselves
useful members of the community. The progress which the Negro has
made in the last fifty years, from slavery, when its statistics are revealed, is marvellous, and it furnishes every reason to hope that in the
next twenty-five years a still greater improvement in his condition as a
productive member of society, on the farm, and in the shop, and in other
occupations may come.

The Negroes are now Americans. Their ancestors came here years ago
against their will, and this is their only country and their only flag.
They have shown themselves anxious to live for it and to die for it. En-
countering the race feeling against them, subjected at times to cruel injustice growing out of it, they may well have our profound sympathy
and aid in the struggle they are making. We are charged with the sacred
duty of making their path as smooth and easy as we can. Any recognition of their distinguished men, any appointment to office from among
their number, is properly taken as an encouragement and an appreciation of their progress, and this just policy should be pursued when suitable occasion offers.

But it may well admit of doubt whether, in the case of any race, an
appointment of one of their number to a local office in a community
in which the race feeling is so widespread and acute as to interfere with
the ease and facility with which the local government business can be

[1]*New York Times*, March 5, 1909.

done by the appointee is of sufficient benefit by way of encouragement to the race to outweigh the recurrence and increase of race feeling which such an appointment is likely to engender. Therefore, the Executive, in recognizing the Negro race by appointments, must exercise a careful discretion not thereby to do it more harm than good. On the other hand, we must be careful not to encourage the mere pretense of race feeling manufactured in the interest of individual political ambition.

Personally, I have not the slightest race prejudice or feeling, and recognition of its existence only awakens in my heart a deeper sympathy for those who have to bear it or suffer from it, and I question the wisdom of a policy which is likely to increase it. Meantime, if nothing is done to prevent it, a better feeling between the Negroes and the whites in the South will continue to grow, and more and more of the white people will come to realize that the future of the South is to be much benefited by the industrial and intellectual progress of the Negro. The exercise of political franchises by those of his race who are intelligent and well-to-do will be acquiesced in, and the right to vote will be withheld only from the ignorant and irresponsible of both races.

2. Woodrow Wilson, 1913

Although Woodrow Wilson stressed democracy abroad, he often overlooked it at home. This was particularly true concerning the Afro-American. "The dearth in administrative circles of any impelling passion for social justice," writes historian Arthur Link, "was nowhere better illustrated than in the government's policy toward Negroes." Wilson had campaigned for the black vote in 1912, but blacks and white sympathizers soon became bitterly disillusioned when Wilson allowed the agencies of the Federal Government to be formally segregated. The following is from a letter to New York Evening Post *editor and owner, Oswald Garrison Villard, and explains Wilson's rationale for official segregation.*[1]

It is true that the segregation of the colored employees in the several departments was begun upon the initiative and at the suggestion of several of the heads of departments, but as much as in the interest of the negroes [sic] as for any other reason, with the approval of some of the most influential negroes I know, and with the idea that the friction, or rather the discontent and uneasiness, which had prevailed in many of the

[1]Reprinted by permission of Rachel Baker Napier in behalf of the heirs of Ray Stannard Baker from Ray Stannard Baker, *Woodrow Wilson, Life and Letters*, Vol. IV, Doubleday, Doran, & Co., New York, 1931, p. 221.

departments would thereby be removed. It is as far as possible from being a movement against the negroes. I sincerely believe it to be in their interest. And what distresses me about your letter is to find that you look at it in so different a light.

I am sorry that those who interest themselves most in the welfare of the negroes should misjudge this action on the part of the departments, for they are seriously misjudging it. My own feeling is, by putting certain bureaus and sections of the service in the charge of negroes we are rendering them more safe in their possession of office and less likely to be discriminated against.

3. Warren G. Harding, 1921

In 1921 President Warren G. Harding launched a "Southern strategy" through which he hoped to gain Republican adherents from among white Southerners. He was neither the first nor the last Republican to make such an appeal; unfortunately, however, such an appeal has invariably been made at the expense of black Americans. On October 26, 1921, President Harding made it quite clear to a Birmingham, Alabama, audience that he understood the Southern position on race, and he extended fatherly advice to both blacks and whites.[1]

Men of both races may well stand uncompromisingly against every suggestion of social equality. This is not a question of social equality, but a question of recognizing a fundamental, eternal, inescapable difference.

Racial amalgamation there cannot be. Partnership of the races in developing the highest aims of all humanity there must be if humanity is to achieve the ends which we have set for it. . . .

The World War brought us to full recognition that the race problem is national rather than merely sectional. There are no authentic statistics, but it is common knowledge that the World War was marked by a great migration of colored people to the North, and West. They were attracted by the demand for labor and the higher wages offered. It has brought the question of race closer to North and West, and I believe it has served to modify somewhat the views of those sections on this question. It has made the South realize its industrial dependence on the labor of the black man and made the North realize the difficulties of the community in which two greatly differing races are brought to live side by side. I should say that it has been responsible for a larger charity on

[1]*New York Times*, October 27, 1921. © 1921 by The New York Times Company. Reprinted by permission.

both sides, a beginning of better understanding and in the light of that better understanding perhaps we shall be able to consider this problem together as a problem of all sections and of both faces in whose solution the best intelligence of both must be enlisted.

Indeed, we will be wise to recognize it as wider yet. Whoever will take the time to read and ponder Mr. Lothrop Stoddard's book on *The Rising Tide of Color* or, say, the thoughtful review of some recent literature on this question which Mr. F. D. Lugard presented in a recent *Edinburgh Review*, must realize that our race problem here in the United States is only a phase of race issue that the whole world confronts. Surely we shall gain nothing by blinking at the facts, by refusing to give thought to them. That is not the American way of approaching such issues. . . .

Men of both races may well stand uncompromisingly against every suggestion of social equality. Indeed, it would be helpful to have that word "equality" eliminated from this consideration; to have it accented on both sides that this is not a question of social equality, but a question of recognizing a fundamental, eternal and inescapable difference. We shall have made real progress when we develop an attitude in the public and community thought of both races which recognizes this difference. . . .

I can say to you people of the South, both white and black, that the time has passed when you are entitled to assume this problem of races is peculiarly and particularly your problem. More and more it is becoming a problem of the North; more and more it is the problem of Africa, of South America, of the Pacific, of the South Seas, of the world. It is the problem of democracy everywhere, if we mean the things we say about democracy as the ideal political state. . . .

With such convictions one must urge the people of the South to take advantage of their superior understanding of this problem and to assume an attitude toward it that will deserve the confidence of the colored people. Likewise, I plead with my own political party to lay aside every program that looks to lining up the black man as a mere political adjunct. Let there be an end of prejudice and of demagogy in this line. Let the South understand the menace which lies in forcing upon the black race an attitude of political solidarity.

Every consideration, it seems to me, brings us back at last to the question of education. When I speak of education as a part of this race question, I do not want the States or the nation to attempt to educate people, whether white or black into something they are not fitted to be. I have no sympathy with the half-baked altruism that would overstock us with doctors and lawyers, of whatever color and leave us in need of people fit and willing to do the manual work of a workaday world. But I would like to see an education that would fit every man not only to do his particular work as well as possible but to rise to a higher plane if he would deserve it. For that sort of education I have no fears, whether it be given to a black man or a white man. From that sort of education, I believe, black men, white men, the whole nation would draw immeasurable benefit.

3
The Scientists and the "Negro Race"

The great outpouring of antiblack writing between the 1890's and 1930's corresponded to the rise of Jim Crow in the South and approval of it in the North. The rationale for Jim Crow was quickly forthcoming, and at times it was difficult to differentiate between the scholars, who presumably based their conclusions on careful research, and the popularizers of race theories, who played on the public's emotions; indeed, the latter often drew upon the findings of the former. The growth of Darwinian thought, nationalism and expansionism, the fear of the new immigrant, and the development of the eugenics movement all contributed to America's general racial attitudes. But above all the period marked the intensive legal, social, and economic removal of the Afro-American from any meaningful role in American society. That the scientists should have been immune to popular movements appears obvious—that they contributed to them seems inexcusable. It was not until the 1930's that much of this scientific race-typing came under serious challenge, and even then those challenging often only cloaked the whole issue in more sophisticated language.

A. ENCYCLOPAEDIA BRITANNICA, 1895

The Encyclopaedia Britannica *has long served as the most trustworthy and prestigious reference work of its kind. For its articles it has generally commanded the leading authorities of the day. The following inclusion under "Negro" well depicts both the scientific and popular views current at the turn of the century. Although this particular* Britannica *came out in 1895 and was labeled the American edition, nine years later*

the Americana *encyclopedia included its own description of the Negro,*
which turned out to be a verbatim use of the Britannica's fourteen points
that are listed below.[1]

(1) The abnormal length of the arm, which in the erect position sometimes reaches the knee-pan, and which on an average exceeds that of the
Caucasian by about two inches; (2) prognathism, or projection of the
jaws (index number of facial angle about 70, as compared with the
Caucasian 82); (3) weight of brain, as indicating cranial capacity, 35
ounces (highest gorilla 20, an average European 45); (4) full black eye,
with black iris and yellowish sclerotic coat, a very marked feature; (5)
short flat snub nose, deeply depressed at the base or frontal suture, broad
at extremity, with dilated nostrils and concave ridge; (6) thick protruding lips, plainly showing the inner red surface; (7) very large zygomatic arches—high and prominent cheek bones; (8) exceedingly thick
cranium, enabling the Negro to butt with the head and resist blows
which would inevitably break any ordinary European's skull; (9) correspondingly weak lower limbs, terminating in broad flat feet with
low instep, divergent and somewhat prehensile great toe, and heel projection backwards ("lark heel"); (10) complexion deep brown or blackish,
and in some cases even distinctly black, due not to any special pigment,
as is often supposed, but merely to the greater abundance of the colour-
ing matter in the Malpighian mucous membrane between the inner or
true skin and the epidermis or scarp skin; (11) short, black hair, eccen-
trically elliptical or almost flat in section, and distinctly woolly, not
merely frizzly, as Prichard supposed on insufficient evidence; (12) thick
epidermis, cool, soft, and velvety to the touch, mostly hairless, and emitting a peculiar rancid odour, compared by Pruner Bey to that of the
buck goat; (13) frame of medium height, thrown somewhat out of the
perpendicular by the shape of the pelvis, the spine, and backward projection of the head, and the whole anatomical structure; (14) the cranial
sutures, which close much earlier in the Negro than in other races. To
this premature ossification of the skull, preventing all further development of the brain, many pathologists have attributed the inherent mental inferiority of the blacks, an inferiority which is even more marked
than their physical differences. Nearly all observers admit that the Negro
child is on the whole quite as intelligent as those of other human varie-
ties, but that on arriving at puberty all further progress seems to be
arrested. No one has more carefully studied this point than Filippo
Manetta, who during a long residence on the plantations of the Southern

---

[1]*Encyclopaedia Britannica*, American Edition, Vol. XVII, Werner Co., New York,
1895, pp. 316–320.

States of America noted that "the Negro children were sharp, intelligent, and full of vivacity, but on approaching the adult period a gradual change set in. The intellect seemed to become clouded, animation giving place to a short of lethargy, briskness yielding to indolence. We must necessarily suppose that the development of the Negro and White proceeds on different lines. While with the latter the volume of the brain grows with the expansion of the brain-pan, in the former the growth of the brain is on the contrary arrested by the premature closing of the cranial sutures and lateral pressure of the frontal bone."

B. THE NEW YORK ZOOLOGICAL SOCIETY AND OTA BENGA, 1906

Many respected scientists at the turn of the century postulated the theory that on the evolutionary ladder the Negro was much closer to the anthropoids than he was to the Caucasian. Illustrating this scientific view was a highly popular special exhibition at the New York Zoological Park, one of the foremost scientific centers in America. In describing the exhibition on page one, the New York Times *pointed out that it had been approved by the directors of the zoological society. The exhibit brought together in the park's monkey cage an African "pygmy" named Ota Benga, who was almost five feet tall, and an orang outang. The cage was to be the man's regular home for the duration of "the purely ethnological exhibit." In response to complaints by "the colored clergymen," the park director, Zoologist William T. Hornaday, told the* Times *on September 11 that the "dwarf" was housed in the monkey cage "because it is the most comfortable place we can find for him." It should be noted that the black ministers found no allies in their fight to free Ota Benga.[1]*

MAN AND MONKEY SHOW DISAPPROVED BY CLERGY

THE REV. DR. MAC ARTHUR THINKS THE EXHIBITION DEGRADING: COLORED MINISTERS TO ACT

THE PYGMY HAS AN ORANG-OUTANG AS A COMPANION NOW AND THEIR ANTICS DELIGHT THE BRONX CROWDS

Several thousand persons took the subway, the elevated, and the surface cars to the New York Zoological Park, in the Bronx, yesterday, and there watched Ota Benga, the Bushman, who has been put by the man-

[1]*New York Times*, September 10, 1906.

agement on exhibition there in the monkey cage. The Bushman didn't seem to mind it, and the sight plainly pleased the crowd. Few expressed audible objection to the sight of a human being in a cage with monkeys as companions, and there could be no doubt that to the majority the joint man-and-monkey exhibition was the most interesting sight in Bronx Park.

All the same, a storm over the exhibition was preparing last night. News of what the managers of the Zoological Park were permitting reached the Rev. Dr. R. S. MacArthur of Calvary Baptist Church last night, and he announced his intention of communicating with the negro [sic] clergymen in the city and starting an agitation to have the show stopped.

"The person responsible for this exhibition degrades himself as much as he does the African," said Dr. MacArthur. "Instead of making a beast of this little fellow, he should be put in school for the development of such powers as God gave to him. It is too bad that there is not some society like that for the Prevention of Cruelty to Children. We send our missionaries to Africa to Christianize the people, and then we bring one here to brutalize him."

Any suspicion that the exhibition was the result of error was contradicted by yesterday's developments. Benga was removed from the chimpanzees' cage to the crescent-shaped construction in the southwestern end of the Primate House, and on the cage was posted this sign:

The African Pigmy. "Ota Benga."
Age, 23 years.   Height, 4 feet 11 inches.
Weight, 103 pounds. Brought from the Kasal River, Congo Free State, South Central Africa, by Dr. Samuel P. Verner. Exhibited each afternoon during September.

To increase the picturesqueness of the exhibition, moreover, an orangoutang named Dohong, which has been widely described as showing almost human intelligence, was put in the cage with the Bushman, and with them the parrot which Dr. Verner brought from Africa with Benga.

The Bushman and the orang-outang frolicked together most of the afternoon. The two were frequently locked in each other's arms, and the crowd was delighted.

There was always a crowd before the cage, most of the time roaring with laughter, and from almost every corner of the garden could be heard the question:

"Where is the pygmy?"

And the answer was, "In the monkey house."

Perhaps as a concession to the fact that it was Sunday, a pair of canvas shoes had been given to the Bushman to wear. He was barefooted on Saturday. He seemed to like the shoes very much. Over and over again the crowd laughed at him as he sat in mute admiration of them on his stool in the monkey cage. But he didn't mind that. He has grown used to the crowd laughing, has discovered that they laugh at everything he does. If he wonders why he does not show it.

The crowd before the cage yesterday fluctuated in size from hour to hour, but there was hardly a time when there were not from 300 to 500 persons standing there. The throng was greatest in the later afternoon.

The performance of man and monkey is not easy to describe. Certainly Dohong is a very patient beast. Many times Benga grabbed him by the forepaws, swung him as though he were a bag, and then dropped him. Then man and monkey grinned. On other occasions Benga pushed the monkey before him. In this attitude the pygmy was not much taller than the orang-outang, and one had a good opportunity to study their points of resemblance. Their heads are much alike, and both grin in the same way when pleased.

Sometimes the man and the monkey hugged each other. That pleased the children, and they laughed uproariously. Next they did individual tricks; the monkey swung on ropes, the pygmy shot his arrow. Occasionally the pygmy mimicked the laughter of the crowd. In one instance a boy yelled, "Shoot."

"Shoot! Shoot!" aped the little Bushman.

From time to time it looked as though the little Bushman was growing out of patience. Then his keeper led him to the soda-water fountain. . . .

Director Hornaday, who recently returned from a trip abroad, was asked last evening whether he saw no impropriety in exhibiting Benga in the monkey cage, and if he was allowing it with the acquiescence of the Directors of the Zoological Society, to which he replied:

"Yes, what is being done in the matter is with the acquiescence of the society. The Secretary, Mr. Madison Grant, was in fact present when I made the arrangement with Dr. Verner for the keep of the little African savage.

"The idea is not exactly new. Zoological societies in Europe frequently resort to it, sometimes to recoup their finances."

"But not in the monkey houses, in a monkey cage?" it was suggested.

"No," replied Mr. Hornaday; "but the little black man is really very comfortable there. The keepers have given up the room to him, and he seems happy."

C. YALE'S ELLSWORTH HUNTINGTON AND THE AMERICAN EUGENICS SOCIETY'S LEON WHITNEY, 1927

In 1927, Ellsworth Huntington, a research geographer at Yale, and Leon Whitney, the Executive Secretary of the American Eugenics Society, published The Builders of America. *Their study, however, not only focused on the "Builders" but also described those who were endangering the foundations that had so carefully been laid by the builders. Among the latter were the new immigrant and, of course, the Afro-American.[1]*

Look, for example, at our industrial system. The desire for gain, coupled with dense ignorance as to the effect of their conduct, led the people of America to demand the importation of cheap labor. First came the blacks, who had increased from 300,000 slaves in the time of Benjamin Franklin to over 12,000,000 freemen today. The army mental tests showed that 86 per cent of the Southern Negroes possess inferior intelligence. Other evidence shows that almost the only Negroes who have accomplished much of importance have been partly white. The blending of white and black has produced something more competent than the pure black, but less competent than the pure white. It has often made a most dysgenic blend, creating a white man's ambition in a black man's lethargic body. A certain group of scientists maintains that within a few hundred years there will be no more pure blacks in America. If that were to happen, the mentality of the nation would be materially lowered by the admixture of the germ-plasm of the blacks with that of the whites. But it is doubtful whether such a complete mixture will ever occur. In many European and Asiatic lands diverse races have been living together for hundreds of years without coalescing. The South has drawn a sharp color line.

The Negroes are assuredly a great problem. They may prove to be either enemies or allies. From the whole United States it might be difficult to collect more than a few thousand pure African blacks who possess the intelligence to rank as Builders, but there are probably hundreds of thousands who possess temperamental qualities of cheerfulness,

---

[1]Ellsworth Huntington and Leon Whitney, *Builders of America*, William Morrow & Co., Inc., New York, 1927, pp. 81–82. Copyright 1927 by William Morrow & Co., Inc. Reprinted by permission.

love of fun, musical ability, willingness to work and the like, which would be of inestimable value to the other Builders. Nevertheless, it seems quite certain that we should be better off without our Negroes and their problems. They and their slavery have been enemies to the children of the Builders.

D. HARVARD'S EDWARD EAST, 1927

Professor of Genetics at Harvard, Edward East believed that science could not only save races but humanize them. "Science will redeem man's hope of Paradise," wrote East in his Heredity and Human Affairs *(1927). East attempted to disassociate himself from the race thinkers of the 1920's, whom he found to be unscientific. East insisted that you could not reject someone simply because he was of a race you did not like. "If the Mexican peon of Arizona is usually dirty and smelly, does this justify avoidance of one who is clean?" he asked. East insisted that if one had to discriminate he do so on scientific grounds, and for East this meant an examination of the genetic stock of the various races. The following passage is from* Heredity and Human Affairs, *and there is little doubt that East's "scientific genetics" had no room for black genes.*[1]

As I have said once before, the geneticist dislikes to recommend union between extreme racial types on theoretical grounds—a position not determined by preconceptions of racial superiorities or inferiorities. But the only conclusion one is entitled to draw from the anthropoligcal facts is that since the yellow and the white races have split into so many diverse subraces, the determining biological factor in the question of intermarriage is the genetic constitution of the contracting parties. On the other hand, there is evidence that the negro [sic] as a group and the American Indian as a group have little of genetic value to contribute to the higher white or yellow subraces. . . .

Mentally the African negro is childlike, normally affable and cheerful, but subject to fits of fierce passion. As an agriculturist and craftsman he has made some progress under the influence of alien races, though his advancement is not comparable to that of his negroid relatives in the Philippines. His religion is a primitive fetishism combined with nature-worship. His whole history drives one to the conclusion that he is not a discoverer. In no case did he produce a written language. . . .

A year or two ago Alain Locke edited a book entitled *The New Negro:*

[1]Reprinted by permission of Charles Scribner's Sons from *Heredity and Human Affairs*, pp. 188–200, by Edward East. Copyright 1927, Charles Scribner's Sons.

An Interpretation. It was a fine performance, despite some nonsense it contained about the value of primitive negro art. Mencken speaks of it as a phenomenon of immense significance, representing the negro's final emancipation from the inferiority complex that has conditioned all his thinking and a determination to point with pride to his own merits. His review is a sincere and courteous approval of a tolerant, dispassionate, meritorious work. When Locke, Johnson, White, Fisher, Miller, and other contributors are compared with some of the present-day Southern writers, the contrast, he says, is pathetic. "The Africans are men of sense, learning, and good bearing; the Caucasians are simply romantic windjammers, full of sound and fury, signifying nothing."

I do not quarrel with the substance of this statement; but it is extraordinary that a man of Mencken's perspicacity, stared out of contenance, while he read, by the polychromic portraits of the contributors with which the volume is illustrated, should speak of them as Africans. No single one is indubitably a negro in the genetic sense. As one who has had a wide experience in making genetic judgments, I am forced to conclude that the developed germ-plasm causing the making of this book is nine-tenths white at least. The whole performance gives no evidence whatever of negro capacity; it simply shows what the mixed-blood can do. . . .

Summing up, the negro as a social group has produced but one man who would be placed among the first 15,000 or 20,000 Great Ones of Earth, as judged by the usual standards. This is Alexandre Dumas, one of whose grandmothers was a negress of San Domingo, though whether a full-blood or not is unknown. In addition, there are perhaps twenty-five individuals who have produced intellectual or artistic work of which most of us might well be proud, but who would have to be placed in the fourth or fifth rank when considering true greatness objectively. And all of these people, so far as I can learn, are mixed-bloods, unless Dunbar is included. In literature there are several poets, critics, essayists, and short-story writers, but they have produced nothing not surpassed by hundreds of white writers during the same period. Countee Cullen and James Weldon Johnson are perhaps the most distinguished poets, and W. E. DuBois the most eminent essayist and critic. Negro music, which is now in great vogue, is interesting but not great. Samuel Coleridge-Taylor is the only composer of real ability, though Roland Hayes is a highly capable performer. In painting, sculpture, and architecture there is nothing. Dramatists are also lacking. Even on the stage, where the reputed ability of the negro as mimic might be expected to produce results, there has been no serious work. . . .

We can find no probability that the negro will contribute hereditary factors of value to the white race, yet the pure negro will gradually die out and the remaining members of our population will vary imperceptibly from black to white. In the social sense the black race will be absorbed. In the genetic sense the black germ-plasm will remain because the inheritance of genes is alternative. What are we going to do about it?

It seems to me that we must make the best of the situation. The negro cannot be deported or sterilized. He must be treated decently, educated up to his intelligence level, and made a part of our political system where qualified. . . .

E. UNIVERSITY OF VIRGINIA'S ROBERT BENNETT BEAN, 1935

As early as 1906, Professor of Anatomy Robert Bennett Bean had written in The Century *magazine that the Negro "lacks reason, judgment, apperception, attention, self-control, will power, orientation, and ethical and esthetic attributes." Unfortunately, 29 years later Professor Bean's Negro had not perceptively improved. Bean was often quoted by fellow scientists, although by the 1930's some of his more extreme views were being rejected. The following selection is taken from* The Races of Man *and deals briefly with the mental and physical characteristics of the three races that Bean distinguished in his work.[1]*

In general, the brain of the White Race is large, the convolutions are rich, with deep fissures. The mental characteristics are activity, nervous and physical vivacity, strong ambitions and passions, and highly developed idealism. There is love of amusement, sport, exploration, and adventure. Art and music are highly developed in appreciation and skill. Poetry is also cultivated to a great extent. Egoism and individuality are strong, but worries and cares are excessive, and psychoses and other brain affections are not only frequent but are on the increase. The religious life of the Whites is varied and highly developed. Their industry is incessant and elaborate. They are more or less immune to certain diseases that affect the other races, but are subject to others.

The brain of the Yellow-Brown Race is about medium human in size, with medium to good convolutions, which are sometimes varied and deep. The mental characteristics of the Yellow-Browns need further study, but they seem to be less vivacious, with emotions and passions less evident when strong than in the other two races. They possess mod-

[1]Robert Bennett Bean, *The Races of Man*, The University Society, Inc., New York, 1935, pp. 94–96.

erate idealism and some love of sport, but have less spirit for exploration and adventure than the White Race. They are artistic, but their musical sense is subdued and they have little ability in poetical composition. They are less subject to cares and worries and are less varied and intense in religious feeling than is the White Race and have few psychoses and brain affections. They are industrious, endure fatigue, and are less likely to succumb to many of the infectious diseases than is either the White or the Black Race.

The size of the brain in the Black Race is below the medium both of the Whites and of the Yellow-Browns, frequently with relatively more simple convolutions. The frontal lobes are often low and narrow, the parietal lobes voluminous, the occipital protruding. The psychic activities of the Black Race are a careless, jolly vivacity, emotions and passions of short duration, and a strong and somewhat irrational egoism. Idealism, ambition, and the co-operative faculties are weak. They love amusement and sport, but have little initiative and adventurous spirit. Within limits the Blacks are rather artistic in music, but not intellectually so. They show some ability in pictorial, decorative, and industrial art, but generally lack steady application. They have poetry of a low order, are rather free from lasting worries, are cursed with superstitious fears, and have much emotionalism in religion. They are only moderately affected by psychoses. Their worst diseases come from sexual promiscuity, contact with the White Race, and lack of acclimatization. . . .

The White Race is more advanced in the evolution of the brain and face and in color, the Yellow-Brown Race in the loss of body hair, and the Black Race in the ear form, hair form, and length of the legs.

4
Historians and the Afro-American

Although many white historians today warn against the using of black history courses for propaganda purposes, they have neglected to examine the full extent to which their fellow historians have contributed to popular ideology concerning black Americans. To be sure, we might expect a good deal of stereotyping by nineteenth-century historians, but unfortunately things did not radically change, even in the years immediately after World War II. Sometimes it is what is left out that distorts the overall picture, but it is also what is overtly stated about such subjects as slavery and reconstruction that has contributed to many a perverted view of the Afro-American. For example, in the 1950 edition of the *Growth of the American Republic* by Henry Steele Commanger and Samuel Eliot Morison, a passage on slavery begins: "As for Sambo, whose wrongs moved the abolitionists to wrath and tears, there is some reason to believe that he suffered less than any other class in the South from its 'pecular institution.'" The authors, two of America's most distinguished and widely read historians, first wrote those words in 1930, and the passing of 20 years had virtually no impact on their interpretation of how the "incurably optimistic Negro" lived under slavery.

A. ULRICH B. PHILLIPS, 1904

U. B. Phillips was born in the South but did most of his productive work while teaching at the universities of Wisconsin, Michigan, and Yale. His publications on slavery represented the first scholarly attempt to reassess slavery as an institution. While Phillips made no attempt to condone the institution of slavery per se, he did find its evils greatly ex-

aggerated, and he thought it the "best school" for those who were so un-prepared for American civilization. He felt the African ideally suited for slavery and found him generally contented with the institution of slavery. Drawing on vast research, his American Negro Slavery *(1918) and* Life and Labor in the Old South *(1929) stood virtually unchallenged among professional historians until well after World War II, when scholars like John Hope Franklin and Kenneth Stampp effectively countered both Phillips' research and his conclusions.*

The following 1904 article, written while he was at the University of Wisconsin, appeared in the Sewanee Review. *In view of the failure of Reconstruction and the succeeding tenant-farmer system, Phillips ap-plied the values of the old plantation system to what he considered present realities. The South needed a cheap and productive laboring force, but it certainly could not revert to slavery. By the same token, blacks had suffered by losing their close contacts with whites. Phillips thus called for a neo-plantation movement that would bring the two "races" back together under the more positive aspects of the earlier system.*[1]

The conditions of our problem are as follows: (1) A century or two ago the negroes [sic] were savages in the wilds of Africa. (2) Those who were brought to America, and their descendants, have acquired a cer-tain amount of civilization, and are now in some degree fitted for life in modern civilized society. (3) This progress of the negroes has been in very large measure the result of their association with civilized white people. (4) An immense mass of the negroes is sure to remain for an indefinite period in the midst of a civilized white nation. The problem is, how can we best provide for their peaceful residence and their further progress in this nation of white men? and how can we best guard against their lapsing back into barbarism? As a possible solution for a large part of the problem, I suggest the plantation system. . . .

The planters of the Old South, within the lifetime of a few generations, developed a fairly efficient body of laborers out of a horde of savages. The negroes became fairly honest, industrious, and intelligent; and even though this may have been at the cost of their sturdiness, initiative, and self-control, the net results were surprisingly good. On the whole, the system of the Old South, with all its limitations, accomplished a good work, which it was perhaps not fitted to carry further. The slavery system had completed its work and was already becoming an anachronism when

[1]U. B. Phillips, "The Plantation as a Civilizing Factor," *Sewanee Review*, July 1904, pp. 257–267.

the Civil War and Reconstruction overthrew it, and with it all system in the South. There followed a period of great social upheaval and industrial demoralization, which was partly remedied by a temporary resort to small farms and tenant cropping.

But none who were well informed have expected that the average negro, with his inevitable shortcomings, would make a successful independent farmer without a large additional amount of training. The plantations were broken up, and the negroes have in name been working for themselves and by themselves. But in truth they have continued to be under the supervision of the landowners, and the merchants, who act in some measure as non-resident planters. But this system of absentee control has such serious faults that it cannot permanently stand. The supervision over the so-called negro farmers is unsystematic, and the economic results are lamentably small. And, still worse, the isolation upon their separate farms is proving injurious to the higher development of the negroes themselves.

For civilization which our negroes have now partly acquired is English civilization, gained from association with the English race. They have advanced exclusively by the help and through their imitation of the Anglo-Americans.

Without the continuance of the inter-racial association there is strong reason to believe that the negroes would gradually lose much of the praiseworthy element in their present attainments. In fact several keensighted students have already detected a tendency of the negroes, where segregated in masses in the black belt, to lapse back toward barbarism. . . .

To secure the best results for all parties, a more sympathetic relationship must be established, which shall include larger numbers of both races. And no system for this purpose has yet been developed which compares in good results with that of the old patriarchal plantation. The patriarchal feature is necessary. The average negro has many of the characteristics of a child, and must be guided and governed, and often guarded against himself, by a sympathetic hand. Non-resident ownership and control of plantations will not do. The absentee system has no redeeming virtue for the purpose at hand. With hired, voluntary labor instead of forced labor, it is the Virginia plantation system and not that of the West Indies which is needed. The presence of the planter and his wife and children and his neighbors is required for example and precept among the negroes. Factory methods and purely business relations will not serve; the tie of personal sympathy and affection is essential to the successful working of the system. The average negro longs for this personal tie. Respect, affection, and obedience for those who earn and encourage his admiration are second nature with him. The negroes are disposed to do their part for securing the general welfare when the proper opportunity is given them. What they most need is friendly guidance and control for themselves, and peace and prosperity for the South as a whole.

B. JAMES FORD RHODES, 1906

James Rhodes was not a university-trained scholar; nevertheless, his multivolume study of American history in the 1850–1877 period was very well received by professional historians. His volumes on Reconstruction were not at variance with the popular Dunning School that proved so sympathetic to the plight of the white Southerners during Radical rule. Nor did Rhodes vary from later historians when he described the inept, unprepared blacks and their misguided quest for freedom. The following passage is taken from Volume V of his History of the United States *and was published in 1906, one year before William Dunning's* Reconstruction, Political and Economic.[1]

The difficulties of the problem were not generally comprehended at the North. Three and a half million persons of one of the most inferior races of mankind had through the agency of their superiors been transformed from slavery to freedom. It was a race the children of which might with favouring circumstances show an intellectual development equal to white children "up to the age of thirteen or fourteen; but then there comes a diminution often a cessation of their mental development. The physical overlaps the psychical and they turn away from the pursuit of culture." "The infernal laws of slavery," declared Thaddeus Stevens, have prevented negroes [sic] from acquiring an education, understanding the commonest laws of contract or of managing the ordinary business of life." "I met," wrote Sidney Andrews, "many negroes whose jargon was so utterly unintelligible that I could scarcely comprehend the ideas they tried to convey."

The negroes' idea of freedom was crude and pitiful. When William Lloyd Garrison was at Charleston, April 15, 1865, he saw at a camp three miles from the city twelve hundred plantation slaves who had been brought thither from the interior by Union soldiers. Their misery and degradation were striking; their manifestations of gratitude affected

[1]James Ford Rhodes, *History of the United States*, Vol. V, Harper and Brothers, New York, 1906, pp. 556–558.

him deeply and he said, "Well my friends, you are free at last, let us give three cheers for freedom!" and he undertook to lead the cheering. "To his amazement there was no response; the poor creatures looked at him in wonder . . . they did not know how to cheer." From a section of the Freedmen's Bureau Act of March 3, 1865 the negroes came to believe that the government purposed to give to each of them "forty acres of land and a mule." The land would be provided from the possessions of their old masters. "When is de land going' fur to be devided?" asked a number of country negroes of Andrews." One old negro would not leave with some of his fellows, who, supposing that the blessings of freedom could only be had near the army, were going to Charleston; he gave as his reason, "De home-house might come to me, ye see, sah, in de dewision" The general impression obtained that the distribution of the land would take place at the holidays, between Christmas and New Year's Day. An old negro at Macon said to Andrews, "One say dis an' one say dat an' we don' know an' so hol' off till Janerwery."

This expectation of what seemed to them a fortune fostered the native laziness and improvidence of the race; they became unwilling to work and wished to wander about—a life which of necessity was partly supported by theft. To many of the negroes freedom meant simply idleness. Andrews, who was opposed to Johnson's policy wrote, "Hundreds of conversations with negroes of every class in at least a dozen towns of central Georgia have convinced me that the race is on a large scale ignorantly sacrificing its own material good for the husks of vagabondage." "What did you leave the old place for, Auntie?" he asked of one who had a comfortable home and had been an indulged favourite of the family. "What fur? 'Joy my freedom!"

C. CLAUDE BOWERS, 1929

Claude Bowers' The Tragic Era was among the ten best-selling non-fiction books of 1929. Bowers felt that although historians were by now sympathetic to the plight of the postwar South, they had still not adequately described the intensive suffering and horror that marked Radical Reconstruction. Bowers was more strident in his treatment of the Radical Era than was Dunning, but he was also more readable. The following passage, taken from the 1957 edition, well depicts the popular fears of what free blacks would do to white women and the heroic proportions of the Klan.[1]

[1]Reprinted by permission of the Houghton Mifflin Company from Claude Bowers, *The Tragic Era*, 1957 edition, Houghton Mifflin Co., Boston, 1957, pp. 307–309.

The crusade of hate and social equality, and more, was playing havoc with a race naturally kindly and trustful. Throughout the war, when men were far away on the battle-fields, and the women were alone on far plantations with the slaves, hardly a woman was attacked. Then came the scum of Northern society, emissaries of the politicians, soldiers of fortune, and not a few degenerates, inflaming the negroes' [sic] egotism, and soon the lustful assaults began. Rape is the foul daughter of Reconstruction. Robert Somers, an Englishman visiting the South, observed the work of "agitators of the loosest type," and noted the utterance of sentiments "in all the circumstances anti-social and destructive," and "a real reign of terror . . . among the whites." An English woman living on a Georgia plantation saw an amazing change in the manner of her servants after the work of the Leagues began to have effect. They walked about with guns on their shoulders, spoke to their employers with studied familiarity, treated the women with disrespect, and worked when they pleased. Through 1869 this woman never slept without a loaded pistol under her pillow. All over the South, white women armed themselves in self-defense. Before the Klan appeared, and after the Loyal Leagues had spread their poison, no respectable white woman dared venture out in the black belt unprotected. "We are in the hands of camp followers, horse-holders, cooks and bottle-washers and thieves," testified a reputable citizen of Alabama. The spectacle of negro police leading white girls to jail was not unusual in Montgomery. Among the poor, the white women of the farms taking their produce to the markets traveled in large companies as a protection against rape. In places the military and the Freedmen's Bureau offered no relief. Negroes who had criminally attacked white women, tried and sent to the penitentiary, were turned loose after a few days' incarceration. It was not until the original Klan began to ride that white women felt some sense of security.

Controlled in the beginning by men of character and substance, the plan was to manage the freedmen by playing on their fears and superstitions. Novel schemes were often tried. Thus a night traveler, provided with a rubber sack, would stop at a negro's hut and ask for water. After "drinking" three bucketfuls, to the consternation of the trembling black, the traveler would observe that he had traveled a thousand miles in twenty-four hours and "that was the best water I have had since I was killed at the battle of Shiloh." The negro, chattering, would take to his heels, and the local paper would significantly announce that he was "a radical negro." Tales would be told of white men sailing through the midnight skies on white horses over neighboring towns. Could the bad negro escape? Not at all—these "spirits always follow them and catch them and no living man hears from them again. . . ." The negroes, clustered together in their cabins, recounted these awful stories and for a time grew humble, industrious, law-abiding. . . .

In the pioneer West, vigilance committees were formed for the protection of horses and cattle; in the South, the Klan was organized for the protection of women, property, civilization itself.

D. JOHN D. HICKS, 1937

The reassessment of slavery and the blacks' role in American society begin after World War II. However, many prominent historians such as John D. Hicks, Samuel Eliot Morison, Henry Steele Commager and Merle Curti stood by the earlier interpretations. Hicks first published his very successful text, The Federal Union, *in 1937, but the University of California professor's 1957 edition still included the following version of the "contented slave."*[1]

The lot of the slave on the Southern plantation was ordinarily quite tolerable. As a valuable piece of property, his good health was a matter of considerable consequence to his master. He was well fed, although no particular pains were taken to vary his diet from the standard corn bread and fat pork that was regarded as entirely adequate to sustain life. In case of illness he was usually cared for by the same physician that attended the master and his family. His living quarters, usually located not far from the "big house" of the planter were apt to be primitive, but they afforded protection from the wind and the rain and a plentiful supply of fuel for cold weather. The slave's clothing was coarse enough, and in summer he was not expected to wear very much, but he was about as well clad as Southern whites of the lower class. By and large, the conditions of his life represented a distinct advance over the lot that would have befallen him had he remained in Africa.

Indeed, the slaves got much positive enjoyment out of life. Extremely gregarious, they delighted in the community life of the plantation, and on special occasions were permitted to indulge in picnics, barbecues, and various other types of celebration. They loved to sing and dance, and contributed ideas along both lines that the whites, at least of a later generation, were not too proud to appreciate. They were generally blessed with a keen sense of humor; they rarely fretted, when treated

[1]Reprinted by permission of the Houghton Mifflin Company from John D. Hicks, *The Federal Union,* 1957 edition, Houghton Mifflin Company, Boston, 1957, pp. 452–454.

well, because of their state of bondage; and they were often deeply devoted to their master and his family. Small children, regardless of color, played together freely, and the affection of white boys and girls for their Negro nurses, or "mammies," was proverbial. The slaves were deeply religious, and almost universally accepted Christianity, usually as interpreted by one of the more emotional denominations, such as the Methodists and the Baptists, whose camp meetings, revivals, and baptizings gave them unbounded joy. A few Negroes were taught to read, but most of them acquired by word of mouth rather than by reading a considerable knowledge of the Bible and of Christian theology. Their devotions were extremely picturesque, and their moral standards sufficiently latitudinarian to meet the needs of a really primitive people. Heaven to the Negro was a place of rest from all labor, the fitting reward of a servant who obeyed his master and loved the Lord.

E.   U. B. PHILLIPS LIVES ON IN HIGH SCHOOL TEXTS

The U. B. Phillips magnolia interpretation of Southern plantation life continued to persist in general textbooks long after his views were attacked by recognized scholars. In the passage below the authors describe "good" and "bad" conditions on the plantation without recognizing that slavery in and of itself was "a bad condition" and that to discuss such an institution in relative terms is to repeat an approach peculiar to white historiography.

Merle Curti, a Pulitzer Prize-winning historian from the University of Wisconsin and long recognized as one of the country's premier intellectual historians, lent his name to the following fourth edition of an original 1950 text that saw the slaves only as objects rather than subjects.[1]

Students of slavery have been handicapped by a lack of adequate records in their effort to decide how slaves were treated. Generally speaking, they have records, diaries, and journals only for the large plantations. There is some evidence however, that the slaves on the small plantations and farms were in general more humanely treated than on the large plantations.

On large plantations the slaves usually worked in gangs under the management of an overseer, whose job it was to get as much work out of the labor force and as big crops as possible. The treatment of slaves

[1]Reprinted by permission of Harcourt Brace Jovanovich, Inc. from Lewis Paul Todd and Merle Curti, *Rise of the American Nation*, 1968 edition, pp. 445–446.

on plantations where the owner was frequently absent and an overseer was in charge was likely to be most severe. It was hard to secure men who were willing to serve as overseers, and some of those who did become overseers were harsh, brutal men. On the other hand, there is some evidence that on the significant plantations of the lower South the slaves often had more food, better quarters, and superior medical care than did those belonging to small owners.

Many planters provided for their slaves as carefully as they did for members of their own families and in turn won the love of the slaves. Thomas Jefferson, for example, belonged to this group of planters. When Jefferson returned to his hilltop home at Monticello after a long absence, his slaves honored him by meeting his coach at the foot of the hill, unhitching the horses, and pulling the coach by hand up the long grade.

Many planters treated their slaves well because they were valuable property. For example, imagine a planter who owned fifty able-bodied slaves. Allowing from $1,000 to $1,500 for each slave . . . his investment in slaves was from $50,000 to $75,000. Death of even a single slave was a setback. Any illness or injury resulting from ill-treatment was contrary to the planter's interests. To protect his investment, therefore, the planter was apt to keep his slaves adequately fed, clothed, and housed.

SELECTED READINGS

Bardolph, Ralph, *The Civil Rights Record*, Thomas Y. Crowell Co., New York, 1970.
    An excellent sampling of the laws, court decisions, and executive pronouncements that served to keep blacks "in their place."

Brown, Sterling, "Negro Character as Seen by White Authors," *Journal of Negro Education*, II, January 1933.
    Although dated, Brown's seven stereotypes are still valuable in understanding black images in American fiction.

Jordan, Winthrop, *White over Black: American Attitudes Toward the Negro, 1550–1812*, University of North Carolina Press, Chapel Hill, 1968.
    A comprehensive treatment of the antiblack actions, attitudes, and motivations of Colonial whites. It is the best work of its kind and needs to be duplicated in other eras of American history.

Litwack, Leon, *North of Slavery: The Negro in the Free States, 1790–1860*, University of Chicago Press, Chicago, 1961.
    An excellent introduction to the post-Revolutionary beginnings of the North's version of Jim Crow.

Logan, Rayford, *The Betrayal of the Negro, From Rutherford B. Hayes to Woodrow Wilson*, Macmillan Co., New York, 1954, 1965.

Of particular value is Logan's sampling of antiblack reporting in the leading newspapers and magazines about the beginning of the twentieth century.

Nash, Gary B., and Weiss, Richard, *The Great Fear: Race in the Mind Of America*, Holt, Rinehart and Winston, Inc., New York, 1970.

Nine helpful essays that examine the historical roots of American racism.

Newby, I. A., *Jim Crow's Defense: Anti-Negro Thought In America, 1900–1930*, Louisiana State University, Baton Rouge, 1965.

Newby's study is particularly valuable on the scholars' contributions to racist thought in the first three decades on the twentieth century.

III
THE CHICANO

It's a long, long way to capture Villa;
It's a long way to go;
It's a long way across the border
Where the dirty greasers grow.
                    Army Ditty, circa 1916

INTRODUCTION

In 1896, California formed her first "pioneer society" in Los Angeles, but not a single Mexican or Spanish name appeared on the membership roster; in fact, the bylaws expressly provided that persons born in the state were not eligible for citizenship. A few years later, when the Native Sons of the Golden West were asked to submit a list of the men who had grown up with Los Angeles, they included only Anglo-American names. Although the Mexican-American, or Chicano, as many now prefer to be called, has long made up America's second-largest visible minority, he has been generally ignored, even by those scholars who have focused on minorities. John F. Kennedy's *A Nation of Immigrants*, for example, dismisses the Mexicans as recent arrivals whose contributions still lie in the future. This is to ignore not only a sizable minority but also the historical effect of Spanish and Mexican culture on the Southwest and California.

When President Kennedy referred to the Mexicans as recent immigrants, he was undoubtedly referring to the thousands who since World War I have come across the border to provide a cheap agricultural labor force. Most twentieth-century debates on the Mexican-American have focused on whether the short-term economic advantages of these migrant workers offset the disadvantage of a people who to many Americans seemed to present permanent social and economic problems. Seldom has anyone suggested that the Mexican immigrant himself might have something beside his labor to add to a country that has often prided itself on the melting-pot concept.

117

As with other minorities, Americans judged the Mexican-American by what was already considered the acceptable norms, and not surprisingly he was found lacking. This was often illustrated by the sociologists and psychologists who seemed incapable of visualizing the Mexican family as anything but a defective Anglo family. Likewise, American schools have worked to eradicate cultural differences and in so doing have only forced many of these children to turn away from the educational system. Even now, when Spanish is proving to be the most popular foreign language in the schools, little attempt is made to connect it to the 10 million Spanish-speaking people who live in the United States.

The first prolonged contact between Americans and Mexicans occurred in Texas, and from the first relations were strained. To the Anglo settlers, the Mexicans were lazy, immoral, and backward. The Mexicans, on the other hand, found these interlopers to be arrogant, conniving, and dishonest. Language, religion, and attitudes toward slavery were also different. In addition, the dark color of most Mexicans was a badge of inferiority to men who had based slavery on the hue of one's skin. Long after these initial contacts, the Mexican would be classified as nonwhite, a designation that in the twentieth century would result in various forms of social, economic, and educational discrimination.

The Mexican War and the Treaty of Guadalupe Hidalgo and its oft-violated guarantee of the rights of the Mexicans living in the annexed territories increased mutual animosity. The fact that the Mexican inhabitants of the annexed areas were quickly and easily pushed into a permanent second-class status helped contribute to the majority view that it was Manifest Destiny that spread the Anglo culture to the frontiers.

The story in California was much the same. The ease and swiftness with which the Mexicans were dispatched also bred a contempt for them and their culture. Early travelers like Richard Henry Dana and Western-fiction writers made their comments on the idle, immoral natives. However, these early writers anticipated many of their later counterparts when they differentiated between the dark-skinned natives, whom they found to be inferior largely because of their Indian background, and the lighter-skinned "ricos," who were held to be the true Spanish descendants.

With the exception of Western literature, the Mexican-American was largely ignored until the 1920's, when a new chapter began. Improved irrigation methods in the Southwest and the expanding production of fruit, vegetables, and sugar beets in the Midwest, coupled with the closing of the gates on foreign labor in 1924, meant new demands for a cheap and mobile labor force. Mexicans responded by the thousands, but with their entrance into the country, cries for restriction were raised by those who regretted that they had not been excluded under the 1924 National Origins Act.

Between 1926 and 1930, the House Committee on Immigration and Naturalization held intermittent hearings on the advisability of restriction. In 1930, a bill to this effect cleared the House, only to be blocked by President Hoover, who was concerned about improving relations with Latin America. For the next decade the State Department used its consulates in Mexico to curtail immigration, while Chicanos within the states fought in vain for better farm wages.

During World War II the need for labor again forced America to open its borders to Mexican workers, and again increased numbers of Mexicans meant increased tensions. In 1943, the infamous "Zoot-Suit" riot in Los Angeles not only soured relations between Anglos and Mexican-Americans, but it also threatened this country's wartime relations with Mexico itself.

The *bracero* labor program continued to be a controversial issue during the 1950's and 1960's, although during the latter decade the Chicano has made his numbers increasingly felt with his demands for a minimum farm-wage scale and his insistence that it is now time for America to notice him. Perhaps his hopes will not be in vain, but before they are realized Americans will have to cast off their image of the indolent, improvident, loose-living Mexican who has been so effectively caricatured by the "Frito Bandito" of television fame.

1
The Mexican in American Literature

Writers of fiction provide a wealth of material for those who would seek popular images and stereotypes of minority groups. This is particularly true regarding the Mexican, since even more than the historian, scientist, or popular journalist, it has been the creators of prose and poetry who have given Americans their most extensive national view of Mexicans. The majority of the early writers treated the Mexicans with disdain and contempt. Their characters were either of a decadent, scheming gentility or the indolent, vicious mixture of inferior races. Later twentieth-century writers found much of the romantic in a culture that they felt contrasted noticeably with their own industrial society. Some of these writers, however, praised their own kind of stereotype—the easygoing, exotic primitive who could always put off his cares until *mañana.*

A. RICHARD HENRY DANA'S
TWO YEARS BEFORE THE MAST, 1840

Dana's masterpiece is primarily a sea story, but he also provided Americans with some of their first glimpses of California. For Dana this was a wondrously rich country that only needed the advantages of "an enterprising people" to become the richest of lands. Dana particularly noted that the difference in skin color could be socially interpreted, with the lighter skin naturally associated with the superior Spanish culture. Finally, there were the obvious differences in justice. Although justice in the American West was to develop its own peculiarities, it was nevertheless held superior to the Mexican variety.[1]

[1]Richard Henry Dana, *Two Years Before the Mast*, Harper and Brothers, New York, 1840, pp. 83–85, 185–187.

The Californians [i.e., Spanish-speaking people] are an idle, thriftless people, and can make nothing for themselves. The country abounds in grapes, yet they buy bad wine made in Boston and brought round by us, at an immense price, and retail it among themselves at a *real* (12½ cents) by the small wine-glass. Their hides too, which they value at two dollars in money, they give for something which costs seventy-five cents in Boston; and buy shoes (as like as not, made of their own hides, which have been carried twice round Cape Horn) at three and four dollars, and "chickenskin" boots at fifteen dollars apiece. . . .

Their complexions are various, depending—as well as their dress and manner—upon their rank; or, in other words, upon the amount of Spanish blood they can lay claim to. Those who are of pure Spanish blood, having never intermarried with the aborigines, have clear brunette complexions, and sometimes, even as fair as those of English women. There are but few of these families in California; being mostly those in official stations, or who, on the expiration of their offices, have settled here upon property which they have acquired; and others who have been banished for state offences. These form the aristocracy; intermarrying, and keeping up an exclusive system in every respect. They can be told by their complexions, dress, manner, and also by their speech; for, calling themselves Castilians, they are very ambitious of speaking the pure Castilian language, which is spoken in a somewhat corrupted dialect by the lower classes. From this upper class, they go down by regular shades, growing more and more dark and muddy, until you come to the pure Indian, who runs about with nothing upon him but a small piece of cloth, kept up by a wide leather strap drawn round his waist. . . .

In their domestic relations, these people are no better than in their public. The men are thriftless, proud, and extravagant, and very much given to gaming; and the women have but little education. Of the poor Indians, very little care is taken. The priests, indeed, at the missions, are said to keep them very strictly, and some rules are usually made by the alcaldes to punish their misconduct; but it all amounts to but little. Intemperance is a common vice among the Indians. The Spaniards, on the contrary, are very abstemious, and I do not remember ever having seen a Spaniard intoxicated.

Such are the people who inhabit a country embracing four or five hundred miles of sea-coast, with several good harbors; with fine forests in the north; the waters filled with fish, and the plains covered with thousands of herds of cattle; blessed with a climate, than which there can be no better in the world; free from all manner of diseases, whether epidemic or endemic; and with a soil in which corn yield from seventy to eighty fold. In the hands of an enterprising people, what a country this might be! we are ready to say. Yet how long would a people remain so, in such a country? The Americans (as those from the United States are called) and Englishmen, who are fast filling up the principal towns, and getting the trade into their hands, are indeed more industrious and effective than the Spaniards; yet their children are brought up Spaniards, in every respect, and if the "California fever" (laziness) spares the first generation, it always attacks the second.

B. JOHN WILLIAM DEFOREST'S *OVERLAND*, 1872

John William Deforest was a successful Eastern writer whose pen traveled west for this popular frontier novel. Deforest had achieved considerable fame with a history of Connecticut Indians and through several romantic novels dealing with European, East Coast, and Civil War themes. Overland was his one excursion into the Southwest, but in it he featured both "rascally" upper-class Spanish-Mexicans and the lower-class, dark-skinned, more common stereotypes. In the novel, Carlos Coronado plots to have his Anglo-Saxon rival in love assassinated during a long overland trip from Sante Fe to Francisco. The heroine, Clara, has to chose between these two beaus and her choice is a popular one. The following are sketches of Coronado's uncle and of the two rivals themselves.[1]

Coronado's Uncle

The uncle was always horrible; he was one of the very ugliest of Spaniards; he was a brutal caricature of the national type. He had a low forehead, round face, bulbous nose, shaking fat cheeks, insignificant chin, and only one eye, a black and sleepy orb, which seemed to crawl like a snake. His exceedingly dark skin was made darker by a singular bluish tinge which resulted from heavy doses of nitrate of silver, taken as a remedy for epilepsy. His face was, moreover, mottled with dusky spots, so that he reminded the spectator of a frog or a toad. Just now he looked nothing less than poisonous; the hungriest of cannibals would not have dared eat him.

Lieutenant Ralph Thurstane

Lieutenant Ralph Thurstane was a tall, full-chested, finely-limbed gladiator of perhaps four and twenty. Broad forehead; nose straight and high enough; lower part of the face oval; on the whole a good physiognomy. Cheek bones rather strongly marked; a hint of Scandinavian an-

[1]John William Deforest, *Overland*, Sheldon & Co., New York, 1872, pp. 6, 9, 11–12, 23, 37, 146.

cestry supported by his name. Thurstane is evidently Thor's stone or altar; forefathers, priests of the god of thunder. His complexion was so reddened and darkened by sunburn that his untanned forehead looked unnaturally white and delicate. His yellow, one might almost call it golden hair, was wavy enough to be handsome. Eyes quite remarkable; blue, but of a very dark blue, like the coloring which is sometimes given to steel; so dark indeed that one's first impression was that they were black. Their natural expression seemed to be gentle, pathetic, and almost imploring; but authority, responsibility, hardship, and danger had given them an ability to be stern. In his whole face, young as he was, there was already the look of the veteran, that calm reminiscence of trials endured, the preparedness for trials to come. In fine, taking figure, physiognomy, and demeanor together, he was attractive.

Coronado

He was a man of medium stature, slender in build, agile and graceful in movement, complexion very dark, features high and aristocratic, short black hair and small black moustache, eyes black also, but veiled and dusky. He was about twenty-eight, but he seemed at least four years older, partly because of a deep wrinkle which slashed down each cheek, and partly because he was so perfectly self-possessed and elaborately courteous. . . .

Let no one expect a stage Spaniard, with the air of a matador or a guerrillero, who wears only picturesque and outlandish costumes, and speaks only magniloquent Castilian. Coronado was dressed, on this spring morning, precisely as American dandies then dressed for summer promenades on Broadway. His hat was a fine panama with a broad black ribbon; his frock-coat was of thin cloth, plain, dark, and altogether civilized; his light trousers were cut gaiter-fashion, and strapped under the instep; his small boots were patent-leather, and of the ordinary type. There was nothing poetic about his attire except a reasonably wide Byron collar and a rather dashing crimson neck-tie, well suited to his dark complexion. . . .

He was not physically a very brave man; he had no pugnacity and no adventurous love of danger for its own sake; but when he was resolved on an enterprise, he could go through with it.

The Author's Conclusion

Profound and potent sentiment of race antipathy! The contempt and hatred of white men for yellow, red, brown, and black men has worked all over earth, is working yet, and will work for ages. It is a motive of that tremendous tragedy which Spencer has entitled "the survival of the fittest," and Darwin, "natural selection."

C. STEPHEN CRANE AND FRANK NORRIS ON CRUELTY

Although docility has often been equated with the Mexican character, so too has cruelty. The English had long considered the Old World Spanish to be a particularly cruel people, and this myth persisted in the New World. Then, too, cruelty has often been associated with a primitive and inferior nature by those feeling more civilized. With the Mexican it was particularly his treatment of animals that seemed so perverse to the Anglo mind.

Both Stephen Crane and Frank Norris included various sketches of Mexicans in their stories. Some of their characters are in the romantic mold, but others reflect the more negative traits attributed to Mexicans.

In this article in the Philadelphia Press *Crane gives some examples of Mexican cruelty.*[1]

Mexican Sights and Street Scenes

When a burdened donkey falls down, a half a dozen Indians gather around it and brace themselves. Then they take clubs and hammer the everlasting daylight out of the donkey. They also swear in Mexican. Mexican is a very capable language for purposes of profanity. A good swearer here can bring rain in thirty minutes.

It is a great thing to hear the thump, thump of the clubs and the howling of the natives, and to see the little legs of the donkey quiver and to see him roll his eyes. Finally, after they have hammered him out as flat as a drum head it flashes upon them suddenly that the burro cannot get up until they remove the load. Well, then, at last they remove his load and the donkey, not much larger than a kitten at best, and now disheveled, weak, and tottering, struggles gratefully to his feet. . . .

It is never just to condemn a class; in returning to the street vendors, it is but fair to record an extraordinary instance of the gentleness, humanity, and fine capability of pity in one of their number. An American lady was strolling in the public park one afternoon when she observed a vendor with four little plum-colored birds seated quietly and peacefully upon his brown hand.

"Oh, look at those dear little birds," she cried to her escort. "How tame they are!"

Her escort too was struck with admiration and astonishment and they went close to the little birds. They saw their happy, restful countenances and with what wealth of love they looked up into the face of their owner.

[1]*Philadelphia Press*, May 19, 1895.

The lady bought two of these birds, although she hated to wound their little hearts by tearing them away from their master.

When she got to her room she closed the door and the windows, and then reached into the wicker cage and brought out one of the pets, for she wished to gain their affection too, and teach them to sit upon her finger.

The little bird which she brought out made a desperate attempt to perch upon her finger, but suddenly toppled off and fell to the floor with a sound like that made by a water-soaked bean bag.

The loving vendor had filled his birds full of shot. This accounted for their happy, restful countenances and their very apparent resolution never to desert the adored finger of their master.

In an hour, both the little birds died. You would die too if your stomach was full of shot.

In the following brief passage, Frank Norris vividly describes the final stage of a massive California rabbit hunt. For the better part of a day the men had been herding the wild rabbits into a corral where their slaughter could begin.[1]

On signal, the killing began. Dogs that had been brought there for that purpose when let into the corral refused, as had been half-expected, to do the work. They snuffed curiously at the pile, then backed off, disturbed, perplexed. But the men and boys—Portuguese for the most part —were more eager. Annixter drew Hilma away, and, indeed, most of the people set about the barbecue at once.

In the corral, however, the killing went forward. Armed with a club in each hand, the young fellows from Guadalajara and Bonneville, and the farm boys from the ranches, leaped over the rails of the corral. They walked unsteadily upon the myriad of crowding bodies underfoot, or, as space was cleared, sank almost waist deep into the mass that leaped and squirmed about them. Blindly, furiously, they struck and struck. The Anglo-Saxon spectators round about drew back in disgust, but the hot, degenerated blood of Portuguese, Mexican, and mixed Spaniard boiled up in excitement at this wholesale slaughter.

D.   O. HENRY AND HIS MEXICANS

William S. Porter (O. Henry) and his short stories have delighted readers for some seven decades. His tales include many settings and a

[1]Frank Norris, *The Octopus*, Doubleday, Page & Co., New York, 1901, p. 214.

variety of characters, and are usually marked by a surprise ending. Unfortunately, his Mexican characters held few surprises for the American reader. This first selection pits the Anglo-Saxon Texas Ranger against a "murderous Mexican." An added element in the story is Alvarita, a fetching Mexican lass who charms not only snakes but also the hero by the end of the story. O. Henry, like many other American authors, found something romantic in Mexican women, but never in their male counterparts. The second selection of O. Henry's is a poem entitled "Tamales," and although it was intended to be humorous, this effect was achieved at the expense of Mexican stereotyping.

An Afternoon Miracle, 1907[1]

"Keep this for me, Billy," said the ranger, handing over his Winchester. Quixotic, perhaps, but it was Bob Buckley's way. Another man—and a braver one—might have raised a posse to accompany him. It was Buckley's rule to discard all preliminary advantage.

The Mexican had left behind him a wake of closed doors and an empty street, but now people were beginning to emerge from their places of refuge with assumed unconsciousness of anything having happened. Many citizens who knew the ranger pointed out to him with alacrity the course of Garcia's retreat.

[A short time later—after the ranger has caught up with his man and while a feminine admirer observes the scene.]

The distance between the two men slowly lessened. The Mexican stood, immovable, waiting. When scarce five yards separated them a little shower of loosened gravel rattled down from above to the ranger's feet. He glanced upward with instinctive caution. A pair of dark eyes, brilliantly soft, and fierily tender, encountered and held his own. The most fearful heart and the boldest one in all the Rio Bravo country exchanged a silent and inscrutable communication. Alvarita, still seated within her vine, leaned forward above the breast-high chaparral. One hand was laid across her bosom. One great dark braid curved forward over her shoulder. Her lips were parted; her face was lit with what seemed but wonder—great and absolute wonder. Her eyes lingered upon Buckley's. Let no one ask or presume to tell through what subtle medium the miracle was performed. As by a lightning flash two clouds will accomplish counterpoise and compensation of electric surcharge, so on that eye glance the man received his complement of manhood, and the maid conceded what enriched her womanly grace by its loss.

[1]O. Henry, "An Afternoon Miracle," from *Heart of the West*, The McClure Co., New York, 1907.

The Mexican, suddenly stirring, ventilated his attitude of apathetic waiting by conjuring swiftly from his bootlet a long knife. Buckley cast aside his hat, and laughed once aloud, like a happy school-boy at a frolic. Then, empty-handed, he sprang nimbly, and Garcia met him without default.

So soon was the engagement ended that disappointment imposed upon the ranger's war-like ecstasy. Instead of dealing the traditional downward stroke, the Mexican lunged straight with his knife. Buckley took the precarious chance, and caught his wrist, fair and firm. Then he delivered the good Saxon knock-out blow—always so pathetically disastrous to the fistless Latin races—and Garcia was down and out, with his head under a clump of prickly pears. The ranger looked up again to the Queen of the Serpents.

TOMALES[2]

This is the Mexican
Don José Calderon
One of God's countrymen.
Land of the buzzard.
Cheap silver dollar, and
Cacti and murderers.
Why has he left his land
Land of the lazy man,
Land of the bull fight,
fleas and revolution.

This is the reason,
Hark to the wherefore;
Listen and tremble.
One of his ancestors,
Ancient and garlicky,
Probably grandfather,
Died with his boots on.
Killed by the Texans,
Texans with big guns,
At San Jacinto.
Died without benefit

[2]O. Henry, *Rolling Stones*, 1912 edition, Doubleday, Garden City, New York, pp. 245–250.

Of priest or clergy;
Died full of minie balls,
Mescal and pepper.

Don José Calderon
Heard of the tragedy.
Heard of it, thought of it,
Vowed a deep vengeance;
Vowed retribution
On the Americans,
Murderous gringos,
Especially Texans. . . .

He hied him to Austin.
Bought him a basket,
A barrel of pepper,
And another of garlic,
Also a rope he bought.
That was his stock in trade;
Nothing else had he.
Nor was he rated in
Dun or in Bradstreet,
Though he meant business,
Don José Calderon,
Seeker of vengeance.

With his stout lariat,
Then he caught swiftly
Tomcats and puppy dogs,
Caught them and cooked them,
Don José Calderon,
Vower of vengeance.
Now on the sidewalk
Sits the avenger
Selling Tamales to
Innocent purchasers.
Dire is thy vengeance,
Oh, José Calderon,
Pitiless Nemesis
Fearful Redresser
Of the wrongs done to thy
Sainted grandfather

Now the doomed Texans,
Rashly hilarious,
Buy of the deadly wares,
Buy and devour.
Rounders at midnight,
Citizens solid,
Bankers and newsboys,
Bootblacks and preachers,
Rashly importunate,
Courting destruction.
Buy and devour.
Beautiful maidens
Buy and devour,
Gentle society youths
Buy and devour.

Buy and devour
This thing called Tamale;
Made of rat terrier,
Spitz dog and poodle.
Maltese cat, boarding house
Steak and red pepper.
Garlic and tallow,
Corn meal and shucks.
Buy without shame
Sit on store steps and eat,
Strewing the shucks around
Over creation.

Dire is thy vengeance.
Don José Calderon.
For the slight thing we did
Killing thy grandfather.
What boots it if we killed
Only one greaser,
Don José Calderon?
This is your deep revenge,
You have greased all of us,
Greased a whole nation
With your Tamales,
Don José Calderon.

E. JOHN STEINBECK AND *TORTILLA FLAT*, 1937

John Steinbeck, like many American writers, found something appealing in the apparent naturalistic simplicity of individuals outside the webb of an industrial society. His Mexican characters are totally free of both time and morality as they move through their uncomplicated lives. This view of a different culture is not unlike that of the "exotic primitive," which was applied to Afro-Americans by well-meaning whites who, during the Harlem Renaissance, sought freedom from their own existence in a Harlem Saturday night.

In the following selection from Tortilla Flat, *Teresina is an uncomplicated person who produces children with a regularity that seemingly baffles this husbandless woman. But she is too natural to be immoral and her fatherless brood too healthy to be pitied.*[1]

Teresina was a mildly puzzled woman, as far as her mind was concerned. Her body was one of those perfect retorts for the distillation of children. The first baby, conceived when she was fourteen, had been a shock to her; such a shock that she delivered it in the ball park at night, wrapped it in newspaper and left it for the night watchman to find. This is a secret. Even now Teresina might get into trouble if it were known.

When she was sixteen, Mr. Alfred Cortez married her and gave her his name and the two foundations of her family, Alfredo and Ernie. Mr. Cortez gave her that name gladly. He was only using it temporarily anyway. His name, before he came to Monterey and after he left, was Guggliemo. He went away after Ernie was born. Perhaps he foresaw that being married to Teresina was not going to be a quiet life.

The regularity with which she became a mother always astonished Teresina. It occurred sometimes that she could not remember who the father of the impending baby was; and occasionally she almost grew convinced that no lover was necessary. In the time when she had been under quarantine as a diphtheria carrier she conceived just the same. However, when a question became too complicated for her mind to unravel, she usually laid that problem in the arms of the Mother of Jesus, who, she knew, had more knowledge of, interest in, and time for such things than she.

---

[1]From *Tortilla Flat* by John Steinbeck. Copyright 1935, 1962 by John Steinbeck. Reprinted by permission of The Viking Press, Inc.

Teresina went often to confession. She was the despair of Father Ramon. Indeed he had seen that while her knees, her hands and her lips did penance for an old sin, her modest and provocative eyes, flashing under drawn lashes, laid the foundations for a new one.

During the time I have been telling this, Teresina's ninth child was born, and for the moment she was unengaged. The vieja received another charge; Alfredo entered his third year in the first grade, Ernie his second, and Panchito went to school for the first time.

At about this time in California it became the stylish thing for school nurses to visit the classes and to catechize the children on intimate details of their home life. In the first grade, Alfredo was called to the principal's office, for it was thought that he looked thin.

The visting nurse, trained in child psychology, said kindly, "Freddie, do you get enough to eat?"

"Sure," said Alfredo.

"Well, now. Tell me what you have for breakfast."

"Tortillas and beans," said Alfredo.

The nurse nodded her head dismally to the principal. "What do you have when you go home for lunch?"

"I don't go home."

"Don't you eat at noon?"

"Sure, I bring some beans wrapped up in a tortilla."

Actual alarm showed in the nurse's eyes, but she controlled herself. "At night what do you have to eat?"

"Tortillas and beans."

Her psychology deserted her. "Do you mean to stand there and tell me you eat nothing but tortillas and beans?"

Alfredo was astonished. "Jesus Christ," he said, "what more do you want?"

In due course the school doctor listened to the nurse's horrified report. One day he drove up to Teresina's house to look into the matter. As he walked through the yard the creepers, the crawlers, and the stumblers were shrieking one terrible symphony. The doctor stood in the open kitchen door. With his own eyes he saw the vieja go to the stove, dip a great spoon into a kettle and sow the floor with boiled beans. Instantly the noise ceased. Creepers, crawlers and stumblers went to work with silent industry, moving from bean to bean, pausing only to eat them. The vieja went back to her chair for a few moments of peace. Under the bed, under the chairs, under the stove, the children crawled with the intentness of little bugs. The doctor stayed two hours, for his scientific interest was piqued. He went away shaking his head.

He shook his head incredulously while he made his report. "I gave them every test I know of," he said, "teeth, skin, blood, skeleton, eyes, co-ordination. Gentlemen, they are living on what constitutes a slow poison, and they have from birth. Gentlemen, I tell you I have never seen healthier children in my life!" His emotion overcame him. "The little beasts," he cried. "I never saw such teeth in my life. I never saw such teeth!"

2
Popular Images of the Chicano

Traditionally, scholars have underemphasized or overlooked the role that popular magazines, newspapers, and books have played in influencing the American mind. Often Americans have examined what people "should have read" rather than what they actually did read. Editors, of course, have been well aware that they must often oversimplify and popularize complex issues, and over the years they have served as an invaluable index of not only the important issues of the day but also what they considered to be the public interpretation of those issues.

With the exception of a few examples of Western fiction, the popular press devoted little space to the Mexican until well into the twentieth century. During the 1920's, when growing numbers of Mexican workers entered the country to replace the now-restricted European immigrants, the number of magazine articles on the Mexican greatly increased. Many of these early articles frankly admitted the racial danger as well as that of unfair economic competition. Later articles concentrated more on the economic questions involved, but the fact that here was a people of vastly different customs and living habits never lurked far beneath the surface.

A. JOHN RUSSELL BARTLETT AND THE SOUTHWEST, 1850–1853

In 1850, President Zachary Taylor appointed John Russell Bartlett as Commissioner for the Survey of the Boundary between the United States and Mexico. In 1854 Bartlett published a two-volume narrative of his experiences. He hoped that his study would provide a guide for im-

134

migrants moving into the area. His work included interesting and lengthy
descriptions of the flora and fauna, but more insidious were his comments
on the Indians and Mexicans, whom he dismissed as vastly inferior to
white Americans. Bartlett also pointed to the Roman Catholic Church as
a factor in separating the Latin and Anglo cultures.[1]

San Antonio contains about 6000 inhabitants, of which number it is estimated two-thirds are Mexicans, Germans, and French. Yet, notwithstanding this preponderance of other nations, the town is essentially American in character. Mexican indolence cannot stand by the side of the energy and industry of the Americans and Europeans; and the newcomers are rapidly elbowing the old settlers to one side. Some few of the Mexicans have the good sense to fall in with the spirit of progress; but the great majority draw back before it, and live upon the outskirts of the town in the primitive style of their forefathers. . . .

The inhabitants of Loreto are of a dingy, opaque, olive green, which shows there is no friendly mixture in the blood of the Spaniard and the Indian. They appear to be the same squalid, flabby, mixed race, which is observed in almost every part of the Mexican coasts. . . .

What a marked difference there is in Spanish and English colonization! Here the zealous Missionary preceded all others, planting the cross along with the manner of his country. Then commenced the work of baptizing; and as soon as a sufficient number of converts had been made, a fertile valley was chosen, and a church erected with buildings to accommodate some hundreds. Next came the colonists, whose main efforts were to support the Mission and its priests. The Anglo-Saxon pioneer entered the wilderness with his axe, his plough, and his rifle; and after he had erected his own dwelling, the mill and blacksmith's shop rose up. Lands were brought into cultivation, the mechanic arts flourished; and when the colony became large enough and rich enough to support a pastor, a church was built. For the results of the two modes of colonization, compare Texas, New Mexico, California, Sonora, and Chihuahua, before the three first became annexed to the United States, and the States of Ohio, Indiana, Illinois, and Michigan. The latter had attained more wealth, more population and importance, and had done quite as much towards promoting Christianity in the first ten years after their settlement, as the former States had in two centuries.

Near by is a fertile valley, a very small portion of which is now tilled

[1]John Russell Bartlett, *Personal Narrative of Explorations and Incidents in Texas, New Mexico, California, Sonora, and Chihuahua,* D. Appleton & Co., New York, 1854, Vol. I, pp. 39–40, 484; Vol. II, pp. 299–300.

—although from appearances, it was all formerly irrigated and under cultivation. I tried in vain to purchase vegetables. A more thoroughly lazy set of people, I never saw. The Pimo and Coco-Maricopa Indians of the Gila are infinitely superior to them. Whether a proximity to the church and the worthless half-civilized Mexicans has reduced them to this state of indolence and poverty, I know not; but if so, they would better have remained in their native valleys, and never seen the faces of white men.

B. W. B. LIGHTON AND "THE GREASER," 1899

One of the early articles analyzing the Mexican character appeared in the Atlantic Monthly *in 1899. W. R. Lighton was a Kansas-Nebraska lawyer who left his practice to write stories on the West. His following contribution is noteworthy for both the number and the simplicity of his stereotypes.*[1]

In the burning noontide comes a slow gray burro, meek and patient; his head dropped, his eyes mere glinting peepholes in his outward shagginess—every line, curve, and movement full of unobtrusive dignity. And this sedate aspect eminently befits his estate, for he is no ordinary beast; he is the bearer of the presiding genius of the desert—the mestizo, the Greaser, half-blood offspring of the marriage of antiquity with modernity. Time cannot take from him the unmistakable impress of old Spain. But his Spanish appearance is not his dominant characteristic. His skin has been sunbrowned for centuries; his nose and cheeks are broad; his lips are thick; his brows are heavy, sheltering eyes soft, passionate, inscrutable. King in his own natural right, master of a blessed content, he is the strange progeny of parents who waged warfare against each other, and all but perished in the strife. They gave him no heritage save a blending of their own warring passions. Anomalous as he is, he is one of the few distinct types in our national life whose origin is fully known to us. . . .

Some one—I think it was Mr. Herbert Spencer—has declared that the unmistakable mark of a high race of men is individualization, differentiation, heterogeneity, and variation from type. If that be a test, then we need not hesitate to say of the Greaser that he stands very low in the scale; for, to lapse into a Western mode of speech, he is all alike. Choose one, and you have a pattern from which all his brethren could be drawn, with only slight modifications in the items of beard and adipose.

[1]W. R. Lighton, "The Greaser," *Atlantic Monthly*, June 1899, pp. 750–760.

Possibly the Greaser may seem more real if we put him down in figures. In 1540 the native population of New Mexico was, by approximation, 150,000. After three centuries it had declined to 45,000. Of the latter number, not more than two percent were of European blood; about twenty percent were considered pure-blooded Pueblans; the others were mestizos. Within the last fifty years, of course, there have been great accessions to the white population, but the numbers of the other classes have not changed materially. And the white distrusts the Indian, the Indian despises the Greaser, the Greaser hates the white; there is a perfect rondo movement of dislike and antagonism. It could not well be otherwise. Inborn and inbred race instincts are strong. The differences are such as cannot be reconciled by the mere dwelling together of conflicting elements. Amalgamation of those elements can never be made complete: the Greaser himself, for example, is not an amalgamation of the characters of his parents; he is only an emulsion. The course of life upon our frontier has been fruitful of practical demonstration of several problems in sociology. One of the clearest is that the Indian problem will not be determined by any process of race absorption. Sometimes, in the exigencies of frontier life, misfit marriages have occurred; but they were only matters of expediency, a compromise with the hard fate which for a time separated the pioneers from women of their own blood. As soon as this condition changed, and white wives had become in some degree commensurate to the demand, those misalliances ceased, and the half-caste households which had been already established served no better purpose than to stand as monuments of connubial folly. There can never be more than a thin overlapping of the margins of these races. As the advance of the whites becomes more aggressive, the red men will simply retreat—grudgingly enough, no doubt—until by and by they are crowded into the last ditch. This is very true of the life of New Mexico; and in that territory the discord is in three notes. . . .

That children of nature are childlike and bland has been often told us, but there is an accompanying element of their disposition which may well cause a thoughtful man to pause. They have a strong way of keeping their mouths shut, and allowing the other fellow to do the talking. That is one of the Greaser's strong points. No one can tell what a Greaser thinks; no one can say what masked batteries of passion lie back of his well-mastered eyes. To trust a Greaser is to take a long jump into utter darkness. That he is treacherous everyone knows who has had to do with him; but he is not wholly blameworthy. We have it upon good authority that the natives of the territory were simple and honest. The trick of deception was caught from the first conquerors and from the later paleface of the much-speaking tongue. But the Greaser's power of deception is a perfect mastery of the art, beside which the skill of the Yankee is merely the bungling of a novice. As we say out West, the Greaser "puts up a good front." One must need be by nature suspicious, or thoroughly schooled in the ways of the smart little man, to detect the danger lurking behind the soft shine of the eyes, in the curves of his smile, and in the few gently breathed words. Only physical courage is wanting to make him what we know as a "bad man." Physical courage he has none—or at best but a little, and that thin. To be sure, he will fight, particularly when in his cups or when his jealousy is aroused; but he must fight with his own weapon, the knife. He is troublesome when he holds a knife, but he dreads the revolver, and of the great American fist he stands in honest fear. When he fights with his knife, so long as the odds are in his favor, he is a demon; but if he is scratched and catches sight of his own blood, that is the end of him. At heart he is the basest of cowards. This alone is enough to seal his doom. When the white nudges with his elbow and demands that the Greaser give more room, the poor little chap has not the "nerve" to jostle him again. . . .

The abode of the Greaser has been styled "headquarters for dirt." He is himself, one could almost say, the apotheosis of dirt, and the nooks of his house and the folds of his raiment are the inns of those skipping, crawling things that provoked Sancho Panza's immortal plaint. But the Greaser is proverbially hospitable; he does not give grudgingly of his substance to his tiny guests; what he has they are free to take. And he has his reward; he gets a little physical exercise now and again. He also gets entertainment. If he had no fleas to bite him, he would be likely to die of ennui. The manner of the Greaser's hospitality is still broader. No matter how poor his hovel or how meagre his board, the stranger is welcome. I should not like to call his apparent generosity a mere feint; but do not be too sure of him because you have eaten of his salt. If you sleep beneath his roof, keep one eye on his handy knife. That is the Spanish of his nature and his creed, and illustrates the uncertainties of life in a neighborhood where forgiveness of sin is a marketable commodity.

C.   CARLETON BEALS AND "THE MEXICAN AS HE IS," 1921

During the 1920's numerous articles on the Mexicans appeared in lead-ing magazines. Most appeared toward the end of the decade when Mexican immigration restriction was being debated in Congress. The following article, however, was published in the North American Review *in October 1921. The author, Carleton Beals, was apparently well quali-*

fied to do such an article. He had spent several years in Mexico City, both as principal of the American High School and as advisor to President Carranza. When he returned to the United States he lectured and wrote on Mexican folkways, but like so many other American observers, it was the stark contrast with his own culture that monopolized his attention.[1]

The Mexican As He Is

The Mexican is a composite of Indian, Oriental and White: small-boned, spare-limbed, short of stature—rarely more than five feet six—with straight black hair, round face, prominent cheek bones, black or deep brown eyes, and a stringy moustache drooping over a somewhat sad, sensitive, full-lipped mouth and weak chin. He is furtive, evasive, distrustful, especially before a person of the higher class or a foreigner; but warm-hearted, impulsive, expansive, and childishly generous if he finds that such a person is simpatico. . . .

The dress of the Mexican is a reflection of his economic status. Under the various regimes that have so quickly "flourished and faded" in Mexico, the peon has discovered that he can live as comfortably in idleness as by toiling long, soul-deadening hours. He will be as likely to be hungry and in rags when he labors as when he does not. He is not the first in the world to have discovered that fact, and in his case it is a happy discovery in that it corresponds to his racial temperament. . . .

His family life, however, is usually happy—perhaps because of its carefree and irresponsible hand-to-mouth character. Yet his wife is virtually his slave. She must do his bidding without question, and she prides herself on her submissiveness and subjection. He may curse her, beat her, have open relations with three or four other women, and she not only has no legal redress, but would not for a moment think of seeking any. The marriage tie, at best, is loose; few peons ever have enough money to pay for a wedding ceremony. Getting married is living together, and is quite the moral thing to do. Yet the man may leave his wife in the lurch with half a dozen children, and return after many years of absence, and she will take him unquestioningly back to her heart! She has no independence and no importance, except to serve as man's slave and minister to his desires. . . .

Before the awe of the greatest Church of the world, the the grandeur and grotesqueness of its Aztec antecedents, poor, torn Jose cringes, with a shaking taper, on his knees before the gorgeousness of the high-flung

[1]Carleton Beals, "The Mexican As He Is," *North American Review*, October 1921, pp. 538–546.

altar. With real and honest worship he watches the tall, but fat, heavy-set, big jowled priest, in his robes of ermine and purple velvet, pass among his tatterdemalion fellows, collecting hand-kisses and pennies; past a poor woman who, without the least sense of embarrassment, nurses her babe at her naked breast; past the boy who munches peanuts as religiously as he recites his prayers; past the great unwashed that knows more of catechism than of soap.

With the drone of the chants, the swelling tones of the full-voiced organ, the sonorous surge of the litany, the peon's emotion masters him, and he bursts into tears. Finally he places his taper beneath his favorite saint, drops two or three day's wages into the pittance-box, and passes with his shaken soul into the sunlight of God.

Outside he thrusts his way through the rotting, blear-eyed beggars, and past the hundreds of clamoring street-venders. A new feeling possesses him—he sheds his emotions easily. The rest of the day is for pleasure.

Most conspicuous are the gambling joints. They announce their presence garishly to eye and ear. From their interiors bursts the rollicking thrum of marimbas. Within may be discovered any number of skin-game contrivances, arranged to appeal to the imagination and the deep-rooted gambling instincts of the Mexican. In such a place, Jose will spend the remainder of the morning, feverishly watching the ebb and flow of his coppers.

At noon he will probably buy his dinner from one of the tag-rag women, squatting by the curb, cooking over a low charcoal fire, her hands and arms streaked with soot and dripping with yellow grease. Crouching down in the gutter, his back to the swirling eddies of dust, a little eathenware bowl of frijoles or some greasy, brick-colored stew, he hastily devours the contents with the aid of a corn tortilla, fashioned in the shape of a trowel.

In some pulqueria, some festively painted saloon, bearing the name of "The Dance of the Gipsies," or "The Promenade of Venus," he will take his place in the midst of the hilarious throng of men, women and children, happy and dirty. Here Jose will dance and play the afternoon away over a floor slippery-wet with spilled pulque in an atmosphere, sweetishly sickening from its stale smell, heavy with tobacco smoke, and foul with vile talk. As the day lengthens into night the fun grows more hilarious, the licentiousness more unrestrained, and then the drinks go around faster. And our Jose drinks; drinks until he has absorbed his share of the 375,000 litres of pulque that are sold on just an ordinary day in the Mexican capital; drinks until he can assure himself that all's well with the world.

D. A *SATURDAY EVENING POST* EDITORIAL, 1930

In 1930, when the debate on Mexican restriction reached the floor of the House, the Saturday Evening Post *editorialized for restriction. The* Post *had run several anti-Mexican articles during the 1920's, and this one reiterated its feeling that in spite of possible economic advantages, The Mexican could only create another racial problem in a country that already had too many.*[1]

Present and Future

The immigration problem, once more to the forefront, resolves itself into a rather simple question despite the endless economic, racial and biological complexities involved. We have to ask ourselves whether we prefer immediate gain or future trouble. However sound or unsound the strictly economic arguments favoring the continued influx of Mexican peon labor may be, the conviction is widespread that this movement must be curtailed unless there is to be a further lowering of American standards. A plausible cause is made out for the Mexicans. They are quiet and docile as compared with certain other types of cheap immigrant labor with which the industries have experimented to their sorrow in years past. Moreover, many of them come into this country for seasonal labor only, returning to their own land as soon as the need is over.

But this very fact raises the major issue. *Do we want the work of the country done by labor which is nonassimilable? To ask the question is to answer it.* The Mexican peons who come into this country for seasonal or even for more permanent labor do not become citizens, the percentage taking out naturalization papers being strikingly small. Grant their domestic and other virtues, they do not become part of us. They fail to assimilate and they delay by that much the harmony which is necessary to continued national success. The point has been reached in this country where the crying need is for unification; the last thing we should have is further national and racial diversity. The native Indian problem is difficult enough, even with only a few hundred thousand aboriginal descendants. Why add a Mexican Indian problem also?

Nor do all the Mexican peon laborers return to their own country when the various crops have been harvested. They seem to be pushing farther north and crowding into the city slums. Because of the difference in economic conditions in Mexico and the United States and the lack of

[1]Editorial, *Saturday Evening Post*, March 15, 1930, p. 28.

immigration restrictions, there is a tremendous suction of labor from the former country to the latter. If we had not shut down on European immigration some years ago, literally millions would have come in from that continent, and for very much the same reasons.

The simple truth is that the dilution of the people and institutions of this country has already gone much too far. Is anyone so simple as to suppose that no connection exists between the unquestioned dilution and the lamentable criminal conditions which obtain in our cities? The country is groping, must grope, toward more rather than less homogeneity. We may be obliged to absorb great numbers of Porto Ricans, Hawaiians and Filipinos; indeed, the Philippine problem has already reared its head in California. With the Mexicans already here, with the as yet unassimilated immigrants from certain European countries, and finally with the vast and growing negro [sic] population, we already have an almost superhuman task to bring about requisite national unity. We are under no obligation to continue to make this country an asylum for the Mexican peon, and we should not do so.

E. *TIME* DISCUSSES THE BRACERO, 1953

The 1930 debate was settled without restrictive legislation when United States consulates in Mexico exercised extreme caution in granting immigration permits. Illegal immigration did continue, but during the Depression America succeeded in returning a great many Mexicans to their homeland. During World War II the human tide again shifted as the need for cheap farm labor forced the Government to lift restrictions. But immigration was still slowed by red tape, and many Mexicans, not without encouragement, crossed the border illegally. These "wetbacks," as they were dubbed in the popular press, once again brought the "Mexican problem" to the fore.

In the following article Time *magazine discusses "the ants" who were illegally streaming into the country. The article is not malicious, but it does little to dispel the traditional view of the Mexican as a simplistic soul who was out of step in modern America.*[1]

The Ants

In 1938, only 3,000 Mexican "wetbacks" were arrested for sneaking illegally across the shallows of the Rio Grande into the U.S. But World

---

[1]"The Ants," *Time*, April 27, 1953, p. 29. Reprinted by permission from TIME, The Weekly Newsmagazine; Copyright by Time Inc., 1953.

War II brought labor shortages to California and Texas harvest fields, and in the years which followed, the wetbacks thronged in by the tens of thousands. The annual invasion has grown bigger and bigger—despite legislation, public clamor, the hardships which the wetbacks suffer, and the best efforts of the U.S. border patrol, which caught and shipped 635,135 of them home (many of them repeaters) during 1952 alone.

There are reasons. At their lowest, U.S. wages seem high to the Mexican border jumper. And in recent years, poor men in all corners of Mexico have heard dazzling tales of the wonders and luxuries to be had in los Estados Unidos—canned chicken soup, pink nylon panties to be taken home to wives and girl friends, sweet paste (wonder of wonders) for scrubbing the teeth, and the little brush to squirt it on. Many a wetback, returning to a small Mexican village, has been hailed as a hero, and has been trailed by every able-bodied man in town when he started north on a new expedition.

The border patrol has taken to jeeps, guided by an eleven-plane airforce, in an effort to stem the tide; it has instituted roadblocks, train searches, and patient patrols in ranch country through the four border states. The wetbacks remain undiscouraged. A good many, smartened up by experience, now try to go as far north as Chicago, Detroit, Toledo, or the apple orchards of Washington and Oregon. Once beyond the patrol's real sphere of activity, a lucky Mexican can live and work for months or years without detection.

Last month, with drought searing Mexico and spring crops ripening in the U.S., the patrolmen caught an army of 73,176 along the 1,700-mile border. All were escorted back across the line. But for every one who was caught, at least one, and probably more, safely got past the patrols. This week the wetbacks were seeping across the border at a record-breaking rate—two a minute, day and night. "Like ants," said Chief Patrol Inspector Ed Parker. "They're swarming over the desert like ants." . . .

F.   THE ZOOT-SUIT RIOTS, 1943

War often creates domestic tensions that manifest themselves in violent ways. Los Angeles had been in a state of nervous crisis since the attack on Pearl Harbor. Half expecting to be bombed, and learning of the "danger" of her indigenous Japanese population, Angelinos were prepared to see the enemy almost anywhere. Along with these wartime apprehensions, was the fact that during 1942 and 1943 the Los Angeles press and police had been waging war on teenage gangs and the crimes and violence that they allegedly produced. At first they were referred to simply as Mexican gangs—although the vast majority of their members had been born in the United States and were, of course, American citizens. When the State Department objected to this labeling, the newspapers labeled gang members "pachucos" or "zoot suiters," after the flashy garb and long haircuts that some of the members sported.

On June 3, 1943, several sailors complained of attacks by Mexican youths. When the police could not find the miscreants, the sailors decided to exact their own revenge, and the "Zoot-Suit War" was on. Several things now stand out about the conflict. The police proved unwilling to get involved, unless it was to pick up the Chicano victims and arrest them for disturbing the peace. Sometimes, too, the police seemed to be cheering on the sailors, as almost all those arrested were Mexican-Americans. Equally disconcerting was the alacrity with which the townspeople joined in on the action. It seemed to be an excellent opportunity to work off frustrations by teaching some youngsters a much-needed lesson. The press coverage only intensified feelings, and not until the State Department intervened did the Los Angeles newspapers tone down their journalism. It also became evident that a great many of those beaten up and arrested were not wearing zoot-suits but were simply Mexican-Americans or, in a few cases, young blacks. A picture carried in the June 21 Life magazine showed a police lineup, and only a minority of those arrested were sporting the infamous suit. Finally, there was the refusal of Los Angeles and Federal officials to admit that there were racial overtones to the violence. Certain officials suggested that a ban on zoot-suits would correct the problem.

The following are some of the Los Angeles Times' articles that were published during the height of the rioting.[1]

ZOOT SUITERS LEARN LESSON IN FIGHTS WITH SERVICEMEN

Los Angeles Times, June 7, 1943

Those gamin dandies, the zoot suiters, having learned a great moral lesson from servicemen, mostly sailors, who took over their instruction three days ago, are staying home nights.

With the exception of 61 youths booked in County Jail on misdemeanor charges, wearers of the garish costume that has become a hallmark of juvenile delinquency are apparently "unfrocked."

These were the conclusions reached last night by Capt. David Crous-

---

[1]Reprinted by permission of the *Los Angeles Times.*

horn, commanding Sheriff's men at the Hall of Justice during night patrols, and Capt. Harry Seager, night Chief of Police. . . .

Strife between the two factions arose as a result of beating of individual sailors by juvenile street bands and, in two cases, assaults on women relatives of servicemen.

These attacks—by zooters occurred over a period of several days. The counterattack did not last as long. . . .

ISSUE NOT RACE DISCRIMINATION, MAYOR DECLARES

Los Angeles Times, June 10, 1943

There is no question of racial discrimination involved in the recent zoot-suit gang riots in Los Angeles, Mayor Bowron yesterday told State Department officials in a telephonic conversation. . . .

"I informed the State Department that assurances could be given to the Mexican Embassy that the occurrences in this city are not in any manner directed at Mexican citizens or even against persons of Mexican descent. There is no question of racial discrimination involved. . . .

"I advised the State Department representatives that I am in close touch with the Mexican Consul and am working with him, and we propose to handle the situation in such a way that there will be no reason for protests on the part of the Mexican government.

"At the same time, I want to assure the people of Los Angeles that there will be no sidestepping and the situation will be vigorously handled. There are too many citizens in this community, some of them good intentioned and a few whose intentions I question, who raise a hue and cry of racial discrimination or prejudice against a minority group every time the Los Angeles police make arrests of members of gangs or groups working in unison. They all look alike to us, regardless of color and the length of their coats. . . .

"The law is going to be enforced and the peace kept in Los Angeles and, under existing circumstances, this requires two-fisted action and it cannot be done with wrists. If young men of Mexican parentage or if colored boys are involved it is regrettable, but no one has immunity and whoever are the disturbers are going to be sternly dealt with, regardless of the protests of the sentimentalists and those who seemingly want to throw so much protection around the disturbing element in the community that the good citizen cannot receive proper protection and the good name of the City of Los Angeles may suffer in the eyes of the rest of the country.

"The police are going to do the job and I propose to back up the police." . . .

BAN ON FREAK SUITS STUDIED BY COUNCILMEN

Los Angeles Times, June 10, 1943

A proposal that it be made a jail offense to wear "zoot suits" with reat pleats within the city limits of Los Angeles was given serious contemplation yesterday by the City Council.

The suggestion was made in a written resolution by Councilman Norris Nelson and immediately set the whole Council off on a baggy pants debate which lasted an hour. . . .

Nelson in advocating a jail sentence ordinance admitted there is a big question if it would be constitutional. He pointed out, in support of his idea, however, that the length of bathing suits had been legislated and that the Federal government as a war measure is now regulating the style and size of clothing. He said that the wearing of zoot suits in Los Angeles has definitely become a "public nuisance" and as such could be abated. . . .

Zooters Escape San Diego Mob

Mobs of servicemen, from a dozen to 300 or 400 strong roamed the downtown streets tonight, on the lookout for zootsuiters reported to be infiltrating into San Diego from Los Angeles.

A mob of more than 100 sailors and marines stormed down a main street after several youths wearing the outlandish garb, but the zootsuiters made a getaway before fists began to swing.

Another gang of servicemen, numbering about 350, gathered at an intersection but were dispersed by city and military police before any zootsuiters were found.

Zoot-suited gang members, who may seek haven here after a series of riots and knife slashings in Los Angeles, will receive rough treatment, Police Chief Clifford E. Peterson warned.

TIME FOR SANITY
[Editorial]

Los Angeles Times, June 11, 1943.

If there was ever a time to avoid hysteria and wild accusations of whatever nature, it is in this so-called zoot suit war now going on in Los Angeles.

Instead there should be a concerted effort to solve a difficult situation as quickly and sanely as possible.

A far greater danger than the gangsterism and its attendant flare-up of retributive violence lies in the perverted purposes to which reports of the difficulties here are being, and will be, put both at home and in other countries.

Attempts by any group, faction, or political philosophy to use the clashes for purposes of stirring up racial prejudice are unwarranted and are serving the aims of Axis propagandists.

There seems to be no simple or complete explanation for the growth of the grotesque gangs. Many reasons have been offered, some apparently valid, some farfetched.

But it does appear to be definitely established that any attempts at curbing the movement have had nothing whatever to do with race persecution, although some elements have loudly raised the cry of this very thing.

In fact, at the outset zoot suiters were limited to no specific race; they were Anglo-Saxon, Latin and Negro.

The fact that later on their numbers seemed to be predominantly Latin was in itself no indictment of that race at all; the American-born boy gangs merely came from certain districts where the Latin population was in the large majority.

No responsible person at any time condemned Latin Americans, as such, because some irresponsibles were causing trouble.

This cardinal fact should be kept in mind.

The present pressing problem, then, not only is to get to the bottom of the social causes which result in zoot suit gangsterism but also during that process to discourage as far as possible the loud and unthinking charges that the fault lies exclusively in racial prejudice, police brutality, or Fascist tendencies of the constituted authorities.

PUNISHMENT FOR ALL URGED IN ZOOT SUIT WAR

Los Angeles Times, June 13, 1943

The Federal government stepped into the local zoot suit picture by obtaining an injunction against a downtown store restraining the sale of zooters' "uniform"—the finger-length and down-to-the-knees coats and ankle-tight pants that cost about $75 each.

The action was directed against Earl Lamm, proprietor of a clothing store at 430 S. Main St., in a suit filed in Federal court charging that the store violated conservation orders of the War Production Board which last October limited the use of wool cloth in clothing.

FIRST SUIT

Los Angeles Times, June 13, 1943

United States District Judge Leon R. Yankwich granted a temporary restraining order, setting a preliminary hearing on the civil action for June 21.

In effect, the suit, first of its kind in the nation, served notice that zoot suits are "out" for the duration—if the government's position is upheld by the courts after a trial.

FOUR MEN WEARING ZOOT SUITS ATTACKED

Los Angeles Times, June 13, 1943

PHILADELPHIA, June 12 (AP) Four Negro boys wearing zoot trousers and "pancake" hats were attacked and badly beaten on a street corner early today by 25 white boys in a melee in which "several shots" were fired, Patrolmen Arthur Pancerie and Thomas O'Neil reported.

The zooters were treated at a hospital for head and face injuries, then were arrested "for their own protection," the patrolmen said, on charges of breach of the peace. Their assailants escaped.

Two of the zooters, booked as Eugene Rochelle, 22, of New York and James Thomas, 21, of Philadelphia, were discharged later today. The others, Charles Emory, 17, and Samuel Satterfield, 17, both of Philadelphia, were held for Juvenile Court.

3
Science and the Chicano

The Chicano has not received the scientific attention that several other minorities have. When scientists and pseudoscientists were preparing the briefs that would help rationalize American immigration restriction laws, the Mexican was scarcely noticed. The fact that the debate over his cheap labor and conflicting culture had not yet reached national proportions undoubtedly contributed to this omission. Then, too, there was no Mexican "race" per se. He was the combination of Indian, Caucasian, and Negro, with the Indian heavily predominating, and the inferiority of the Indian had already been firmly established by numerous scientists. Thus, most of the scientific writing on the Chicano has had a local color tinge to it, with the Southwest and California providing the usual locale.

A. WILLIAM A. SHELDON AND THE INTELLIGENCE OF MEXICAN-AMERICAN CHILDREN, 1924

Although for the most part the Chicano escaped the broad scientific attack that the black and Native American suffered, the intelligence of his children often came under examination during the 1920's and 1930's. His offspring did not score as well on the tests as did the Anglos, and various educational and psychological journals carried articles on the subject. Some of these articles did mention possible language and economic factors that might have a bearing, but none suggested that the type of test itself might be invalid. In addition to the standard I.Q. tests of the day, color-preference tests were also given. These usually showed the Chicano child to be closer to the Indian than to the Anglo in his choice of colors.

The following article by University of Texas educational psychologist, William A. Sheldon appeared in School and Society *and is fairly typical of those making intelligence comparisons. Four years later in the same journal, Thomas Garth, perhaps the best-known educational psychologist of this period, thought that Sheldon had underestimated the differences in intelligence scoring, but Garth was careful not to draw any overt inferences of racism.*[1]

Since it is now well established that intelligence tests enable us to compare accurately the ability of one child with another, of approximately the same age, it seems probable that in the same way we can reliably compare the intelligence of children of different races by means of such tests. . . .

In school systems having a large admixture of foreign children, it is essential that the intelligence of the foreigners be known as accurately as possible, and that every effort be put forth to use such knowledge to the best advantage. As this problem is rendered important in southwestern United States by the presence of a considerable Mexican population, it was suggested by Professor L. W. Cole, of the University of Colorado, that I test for comparative purposes, one hundred white and one hundred Mexican children, of the same age and school environment.

The work was done in the spring of 1923 at Roswell, N. M., where the desired conditions could be fulfilled. All the two hundred children tested were in school at the time. They were all enrolled in the first grade, excepting twenty of the Mexicans, who were unclassified. For the most part, these Mexican children were able to understand English as well as their white schoolmates; they were not separated from the whites, but taught in the same classes with them. However, one school in this city was found to be devoted entirely to Mexicans, and here the children understood English very imperfectly. To overcome the difficulty in this school, it was necessary that the children tested (about forty) be given the group tests by their respective teachers. These teachers were able to make themselves understood by the use of a sort of Spanish-English dialect colloquially called "spic," and mongrel Spanish. With this exception, all the tests were given by the writer. . . .

The comparison becomes much' clearer when expressed in the form

[1]Reprinted by permission of *School and Society* from William Sheldon, "Educational Research and Statistics: The Intelligence of Mexican Children," *School and Society,* February 2, 1924, pp. 139–142.

of intelligence quotients. The average Binet intelligence quotient for the white children was 104.8, while that of the Mexicans was 89. This gives a difference of 15.8 between the two groups, which places the Mexicans at an intelligence level almost exactly 85 percent of that of the whites. Considering the Mexican children as a group, then, we may say roughly that the tests rated their intelligence at about 85 percent of that of a normal group of white children of the same age and school environment.

The figures given in Table I will doubtless be revised by the use of standardized mental tests, but at present the relative intelligence of the races listed seems to be about as set forth.

TABLE 1

Nationality	Average I.Q.
American	100
English	100
Hebrew	98
Chinese	90
Mexican (American)	85
Indian (American)	83
Slavish	83
Italians	77
Negroes	75

In addition to the facts already mentioned, a study of the results of the Binet tests shows that the Mexicans were about equal to the whites in tests or rote memory, visual memory, and interest in numbers, including comprehension of time periods. The whites were decidedly superior in tests involving comprehension (all degrees), judgment, and the higher associative processes, especially where sustained attention and accurate observation were necessary. The Mexican children showed a slightly greater range in mental age than did the whites, and much greater range in chronological age, but the whites had the greater range in intelligence quotients, because of a few very high scores made by young children.

B. EUGENICS AND THE MEXICAN IMMIGRANT

When Congress debated Mexican immigration restriction in the late 1920's, the eugenics experts volunteered their comments on what the Mexican influx would mean to this country's native stock. Several eugenicists testified before the House Committee on Immigration and

Naturalization on the undesirability of Mexican immigrants, and their publications likewise upheld restriction.

The American Genetics Society's Journal, Eugenics, *first appeared in 1928, and although it was destined to be rather short-lived, its Advisory Council did include some of America's leading scholars. The following article appeared in 1929 and is a good, albeit somewhat extreme, example of how the eugenicists could connect social, economic, and cultural differences to inferior bloodlines. The "Amerinds" are the "non-white" Mexicans.*[1]

The Influx of Mexican Amerinds

The doctor was careful to distinguish between the Castillian (white) Mexican, and the peon of Amerind (American-Indian) blood. It is doubtful whether 10 per cent of Mexico's, say, 15,000,000, are free from Amerind blood. Eugenically as low-powered as the Negro, the peon is from a sanitation standpoint, a menace. He not only does not understand health rules: being a superstitious savage, he resists them. Vicente Espinosa's case is typical. Two Espinosa children contracted smallpox. Their home was quarantined. Vicente had, however, the Mexican passion for gambling. Despite the quarantine he slipped out to the poolroom. Two men contracted the disease from him. Both died. Before dying, they passed the disease on to ten others. Of these three more died. Vicente was sentenced to thirty days in jail. . . .

Venereal disease is widespread among peons. In our border counties, the commercialized brothel has, under red-light abatement acts, practically disappeared. South of the line it persists as an institution. It is common to find a Mexican sitting outside one until a daughter, forced therein, has earned enough for his coming spree of pulque. There could hardly be a greater gulf between the peon's attitude toward his womenfolk and that of the typical American. The former's being Amerind, it is still that of an Indian buck toward his squaw. . . .

California's early miners thus frequently named new camps with location names from "back home." These latter had, in 1849, nearly 100 per cent Nordic populations. The pioneers were, almost to a man, red or yellow-bearded Nordics with blue or grey eyes. They were Longobards of a later age who had crossed, not Alps, but Sierras, to delve into the red dust for gold. While the Placer Age changed into the beginnings of the Quartz Epoch, they persisted. Then came industrial organi-

[1]C. M. Goethe, "The Influx of Mexican Amerinds," *Eugenics,* January 1929, pp. 6–9.

zation of quartz mining with insistence on ever cheaper labor. Followed successive invasions of Irish, Sicilians, Slavonians. Each group displaced its predecessor. Today pour in from Guanajuato, Zacetecas, Sonora, peons of the notch-pole-mining-ladder type. . . .

Near Aguascalientes a squealing porker, seven chickens, some thirteen children were co-tenants of a rural adobe. . . . The father of this brood was a County Kerry man, strayed hither years ago. He long had consorted with, later abandoned, a native woman. He was what north of the Rio Grande is called a "squaw man." Amerind women are markedly prolific. The peons' northward trek, now a mass movement, has, therefore become a menace to the old American seed stock. . . .

An Anglo-Saxon farmer complained, that with Mexican competition, he dared bring only three kiddies into the world. At the three-rate, he would have twenty-seven great-grandchildren. At a nine-child rate, the Mexican would have 729. If one week's automobiles carried 322 families, if train plus stage influx were the same, at such a nine average, we, in that week, admitted the forbears of 469,476 peons to compete for food with 17,388 great-grandchildren from a similar present-day American group.

America today enjoys a material prosperity hitherto unknown in history. This is the result of generations of those eugenically high-powered. America feasts unthinkingly, heedless of The Back Door. Though Ellis Island's portal be closed, this Back Door remains wide open. Through it are coming five people: Mercedes Ramirez, chambermaid, disease carrier; the brothers Gomez, miners, highgraders, fathers of social inadequates; Guadelupe and Patrick, hybrids from an Amerind stock with a menacingly prolific birth rate.

One thinks of the description in Maeterlinck's *Bluebird* of the unborn generations of the Tomorrow. Will they not have the right to rise up and curse us, Americans of today, for failing to close, by adequate legislation, that Back Door? . . .

C.   UNIVERSITY OF CALIFORNIA'S S. J. HOLMES
AND THE MEXICAN IMMIGRANT, 1936

Perhaps the best known scientific scholar to lend his name to Mexican exclusion was the University of California's Professor of biology, S. J. Holmes. Holmes wrote a great deal on genetics and the accompanying social problems, and he was often quoted on the "Mexican Problem" by popular journalists of the 1920's and early 1930's. The following passage is taken from his Human Genetics and Its Social Import *and is another example of how easily some of these scholars slipped from the realm of pure science into that of social and political speculation.*[1]

The establishment of the quota system limiting the proportion of immigrants who could enter from any one country led to a great reduction of immigration from southern Europe. The aim of the assignment of quotas was to preserve approximately the existing ethnic composition of the American people. This was accomplished in accordance with a general rule without making invidious discriminations against any European nation. The quota system was not applied to nations in the Western Hemisphere, and immigrants from Canada, Mexico, the West Indies, and Central and South America could enter in any desired numbers, subject only to the literacy test and a small fee required of all incoming aliens. The reduced numbers of laborers coming from southern Europe had the effect of stimulating immigration from the countries of the Western Hemisphere, and especially from Mexico. The Mexican invasion threatened to give rise to race problems second only to those created by the presence of the Negro. The great majority of Mexican immigrants consisted of peon laborers mostly of Indian blood. . . .

Many of the employments of Mexicans are seasonal, and they trek with their families from one place to another as opportunities for employment determine. Frequently they are unemployed and become a burden upon charity. Although they possess many attractive qualities, it cannot be said that they contribute much to the cultural life of the communities they enter. Politically they are largely under the sway of bosses who determine how they shall vote. Their record for crime is distinctly bad, and in many communities they create embarrassing social and educational problems. Their birth rate is very high and in many localities the majority of the children in the schools are Mexicans. The studies which have been made on the intelligence of Mexican children indicate that their average I.Q. is low, but to what extent this is due to the disadvantages of their upbringing instead of their heredity is not determined. At least the Mexican peon has shown little evidence of intellectual superiority. But granting that his defects are cultural and not genetic it remains true that the average Mexican is singularly slow of assimilation. Even today there are numerous Mexicans in New Mexico, descended from the population of the territory when it was taken over

[1]From *Human Genetics and its Social Import* by S. J. Holmes, pp. 337–341. Copyright 1936 by McGraw-Hill Book Company. Used with permission of McGraw-Hill Book Company.

by the United States, who are unable to speak the English language; and even in the state legislature the proceedings have to be published in both English and Spanish for the benefit of constituents who are unable to read the English language.

The race mixture which occurs between Mexican peons and whites is largely on the basis of illegitimate unions between white males and Mexican females. There is a good deal of miscegenation between Mexicans and Negroes and between Mexicans and American Indians. Some Mexicans are of pure Spanish extraction, but these constitute a small minority. More have some admixture of Spanish or other white blood, but the rank and file of Mexican laborers are almost pure Indians.

D. STANFORD'S L. L. BURLINGAME AND THE BIOLOGY OF THE MEXICAN, 1940

In 1940, Stanford University biologist L. L. Burlingame published a textbook in the McGraw-Hill Zoological Science series entitled Heredity and Social Problems. *It was the author's hope that such a study would not only aid students but would also accelerate the growing rapprochement between the biological and the social sciences; thus, he attempted to apply his scientific theories to social realities.*

Quite naturally race came under his attention, and although his writing contains nothing that is particularly new, his conclusions are nevertheless significant if for no other reason than that they appeared in a nationally recognized textbook series. The following passage is on the biological problem of the Mexican.[1]

The problems connected with relatively large immigration of Mexicans is biologically a rather serious one. The need for cheap labor, particularly in California, is the prime cause of this immigration. So long as this need is not supplied in some other way, Mexicans will continue to come to supply it, create labor troubles and greatly aggravate the various relief problems. This immigration has been and will continue to be difficult to control. With the purely social and economic aspects of this problem this book is not directly concerned. But what of the biological aspects?

Racially the Mexican immigrants are largely Amerind or hybrids with

[1]From *Heredity and Social Problems* by L. L. Burlingame (pp. 251–252, 257). Copyright 1940 by McGraw-Hill Book Company. Used with permission of McGraw-Hill Book Company.

other races. Physically they are not a particularly desirable group to introduce into the population. Intellectually they seem from the scanty
evidence available to be even less desirable. Tests have been few, and
the results are probably less reliable than those for more settled groups.
Since their social and economic status is very low, whatever this may
do to lower test scores should be allowed for in considering the results.
However, with even the most liberal allowance, they would still rank
very low. They have of course produced no persons of eminence in the
United States. In Mexico some leaders have risen from the pure or almost
pure Amerind stocks. The immigrants are themselves chiefly peons and
have here practically no opportunity to attain eminence. The very similar ethnic groups long settled in New Mexico have, of course, much
fuller opportunity but have also failed to produce eminent men in numbers even approaching their numerical proportion in the population of
the state.

At the lower end of the intelligence scale mental deficiency is almost
surely high. Mexicans constitute a large fraction of the relief load of
all sorts in those parts of California where they live or work. This is
partly due to the seasonal nature of their occupation. It approaches the
truth to say that they work in the seasons when work is available and
are on relief of some kind at other times.

Fertility and mortality are both very high among this group. Net
fertility is probably higher by a very wide margin than that of any other
considerable group in the entire population. . . .

[In conclusion], Mexicans present the second most serious race problem. They are apparently of distinctly low mental caliber, have not yet
produced eminence and do contribute heavily to various dependent
classes. They work cheaply, aggravate labor troubles and impose heavy
tax burdens.

The only biological remedy so far applied to this problem is that of
emigration. It is good as far as it goes but is unlikely to be particularly
effective unless the situation changes materially. The socially inadequate
part of this population will presumably be handled in the future by the
same methods adopted for control of the social inadequates of all origins.

4
Congress and Mexican Immigration Restriction

The curtailment of European immigrants in 1924 meant increased demands for labor, and thousands of Mexicans came over the border to fill this need. While the 1924 National Origins Act was being debated, an amendment to include the countries of the Western Hemisphere under the quota system was decisively defeated. With the total immigration restricted to some 150,000, the additional 50,000 Mexicans made up a sizable proportion of our annual immigration. By 1925, pressure was again being exerted to place Latin Americans and, more specifically, Mexicans, under the quota system. The groups behind this movement were familiar ones. Patriotic societies, eugenics organizations, and the labor unions demanded that we now "close the back door." Opposition to restriction came from large economic interests that used Mexican labor and from the State Department, which feared a worsening of relations with Latin America.

Restrictionists tried to focus their arguments on economic issues, but racial fears were usually evident. Canada was then sending some 75,000 immigrants into the United States each year to compete with our labor force, but there was little demand for Canadian restriction. In 1926, a restrictionist bill for the Western Hemisphere was introduced in the House, and for four years its Committee on Immigration and Naturalization held hearings on the subject. Finally, in 1930, the original bill, which by this time had been changed to include only Mexicans, passed the House. At this point, and largely for diplomatic reasons, the Administration stepped in and blocked the bill.

A. REPRESENTATIVE JAMES L. SLAYDEN AND MEXICAN IMMIGRATION, 1921

Rep. James Slayden was President of the American Peace Society, a Trustee of the Carnegie Endowment for International Peace, and a member of the World Court. At home, however, he felt that tranquillity would best prevail if America followed a strict immigration policy, and this must include Mexicans. The Texas representative made it unmistakably clear that here was a people who simply could not be assimilated into his America. This paper was presented to the Academy of Political and Social Sciences in January, 1921.[1]

The importance of the question of immigration from Mexico can hardly be overestimated. It has a direct bearing on the general subject of immigration which Congress has been considering for years, and which has not yet been solved. It is tied up with the greatest of all of our problems, that of race mingling. . . .

This steady incoming of an alien race, not altogether white, is welcomed by some Americans, tolerated by others and utterly abhorred by those who look beyond the next cotton crop or the betterment of railway lines.

Large planters short of labor, because of the extraordinary hegira of Negroes in the last few years, know their value and welcome the Mexican immigrants as they would welcome fresh arrivals from the Congo, without a thought of the social and political embarrassment to their country. On the other hand, the small southern farmers (and they are the greater number) who cultivate their land with the help of their children, do not want the Mexicans, and would gladly see the movement of Negroes go on until the last one was settled in New England or Illinois or wherever they may be most happy, prosperous and welcome.

But both Negroes and Mexicans are here yet in large numbers, and close observers begin to detect a feeling of jealousy and dislike between them. In Texas and other southern states the Mexican is classed as white in public conveyances, hotels and places of amusement which does not make for good feeling between him and the Negro, and the Mexican,

---

[1]James L. Slayden, "Some Observations on Mexican Immigration," *The Annals, The American Academy of Political and Social Science,* January 1921, pp. 121–126.

even of very low class, is not much inclined to social intimacy with the latter.

That to substitute one for the other may be jumping from the frying-pan into the fire is a thought that will intrude itself. . . .

In Texas the word "Mexican" is used to indicate the race, not a citizen or subject of the country. There are probably 250,000 Mexicans in Texas who were born in the state but they are "Mexicans" just as all blacks are Negroes though they may have five generations of American ancestors.

Most Mexicans are Indians or Mestizos (mixed white and Indian blood) and between them and the other inhabitants of Mexico there is a sharply defined social distinction. The upper classes, of European ancestry, are frequently educated in Spain, France or the United States, and few of them become immigrants unless forced out by revolutions, when they go to San Antonio, El Paso or Los Angeles. At home they are the merchants, big planters, bankers and professional men.

With rare exceptions these people stay at home, look after their private affairs and do not meddle with politics. They would make good and useful citizens of any country. When one of them does go in for politics (or revolution, which is the same thing in Mexico) he does more mischief, because above his wicked heart is a cleverer head. He easily becomes the leader of the low-browed, poverty-stricken peon class, and by perfervid appeals to the prejudice of the thoughtless and uneducated mass of Indians and the promise of an impossible Utopia quickly converts them into murderous bandits. Resounding phrases about the Constitution, whether that of 1857 or that of Queretaro, makes no difference—and the rights of the Indians, mixed with contemptuous remarks about the "Gringoes" and the hated "Colossus of the North" soon can make fiends of otherwise quiet and useful men. . . .

These are the people, high and low, from whom thousands of immigrants are coming to the United States. What it may mean for Americans in the future no one can tell. Probably our safety and peace lie in the fact that as yet so few of them, comparatively are coming.

B.   REPRESENTATIVE THOMAS A. JENKINS
SUPPORTS RESTRICTION, 1930

Not all supporters of Mexican restriction were from the South. Ohio's Representative Thomas A. Jenkins had worked with Texas Representative

John Box on the latter's 1926 attempt to push a restriction bill through Congress. The following comments were from testimony he gave to the House Committee on Immigration and Naturalization in 1930. For Jenkins it was also easy to slip from the economic argument into the racial one.[1]

All this substantiates the thousands of reports received by Judge Box and myself in the survey made by us and a part of which we have heretofore made to your honorable committee.

By song and ballad the negro [sic] has been identified with the cotton fields and the watermelon patches of the South and Southwest for generations. The story of the heroic plainsmen of Texas has spurred our youth to high resolves to be courageous and valorous ever since the day of Sam Houston and Davy Crockett, but each of these admirable classes of our population has been driven from its throne by the sinister, silent flood of Mexican immigration that has washed it far back from its once secure moorings. In fact, the negro has been supplanted almost altogether by the Mexican in the territory 200 miles north from the Rio Grande. And the plainsman has receded before the onrush of Mexicans that have supplanted his cattle ranches with cotton fields which yield a larger return to the big plantation man of the Southwest, and has now lost himself in the population of the large cities or has moved on to the highlands of the Northwest. The Mexicans have so preempted the track work of the railroads that practically all of it in the Southwest is done by them, and even as far north as Chicago nearly 50 per cent of all track workers are Mexicans—and practically all this is the result of a desire to employ cheap labor. If we are to keep American business for Americans, we must keep American jobs for Americans.

There can be no question but that economic and hygienic conditions among the Mexicans in our country are very bad in many cases. The average is far below that maintained by Americans. Crime and vagrancy among Mexicans are serious handicaps to their desirability as citizens and lowers their efficiency as laborers. General undesirability of the Mexican because of his shiftlessness and propensity to shirk is clearly established from the reports that we received. This summary, together with other data procured by us, lead me to believe that there are at present about 2,000,000 Mexican-born Mexicans in the United States.

[1]"Western Hemisphere Immigration," *Hearings Before the Committee on Immigration and Naturalization*, House of Representatives, 71st Cong., 2nd Sess., 1930, p. 419.

The Mexican can not be blamed for his desire to come to the United States and to enjoy the superior facilities of our country. A visitor to El Paso, Texas, or to Nogales, Arizona, or to any of the other border cities will see a contrast between the standards of living in the United States and those of Mexico that will be most astonishing. Nogales is a small city on the boundary between the United States and Mexico. It is located in a valley probably one-quarter of a mile wide, which runs north and south. From the top of the bordering mountains on the east side of the valley runs an international wire fence to the top of the opposite mountains. This fence runs directly through the city and divides it into two parts—American Nogales and Mexican Nogales. A railroad track runs up and down the valley. Trains coming north stop at Nogales, Mexico. A watchman opens a large wire gate and the train, after passing the inspection of American customs and immigration officials, pulls into Nogales, Arizona, and stops.

The contrast between the general conditions on either side of this wire fence is unbelievable. The American city is a clean, healthy, and prosperous community. The Mexican city is typically Mexican—poor buildings, poor streets, ragged children, dirty foodstuffs sold by dirty men and women. Loafers on every curb and corner, and listless lollers everywhere.

The Mexican has been most unfortunate. Of an ancestry which promises little—a mixture of native Indian with West Indian negro and Spaniard—with an environment that can hardly be expected to conduce to progress, with a political background of hundreds of years of banditry, murder, rapine, mobs, and assassinations, what can be expected of him? The so-called higher classes have utterly failed to appreciate the rights of the unfortunate. The unfortunate has been oppressed and enslaved until the peon class far exceeds the upper class in the population. Illiteracy is almost universal in many sections; poverty stalks everywhere; immorality is so common that decency is a rare virtue, but over it all are the dishonest, debased, grafting officials who live off of the oppression of various kinds heaped on a poor benighted people. It has been said that no nation can outlast the patience of its poor. May the time soon come when this maxim will be again proved by another enslaved people losing their patience and demanding their rights.

It is not my object in this article to discuss any special plan for effecting the restriction of Mexican immigration. Any plan that will adequately restrict should be approved by Congress. Since restriction is our natural policy, it is folly to apply this doctrine to the front door and neglect to apply it to the back door.

SELECTED READINGS

McWilliams, Carey, *North from Mexico*, J. B. Lippincott Co., New York, 1948, 1961.
   Although this study first appeared in 1948, it still remains the most widely used survey of the Mexican-American experience.

Moore, Truman, *The Slaves We Rent*, Random House, New York, 1965.
   A moving journalistic account of the migrant workers and the system that uses and abuses them.

Robinson, Cecil, *With the Ears of Strangers; the Mexicans in American Literature*, University of Arizona Press, Tucson, 1963.
   This is the kind of study that needs to be done for all our minorities: of their image as portrayed in American literature.

Romano-V., Octavio I., "The Anthropology and Sociology of the Mexican Americans," *El Grito*, II (Fall 1968).
   An incisive attack on the well meaning social scientists who needed a stereotyped Chicano to fit their case studies.

Samora, Julian, Ed., *La Raza: Forgotten Americans*, University of Notre Dame Press, Notre Dame, Indiana, 1966.
   A series of useful political, economic, sociological, and historical essays by both Anglo and Chicano scholars.

Steiner, Stan, *La Raza*, Harper Row, New York, 1970.
   In addition to complementing McWilliams' earlier study, Steiner examines the thoughts of today's activist Chicanos.

IV
CHINESE-AMERICANS

I am satisfied that the present Chinese labor invasion is pernicious and should be discouraged. Our experience in dealing with the weaker races—the Negroes and Indians, for example—is not encouraging . . . I would consider with favor any suitable measures to discourage the Chinese from coming to our shores.

President Rutherford B. Hayes, 1879

INTRODUCTION

Because they were barred from settling on our soil a half century before the 1927 National Origins Act, the Chinese occupy a unique place among ethnic minority groups in America. Chinese first began to arrive in California in 1847, and were welcomed by all segments of the population. Yet by 1882, when they numbered approximately 105,000, anti-Chinese agitation had become so intense and so widespread that Congress acted to restrict their immigration.

The anti-Chinese movement gained its strength in the 1870's among the economically depressed working classes of California. It then spread rapidly to worker groups elsewhere in the country. Although there was some use of Chinese as strikebreakers in the East, most Americans had never seen the "Chink" they raged against. By 1876, the popular sentiment in the country prompted both the Democrats and Republicans to approve anti-Chinese planks in their national platforms. In 1879, Californians voted 154,638 to 883 in favor of a proposed exclusion measure. Congress also acted in 1879 to halt virtually all Chinese immigration, but President Hayes vetoed the bill because of U.S. treaty commitments with China. The anti-Chinese movement, however, continued to gain strength, and, in 1880, the treaties with China were altered; two years later approval was given to a Chinese exclusion law. Others followed—in 1888, 1902, and 1904—and they effectively barred the Chinese for an indefinite period. It was not until 1943 that Congress, after con-

163

siderable debate, decided to repeal the exclusion acts in hopes of boosting the morale of its loyal ally in the fight against Japan. China was thus brought under the quota system established by the 1924 immigration act, which meant that 105 persons of Chinese ancestry could enter the country annually.

Why were the Chinese specifically excluded from the United States on racial grounds? The overriding reasons for exclusion were purported to be economic, but anti-Chinese sentiment began long before California was plagued by any serious economic problems. It is true that the Chinese in California became a symbol for the white man's economic problems there in the 1870's, but in the hysteria that took hold of the state at that time, it is easy to see the ingrained racial hostility toward the "Heathen Chinee." To Californians, these little "yellow" people with their slanted eyes, long pigtails, strange language, and barbaric customs were industrious—no one denied that—but they were also cunning, cruel, stolid, and generally inhuman. They could never be assimilated, it was argued, because they retained their loyalty to their Emperor, to their ancestors, and to Confucius. They had filthy social habits, were too clannish, gambled incessantly, corrupted young white girls and boys in their opium dens, and plotted to take control of the "Pacific Slope." Thus, their very presence was a threat to the Western way of life; if not restrained, "this inferior yellow race" would endanger America's very way of life. The Chinese stereotype, so firmly etched in the popular mind in the 1870's and 1880's, has continued well into the twentieth century in some of America's best-selling mystery and suspense fiction.

The stream of Chinese immigration, which in the late 1800's many said would soon become a torrent if not checked, effectively began in the late 1840's when floods and revolution wreaked havoc among the poverty-stricken peasants of Southeastern China. Then gold was discovered in California, creating jobs and prompting the encouragement of Chinese immigration. By the end of 1851, it was estimated that there were 25,000 Chinese in California, engaged in either mining or domestic and manual labor. The business and commerical class of California welcomed "John Chinaman," but before long the miners became fearful of the Chinese intrusion into the mining areas. The cry "California for Americans" was soon followed by violence and then official discrimination. In Congress, Western representatives began to agitate for stiff Federal laws that would halt Chinese immigration and discourage those living here from staying. The Chinese race, said one congressman in 1862, was so "deeply sunk in barbarism" that mere contact with it was "demoralization." The press in the West generally agreed with such comments; in fact, there were few public defenders of the Chinese anywhere in the country.

For Californians, the 1866 Burlingame Treaty with China contained dangerous implications. The treaty stated that the two countries recognized the mutual rights of emigration and immigration. Then, with the adoption of the Fifteenth Amendment, Californians were filled with fear that Chinese would soon be naturalized, gain the vote, and hold public office.

By 1876, because of widespread unemployment and growing violence, San Francisco public officials and California legislators were pressuring Washington for a revision of the Burlingame Treaty in order to halt "the immigration of a servile laboring element" that would soon make San Francisco "a purely Asiatic City." The platforms of the two major political parties in 1876 promised that something would be done; in addition, Congress appointed a special six-member joint committee to examine the Chinese problem in California. The committee, which did not call a single Chinese witness, urged Congress to restrain immigration of Asiatics and requested the President to modify American treaties with China.

The anti-Chinese crusade soon enlisted the aid of prominent Eastern politicians, particularly Senator James Blaine of Maine, who envisioned California support for a planned bid for the presidency. The strength of the crusade was apparent in January when the House passed a bill stating that no ship could carry more than 15 Chinese passengers to any U.S. port on any one voyage. The bill passed the Senate a month later, but was vetoed by President Hayes, who favored Chinese exclusion but declared that the legislation usurped the Executive's treaty-making power. Anti-Chinese riots followed in Wyoming, Colorado, and Washington, as well as in California, and local legislation against the Chinese in these states became increasingly oppressive.

In a matter of months, a new treaty with China was negotiated, clearing the way for Congress to act. President Arthur in 1882 vetoed a bill excluding Chinese laborers for 20 years, but approved a 10-year ban and denial of citizenship to all Chinese already in the country who had not been born here. Complaining that the new act did not effectively stem the tide of Chinese immigration, the anti-Chinese forces remained mobilized and finally prodded Congress into passing a measure in 1888 barring both skilled and unskilled laborers and refusing readmittance to Chinese leaving the country. Other exclusion acts were passed in 1892 and 1902. Finally, in 1904, the Chinese were indefinitely barred from settling here. Four decades later, America's fear of the military power of another "yellow" race prompted a change in attitude toward the Chinese and led to their inclusion under the national quota system. They also became eligible for citizenship, but even after World War II several states continued to bar Chinese-Caucasian marriages.

1
Popular Images of "The Heathen Chinee"

Soon after the "Celestials" began to arrive in the late 1840's, a negative popular image started to emerge in various articles, stories, songs, and poetry. Anti-Chinese songs were known to be popular among the miners and laborers of California as early as 1855. Anti-Chinese poetry of the type Bret Harte was later to popularize had also appeared in newspapers and magazines in the decade before the Civil War. But it was in the postwar era that increasing numbers of social reformers, missionaries, politicians, and intellectuals, distressed about the possibilities of a Chinese "invasion," published their assessments of Chinese habits, customs, and character.

That criticism of the Chinese was sometimes warranted cannot be denied; however, most of the criticism—implicitly or explicitly—attributed much of their behavior to racial flaws; and it became increasingly difficult to find a balanced, or even a rational, article on the Chinese immigrants. They looked and acted different from the majority of Americans, and for most critics "different" meant "inferior." Thus those who might have positively influenced public opinion, sought simplistic solutions instead: prohibit Chinese immigration, deny entry to the wives of the overwhelmingly male population, refuse reentry to those who left the country, and forbid the rights of citizenship to those who remained in America.

A. ANTI-CHINESE SONGS OF CALIFORNIA

The three songs that follow offer an excellent reflection of popular opinion concerning the Chinese in California in the three decades prior

167

to the first exclusion act. "John Chinaman" illustrates the miners' fear that the Chinese were becoming too numerous in the gold-mining areas. Forced out of the mine fields by violence and restrictive legislation, the Chinese turned to the cities and sought there to make a living. "Since the Chinese Ruint the Thrade" exemplifies how urban laborers, many of them Irish, reacted to the new competition. The 1877 song, "Twelve Hundred More," reflects the growing hysteria in California over the continuing immigration of Chinese workers.[1]

JOHN CHINAMAN (1855)[2]

John Chinaman, John Chinaman,
    But five short years ago,
I welcomed you from Canton, John—
    But wish I hadn't though;

For then I thought you honest, John,
    Not dreaming but you'd make
A citizen as useful, John
    As any in the State

I thought you'd open wide your ports
    And let our merchants in
To barter for their crapes and teas
    Their wares of wood and tin.

I thought you'd cut your queue off, John,
    And don a Yankee coat,
And a collar high you'd raise, John,
    Around your dusky throat.

I imagined that the truth, John
    You'd speak when under oath,
But I find you'll lie and steal too—
    Yes, John, you're up to both.

[1]These songs and others are reproduced in Richard Lingenfelter, Richard Dwyer, and David Cohen, *Songs of the American West*, Univ. of Calif. Press, Berkeley, 1968.

[2]"John Chinaman," *The California Songster*, David E. Appleton & Co., San Francisco, 1855, p. 44.

I thought of rats and puppies, John
    You'd eaten your last fill;
But on such slimy pot-pies, John,
    I'm told you dinner still.

Oh, John, I've been deceived in you,
    And in all your thieving clan,
For our gold is all you're after, John,
    To get it as you can.

SINCE THE CHINESE RUINT THE THRADE (n.d.)[3]

From me shanty down on Sixth Street,
    It's meself have jist kim down;
I've lived there this eighteen year—
    It's in phat they call Cork Town.
I'm on the way to the City Hall
    To get a little aid;
It's meself that has to ax it now
    Since the Chinese ruint the thrade.

CHORUS: For I kin wash an' iron a shirt,
        An' I kin scrub a flure;
An' I kin starch a collar as stiff
    As any Chineseman, I'm sure;
But there dhirty, pigtailed haythens,
    An' ther prices they are paid
Have brought me to the state you see—
    They've entirely ruint the thrade

I'm a widdy woman, I'd have ye know—
    Poor Mike was kilt at work.
He got a fall from the City Hall,
    For he was a mason's clerk.
An' me daughter Ellen is gone this year
    Wid a Frinch bally troupe, ther jade,
So I find it hard to get along
    Since the Chinese ruint the thrade.

---

[3]"Since the Chinese Ruint the Thrade," *The Poor Little Man and the Man in the Moon Is Looking, Love, Songster*, G. W. Greene, San Francisco, p. 11.

It makes me wild, whin I'm on the street,
    To see those haythens' signs:
Ah Sung, Ah Sing, Sam Lee, Ah Wing,
    An' ther ilegatt sprid on ther lines.
If iver I get me hands on Ah Sing,
    I'll make him Ah Sing indade—
On me clothesline I'll pin th' leather skin
    Of the haythen that ruint the thrade.

TWELVE HUNDRED MORE (1877)[4]

O workingmen dear, and did you hear
The news that's goin' round?
Another China steamer
Has been landed here in town.
Today I read the papers,
And it grieved my heart full sore
To see upon the title page,
O, just "Twelve Hundred More!"

O, California's coming down,
As you can plainly see.
They are hiring all the Chinamen
and discharging you and me;
But strife will be in every town
Throughout the Pacific shore,
And the cry of old and young shall be,
"O, damn, 'Twelve Hundred More' "

They run their steamer in at night
Upon our lovely bay;
If 'twas a free and honest trade,
They'd land it in the day.
They come here by the hundreds—
The country is overrun—
And go to work at any price—
By them the labor's done.

---

[4]"Twelve Hundred More," *The Blue and Grey Songster*, S. S. Green, San Francisco, 1877, pp. 16–17.

If you meet a workman in the street
And look into his face,
You'll see the signs of sorrow there—
Oh, damn this long-tailed race!
And men today are languishing
Upon a prison floor,
Because they've been supplanted by
This vile "Twelve Hundred More!"

Twelve hundred honest laboring men
Thrown out of work today
By the landing of these Chinamen
In San Francisco Bay.
Twelve hundred pure and virtuous girls,
In the papers I have read,
Must barter away their virtue
To get a crust of bread.

This state of things can never last
In, this our golden land,
For soon you'll hear the avenging cry,
"Drive out the China man!"
And then we'll have the stirring times
We had in days of yore,
And the devil take those dirty words
They call "Twelve Hundred More!"

B.   BRET HARTE'S CHINESE POETRY

A native of Albany, New York, Bret Harte moved to San Francisco in 1854 when he was eighteen. By 1860, his romantic local color poems and stories were being published, and by the end of the decade his reputation was widespread. Part of his fame was based on humorous writings called "Plain Language from Truthful James." From this collection is taken the 1870 poem, "The Heathen Chinee."[1]

[1]Bret Harte, "The Heathen Chinee," from *Plain Language from Truthful James*, Western News Co., Chicago, 1870.

THE HEATHEN CHINEE

Which I wish to remark—
And my language is plain—
That for ways that are dark
And for tricks that are vain,
The heathen Chinee is peculiar
Which the same I would rise to explain.

Ah Sin was his name;
And I shall not deny
In regard to the same
What that name might imply
But his smile it was pensive and childlike,
As I frequent remarked to Bill Nye.

It was August the third;
And quite soft was the skies;
Which it might be inferred
That Ah Sin was likewise;
Yet he played it that day upon William
And me in a way I despise.

Which we had a small game,
And Ah Sin took a hand:
It was Euchre, the game
He did not understand;
But he smiled as he sat by the table,
With the smile that was childlike and bland.

Yet the cards they were stacked
In a way that I grieve,
And my feelings were shocked
At the state of Nye's sleeve:
Which was stuffed full of aces and bowers,
And the same with intent to deceive.

But the hands that were played
By that heathen Chinee,
And the points that he made,

Were quite frightful to see—
Till at last he put down a right bower,
Which the same Nye had dealt unto me.

The I looked up at Nye,
And he gazed upon me;
And he rose with a sigh,
And said, "Can this be?
We are ruined by Chinese cheap labor"—
And he went to that heathen Chinee

In the scene that ensued
I did not take a hand
But the floor it was strewed
Like the leaves on the strand
With the cards that Ah Sin had been hiding,
In the game "he did not understand."

In his sleeves, which were long,
He had twenty-four packs—
Which was coming it strong,
Yet I state but the facts;
And we found on his nails, which were toper,
What is frequent in tapers—that's wax.

Which is why I remark,
And my language is plain,
That for ways that are dark,
And for tricks that are vain,
The heathen Chinee is peculiar—
Which the same I am free to maintain.

C. THE EX-GOVERNOR OF NEW YORK COMMENTS ON CHINESE "BARBARISM," 1870

With remarkable speed the anti-Chinese movement found support in the East where there were few Chinese. Because of the working-class alarm in California, labor leaders throughout the country took up the cry, "The Chinese must go." Responding to this attitude was the ex-governor of New York, Horatio Seymour, who in 1868 also had been the Democratic nominee for the presidency. Seymour had been asked to ad-

dress a working-men's association in Rochester, but when unable to attend, he sent the following letter, which appeared in the New York Times.[1]

Sir: I put off until this time my answer to your letter asking me to speak to a meeting at Rochester upon the subject of Chinese immigration, as I hoped it would be in my power to do so. I am sorry that I cannot attend. All agree that this is a grave subject. It is one that must be met, and it must be met now. Strong influences are at work to open the flood-gates and pour in upon us the worst classes of over-crowded China. They can get to our shores at less cost, and in greater numbers than the people of Europe. If they continue to crowd in, they will over-throw the customs, civilization and religion of the whole Pacific coast, and they will also crush down the position of laboring classes throughout our country. I am against this. I am not willing they should gain a foothold here. No nation in Europe would suffer such an invasion. If Britain, Germany, or France should allow anything of the kind, their governments would be overthrown. Why should we give up our civilization in any part of our country for that of Asia? . . .

It is said by some, if we shut our Chinese immigration, we do so in the face of all our former professions. This is not so. We invite European immigration, because it adds to our power and happiness. Europeans do not overthrow our customs, religion or civilization. They do not bring here any strange blood. It has always been our practice to shut out any immigration that is hurtful. We send back to Europe criminals or paupers, by virtue of state and national laws. Every city and town guards against incomers who endanger social order or safety. We are in no way bound to take into our public system any mischievous elements, or to destroy it by personal influences. If we believe in our religious creeds, in the form and principles of our Government, then we must believe that Asiatic creeds and customs are baleful. Today we are dividing the lands of the native Indians into States, counties and townships. We are driving off from their property the game upon which they live, by railroads. We tell them plainly, they must give up their homes and property, and live upon corners of their own territories, because they are in the way of our civilization. If we can do this, then we can keep away another form of barbarism which has no right here.

I have no doubt the Chinese have useful qualities. They are said to be good servants, ready to do the work of men or women, but they have not the traits which will build up on this Continent a great and high-

[1] *New York Times*, August 6, 1870.

toned power. We must not judge of those who come here by those who stay at home. We get only the dregs. . . . There is but one way of dealing with this matter. The policy of exclusion must be as sharp and as vigorous as that of Massachusetts or New York against the coming pauperism. It must be borne in mind that, under the late amendments to our national Constitution, you can give them no qualified condition; you put upon them no political restraint, made necessary by their peculiarities. They can grasp the rights of voting and law making despite all State legislation. It is to be hoped that this subject will be taken up and discussed in a fair and temperate way by all classes. We must not let it drift and settle itself. Unless we are ready to give up the consequences of this new danger to the public peace and home happiness of our people, we must confront the problem at the outset.

D. "THE CHINESE MUST GO," *UNITARIAN REVIEW,* 1879

Generally, those persons affiliated with churches that sponsored missions in China tended to take a moderate position on the question of Chinese exclusion. Although they often admitted that the Chinese were an inferior race that could cause severe problems for the dominant race in America, they nevertheless insisted that the Chinese should be treated with kindness and brought to the altar of God. In this article, however, David N. Utter is skeptical about Christianity's impact on the Chinese, and because "blood will tell," he suggested that his fellow churchmen spend their energy developing a higher form of Christianity among the American people. As far as the Chinese were concerned, exclusion was his answer to this "cancer" that was threatening the American system.[1]

It is confessedly true that in many points of manhood and morals the average Chinaman is superior to the average American. We may mention two qualities in particular in which he excels: industry and patience. His industry may be inherited from a line of ancestors who were slavers, but he has it. Patience is almost among the forgotten virtues with us, but it is a virtue, and the Chinaman has it. When we come to the more robust virtues, we must speak in qualified phrase. Courage the Chinaman has to such an extent as to be absolutely indifferent to pain or death, when he has made up his mind that a certain course is to be pursued or a certain thing done; but only a Chinaman can calculate accurately what will bring this courage out. Ordinarily two Pacific Coast

[1]David N. Utter, "The Chinese Must Go," *Unitarian Review,* July 1879, pp. 48–56.

"hoodlums" will drive six or more full-grown Chinamen from a common fishing-ground or other desirable situation. This may be because the Chinamen think that they have no rights; but the fact that they allow even our boys to impose upon them shows a real lack of some qualities that make up what we are accustomed to call manliness. And the people of the Pacific Coast would speak with almost entire unanimity and great confidence that, as a whole, the race is inferior to our own. And the Chinamen themselves seem to understand the matter thus, though it would be very hazardous to attempt to say what a Chinaman understands or thinks or feels.

One of the first things thought of, when a proof of their inferiority is sought, is, that as a race the Chinese do not change or improve. They do not learn our language, nor care for our literature or science. The results of science they are quick to use, but the science they would like better if it were magic. They accept the position of servants and expect to remain there. They never even think of employing a white man except as teacher or overseer. They seem to have no ambition to be other than what they are in any way, except it be to be richer.

But it is perhaps better to leave out of the question the matter of inferiority or superiority as a race, and consider the fact that the Chinese have fixed habits, language, customs, and modes of life, which they do not and will not change, and that these modes of life are not so good as our own. Whether the Chinese themselves are inferior or not, there is no question that their civilization is inferior. That is what is meant when they are called barbarians. Their way of living is semi-barbarous when compared with our way. . . .

There are those who think that this tendency toward the wide separation between the laborer and the employer will be checked in a natural way through the ambition of the Chinaman. We might hope for this, trust in it, but for the three million more who wait in Asia ready to come as soon as wages should rise to a certain point. The continual immigration would probably effectually prevent either any considerable rise in wages or the arising of any large class of Americanized Chinamen. If we could stop with those we have and cut off all hope of return to the mother country, a century or two would make all our Chinamen into some kind of American citizens, no doubt. But what kind of citizens would they make? "Industrious, peaceable, patient, and meek," is answered by a hundred Eastern theorists. True! And thieves and liars also, just as certainly. Not occasionally one, but a race in whom truth and veracity is not. Prudence and policy you may count on, truthfulness and honor you cannot even teach them. Chastity, as we understand it, they do not know. All is prudence and nicely calculated policy. And, humanly speaking, they cannot be improved. Their virtues and their vices are bred in them by a civilization older than our ancient world, and there is nothing in human character, on the face of the whole earth so stable, so fixed, and sure and changeless, as the character of a Chinaman. To think that our Pacific Coast type of civilization, green, luxuriant, and sappy, as it is, can and will absorb these polished pebbles from Asia, or warm them into life so that they will sprout, take root, and grow in our soil, is a pleasing dream and nothing more. If they become citizens, we have simply annexed a Chinese state. If they make homes, they will be Chinese homes. If they build towns, they will be suburbs of Canton and Peking. . . .

E.   JACOB RIIS' VIEW OF CHINATOWN, 1890

Born, raised, and educated in Denmark, Jacob Riis came to New York City and soon earned a reputation as a police reporter for the New York Sun. *Later, he became a major force for social reform and good government in the city. His book,* How the Other Half Lives, *first published in 1890, described the horrors of tenement life for immigrants and sets forth his personal racial views.*[1]

Between the tabernacles of Jewry and the shrines of the Bend, Joss has cheekily planted his pagan worship of idols, chief among which are the celestial worshipper's own gain and lusts. Whatever may be said about the Chinaman being a thousand years behind the age on his own shores, here he is distinctly abreast of it in his successful scheming to "make it pay." It is doubtful if there is anything he does not turn to a paying account, from his religion down, or up, as one prefers. At the risk of distressing some well-meaning, but I fear, too trustful people, I state it in advance as my opinion, based on the steady observation of years, that all attempts to make an effective Christian of John Chinaman will remain abortive in this generation; of the next I have, if anything, less hope. Ages of senseless idolatry, a mere group-worship, have left him without the essential qualities for appreciating the gentle teachings of a faith whose motive and unselfish spirit are alike beyond his grasp. He lacks the handle of a strong faith in something, anything, however wrong, to catch him by. There is nothing strong about him, except his passions where aroused. I am convinced that he adopts Christianity,

[1]Jacob Riis, *How the Other Half Lives*, C. Scribner's Sons, New York, 1901 edition, pp. 67–75.

when he adopts it at all, as he puts on American clothes, with what the politicians would call an ulterior motive, some sort of gain in the near prospect—washing, a Christian wife, perhaps, anything he happens to rate for the moment above his cherished pigtail. It may be that I judge him too harshly. Exceptions may be found. Indeed, for the credit of the race, I hope there are such. But I am bound to say my hope is not backed by lively faith. . . .

From the teeming tenements to the right and left of it come the white slaves of its dens of vice and their infernal drug, that have infused into the "Bloody Sixth" Ward a subtler poison than ever the stale-beer dives knew, or the "sudden death" of the Old Brewery. There are houses, dozens of them, in Mott and Pell Streets, that are literally jammed, from the "joint" in the celler to the attic, with these hapless victims of a passion which, once acquired, demands the sacrifice of every instinct of decency to its insatiate desires. There is a church in Mott Street, at the entrance to Chinatown, that stands as a barrier between it and the tenements beyond. Its young men have waged unceasing war upon the monstrous wickedness for years, but with very little real result. I have in mind a house in Pell Street, that has been raided no end of times by the police, and its population emptied upon Blackwell's Island, or into the reformatories, yet is today honeycombed with scores of the conventional households of the Chinese quarter: the men worshippers of Joss; the women, all white girls, hardly yet grown to womanhood, worshipping nothing save the pipe that has enslaved them body and soul. Easily tempted from homes that have no claim upon the name, they rarely or never return. . . .

One thing about them is conspicuous: their scrupulous neatness. It is the distinguishing mark of Chinatown, outwardly and physically. It is not altogether by chance the Chinaman has chosen the laundry as his distinctive field. He is by nature as clean as the cat, which he resembles in his traits of cruel cunning, and savage fury when aroused.

F. A SOCIOLOGIST DESCRIBES "THE RACE FIBER OF THE CHINESE" 1911.

Long before he discarded his belief in the ability of America to assimilate European immigrants, E. A. Ross, prominent University of Wisconsin sociologist, warned the country about the Chinese threat. In 1901, a decade before the term "race suicide" became popular, Ross claimed that unchecked Chinese immigration might lead to the extinction of the

American people. In his 1911 book, The Changing Chinese, *he devoted the chapter that follows to explaining the "special race vitality" of the Chinese that threatened this country in several ways.*[1]

Out of ten children born among us, three, normally the weakest three, will fail to grow up. Out of ten children born in China these weakest three will die and probably five more besides. The difference is owing to the hardships that infant life meets with among the Chinese. If at birth the white infants and the yellow infants are equal in stamina, the two surviving Chinese ought to possess greater vitality of constitution than the seven surviving whites. For of these seven the five that would infallibly have perished under Oriental conditions of life are presumably weaker in constitution than the two who could have endured even such conditions. The two Chinese survivors will transmit some of their superior vitality to their offspring; and these in turn will be subject to the same sifting, so that the surviving two-tenths will pass on to their children a still greater vitality. Hence these divergent child mortalities drive, as it were, a wedge between the physiques of the two races. If now for generations we whites, owing to room and plenty and scientific medicine and knowledge of hygiene, have been subject to a less searching and relentless elimination of the weaker children than the Chinese, it would be reasonable to expect the Chinese to exhibit a greater vitality than the whites. . . .

Many never get over being astonished at the recovery of the Chinese from terrible injuries. I am told of a coolie who had his abdomen torn open in an accident, and who was assisted to the hospital supported by a man on either side and holding his bowels in his hands. He was sewed up, and, in spite of the contamination that must have gotten into the abdomen, made a quick recovery! Amazing also is the response to the treatment of neglected wounds. A boy whose severed fingers had been hastily stuck on any how and bound up with dirty rags came to the hospital after a week with a horrible hand and showing clear symptoms of lockjaw. They washed his hand and sent him home to die. In three days he was about without a sign of lockjaw. A man whose fingers had been crushed under a cart some days before came in with blood-poisoning all up his arm and in the glands under the arm. The trouble vanished under simple treatment. A patient will be brought in with a high fever from a wound of several day's standing full of maggots; yet after the wound is cleansed the fever quickly subsides. A woman who

[1]E. A. Ross, *The Changing Chinese*, Century Co., New York, 1911, pp. 33–48.

had undergone a serious operation for cancer of the breast suffered infection and had a fever of 106 during which her husband fed her with hard water chestnuts. Nevertheless, she recovered. . . .

While they make wonderful recoveries from high fevers they are not enduring of long fevers. Some think this is because the flame of their vitality has been turned low by unsanitary living. They have a horror of fresh air and shut it out of the sleeping apartment, even on a warm night. In the mission schools, if the teachers insist on open windows in the dormitory, the pupils stifle under the covers lest the evil spirits flying about at night should get at them. The Chinese grant that hygiene may be all very well for these weakly foreigners, but see no use in it for themselves. It is no wonder, therefore, that their schoolgirls cannot stand the pace of American schoolgirls. Ofter they break down, or go into a decline, or have to take a long rest. In the English mission schools with their easier pace the girls get on better. . . .

Of course, with the coming in of Western sanitation, the terrible selective process by which Chinese toughness has been built up will come to an end, and this property will gradually fade out of the race physique. But for our time at least it is a serious and pregnant fact. It will take some generations of exposure to the relaxing effects of drains, ventilation, doctors, district nurses, food inspectors, pure water, open spaces and out-of-door sports to eradicate the peculiar vitality which the yellow race has acquired. During the interim the chief effect of freely admitting coolies to the labor markets of the West would be the substitution of low wages, bad living conditions and the increase of the yellow race for high wages, good living conditions and the increase of the white race.

2
The Exclusion Debate in Congress

In the early 1870's, soon after organized labor began to clamor against Chinese competition, California's representatives in Congress began to agitate for a ban on the immigration of Chinese workers. Denis Kearney's subsequent forming of the California Workingman's Party, dedicated to Chinese exclusion, quickly forced both political parties to take notice of the issue. Under pressure from public officials in California, who had seen their state exclusion measures struck down by the courts, Congress in 1876 approved the first of many investigations into the Chinese question. Over the years, these investigations followed the same general pattern: A Congressional committee would take testimony from a variety of witnesses who, like the committee itself, were generally anti-Chinese; and, in due course, the committee would recommend Federal action to stop the flood of Chinese immigration.

Politicians from the Midwest, East, and South, areas where there was a negligible Chinese population, also agreed with their West Coast counterparts that "the Chinese must go." In 1882, Congress invoked the first of several restrictive measures that by the early twentieth century had excluded Chinese immigration for an "indefinite" period. For this reason, the Chinese were rarely mentioned during the immigration debates of the 1920's, when other Orientals were being systematically excluded. It was not until 1943 that Congress again took up the Chinese exclusion question. Under prodding from friends of China in this country, Congress was urged to repeal exclusion in order to boost the morale of America's wartime ally. Significant opposition lurked beneath the surface, but it was rarely heard in public debate. The repeal was thus approved, and the Chinese received an annual quota of 105 immigrants.

A. SENATOR JAMES G. BLAINE OF MAINE JOINS
THE ANTI-CHINESE CRUSADE, 1879

The first notable Eastern convert to join the Californians in calling for restrictions on Chinese immigration was Senator James G. Blaine of Maine. Blaine, who had served six years as Speaker of the House, had been a Republican presidential hopeful in 1876, and by 1879 he was working for the following year's nomination. With his support a restriction law was passed in 1879 that prohibited more than 15 Chinese passengers on any ship bound for the United States, but President Hayes vetoed it. Later, as Secretary of State, Blaine was involved in some delicate treaty negotiations between the United States and China, but his fear of the "incalculable hordes" of Chinese was already well established. Blaine made the following remarks in an 1879 Congressional debate on Chinese exclusion.[1]

Ought we to exclude them? The question lies in my mind thus: either the Anglo-Saxon race will possess the Pacific slope or the Mongolians will possess it. You give them the start today with the keen thrust of necessity behind them, and with the ease of transportation before them, with the inducements to come, while we are filling up the other portions of the continent, and it is entirely inevitable if not demonstrable that they will occupy that great space of country between the Sierras and the Pacific coast. They are themselves today establishing steamship lines; they are themselves today providing the means of transportation and when gentlemen say that we admit from all other countries, where do you find the slightest parallel? And in a republic especially, in any government that maintains itself, the unit of order and of administration is in the family. The immigrants that come to us from all portions of the British Isles, from Germany, from Sweden, from Norway, from Denmark, from France, from Spain, from Italy, come here with the idea of the family as much engraven on their minds and in their customs and in their habits as we have it. The Asiatic cannot go on with our population and make a homogeneous element. The idea of comparing European immigration with an immigration that has not regard to family, that does not recognize the relation of husband and wife, that does not observe the tie of parent and child, that does not have the slightest degree of the ennobling and civilizing influences of the hearth stone and the fireside! Why when gentlemen talk loosely about emigration from

[1]*Congressional Record*, 46th Cong., 1st Sess., February 14, 1879, pp. 1299–1303.

European states as contrasted with that, they certainly are forgetting history and forgetting themselves. . . .

Treat them like Christians, my friend says; and yet I believe the Christian testimony from the Pacific coast is that the conversion of Chinese on that basis is a fearful failure; that the demoralization of the white is much more rapid by reason of the contact than the salvation of the Chinese race, and that up to this time there has been no progress whatever made. I think I heard the honorable Senator from California who sits on this side of the Chamber (Mr. Booth) say that there was not, as we understand it, in all the one hundred and twenty thousand Chinese, more or less (whether I state the number right or not does not matter), there did not exist among the whole of them the relation of family. There is not a peasant's cottage inhabited by a Chinaman; there is not a hearth stone, in the sense we understand it, of any American home, or an English home, or a German home, or a French home. There is not a domestic fireside in that sense; and yet you say that it is entirely safe to sit down here and permit that to grow up in our country. . . .

I only rose, Mr. President, to speak briefly. I have had many interruptions or I should have long since taken my seat. In conclusion, or by summary, I maintain that this legislation is in the strictest accord with international obligation. We have given notice, and the Chinese Empire has itself violated the treaty. Whether you take it on the one ground or the other, we are entirely justified in the legislation proposed. They have never lived for one month on their side by the terms of the treaty. A treaty, I repeat, which is interminable, so far as its own language is involved, when one party or the other desires it to be terminated, must be terminated by just such action as this bill proposes. That question out, the only one we have to regard is whether on the whole we will devote that interesting and important section of the United States to be the home and the refuge of our own people and our own blood, or whether we will continue to leave it open, not to the competition of other nations like ourselves, but to those who, degraded themselves, will inevitably degrade us. We have this day to choose whether we will have for the Pacific coast the civilization of Christ or the civilization of Confucius. (Applause in the galleries)

B.   SENATOR PENDLETON OF OHIO
URGES RESTRICTION, 1882

In attacking President Garfield's veto of the 20-year ban on the immigration of Chinese workers, Senator George A. Pendleton of Ohio expressed the hope that all races would one day find their own special place on earth. He further commented that by excluding the Chinese, America could help them realize where their correct place was. In 1883, Pendleton sponsored a much-needed civil service reform bill, but his comments a year earlier on the "corrupt and barbaric" habits of the Chinese help set the vulgar tone of the 1882 debate, which culminated in a 10-year exclusion of Chinese workers.[1]

I recognize that mysterious and almost mystic tie which binds together the nations and the races of the earth. "I am a man, and therefore nothing human is entirely alien to me." I believe in "the brotherhood of man." The very points of repulsion between nations and races are points of contact. These nations and races are scattered over all the world. Under every condition of climate, of habit, of tradition, of history, of association, of institutions, they are working out their several functions in the advancement of their civilizations. Some of them are drinking to the dregs waters that are foul with all the vices and the crimes which the taste and the passions and the utterly depraved imagination of the human heart can invent; others are reaping the reward of attempts, however imperfect, to attain to that divine humanity whose highest expression, in the words of the Master, was "Bear ye one another's burdens." They are all men, they are all human beings; I believe they are all working out, in one form and another, their progress and advancement and improvement. I would do nothing here or elsewhere, as an individual, as a legislator, as a patriot, as a cosmopolitan which I believe would not aid them in this effort.

But, sir, we must remember that contact, association, immigration are not the only means of aiding them. We must remember that you cannot touch pitch and remain undefiled; we must remember that you cannot plant virtue in the midst of surrounding and overwhelming vice and expect it to be uncontaminated; we must remember that you cannot plant the best virtues of the human heart in the foul pollutions of crime and vice and expect them to increase and grow. Mr. President, you cannot put the spot upon the camelia and expect it to retain its unsullied purity and whiteness. The spot will not grow white, but the camelia will be discolored and decay. In our practical life we do not take the pure virgins who are to be the mothers of the next generation and plant them in the haunts of vice in order to reclaim the vicious. We do not take the young men who will come to be the guardians of our civilization almost before we are able to realize the fact and associate them with the corrupt and licentious and depraved in order to win them from their

[1]*Congressional Record*, 47th Cong., 2nd Sess., April 28, 1882, pp. 3409–3410.

evil ways. We cannot bring upon our civilization on the Pacific coast the hordes of Chinese devoted to everything which is repugnant to our religion, to our morals, to our habits, to our civilization and expect it to increase in purity and power there.

It may be, sir, that this very bill we are passing to-day will awaken the authorities of the Chinese Empire to such an appreciation of the fact that their hordes are down in the very depths of a most degraded corruption—will so startle them with the conviction that we, their best friends and neighbors, can not endure the contact—that they will bring all the resources of government and institutions of education and example, to lift up their people until they shall also be fitted to join in the advancement of the races.

I said that the nations and the race were all working out, each in its appropriate sphere in different ways, in different conditions, under different circumstances, its own advancement. . . .

Mr. President, let us, our American nation, our American civilization, lead in the van of that effort, and let us do it by purifying, preserving, maintaining, consecrating the virtues which we have thus far attained, let us not endanger them by association with vice and corruption, which can only contaminate and destroy.

C.   HOUSE IMMIGRATION COMMITTEE REQUESTS NEW LAW TO BAN CHINESE, 1892

"Impelled by natural laws of self-preservation," the House Committee on Immigration and Naturalization in 1892 strongly recommended passage of a bill renewing the restrictions on Chinese immigration. The Committee's recommendation, was heeded, and Congress passed a tough law that closed the loopholes, broadened the definition of laborer, and placed the burden of proof regarding legality of residence on the Chinese themselves. Representative Herman Stump of Maryland presented the committee report, and in the following year he was named Superintendent of Immigration by President Cleveland.[1]

There is urgent necessity for prompt legislation on the subject of Chinese immigration. The exclusion act approved May 6, 1882, and its supplement expires by limitation of time on May 6, 1892, and after that time there will be no law to prevent the Chinese hordes from invading

[1]U.S. Congress, House of Representatives, Report No. 255, February 10, 1892, pp. 1–5.

our country in number so vast, as soon to outnumber the present population of our flourishing States on the Pacific slope. . . .

The popular demand for legislation excluding the Chinese from this country is urgent and imperative and almost universal. Their presence here is inimical to our institutions and is deemed injurious and a source of danger. They are a distinct race, saving from their earnings a few hundred dollars and returning to China. This they succeed in doing in from five to ten years by living in the most miserable manner, when in cities and towns in crowded tenement house, surrounded by dirt, filth, corruption, pollution, and prostitution; and gambling houses and opium joints abound. When used as cooks, farm-hands, servants, and gardeners they are more cleanly in habits and manners. They, as a rule, have no families here; all are men, save a few women, usually prostitutes. They have no attachment to our country, its laws or its institutions, nor are they interested in its prosperity. They never assimilate with our people, our manners, tastes, religion, or ideas. With us they have nothing in common.

Living on the cheapest diet (mostly vegetable), wearing the poorest clothing, with no family to support, they enter the field of labor in competition with the American workman. In San Francisco, and in fact throughout the whole Pacific slope, we learn from the testimony heretofore alluded to, that the Chinamen have invaded almost every branch of industry; manufacturers of cigars, cigar boxes, brooms, tailors, laundrymen, cooks, servants, farm-hands, fishermen, miners and all departments of manual labor, for wages and prices at which white men and women could not support themselves and those dependent upon them. Recently this was a new country, and the Chinese may have been a necessity at one time, but now our own people are fast filling up and developing this rich and highly favored land, and American citizens will not and can not afford to stand idly by and see this undesirable race carry away the fruits of the labor which justly belongs to them. A war of races would soon be inaugurated; several times it has broken out, and bloodshed has followed. The town of Tacoma, in 1887, banished some 3,000 Chinamen on twenty-four hours' notice, and no Chinaman has ever been permitted to return.

Our people are willing, however, that those now here may remain, protected by the laws which they do not appreciate or obey, provided strong provision be made that no more shall be allowed to come, and that the smuggling of Chinese across the frontiers be scrupulously guarded against, so that gradually, by voluntary departures, death by sickness, accident, or old age, this race may be eliminated from this country, and the white race fill their places without inconvenience of our own people or to the Chinese, and thus a desirable change be happily and peacefully accomplished. It was thought that the exclusion act of 1882 would bring about this result; but it now appears that although at San Francisco the departures largely exceed the arrivals, yet the business of smuggling Chinese persons across the lines from the British Possessions and Mexico has so greatly increased that the number of arrivals now exceed the departures. This must be effectually stopped.

D. TO SAVE THE MORALS OF AMERICAN GIRLS, THE CHINESE MUST BE EXCLUDED, 1902

Mrs. Charlotte Smith of the Women's National Industrial League of America. did not have the political influence of Samuel Gompers, but her testimony before the Senate Immigration Committee succinctly summed up labor's longtime arguments against the Chinese. Gompers and other A.F. of L. officials might have been more subtle in their testimony, but like Mrs. Smith, they used more than economics in their argument. Congress responded favorably to such testimony by extending the ban on the Chinese until 1904, at which time their exclusion was extended indefinitely.[1]

I should like to discuss the question of women as moral and industrial factors. How do the Chinese effect women in the United States! I probably had more to do with the passage of the Geary act than anybody else in this room, not excepting Mr. Gompers. Today I am working hard in this movement because I am interested in women as industrial factors. As president of the Woman's National Industrial League I receive no salary. Women could not afford to pay me, but I give my time in behalf of women as industrial factors for nearly twenty years.

I have sat here for hours listening to elaborate speeches made by lawmakers in regard to how the Chinese affect the financial interests, principally. Very lightly do you touch on the moral situation. You remember that the captain of the steamship discussed the question here, if a man's wife were lying sick in the cabin of a vessel whether he would prefer to have a white man or a Chinaman wait on her.

My efforts for the rescue and reform of fallen women in the United States have been I think more extensive than those of any other woman in this country, and in my work among those women I have had fre-

[1]U.S. Congress, 5th Cong., 1st Sess., Senate, Report No. 776, Pt 2, January 27, 1902, pp. 442–447.

quent occasion to see the shocking results of the immorality of the Chinamen who come to this country, very few of them who bring their wives,
and who prey upon white girls. . . . The Chinese are like the sponge;
they absorb and give nothing in return but bad odors and worse morals.
They are a standing menace to the women of this country. Their very
presence is contaminating. They have sown the seed of vice in every
city, town, and hamlet in this country. They encourage, aid, and abet
the youths of the land to become opium fiends, for in the sale of opium
is where their greatest revenues are derived. Through the introduction
of importing and experimenting in cheap labor of the Chinese the result
is our insane asylums are full to overflowing, and Americans are fast becoming addicted to the use of opium, largely through the Chinese, who
have for centuries been addicted to the use of opium.

I said before the Silver Jubilee Total Abstinence Convention of America, in 1895, in New York: "In my investigations as president of the
Woman's Rescue League, which is a branch of the Woman's National
Industrial League, I found 175 women who had been baptized in the
Christian faith living with Chinamen in New York in 1892. These women
bring young pagans into the world, who, with their so-called husbands,
worship in joss-house temples and become disciples of Confucius as well
as opium fields."

Furthermore, 99 out of every 100 Chinese are gamblers. This undesirable class come in direct competition with women who are breadwin-
ners. The beastly and immoral lives that these Mongolians lead is only
too well known in the police courts in all our large cities, where patrol
wagons filled with Chinese gamblers and Sunday school scholars every
Monday morning goes to prove as an object lesson that they never can
be "Christianized." . . .

During the year 1889, in Washington, D.C. 564 Chinese were arrested;
the majority were members of the Metropolitan Church Sunday school.
Men and women, pipes and opium joint paraphernalia were brought into
the police court. Furthermore, the worst gamblers and most immoral
opium-joint keepers were so-called Sunday school Chinese pupils.

Gentlemen, I was interested in having these Chinese "Christians"
raided, because of their contaminating young children, and the result was
published in the newspapers at the time. I have there a copy of the
Working Woman, which I published, giving the full report.

In Boston, June 23, 1894, 15,000 unfortunate girls were turned loose
to forage upon the community because of a moral crusade inaugurated
against vice. What was the result? American born, educated girls, became
the mistresses of the Chinese of Boston. The Tenderloin floating population was soon after transferred to Chinatown, and the Chinese were per-

mitted to go into the business of keeping houses of ill-repute, and engaged extensively in this illicit traffic. This is puritanical Boston, where educated, American-born white slaves were bought and sold for as low as $2 per head, while Chinese women were prized at $1,500 to $3,000 each. This was the market price at that time in New York and Boston. The Chinese, with few exceptions, do not bring their wives and children to this country, therefore they prey upon American girls because they can be procured so much cheaper. They place a much higher value on their women than do Americans upon theirs. . . .

It is time Christian women began missionary work in the slums of our large cities. The heathens are making more converts to Confucius than the missionaries are making converts to Christianity. Therefore it would be well to keep the missionaries at home and help save the bodies as well as the souls of our girls.

E. CONGRESS PONDERS THE ANNUAL ENTRY OF 105 CHINESE, 1943

The overt racism of the turn of the century all but disappeared from the 1943 public debate in Congress over the repeal of the Chinese exclusion acts; nevertheless, a lingering animosity toward the Oriental could easily be detected in many of the recorded speeches. Despite China's role in the war, Congressional reluctance to allow the Chinese again to settle here stood in sharp relief to the almost pathetic appeals of Representative Samuel Dickstein of New York, who championed the repeal cause in the Lower House. Dickstein, a Jewish émigré from Russia, could not comprehend why his colleagues criticized a bill that would allow only 105 Chinese annually into the country. One of the few men in the Congress who openly expressed his anti-Chinese sentiment was Idaho Representative, Compton I. White.[1]

MR. DICKSTEIN. There is too much fighting over legislation that comes from certain committees, too much objection to certain racial groups. We talk about unity in the outside world, we talk about being in a great war—we all know it and we all want to win this war—but we have got to keep our forces united so that people of every race, religion, and nationality will join in this great struggle to win the war. . . .

On page 5830 of the *Record* you will see I am charged with having

[1]*Congressional Record*, 78th Cong., 1st Sess., June 16, 1943, pp. 5966–5967, and October 21, 1943, pp. 8625–8627.

introduced bills on the Chinese exclusion question. Since when must I apologize to Members of Congress for the bills I introduce? Since when does anyone have to ask for permission to introduce any bill in the Congress of the United States? Just because some people disagree with the provisions in bills to repeal the Chinese exclusion laws they have started a rumor that we are going to flood this country with cheap Chinese labor. I say it is unfair and unjust to the American people to stifle any bill that has merit in committee. I introduced two bills to repeal Chinese exclusion and I am proud of it. They did not go far enough and I withdrew them, but there are other bills pending in my committee now that I think deserve the most earnest consideration of this Congress. . . .

China may not be in the war unless we give her some sort of moral support. All she is asking now to bring up her morale and to unite her people is to give her a quota on the same basis as we gave Germany, Italy, and the other countries of the world, which in the case of China would amount to 100 or, tops, 107 persons a year. Yet I have been criticized from this end of the aisle and from that end of the aisle in statements to the effect that I am trying to open the doors to bring in a lot of Chinese coolie labor. . . .

Mr. Speaker, I want to say now that I do not intend to be abused by any Member of this House because I have a different philosophy of life than he does. I do not mind Members disagreeing with me; I do not mind their voting against any proposition that I suggest, but this sniping and the cruel objections to deserving legislation that are made on the floor by some of the Members from my side of the aisle have to stop. . . .

MR. WHITE. Mr. Chairman, we are considering a most important policy in dealing with the Chinese immigration today. We are dealing with a policy that undermines civilization. We are dealing with the kind of a policy that undermined the Roman civilization. I know something about the Chinese. As a boy of 12, I was immigrated from the State of Iowa to the State of Idaho, and at the point where I landed, where my father was a railroad station agent, there were nothing but Chinese inhabitants. I think there were 200 Chinese coolies employed in the immediate environs of the little town where I landed. It was simply a station along the railroad line. I saw the Chinese. I know something of the Chinese mentality. I wonder how much these people here who want to open the gates to Chinese immigration know of the perils that the Chinese immigration raised in California in the early days, and all the troubles that the people had to maintain themselves against being displaced wholly and bodily by the Chinese coolies, exploited by a few whites. It was the exploitation of cheap Asiatic people by the people of Rome that drove out the best fighting class in the world, their own Roman nationals, the people who had conquered the world. They were displaced by the importation of Asiatics and immigrants from Egypt, and when the barbarians came down upon Rome, where were the fighting men? They had been gone for hundreds of years, and Rome fell a victim to the invasion of the barbarians. . . .

I have no animosity against the Chinese. We children loved the Chinese cooks and laundrymen who lavished Chinese "goodies" on us on Chinese New Year's—and even remembered our own Christmas.

3
The Chinese and American Law

The Chinese who lived in this country between the mid-nineteenth and mid-twentieth centuries could well understand the black man's lament over "second-class citizenship." Less than a decade after the Chinese began to arrive in appreciable numbers on the West Coast, the California Supreme Court ruled that Chinese, like Indians and blacks, could not testify against whites. The 1854 decision reflected the racial attitudes of most whites in the state; later whites approved innumerable anti-Chinese measures on the local and state levels. Discrimination sanctioned by law and violence unchecked by the authorities were endemic in the West throughout the 1860's and 1870's. By 1882, the clamor against the Chinese in California had reached such proportions that Congress took action to exclude Chinese laborers from the country for 10 years. In 1888, Congress passed new legislation, closing loopholes in the 1882 act and restricting Chinese immigration even more. Challenged in the courts, this law was upheld by the U. S. Supreme Court. Chinese immigration was banned in 1904 for an indefinite period, and for the Chinese who remained here there was little opportunity to enter into the mainstream of American life. They lived in ghettoes called "Chinatowns" and were forced to attend their segregated schools. The U. S. Supreme Court in 1927 illustrated the dilemma of the Chinese when it ruled that a Chinese-American citizen of Mississippi must go to a "colored school" although she was not black. Because she did not belong to the Caucasian race, she was ineligible to attend the all-white school in her neighborhood.

A. PROHIBITING CHINESE FROM TESTIFYING AGAINST WHITES, 1854

Convicted of murder in 1854 on the testimony of Chinese witnesses, George W. Hall appealed the court decision to the California Supreme Court. In arriving at its decision to bar the testimony of Chinese and to free the appellant, the court held that the Chinese and Indians were of the same race, and thus, the law barring Indian testimony against whites applied also to the Chinese. Chief Justice Hugh C. Murray held that it "would be an insult to the good sense of the Legislature" to think that existing laws did not apply to "the more degraded tribes" (i.e., Chinese) of Indians. The decision was not overturned for almost 20 years. The following selection is from Chief Justice Murray's majority opinion.[1]

The appellant, a free white citizen of this State, was convicted of murder upon the testimony of Chinese witnesses.

The point involved in this case, is the admissibility of such evidence.

The 394th section of the Act Concerning Civil Cases, provides that no Indian or Negro shall be allowed to testify as a witness in any action or proceeding in which a White person is a party.

The 14th section of the Act of April 16th, 1850, regulating Criminal Proceedings, provides that "No Black, or Mulatto person, or Indian, shall be allowed to give evidence in favor of, or against a white man."

The true point at which we are anxious to arrive, is the legal significance of the words, "Black, Mulatto, Indian and White person," and whether the Legislature adopted them as generic terms, or intended to limit their application to specific types of the human species.

When Columbus first landed upon the shores of this continent, in his attempt to discover a western passage to the Indies, he imagined that he had accomplished the object of his expedition, and then the island of San Salvador was one of those islands of the Chinese sea, lying near the extremity of India, which had been described by navigators.

Acting upon the hypothesis, and also perhaps from the similarity of features and physical conformation, he gave to the islanders the name of Indians, which appellation was universally adopted, and extended to the aboriginals of the New World, as well as of Asia.

From that time, down to a recent period, the American Indians and

---

[1]"The People v. Hall," California Supreme Court, 4 Cal., October 10, 1854, pp. 390–405.

the Mongolian, or Asiastic, were regarded as the same type of the human species. . . .

We have adverted to these speculations for the purpose of showing that the name of Indian, from the time of Columbus to the present day, has been used to designate, not only the North American Indian, but the whole of the Mongolian race, and that the name, though first applied probably through mistake, was afterwards continued as appropriate on account of the supposed common origin.

That this was the common opinion in the early history of American legislation, cannot be disputed, and, therefore, all legislation upon the subject must have borne relation to that opinion.

We are not disposed to leave this question in any doubt. The word "White" has a distinct signification, which *ex vi termini*, excludes black, yellow, and all other colors. It will be observed, by reference to the first section of the second article of the Constitution of this State, that no one but white males can become electors, except in the case of Indians, who may be admitted by special Act of the Legislature. On examination of the constitutional debates, it will be found that not a little difficulty existed in selecting these precise words, which were finally agreed upon as the most comprehensive that could be suggested to exclude all inferior races. . . .

The same rule which would admit them to testify, would admit them to all the equal rights of citizenship, and we might soon see them at the polls, in the jury box, upon the bench, and in our legislative halls.

This is not a speculation which exists in the excited, and over-heated imagination of the patriot and statesman but it is an actual and present danger.

The anomalous spectacle of a distinct people, living in our community, recognizing no laws of this State except through necessity, bringing with them their prejudices and national feuds, in which they indulge in open violation of law; whose mendacity is proverbial; a race of people whom nature has marked as inferior, and who are incapable of progress or intellectual development beyond a certain point, as their history has shown; differing in language, opinions, color, and physical conformation; between whom and ourselves nature has placed an impassable difference.

B.   U. S. SUPREME COURT UPHOLDS
CHINESE EXCLUSION, 1889

Designed mainly to close loopholes in the 1882 Chinese Exclusion Act, the 1888 act, in reality, did much more. It altered the language of the

1882 act to prohibit the reentry of any Chinese laborers who left the country, even those who left prior to the passage of the 1888 act on October 1. In addition, the act clearly violated the terms of American treaties with China. Nevertheless, the U. S. Supreme Court rejected the appeal of a Chinese laborer who sought to reenter the United States with a valid (under the 1882 act) return certificate. The following is from Justice Stephen Field's majority opinion, and of particular note is his use of history to explain the Court's decision.[1]

The appeal involves a consideration of the validity of the Act of Congress of October 1, 1888, prohibiting Chinese laborers from entering the United States who had departed before its passage, having a certificate issued under the Act of 1882 as amended by the Act of 1884, granting them permission to return. The validity of the Act is assailed as being in effect an expulsion from the country of Chinese laborers in violation of existing treaties between the United States and the Government of China, and of rights stated in them under the laws of Congress. . . .

The differences of race added greatly to the difficulties of the situation. Notwithstanding the favorable provisions of the new articles of the Treaty of 1868, by which all the privileges, and exemptions were extended to subjects of China in the United States which were accorded to citizens or subjects of the most favored nation, they remained strangers in the land, residing apart by themselves, and adhering to the customs and usages of their own country. It seems impossible for them to assimilate with our people or to make any change in their habits or modes of living. As they grew in numbers each year the people of the coast saw, or believed they saw, in the facility of immigration, and in the crowded millions of China, where population presses upon the means of subsistence, great danger that at no distant day that portion of our country would be overrun by them unless prompt action was taken to restrict their immigration. The people there accordingly petitioned earnestly for protective legislation.

In December, 1878, the Convention which framed the present Constitution of California, being in session, took this subject up, and memorialized Congress upon it, setting forth in substance, that the presence of Chinese laborers had a baneful effect upon the material interests of the State, and upon public morals; that their immigration was in numbers approaching the character of an Oriental invasion, and was a menace to our civilization; that the discontent from this cause was not

[1]"Chae Chang Ping v. U.S.," U.S. *Supreme Court Reports*, 130 U.S., May 13, 1889, pp. 1068–1077.

confined to any political party, or to any class or nationality, but was well nigh universal; that they retained the habits and customs of their own country, and in fact constituted a Chinese settlement within the State, without any interest in our country or its institutions; and praying Congress to take measures to prevent their further immigration. This memorial was presented to Congress in February, 1879.

So urgent and constant were the prayers for relief against existing and anticipated evils, both from the public authorities of the Pacific Coast and from private individuals, that Congress was impelled to act on the subject. . . .

Whatever license, therefore, Chinese laborers may have obtained previous to the Act of October 1, 1888, to return to the United States after their departure, is held at the will of the Government, revocable at any time, at its pleasure.

C. THE U.S. SUPREME COURT HOLDS THAT CHINESE MUST GO TO "COLORED SCHOOLS," 1927

In Gong Lum v. Rice, the U.S. Supreme Court upheld a Mississippi court decision to exclude a young Chinese girl from a white high school even though there was no other school for her to attend in her school district. Chief Justice William Howard Taft delivered the majority opinion, and he "assumed" that somewhere in the entire county there must be a school for the "colored children" and thus the plaintiff's rights were still being upheld under the "separate but equal" decision.[1]

Gong Lum is a resident of Mississippi, resides in the Rosedale Consolidated High School District, and is the father of Martha Lum. He is engaged in the mercantile business. Neither he nor she was connected with the consular service of the government of China, or any other government, at the time of her birth. She was nine years old when the petition was filed, having been born January 21, 1915, and she sued by her next friend, Chew How, who is a native born citizen of the United States and the State of Mississippi. The petition alleged that she was of good moral character and between the ages of five and twenty-one years, and that, as she was such a citizen and an educable child. It became her father's duty under the law to send her to school; that she desired to attend the Rosedale Consolidated High School; that at the opening of the school she appeared as a pupil, but at the noon recess

---

[1] "Gong Lum v. Rice," *U.S. Supreme Court Reports*, 275 U.S., November 21, 1927, pp. 172–177.

she was notified by the superintendent that she would not be allowed to return to the school; that an order had been issued by the Board of Trustees, who are made defendants, excluding her from attending the school solely on the ground that she was of Chinese descent and not a member of the white or Caucasian race, and that their order had been made in pursuance to instruction from the State Superintendent of Education of Mississippi, who is also made a defendant.

The petitioners further show that there is no school maintained in the District for the education of children of Chinese descent, and none established in Bolivar County where she could attend.

The petition was demurred to by the defendants on the ground, among others, that the bill showed on its face that plaintiff is a member of the Mongolian or yellow race, and therefore not entitled to attend the schools provided by law in the State of Mississippi for children of the white or Caucasian race.

The trial court overruled the demurrer and ordered that a writ of mandamus issue to the defendants as prayed in the petition.

The defendants then appealed to the Supreme Court of Mississippi, which heard the case. Rice v. Gong Lum, 139 Miss. 760. In its opinion, it directed its attention to the proper construction of 207 of the State Constitution of 1890, which provides:

"Separate schools shall be maintained for children of the white and colored races."

The Court held that this provision of the Constitution divided the educable children into those of the pure white or Caucasian race, on the one hand, and the brown, yellow, and black races, on the other, and therefore, that Martha Lum of the Mongolian or yellow race could not insist on being classed with the whites under this constitutional division. . . .

As we have seen, the plaintiffs aver that the Rosedale Consolidated High School is the only school conducted in that district available for Martha Lum as a pupil. They also aver that there is no school maintained in the district of Bolivar County for the education of Chinese children and none in the county. How are these averments to be reconciled with the statement of the State Supreme Court that colored schools are maintained in every county by virtue of the Constitution? This seems to be explained, in the language of the State Supreme Court, as follows:

> By statute it is provided that all the territory of each county of the state shall be divided into school districts separately for the white and colored races; that is to say, the whole territory is to be divided into white school districts, for the particular race, white or colored, so that the territorial limits of the school district for the colored race

may not be the same territory embraced in the school district for the white race, and vice versa, which system of creating the common school districts for the two races, white and colored, does not require schools for each race as such to be maintained in each district, but each having the same curriculum, and each having the same number of months of school term, if the attendance is maintained for the said statutory period, which school district of the common or public schools has certain privileges, among which is to maintain a public school by local taxation for a longer period of time than said term of four months under named conditions which apply alike to the common schools for the white and colored races.

We must assume then that there are school districts for colored children in Bolivar County, but that no colored school is within the limits of the Rosedale Consolidated High School District. This is not inconsistent with there being at a place outside of that district and in a different district, a colored school which the plaintiff Martha Lum, may conveniently attend. If so, she is not denied, under the existing school system, the right to attend and enjoy the privileges of a common school education in a colored school. If it were otherwise, the petition should have contained an allegation showing it. Had the petition alleged specifically that there was no colored school in Martha Lum's neighborhood to which she could conveniently go, a different question would have been presented, and this, without regard to the State Supreme Court's construction of the State Constitution as limiting the white schools provided for the education of the white or Caucasian race. But we do not find the petition to present such a situation.

The case then reduces itself to the question whether a state can be said to afford to a child of Chinese ancestry born in this country, and a citizen of the United States, equal protection of the laws by giving her the opportunity for a common school education in a school which receives only colored children of the brown, yellow or black race. . . .

The question here is whether a Chinese citizen of the United States is denied equal protection of the laws when he is classed among the colored races and furnished facilities for education equal to that offered to all, whether white, yellow or black. Were this a new question, it would call for very full argument and consideration, but we think that it is the same question which has been many times decided to be within the constitutional power of the state legislature to settle without intervention of the federal courts under the Federal Constitution. . . .

The decision is within the discretion of the state in regulating its public schools and does not conflict with the Fourteenth Amendment. The judgment of the Supreme Court of Mississippi is Affirmed.

4

The Lingering Stereotype

In 1904, Chinese immigration was halted for an indefinite period by an act of Congress, and, correspondingly, the number of anti-Chinese articles in magazines and newspapers greatly diminished. After the Immigration Law of 1924 had finalized the exclusion of the Oriental, there was little reason to discuss the Chinese; yet the image of the Chinese as members of a sinister, cunning, inscrutable race persisted, particularly in the popular fiction of various mystery and suspense writers. The character traits of the Chinese served to produce the perfect villain for adult writers like Van Wyck Mason and Sax Rohmer and for children's adventure series like the Hardy Boys, and their readers numbered in the millions. Even lovable Charlie Chan owed much of his appeal to his inscrutable nature and his Oriental cleverness, and many of the villains he brought to justice were tried-and-true non-Western types. Finally, the popular magazines did, on occasion, continue to carry "informative" articles that all too often only reinforced American attitudes about the Orient.

A. SAX ROHMER'S DR. FU-MANCHU

Sax Rohmer, the pen name of Arthur Sarsfield Ward, made his fortune writing about the evil and cunning Chinese. In 1913, he introduced his infamous Dr. Fu-Manchu, a diabolically evil and cunning character who four decades later would still be thrilling his readers. For Rohmer, Dr. Fu-Manchu made the perfect adversary for Nayland Smith, the great white hope whose race and civilization stood in stark contrast to those of Dr. Fu-Manchu's. Long before Ward died in 1959, the name of Dr.

199

Fu-Manchu was virtually a household word in America and England, and his wicked schemes were serialized in Collier's, which simply introduced him as "an old enemy of Western civilization." Actually, a change had overcome the erstwhile schemer, since the American Government after World War II urged Ward to alter the image of the popular character. He did so, making Dr. Fu a misunderstood but still dangerous genius who now waged unceasing war against the Communists.

The following selection is from the original Dr. Fu story, published in 1913.[1]

My head throbbed madly; my brain seemed to be clogged—inert; and though my first, feeble movement was followed by the rattle of a chain, some moments more elapsed ere I realized that the chain was fastened to a steel collar—that the steel collar was clasped about my neck.

I moaned weakly.

"Smith!" I muttered, "Where are you? Smith!" . . .

Groping in the darkness, my hands touched a body that lay close beside me. My fingers sought and found the throat, sought and found the steel collar about it.

"Smith," I groaned; and I shook the still form. "Smith, old man—speak to me! Smith!"

Could he be dead? Was this the end of his gallant fight with Dr. Fu-Manchu and the murder group? If so, what did the future hold for me—what had I to face?

He stirred beneath my trembling hands.

"Thank God!" I muttered, and I cannot deny that my joy was tainted with selfishness. For, waking in that impenetrable darkness, and yet obsessed with the dream I had dreamed, I had known what fear meant, at the realization that alone, chained, I must face the dreadful Chinese doctor in the flesh.

Smith began incoherent mutterings. . . .

"Why have we been spared, Smith? Do you think he is saving us for—"

"Don't, Petrie! If you had been in China, if you had seen what I have seen—"

Footsteps sounded on the flagged passage. A blade of light crept across the floor towards us. My brain was growing clearer. The place had a

[1]Sax Rohmer, *The Insidious Dr. Fu-Manchu: Being A Somewhat Detailed Account of the Amazing Adventures of Nayland Smith in His Trailing the Sinister Chinaman,* McBride, Nast and Co., New York, 1913, pp. 165–173.

damp, earthen smell. It was slimy—some noisome cellar. A door was thrown open and a man entered, carrying a lantern. Its light showed my surmise to be accurate, showed the slime-coated walls of a dungeon some fifteen feet square—shone upon the long yellow robe of the man who stood watching us, upon the malignant, intellectual countenance.

It was Dr. Fu-Manchu.

At last they were face to face—the head of the great Yellow Movement, and the man who fought on behalf of the entire white race. How can I paint the individual who now stood before us—perhaps the greatest genius of modern times?

Of him it had been fitly said that he had a brow like Shakespeare and a face like Satan. Something serpentine, hypnotic, was in his very presence. Smith drew one sharp breath, and was silent. Together, chained to the wall, two mediaeval captives, living mockeries of our boasted modern security, we crouched before Dr. Fu-Manchu.

He came forward with an indescribable gait, cat-like yet awkward, carrying his high shoulders almost hunched. He placed the lantern in a niche in the wall, never turning away the reptilian gaze of those eyes which must haunt my dreams forever. They possessed a viridescence which hitherto I had supposed possible only in the eye of the cat—and the film intermittently clouded their brightness—but I can speak of them no more.

I had never supposed, prior to meeting Dr. Fu-Manchu, that so intense a force of malignancy could radiate—from any human being. . . .

"Mr. Smith and Dr. Petrie, your interference with my plans has gone too far. I have seriously turned my attention to you."

He displayed his teeth, small and evenly separated, but discolored in a way that was familiar to me. I studied his eyes with a new professional interest, which even the extremity of our danger could not wholly banish. Their greenness seemed to be of the iris; the pupil was oddly contracted —a pin-point. . . .

He rested one bony hand on his hip, narrowing the long eyes as he looked down on us. The purposeful cruelty of the man was inherent; it was entirely untheatrical. Still Smith remained silent.

"So I am determined to remove you from the scene of your blunders!" added Fu-Manchu.

"Opium will very shortly do the same for you!" I rapped at him savagely.

Without emotion he turned the narrowed eyes upon me.

"That is a matter of opinion, Doctor," he said. "You may have lacked the opportunities which have been mine for studying that subject—and

in any event I shall not be privileged to enjoy your advice in the future.
. . .

I stifled a cry that rose to my lips; for, with a shrill whistling sound, a small shape came bounding into the dimly lit vault, then shot upward. A marmoset landed on the shoulder of Dr. Fu-Manchu and peered grotesquely into the dreadful yellow face. The Doctor raised his bony hand and fondled the little creature, crooning to it.

"One of my pets, Mr. Smith," he said, suddenly opening his eyes fully so that they blazed like green lamps. "I have others, equally useful. My scorpions—have you met my scorpions? No? My pythons and hamadryads? Then there are my fungi and my tiny allies, the bacilli. I have a collection in my laboratory quite unique. Have you ever visited Molokai, the leper island, Doctor? No? But Mr. Nayland Smith will be familiar with the asylum at Rangoon! And we must not forget my black spiders, with their diamond eyes—my spiders, that sit in the dark and watch—then leap!" . . .

"O God of Cathay!" he cried, "by what death shall these die—these miserable ones who would bind thine Empire, which is boundless!"

Like some priest of Tezcat he stood, his eyes upraised to the roof, his lean body quivering—a sight to shock the most unimpressionable mind.

"He is mad!" I whispered to Smith. "God help us, the man is a dangerous homicidal maniac!"

Nayland Smith's tanned face was very drawn, but he shook his head grimly.

"Dangerous, yes, I agree," he muttered; "his existence is a danger to the entire white race which, now, we are powerless to avert."

Dr. Fu-Manchu recovered himself, took up the lantern and, turning abruptly, walked to the door, with his awkward, yet feline gait. At the threshold he looked back. . . .

"You were in Rangoon in 1908?" continued Dr. Fu-Manchu—"you remember the Call?"

From somewhere above us—I could not determine the exact direction —came a low, wailing cry, an uncanny thing of falling cadences, which, in that dismal vault, with the sinister yellow-robed figure at the door, seemed to pour ice into my veins. Its effect upon Smith was truly extraordinary. His face showed grayly in the faint light, and I heard him draw a hissing breath through clenched teeth. . . .

"Smith," I said, "what was that?" The horrors about us were playing havoc with my nerves.

"It was the Call of Siva!" replied Smith hoarsely.

"What is it? Who uttered it? What does it mean?"

"I don't know what it is, Petrie, nor who utters it. But it means death!"

B. VAN WYCK MASON'S CAPTAIN NORTH FACES THE CHINESE TORTURE TEST, 1933

For two decades, Van Wyck Mason's many books about the exploits of Capt. Hugh North of U.S. Military Intelligence were perennial best-sellers. Mason traveled extensively collecting background information for the series, which usually featured a foreign setting. In The Shanghai Bund Murders, *the hero has to survive a diabolical system of torture before he triumphs over the evil Chang. But even the invincible Capt. North is hard pressed to maintain "face" when confronted by the heinous methods of torture that so long have seemed a Chinese speciality.*[1]

Silently, their bloodshot eyes alert, all three invaders now closed in.

"No noise. You go 'long ladder top side," directed the leader, who polluted the garden freshness with the rank exhalations of garlic.

North's rising hope that his shoulder holster might go unnoticed was eclipsed when, just before he quit the pergola, a powerful coolie lacking two front teeth ran hands over his person. Emitting a grunt he snatched out North's cherished .32 and thrust it into a rope belt above the skin of his gaunt and very dirty belly.

Ruby at first seemed unable to stand, so great was her fear, but a man in ragged black coat snatched at her wrist and hauled her to her feet. Losing her head, she tried to cry out, but the coolie, who wore a queue coiled about his conical skull, instantly clapped one hand over her mouth and with the other snatched out a dagger which he pressed threateningly against the agitated curve of her breast.

"Plenty quiet," was the soldier-leader's warning hiss, "or make dead. Savvy?" . . .

"Look here," North began in that unimpressed tone which alone can inculcate respect in ignorant Chinese, "me no savvy what want. No have got money."

"Pa ya!" The leader dealt his prisoner a cuff that neatly tripped him and sent him sprawling onto the dirty floor. Damn! So they were going to lash his ankles, too. Blacker still grew the outlook when a gag of dingy cotton cloth was thrust between his teeth.

Helpless as a mummy, he lay quite still, watching his captors paw and gloat over the unconscious woman. Many were the smiles and the

---

[1]Van Wyck Mason, *The Shanghai Bund Murders*, Doubleday & Co., New York, 1933, pp. 241–246, 258–260, 268–271. Copyright 1933, 1961 by F. van Wyck Mason, reprinted by permission of the Harold Matson Company, Inc.

loose-lipped grins of the starvelings as they worked to secure the coaster's delicate limbs. . . .

North's faint hopes grew even paler when he reasoned that he and the other prisoner were soon to be carried to some destination doubtless very far from Caucasian eyes. Back into his retentive memory crept tales of certain horrors known to have occurred amid the stewing slums of Chapel and the Native City.

What was that story of the Belgian whose eyelids had been stitched together before he had been sent naked to reel about a room studded, floor and walls, with razor-edged blades? To the last detail he could recall his sight of the Swede who had died because, disemboweled his ventral cavity had been filled with redhot sand. Sweat coursed in acid torrents into his eyes as he recollected the contorted features of— Enough! He must think no more of such things. [But a short time later North is forced to think of such things as he and his lady friend face the horrors of Chinese torture]. . . .

Now that talk was ended, he looked once more about the dusty and cavern-like chamber and noted several objects which had heretofore escaped his attention. One was a long-coffin-like box curiously contrived and standing on end; beyond it a heavy board table supported a small green painted box and a bamboo cage containing perhaps a dozen enormous black rats.

He was, North realized, a reasonably brave man, but somehow the sight of the red famished eyes of those rats aroused a terrible fear. With the cord halter still danging from his neck and his hands tightly secured to one of the several rings set into the stonework, he must stand back to the wall and watch what took place. . . .

Their calloused bare feet making very little noise; the four coolies secured Ruby's arms wide apart to two rings set in the wall opposite North. Then, with a powerful jerk, Sergeant Hsu ripped the jacket of her pajamas into gleaming shreds.

At this she began to scream, and her pale body twisted and squirmed with panic-stricken violence, its muscles rippling smoothly beneath skin which, in the dim light, seemed lustrous as mother of pearl.

"Oh, you devils—let me go! Don't hurt me!" panted the terrified woman, and tears streamed down her smooth cheeks. "I—I don't know. I—I swear I don't know!"

"You lie!" Mr. Chang from behind the devil screen sounded quite moved. "You, Number One boy, the green box."

Panting and silently cursing Ruby's unsuspected courage, North gazed helplessly on as the coolie with the queue selected a small pair of iron tongs from a box of instruments on the floor. Meanwhile, Sergeant Hsu crossed to the table, removed from it the little green-painted box, whose cover he slid back. Next, with great wariness, Hsu dipped the tongs into it and brought out a small struggling object.

At first North could not tell what the creature was, but as the evil faced soldier passed one of the lanterns he perceived it to be a large reddish-brown scorpion, its many legs writhing and its death-laden tail lashing furiously back and forth.

Grinning, the sergeant held it a few inches before Ruby Braunfeld's enormous staring eyes. She flung herself violently back and uttered dreadful cries of purely animal fear. . . .

Chang said nothing but turned angrily away, his high field boots tapping loud on the greasy flagstones. Meanwhile Sergeant Hsu laid flat on the floor the long, narrow box which North had previously noted. It was hinged on top and roughly divided into four segments. . . .

From puzzled, hopeless eyes, North looked on and saw how segments attached to the lid met other segments below which were roughly carved to admit the contours of a human body.

Once the lid was dropped, Ruby Braunfeld lay as though in a wire topped coffin perpendicularly divided into four segments. The first division was empty; the second contained the captive's feet and legs; the third included her body from her knees to her waist; and the fourth contained the rest of her body.

Curious, despite his own impending doom, North was wondering, what would happen next when one of the coolies took a square of what looked like very thick bacon rind and tacked it across a hole in the partitions separating the empty segment and the one containing the prisoner's legs.

"Hole in there," remarked Hsu for the benefit of the victim. "Pigskin hold back visitors a while."

Meanwhile the coolie with the queue raised a trapdoor at the foot of the coffin and to North's indescribable horror spilled into the empty compartment a dozen of the largest rats he had ever seen. Once the fierce creatures, starved to the verge of madness, had smelt the rind they set up a terrific clamor, but Ruby, writhing in her narrow prison; drowned them out with shrieks that made the whole grim chamber reverberate.

While the dreadful cries of the doomed woman rang in his ears North had not even conjectured on his own fate, but now the heavy table on which the rat cage had stood was cleared, and a quarter of guards laid him flat upon it. Despite an instinctive revolt at this fate, North forced himself to lie still; reason told him it was quite useless to struggle and that perhaps a passive attitude might cause his jailers not to bind the ropes so tightly.

Swiftly he was lashed head and foot to the table with a powerful rope passed around and around it. Then one of the soldiers brought forward a strange contrivance which, with a pair of guiding rings, held perpendicular a short, double edged sword. When the point of this sword was poised directly over his heart North could see that lashed to its handle was an earthen jar. Above this, on a cleverly contrived platform, was placed a barrel containing a liquid of some sort. So delicately adjusted was the weight of the short, straight sword that its point did not even penetrate the prisoner's shirt but rose and fell gently with his breathing.

"So," North told himself, "It's going to be one of those slow things." He quickly guessed that the little barrel above would slowly drip water into the jar fixed to the sword's handle until the jar supported enough weight to drive the sword into his heart.

Despite himself, his fingers spasmodically gripped at the edge of the table when Chang opened a pet-cock projecting from the barrel end. Pst! A drop of water fell into the jar lashed to the bayonet handle, and, faint though the impact was, the steel shivered, and he felt a tiny pang.

"After a few hours of that, Captain," Change grimly remarked, "you will be ready to talk—say around one o'clock!" . . .

After a final inspection Sergeant Hsu closed and locked the door behind the devil screen through which Chang had disappeared. His soldiers looked dumbly on—stupid cattle, obeying blindly, with no conviction of right or wrong, stumbling, fighting on and on until the inevitable bullet cut short their quest for women and a full belly.

C. MAKING THE STEREOTYPE A REALITY, 1945

The 1943 repeal of the various acts that excluded Chinese immigrants and withheld citizenship from those already here in no way altered the image of the Chinese for some Americans. John J. Espey wrote an article for the New Yorker *in 1945 that illustrated that even the son of a missionary who lived in China was not free of an extremely narrow view of the Chinese people. Although Espey was writing about his childhood, it seems inconceivable that as an adult he and his editors should think his story was humorous and worth repeating for the thousands of* New Yorker *readers.*[1]

When I was eleven and my sister fourteen, we came to realize that one thing was lacking to complete the comfort of whatever guests our

[1]John J. Espey, "No Man Can Serve Two Masters," *New Yorker*, February 3, 1945, pp. 20–23.

parents entertained at our home in Shanghai. . . . In these other homes all the servants spoke English. If you wanted another fork, you simply said, "I'd like another fork," and the table boy would produce one. In fact, if you took the trouble to say it in Chinese, the table boy would look down his nose at you and probably bring you a dirty spoon just to let you know that he understood English. At our house, if you said in English to the table boy, or the cook, "I'd like another fork," he would stare at you blankly and wait for a member of the family to translate. Not, of course, that we ever failed to have the correct number of forks on the table, but any sort of request addressed in English to our servants got nothing but a blank stare in return. . . .

The cook really understood a great deal of English, but he never admitted this. When my sister and I offered to give him English lessons, he informed us that Chinese was an ancient mode of expression which had been found adequate by his people since the beginning of time. Was there anything anyone wanted to say that couldn't be said in Chinese? We granted there wasn't anything we knew of. We could never get the cook to see why he should learn to speak English.

It was because of this that we looked at Oo-zong with great interest when he came to work for us as outside coolie. . .

Oo-zong was the cook's nephew, a large, raw-boned fellow who was about twenty when he came from the home village to work for us. His gown was narrow at the shoulders and ended at his calves. His teeth were always in evidence, because he went about his duties with an idiotic grin spread over his face. His hair was cut very short, exposing all the bumps of his skull. Furthermore, Oo-zong, with his enormous hands and feet, was about the clumsiest individual we had ever encountered. Whenever he ventured into the house, something was certain to be smashed to bits and Oo-zong would be found sprawling on the floor in the midst of the wreckage.

My sister and I agreed that he didn't look promising but, having been raised in the Presbyterian atmosphere of South Gate, we knew the value of attempting the impossible. We decided to give Oo-zong a chance. After he had become accustomed to our yard work, he was gradually introduced by Mother and the cook into the subtleties of being a table boy. This meant that he was going to stay on at South Gate, so my sister and I cornered him in the servants quarters one afternoon and broached our scheme. By devious means we told him of the qualities of the English language. The Chinese tongue, we admitted readily, was a beautiful thing but English had its own advantages. Wouldn't Oo-zong like to have us teach him English so that he could understand what our guests wanted when they spoke to him? No, "goddam" was not the only phrase aside from "damfole" that was useful in speaking English. We could teach him many phrases if he wanted to learn them.

Once Oo-zong had understood our plan, he was most enthusiastic. After lesson 1, which consisted of teaching him that my sister must always be addressed as Miss Espey and I as Master John, we dragged out our old primer and started in with "This is a dog. This is a cat. The dog is chasing the cat." No one I am sure, had ever paid much attention to Oo-zong's mind, yet it took us only a few hours to make him grasp the basic concepts of Western civilization, and, once started, there was almost no holding him back.

After a few weeks we used the direct method. Oo-zong would come into the room with a freshly laundered tablecoth in his hands. "What are you carrying, Oo-zong?" I would ask.

"I do not know the English name Master John," Oo-zong would reply in slow syllables.

"That article is called a tablecloth, Oo-zong," I would say.

"Then I carrying a tablecroth, Master John."

"No, you are not carrying a tablecroth, Oo-zong. You must learn the difference between "l" and "r". It's a tablecloth, Now say it again."

"Yes, Master John. Tabblecloth."

"That's better, Now listen. Not tabblecloth, but tablecloth."

"Yes, Master John, thank you very much. Tablecloth."

"That's very good, Oo-zong, Say it again."

"Thank you, Master John. Tablecloth, tabru—no, tablecloth, tablecloth, tablecloth.

"Good work, Oo-zong." . . .

Meanwhile Mother was guiding Oo-zong through the intricacies of serving from the left and removing from the right, and the ways of distinguishing the rank and importance of male and female guests. Oo-zong was puzzled by the serving of ladies first. To him it was obvious that Miss Espey and Master John were the most important mouths to be filled. We agreed with him in private but told him he had better do as Mother instructed. . . .

Oo-zong's progress was not a constant, unmixed triumph. At first he was so awkward that he kept breaking dishes right and left. The grin would immediately leave his face and he would fall screaming to his knees to beg forgiveness. My sister and I took him aside after this had happened two or three times. It was not good taste we informed him, to bawl this way. Everyone knew that the Chinese were emotionally very reserved, so he would please in the future just pick up the pieces and walk with dignity to the pantry.

As we got to thinking about it, there were many things in Oo-zong's nature that weren't a bit Chinese, so we began to remold him into a member of his own race. There was his grin, for example. We had to explain to Oo-zong that the Chinese are an inscrutable people who rarely show joy or sorrow in public. He was to make his face, we told him, blandly intelligent. The effect, we added, would be heightened if he were to droop his eyelids a little. Then, when he was addressed, he was to tighten the corners of his mouth ever so slightly, which was as far, he should know, as any Chinese ever went in showing amiability. The cook and the amah whinnied in constant entertainment at the frozen mask of detachment we finally got Oo-zong to assume. It took hours of patient work in front of a mirror, but the result was the most Orientally bland face in all China.

Once we had given Oo-zong a truly Chinese face, we set to work on his clothes. He was still stumbling about in the short, narrow, rusty-black gown which the village tailor had probably fubbed off on him as the latest Shanghai style. We contributed some money of our own and gave him careful instructions. . . .

When he had been outfitted. . . . we got to work on his posture and walk, for Oo-zong still loped into a room, head stretched forward, as if he were in pursuit of a water buffalo. We made him stand up straight. This at first produced an appalling result: he thrust his Adam's apple out in front, his rump out and up in the rear, the shirts of his gown riding high on its rounded eminence. After great effort we taught him to pull in his chin and tilt his pelvis forward, so that his truly elegant gown fell in an unbroken line from the back of his shoulders to the floor, while in front it left his broad chest in another beautiful straight line. This, we were happy to tell him, was what made Chinese clothes, so pleasing to the eye and so superior to the chaotic and contradictory lines of Western dress. Oo-zong had never before realized this, and he was happy to agree with Miss Espey and Master John.

Once Oo-zong had been taught to stand correctly, we had to teach him to walk. His normal step was about four feet long, which made his gown fly in all directions and exposed his trousers well up the leg if he was turning a corner. Patiently we taught him to flex his knees slightly and take smaller, more deliberate steps. After some weeks we were delighted by the sight of Oo-zong, swimming, as it were, over the floor, the light forward motion carrying his gown quivering along with him, always on the point of breaking its lovely lines but never quite doing so, its sharp cut modified in movement by softening modulations. At last, we congratulated ourselves, we had taught him the Oriental glide for which Chinese servants have ever been justly world-famous.

The more I think of it, the more I realize how essentially responsible my sister and I were for making Oo-zong conscious of the habits of his own race, for making him, indeed, really Chinese. Without us he would probably never have known the true qualities of his own nationality. . . .

The complete process took us about a year. At the end of that time Oo-zong, was an unparalleled table boy, and in the Western phrase, a true son of Man.

SELECTED READINGS

Coolidge, Mary Roberts, *Chinese Immigration*, Henry Holt and Company, New York, 1909.

Despite its antiquity, this study has no parallel. It covers the Chinese immigration issue from its inception in 1848 until the San Francisco fire of 1906, when the Chinese quarter was destroyed.

Lee, Rose Hum, *The Chinese in the United States of America*, Hong Kong University Press, Hong Kong, 1960.

A study of the social, cultural, intellectual, and economic life of the Chinese in America.

Miller, Stuart Creighton, *The Unwelcome Immigrant; the American Image of the Chinese, 1785–1882*, University of California Press, Berkeley, 1969.

A scholarly treatment of the West Coast and national attitudes that led to the Chinese exclusion measures in Congress.

Oberheltzer, Ellis Paxson, *A History of the United States Since the Civil War*, Vol. IV, Macmillan Company, New York, 1931.

Despite some flaws, a 95-page chapter on the Chinese, from the Burlingame Treaty of 1868 to the first exclusion act of 1882, is a valuable source of information on the Chinese travails on the Pacific Coast.

Wollenberg, Charles, Ed., *Ethnic Conflict in California History*, Tinnon-Brown, Santa Monica, California, 1969.

Dr. Stanford M. Lyman contributes a valuable chapter to this anthology, entitled "Strangers in the Cities: the Chinese on the Urban Frontier."

V
JAPANESE-AMERICANS

In the matter of Chinese and Japanese coolie immigration I stand for the national policy of exclusion. The whole question is one of assimilation of diverse races. We cannot make a homogeneous population out of people who do not blend with the Caucasian race. . . . Democracy rests on equality of the citizens. Oriental coolieism will give us another race problem to solve, and surely we have had our lessons.

Woodrow Wilson, 1912

INTRODUCTION

Japan's devastating surprise attack on Pearl Harbor and the ensuing war inspired harsh reaction against Americans of Japanese ancestry. Individual acts of violence and harassment were followed by the relocation of the entire West Coast Japanese-American population in internment camps in the interior. The fact that the majority of these individuals were American citizens who were being deprived of their rights without "due process of law" was overlooked by a nation caught up in wartime hysteria. Hostility toward a military enemy is not unusual, but the reaction in this country against Japanese-Americans was unquestionably the product of long-standing racial feelings. Japanese-Americans had earlier been denied the privilege of becoming citizens of the United States. They also had been denied the right to own land in several states. Finally, in 1924, the United States Government refused to grant a quota for Japanese immigrants.

Between 1865 and 1924, while some 30 million European immigrants were settling in America, approximately 275,000 Japanese entered our West Coast portals. By 1940, because of departures, deaths, and a low

211

birth rate, less than 135,000 Japanese-Americans were counted in the census. On the West Coast in 1940, there were only 112,353 persons of Japanese ancestry in a total population of almost 10 million. Because of their small numbers, the Japanese posed no real threat to American society. And because by World War I they were either small farmers or small businessmen, they did not threaten the laboring man's job. In general, the Japanese who came to this country at the turn of the century exhibited qualities not unlike those of the old European immigrants whom Americans so admired: they were generally literate, almost always law-abiding, industrious, and ambitious to rise in the world. By the 1920's, their diligence and skill had produced a standard of living just below that of the average American and well above that of the average immigrant. In addition, the scientists could find no trace of inferiority. Intelligence tests showed that Japanese-Americans approached national norms, and in academic achievement they surpassed national averages. Thus the problem did not lie with the Japanese, but with the white majority that refused to believe that it was possible to assimilate them into American society. General John DeWitt, the man who directed the 1942 relocation, succinctly stated the nature of the problem when he was quoted in a West Coast newspaper as saying, "A Jap's a Jap." Reflecting widespread opinion in America, DeWitt did not believe the Japanese could become "American" as readily as those immigrants of German or Italian extraction, who, on the whole, escaped discrimination and oppression during World War II.

After Commodore Perry "opened" Japan in 1853, the first Japanese to take up residence in the United States were students. Until the 1880's permanent emigration was forbidden by Japan, but when this restriction was eased, Japanese immigration gradually increased until our 1920 census listed 139,000 Americans of Japanese descent. During the early years of this migration, most Issei (those born in Japan) worked as farm hands or were wage earners in towns. As they competed in the labor-market in increasing numbers, they began to antagonize white workers. During the 1890's, Dennis Kearney, an Irish labor leader, helped organize the first concerted attacks on the Japanese. His campaign assured their exclusion from West Coast labor unions, and thereafter, organized labor was an effective anti-Japanese force. In 1905 the Japanese and Korean Exclusion League was formed in California. Later it would be renamed the Asian Exclusion League and include elements other than labor. Also in 1905, the California legislature adopted a 10-point resolution condemning the Japanese of the state. By 1911, twenty more bills of a similar nature had been proposed in the state. During this same period, the West Coast press generally, and the Hearst newspapers in particular, began to publish considerable anti-Japanese material. By 1906, when San Francisco attempted to segregate its Japanese-American school children, the West Coast labor unions and patriotic organizations were well organized and increasingly vocal.

Although the Japanese vigorously opposed intermarriage with whites, this "peril" was also raised in the press and by politicians. As early as 1872, a California antimiscegenation law forbade marriages between Japanese and Caucasians. In the early 1900's the state's civil code was amended to declare that mixed marriages already existing were null and void. It was not until 1948 that such laws were declared unconstitutional in California, but fourteen other states retained similar laws. Charges of immorality were also leveled at the Japanese over their "picture brides." The shortage of Japanese women in the United States and the lack of social contact with American women forced many Japanese men to have their families in Japan select wives for them. The wife would then be sent to America to meet her husband, but only after the wedding ceremony already had been conducted in Japan.

In 1913, California passed an alien land act that was aimed at the Japanese. Any alien ineligible for citizenship was not allowed to own land and could lease it only for a period up to three years. The restrictive legislation was not enacted because the Japanese-Americans ruined valuable land; quite the contrary, it was their success in producing bumper crops from land often thought to be quite worthless that proved frightening to their white competitors. The national dimension of anti-Japanese feeling was illustrated by the fact that similar land restrictions were passed in Arizona, Delaware, Idaho, Louisiana, Nebraska, New Mexico, Missouri, Nevada, Texas, and Washington. Indeed, with the exception of Utah, discriminatory legislation was passed in every state containing a significant number of Japanese. Attempts of the Issei to turn over their land to their sons (Nisei) were blocked, even though their sons, because of American birth, were citizens. The Issei either had to sign over their land to a trusted white or begin share-cropping. Even the latter form of farming was later effectively restricted in California.

In 1924, the Native Sons and Daughters of the Golden West, along with West Coast units of the American Legion, American Federation of Labor, and the Grange, successfully pressured Congress into permanently excluding Japanese immigrants. Two years earlier the United States Supreme Court had helped brand the Japanese as undesirable residents by upholding their ineligibility for American citizenship. After 1924, anti-Japanese sentiment was less overt, but the attack on Pearl Harbor again made it painfully clear that Japanese-Americans did not have the same rights as other Americans.

1
Popular Images of the Japanese

Although the Japanese occasionally had been mentioned along with Chinese as undesirable aliens, it was not until the early twentieth century that they came under major attack in the popular press. In 1900, San Francisco's Mayor James Duval Phelan warned his constituents that the Japanese "were not the stuff of which American citizens can be made," and he insisted that they be kept at a "respectful distance." His sentiments were often repeated in newspapers, magazines, and novels in the following decades.

In 1901, the 1000 delegates to the Chinese Exclusion Convention were informed of the growing menace of the Japanese, a menace that might well overshadow that of the Chinese because the former were "more intelligent and civilized than the Chinaman." By 1906, the anti-Japanese agitation had influenced most Americans.

A. JACK LONDON AND THE RUSSO-JAPANESE WAR, 1905

In 1905 Japan shocked the Western world with her quick victory in the Russo-Japanese War. Although President Roosevelt acted as peace mediator, it was disconcerting to many that a "yellow, inferior race" could defeat the Russians, a white people. In the following selection, Jack London, whose novels and short stories so often exalted the image of the Anglo-Saxon, briefly described his reactions upon seeing Russian soldiers in a Japanese prison camp.[1]

[1]*New York American and Journal*, June 12, 1905.

The sight I saw was a blow in the face to me. On my mind it had all the stunning effect of the sharp impact of a man's fist. There was a man, a white man, with blue eyes, looking at me. He was dirty and unkempt. He had been through a fierce battle. But his eyes were bluer than mine, and his skin was as white. And there were other white men in there with him, many white men.

I caught myself gasping. A choking sensation was in my throat. These men were my kind. I found myself suddenly and sharply aware that I was an alien among the brown men who peered in through the windows at me. And I felt myself strangely alone with those other men behind the window, felt that my place was there inside with them in their captivity rather than outside in freedom among the aliens.

B. A REPORT ON THE NEW JAPANESE NATION, 1907

After the Japanese victory over the Russians and the growing California agitation, several national magazines started to take an increasing interest in the Japanese, both as a people and as a nation. In several cases returning Americans published accounts of their experiences in the Orient. The following article in the North American Review *was the product of a three-and-one-half-month trip to Japan by William T. Ellis.*[1]

Every Occidental is expected to take off his hat to "the Oriental mind," as something inscrutable, unfathomable and mysteriously potent. After a time, the hard-headed Westerner who has dwelt long in the Orient is likely to use plain speech about this. To him, the Oriental mind is merely selfishness, plus superstition, plus complete disingenuousness. What is euphemistically called "Orientalism" is often nothing but plain lying and dishonesty. The Oriental, accustomed for ages to oppression and deceit, has become a past master in craftiness and guile. For sinuous and subterranean ways, he outclasses anything known in the West. But the aforesaid hard-headed man, who should know, says that it is foolish to apply to a people, be their skins yellow, brown or white, any other standards than the old, old ones of fair and open dealing, plain speech and true words. If the yellow man is to sit with the white in the game of nations, he must obey the ancient and tested rules of the game. . . .

The question is often raised among European businessmen in the Orient, whether Japan is really a civilized or a barbarous nation. This sort

[1]William T. Ellis, "Some Guesses at Japan," *North American Review*, October, 1907, pp. 237–244.

of discussion is not carried on in the newspapers published in Japan; for the Japanese are more sensitive upon this point than upon any other. Their chief source of pride is that they are one of the world's great civilized and civilizing Powers. Those who contend that Japan has experienced no change of heart, but has merely put on the new manners and forms of civilization, like a new garment, with the same zest that she has displayed in adopting the frock coat and the top-hat, point to various phases of Japanese character and conduct to justify their contention. They say that Japan is a cruel, pitiless nation. Her boys find their sport in torturing insects and small animals—everybody who has been in Japan a week has seen the little children with bamboo poles, tipped in birdlime, hunting the cicada. The merciless bit worn by the Japanese horse, and the cruel loads it carries, and the beatings it endures, are the reasons for the proverbially vicious character of this beast. Look a Japanese ox in the face, as he plods along with the load of half a dozen American horses, and the way his nose-ring is drawn taut over his bleeding nostrils will haunt you for days. Nor is this disregard of life and suffering confined to the lower animals. The frightful and, at times, needless slaughter of soldiers before Port Arthur and Mukden is significant of something more than military discipline. Life is not a sacred thing to the Japanese. A Japanese soldier, bound for the war, was saying farewell to his sister at the train, and did not hear the captain's command to "fall in." The latter drew his sword and stabbed the man to the heart. That's a way they have in the army; it promotes discipline. Could the practice of selling their daughters into a slavery of shame be permitted and approved in any civilized country? It is counted a point of virtue for a Japanese girl to enter a brothel, in order to raise money to pay her father's debts. And I do not believe that Tokio's infamous "Yoshiwara," where young girls are displayed to the street in cages, could exist anywhere else outside of A´rica. . . .

A guess at the future of Japan is inevitable. Will she have a great reaction against the Western ways which she has adopted? One day I saw a "high collar," as the modern Japanese dude is called, ride full tilt on his bicycle against an old peasant woman, carrying across her shoulders a yoke with two panniers of vegetables. The woman was knocked down and her burden spilled, but seemingly no serious injury was done her. The bicycle, however, was hopelessly smashed, a case of poetic justice. I wondered, at the moment, if this was a picture of the conflict between Old and New Japan. Will the stolid peasant, brutalized, provincial and wedded to his idols, which line every highway, come off the better in a struggle with the fashionable "foreign style"? I think not, despite the parable just cited. The whole nation is going to school. It cannot escape the thought and ideals of civilization. The general study of English means an acquisition of the principles that are embodied in our language. Self-government and real liberty will come to the people, after they have learned how to use them. . . . Christianity, which is slowly, but steadily, supplanting the superstition, idolatry and ignorant spirit-worship of Buddhism and Shintoism, will elevate the national character, and temper the all-absorbing, inconsiderate and relentless selfishness of the nation. In a word, time, education, and hard knocks will fit Japan to take her place alongside of the great Powers of the earth.

C. *COLLIER'S* INVESTIGATES THE CALIFORNIA LAND PROBLEM, 1913

In 1913, and again in 1920, the California legislature led the way in restricting the Japanese from land ownership. The 1913 act limited leases of agricultural and to Japanese to maximum terms of three years, and it barred further land purchases by "aliens who were excluded from citizenship." This 1913 act, however, was often circumvented by the foreign-born fathers turning their land over to their Nisei children who were American citizens. The 1920 act, which passed as an initiative measure by a more than three-to-one margin, tried to plug the loopholes of the 1913 act. These California acts were emulated in many other states that wished to exclude Japanese-Americans from the land.

In the spring of 1913 the editors of Collier's *commissioned Peter Clark Macfarlane "to find out . . . the conditions that led California to the conviction that the agricultural invasion of Japanese must be stopped by legislation." The following is taken from Macfarlane's report.[1]*

This unanimity [on the land question] shows that it was not a class but a race issue. It was the clash of two races meeting upon the frontiers of their respective civilizations. It is not a question of inferiority or superiority. It is a question of existence, and of social existence at that. At the present time, and until the Panama Canal is opened, bringing fuller tides of European immigration, there is an industrial place for the Japanese in California. But socially there is no place. It is this which makes the complication. Socially the two races will not coexist. When the Japanese farmers move in American farmers move out. This has been the inevitable result. . . .

Just at the moment the classic instance of Japanese agrarian aggression

[1] Peter Clark Macfarlane, "Japan in California," *Collier's,* June 7, 1913, pp. 5–6.

is the town of Florin, which is but eight miles southeast of Sacramento, and therefore an object lesson right at the doors of the Legislature. . . . To see an American community that had been representative of the very best elements of our fine life thus completely displaced by Orientals gives one a strange sensation. This sensation deepens when one drives up to an American farm only to find it inhabited by Japanese. Imagine bowling along a splendid California roadway with the finest of fruit farms on every hand. We see the fence by the side of us and know an American built it; we see the house designed after American architectural plans, surrounded by trees and shrubs and that profusion of flowers with which California's soil and climate repay so bountifully the work of an affectionate hand. The house is environed by beautiful vineyards or orchards, and the whole is a scene of independence and contentment that makes the life of the California rancher seem ideal.

But driving in at the big gate we are pained to notice an air of neglect about the garden and the yard. The grass is uncut, the flowers look wilted. The very house has an absentee air about it. There are no lace curtains at the windows, only shades. One of the shades goes up and a face is seen, staring, inquisitive, suspicious. It is the face of an Oriental. We round the corner and Japanese babies are sprawling before the door. We turn toward the backyard and a pair of Japanese boys are romping about. The barnyard itself has an empty look. There are no cows or calves, not even a fowl, for these Japanese of Florin are tillers of the soil pure and simple. Behind the barn one sees a Japanese plowing. In a berry patch to the left, half a dozen men and women are squatting in the rows, pushing their picking trays ahead of them. If we could look inside of this American house and see how it is furnished and occupied by its Japanese owners we should be still more depressed. Pictures of cherry-blossom festivals and stories of the wizardry of Japanese farmers would lead one to suppose these Japanese "carnations" would be found blossoming with floral finery and fragrance. The contrary is true. Nothing appears to receive attention but that which can be sold for money.

The rainbow hues fade out as we see these people in the midst of a Western environment. Sordid realism takes the place of romance. We see merely an alien race with likes that are not our likes, ambitions that are not our ambitions, satisfactions that are not our satisfactions, with morals that to us are no morals, and habits of life that make social relation with them utterly impossible. . . .

The Japanese—without meaning any disrespect to the little brown man —does not commend himself to the average American farmer family as a desirable neighbor. He is not overly clean. He is accused of being unmoral. It is claimed the Japanese have no marriage tie as we know the institution. Women, if scarce, may be held pretty much in common. The white farmer's wife does not run in and sit down to gossip with the Japanese farmer's wife and she does not want the Japanese farmer's wife running in to gossip with her. Their children cannot play together. Jenny Brown cannot go for a buggy ride with Harry Hirada. The whole idea of social intercourse between the races is absolutely unthinkable. It is not that the white agriculturist cannot compete with the Japanese agriculturist. It is that he will not live beside him.

D. TWO ANTI-JAPANESE NOVELS OF THE 1920's

1. Wallace Irwin's *Seed of the Sun* (1921)

Popular literature also did its part to publicize the growing "yellow peril." Wallace Irwin's Seed of the Sun, *a popular anti-Japanese novel, appeared first in 1920 in serialized form in the* Saturday Evening Post *and cleverly played on the fears of white Californians. In the story, a comely widow, her two children, her sister, and their Irish maid try to make a success of a California prune ranch. Unfortunately, her land is located in a district on which the Japanese have "imperial designs." After coming perilously close to succumbing to the wily charms of a Japanese diplomat, and after losing most of her prune crop because of the sabotaging effects of her Japanese help, the widow Anna Bly realizes a happy ending in the strong arms of the Anglo-Saxon farmer from down the road.*

(a) The first selection contains a description of the town named after Anna's family and the oft-criticized practice of the "picture bride."[1]

Now the little town of Bly . . . sits near the river bank and not many miles distant from the busy city which the people of Nippon call Ofu—City of Cherries—and the long-haired ones of the West call Sacramento. Aviators, flying over from the government fields beyond, look down on the huddle of mean buildings in the midst of neatly squared orchards and plantations, and as they pass over they say, "Japtown!" and let it go at that.

The casual Californian, motoring between his farm and the city, gets a more human view of this modern phenomenon; a transplanted race with their elfin peculiarities—different from us, as though the people of

[1]Wallace Irwin, *Seed of The Sun*, George H. Doran & Co., New York, 1921, pp. 55–63.

Mars had plumped down upon America and had schooled themselves to wear American shoes on their three-legged bodies. . . .

Here in Bly you will find nothing of the fairyland charm, the quaintness of composition, the age-old prettiness which we have learned to associate with Japan. The stores, it is true, are marked with the delicate Chinese characters which never disfigure a building as our Roman letters often do. Brown, slant-eyed men in baggy overalls, rough sweaters and swampers' boots, muddy from the irrigation ditches, come slouching in toward the general store. In and out of the local garage small tinnish automobiles are charging noisily all day long. Little brown men sit at the wheel and gossip of grease cups and gear shifts in the language of Nippon. . .

Now the strip of land known even to the Japanese as the Bly tract lies on the river verge a good sling's shot from the town of Bly; and it was on a bright Saturday morning early in March that Mr. Shimba, Esquire, came slopping in from the fields, his boots caked with the mud of river loam. The rain god had been moderately liberal, he concluded, since there had been two good days of downpour, and only at dawn had the brisk north wind managed to drive the clouds toward Fresno. But the ground would be too wet for working yet a while unless the dry wind continued. The prune trees were budding healthfully and blossoms were appearing in the four-acre strawberry patch. It would be a fair year for him and for the strange white woman who had insisted on occupying the ranch house.

It was about time for the noon meal when Shimba plodded over irrigation ditches and through burgeoning orchards. He was a knotty little man with a face all puckered in curly lines. His front teeth protruded, giving him the appearance of a brindle bulldog. His ears, which were reddened with sunburn, stood out straight under his battered gold cap. Rather gracelessly he wore the mask of Asia, and through the slitlike eyeholes living fires glittered constantly, fed forever by his restless thoughts. . . .

On the rough board table by the window places had been laid for four; bowls for rice and tea, plates for fish, little dishes of shoyu sauce and chopsticks—the latter brown with use, not unsplit and cased with paper as they are provided in fashionable restaurants.

Matsu, who was younger and handsomer than Shimba, read the Japanese papers, while his wife attended the rice kettle. Shimba went into an inner room and prepared to shave. It was a chaos of a room, but he was accustomed to that. Since his separation from his wife Mrs. Matsu had taken to piling superfluous household goods on the sleeping platform where at night his mat was spread. . . .

Shimba took a safety razor from his trunk, lathered and proceeded to

shave; but the blade had scarce passed across his stubby chin when
Matsu entered smilingly. The Matsus and their four children slept in
the room beyond, but Matsu's social hours were spent with Shimba.
Whom, otherwise, could he talk to?

"So you are going somewhere?" he asked, viewing the unusual prepa-
rations of his successor in management.

"To Ofu," declared Shimba, meaning Sacramento.

"Ah"—Matsu came a little closer, and his eyes were wide with curiosity—"then it is a great occasion."

"And let me tell you, Matsu-san," said Shimba through his lather, "you
will also shave and dress yourself ceremoniously. I have need of your
superior knowledge this afternoon."

"So? And what can my poor ability do for you?"

"You must know, Matsu-san, that I have been married again."

"That I have been told," admitted Matsu. "But I have never been
permitted to see the honorable photograph of your lady."

"I shall show you."

Shimba, who had finished wiping his chin, opened his trunk again and
brought two photographs from its flimsy upper tray. The one he handed
Matsu was done in the stereotype manner of the cheap gallery, but the
face it showed was young and wistful. The little maid in the picture
looked to be about sixteen. Her mouth was small and soft as a baby's; a
modest kimono was folded sweetly across her breast.

"You have done well, Mr. Shimba!" exclaimed Matsu. "And the other
picture, I suppose, is of yourself?"

"Eh!" grunted Shimba, and handed over the photograph he had been
holding back.

It was small wonder that Matsu puzzled a while over the hard-glazed
surface which bore the imprint of the Rising Sun Photo Parlor, Sacramento. Could the perfect young Japanese in a dinner jacket and white
dress tie be any kin to the hard-faced Shimba? A younger brother perhaps—the resemblance was unmistakable.

"A splended portrait!" declared the polite Matsu.

"A little fashionable, perhaps," admitted Shimba. "But this is like the
one I sent the lady. The photographer, who is a wise man, cautioned me
that a bridegroom should appear especially stylish when he has never
met his bride and is forced to be absent from the ceremony. Therefore
he was very artistic. From a photograph I had taken in youth he cut
the head and joined it nicely to this American dress suit which he had
in stock. It costs me twenty yen—very reasonable in these times. In this
bargain he included a few touches to beautify my features."

"What lady could resist so beautiful a thing?" sighed Matsu.

(b) Later in the novel occurs a series of interesting exchanges between Anna and the white farmer for whom her love will grow in direct proportion to her increasing awareness of the insidious nature of the smiling, ubiquitous Japanese.²

Anna switched on the light in the sitting room and unbolted the door. Reaction had set in. After what she had seen she could fear nothing. A tall, raw-boned man in a leather coat stood in the square of light, his florid, well-fed face beaming amiably under the brim of a greenish motor hat. His Anglo-Saxon look of health and well-being seemed to bring clean air into the poisoned atmosphere:

"Is this Mrs. Bly?" he asked, removing his cloth hat and showing a head of blond hair combed back pompadour fashion.

"Yes," she faltered, "I'm Mrs. Bly."

"I hope you'll forgive my walking in on you at this time of night," he grinned. "But I heard in Japtown that there'd been some trouble here."

"My foreman's wife has just—[committed suicide]."

"I know," he replied consolingly. "The Japs are always pulling something like that. I heard there weren't any men on the place, so I thought you might let me poke round a bit and straighten out this mess for you. . . . My name's Leacy," he said, apparently recognizing the necessity for an introduction. "I'm a farmer, too. I run an asparagus ranch down on the delta."

"I'm so grateful to you—" she began, and stopped in time to save herself from crying.

It was good to know that an American was on the place.

. . .

[Sometime later] "Well," said Leacy, "I don't know why there has been so much bunk circulated about the Japs, unless they've circulated it themselves—they're grand little circulators, you know. Sentimental missionaries are always moaning round about the wonderful little people who are so economical that they grow three hills of beans on grandmother's grave, water it with their tears, take the plants in at night and thus produce enough grub to feed the whole darned family for a year. Now there's just a grain of truth in that. The Jap is a one-horse farmer; the American is a thousand-horse farmer. Our imagination takes in the whole landscape, while a Jap gets down on his haunches and rubs a dinky piece of dirt between his hands. . . .

[A short time later Leacy tries to warn her about losing her land.] "Well, they haven't grabbed my land, you see!"

²*Op. cit.*, pp. 128, 135, 215–217.

"I've been worrying about you, " he confessed.

"About me?"

She scarcely knew it, but her heart fluttered.

"Of course you're going to hang onto this strip—or sell out to a white man," was his next decision.

"Why shouldn't I sell out to anybody I want to?" she asked perversely.

"A few weeks ago," said Dunc slowly, "I couldn't have answered your question. But right now, today, I've been forced to a conclusion. A lot of that stuff I've been calling cheap politics and newspaper tommyrot is only too true. The Japanese thirst for land isn't just individual and natural. It's inspired, concerted and directed."

"Inspired, concerted and directed by what?" she persistently smiled.

"The Japanese Government. . . ."

"Aren't you exaggerating a little?" asked Anna.

"I wish I were. We're yellow down on the island too, but the situation there's a little different. We've got the yellow peril working for us, and any time we find enough white labor to do the trick we can clear the Japs and Hindus and Mexicans off the lot and make it a white man's country again. But here the situation is different."

.   .   .

[Later when Anna is faced by a proposal of marriage from Baron Tazumi, a Japanese diplomat, it is the image of the strong-willed Anglo Saxon that interrupts her thoughts.] His skin, to be sure, was a shade sallower than hers, his eyes a little different. Many women of her acquaintance had married hideously ugly men and loved them to distraction. What then was the invisible wall between her and the aristocratic Tazumi?

In that searching flash she thought of Dunc Leacy—or was it the mind behind the mind that brought his picture to her? There had been an hour when she had considered him. That hour had passed. . . .

"Much as I have admired your fight against fate," Tazumi was saying, "I have hated to think of you struggling against the rough elements— alone. I am no worshiper of money, Anna, but I have a great deal of it. You would enjoy among my people the place you deserve. You would be a figure in court society. You could live again among the great of the earth."

"The great of the earth! Who are they? Big-framed men, blond and boisterous, fighting for the fruits of the soil with the spirit of boys? Fine-boned yellow men, keen eyed, studious and thoughtful, planning their destiny with the skill of engineers? Soul strength against soul strength—who are the great of the earth?"

Anna glanced at the silk-skinned little man beside her. Candid, earnest, honorable, she knew that he admired her because he, too, was admirable. He had gone into a strange land and fought for his people with an ethical code as pure as Galahad's. And yet she gazed in wonder, trying to imagine them in the relation of husband and wife.

"I shall be called home soon," he urged, "and I should like your answer, Anna."

"He touched her hand for an instant, but she withdrew it. His fingers were soft as silk, but cold to the touch.

2. Gene Stratton-Porter's *Her Father's Daughter*, 1921

Gene Stratton-Porter entertained millions of young readers with her many novels in the early decades of the twentieth century. Several times her books made the best-seller list, and Her Father's Daughter *ranked eighth in 1921. This particular story focuses on a young lady who well understands the tradition she has inherited from her elders and her responsibility to pass it on to her fellow Anglo-Saxon students at a Los Angeles high school. In the following passages Linda urges a young male friend to rise to the challenge of a Japanese-American student who is leading his class.[1]*

An angry red rushed to the boy's face. It was an irritating fact that in the senior class of that particular Los Angeles high school a Japanese boy stood at the head. This was embarrassing to every senior.

Shortly after this, Sweet Linda is discussing the problem with a fellow student:

"I am getting at the fact that a boy as big as you and as strong as you and with as good brain and your opportunities has allowed a little brown Jap to cross the Pacific Ocean and in a totally strange country to learn a language foreign to him, and, with the same books and the same chances, to beat you at your game. You and every other boy in your class ought to be thoroughly ashamed of yourselves. Before I would let a Jap, either boy or girl, lead in my class, I would give up going to school and go out and see if I could beat him growing lettuce and spinach." . . .

"For God's sake, Linda, tell me how I can beat that little coconut-headed Jap."

Linda slammed down the lid to the lunch box. Her voice was smooth and even but there was battle in her eyes and she answered decisively:

---

[1]From *Her Father's Daughter* by Gene Stratton-Porter. Copyright 1921 by Gene Stratton-Porter, pp. 6–7, 114–118, 162–163, 264–265. Reprinted by permission of Doubleday & Company, Inc.

"Well, you can't beat him calling him names. There is only one way on God's footstool that you can beat him. You can't beat him legislating against him. You can't beat him boycotting him. You can't beat him with any tricks. He is as sly as a cat and he has got a whole bag full of tricks of his own, and he has proved right here in Los Angeles that he has got a brain that is hard to beat. All you can do, and be a man commendable to your own soul, is to take his subject and put your brain on it to such purpose that cut pigeon wings around him. . . . There is just one way in all this world that we can beat Eastern civilization and all that it intends to do to us eventually. The white man has dominated by his color so far in the history of the world, but it is written in the Books that when the men of colour acquire our culture and combine it with their own methods of living and rate of production, they are going to bring forth greater numbers, better equipped for the battle of life, than we are. When they have got our last secret, constructive or scientific, they will take it, and living in a way that we would not, reproducing in numbers we don't, they will beat us at any game we start, if we don't take warning while we are in the ascendency, and keep there." . . .

"I'll do anything in the world if you will only tell me how," said Donald. "Maybe you think it isn't grinding me and humiliating me properly. Maybe you think Father and Mother haven't warned me. Maybe you think Mary Louise isn't secretly ashamed of me. How can I beat him, Linda?"

Linda's eyes were narrowed to a mere line. She was staring at the wall back of Donald as if she hoped that Heaven would intercede in her favour and write thereon a line that she might translate to the boy's benefit.

"I have been watching pretty sharply," she said. "Take them as a race, as a unit—of course there are exceptions, there always are—but the great body of them are mechanical. They are imitative. They are not developing anything great of their own in their own country. They are spreading all over the world and carrying home sewing machines and threshing machines and automobiles and cantilever bridges and submarines and aeroplanes—anything from eggbeaters to telescopes. They are not creating one single thing. They are not missing imitating everything that the white man can do anywhere else on earth. They are just like the Germans so far as that is concerned." . . .

Donald started up and drew a deep breath.

"Well, some job I call that," he said. "Who do you think I am, The Almighty?"

"No," said Linda quietly, "you are not. You are merely His son, created in his own image, like Him, according to the Book, and you have got to your advantage the benefit of all that has been learned down through the ages. . . . All Oka Sayye knows how to do is to learn the lesson in his book perfectly, and he is 100 per cent. I have told you what you must do to add the plus, and you can do it if you are that boy I take you for. People have talked about the 'yellow peril' till it's got to be a meaningless phrase. Somebody must wake up to the realization that it's the deadliest peril that ever has menaced white civilization. Why shouldn't you have your hand in such wonderful work?"

"Linda," said the boy breathlessly, "do you realize that you have been saying 'we'? Can you help me? Will you help me?"

"No," said Linda, "I didn't realize that I had said 'we.' I didn't mean two people, just you and me. I meant all the white boys and girls of the High School and the city and the state and the whole world. If we are going to combat the 'yellow peril' we must combine against it. We have got to curb our appetites and train our brains and enlarge our hearts till we are something bigger and finer and numerically greater than this yellow peril. We can't take it and pick it up and push it into the sea. We are not Germans and we are not Turks. I never wanted anything in all this world worse than I want to see you graduate ahead of Oka Sayye. And then I want to see the white boys and girls of Canada and of England and of Norway and Sweden and Australia, and of the whole world doing exactly what I am recommending that you do in your class and what I am doing personally in my own. I have had Japs in my classes ever since I have been in school, but Father always told me to study them, to play the game fairly, but to *beat* them in some way, in some fair way to beat them at the game they are undertaking."

"Well, there is one thing you don't take into consideration," said Donald. "All of us did not happen to be fathered by Alexander Strong. Maybe we haven't all got your brains."

"Oh, bother!" said Linda. "I know of a case where a little Indian was picked up from a tribal battlefield in South America and brought to this country and put into our schools, and there was nothing any white pupil in the school could do that he couldn't as long as it was imitative work. You have got to be constructive. You have got to work out some way to get ahead of them; and if you will take the history of the white races and go over the great achievements in mechanics, science, art, literature—anything you choose—when a white man is constructive, when he does create, he can simply cut circles around the coloured races. The thing is to get the boys and girls of today to understand what is going on in the world, what they must do as their share in making the world safe for their grandchildren." . . .

[Later, Linda reflects on the situation.] "In all my life I have never seen anything so mask-like as the stolid little square head on that Jap. I have never seen anything I dislike more than the oily, stiff, black hair standing up on it like menacing bristles. I have never had but one straight look deep into his eyes, but in that look I saw the only thing that ever frightened me in looking into a man's eyes in my whole life. And there is one thing that I have to remember to caution Donald about. He must carry on this contest in a perfectly open, fair, and above-board way, and he simply must not antagonize Oka Sayye. There are so many of the Japs. They all look so much alike, and there's a blood brotherhood between them that will make them protect each other against any white man. It wouldn't be safe for Donald to make Oka Sayye hate him. He had far better try to make him his friend and put a spirit of honest rivalry into his heart; but come to think of it, there wasn't anything like that in my one look into Oka Sayye's eyes. I don't know what it was, but whatever it was it was repulsive." . . .

[A short time later, Donald relates how he is doing.] "We got so in earnest that I am afraid both of us were rather tense. I stepped over to his demonstration to point out where I thought his reasoning was wrong. I got closer to the Jap than I had ever been before; and by gracious, Linda! scattered, but nevertheless still there, and visible, I saw a sprinkling of grey hairs just in front of and over his ears. It caught me unawares, and before I knew what I was doing, before the professor and the assembled classroom I blurted it out: 'Say, Oka Sayye, how old are you?' If the Jap had had any way of killing me, I believe he would have done it. There was a look in his eyes that was what I would call deadly. It was only a flash and then, very courteously, putting me in the wrong, of course, he remarked that he was 'almost ninekleen'; and it struck me from his look and the way he said it that it was a lie. If he truly was the average age of the rest of the class there was nothing for him to be angry about. Then I did take a deliberate survey. From the settled solidity of his frame and the shape of his hands and the skin of his face and the set of his eyes in his head, I couldn't see that much youth. I'll bet he's thirty if he's a day, and I shouldn't be a bit surprised if he has graduated at the most worthwhile university in Japan, before he ever came to this country to get his English for nothing."

2
The San Francisco School Board Case and the Dangers of Integration

In 1906, the mayor of San Francisco, Eugene Schmitz, was under attack for corrupt administrative practices. Partly because he wished to divert public attention and partly because he was a representative of organized labor who had campaigned on an anti-Japanese platform, the mayor insisted that "all Chinese, Japanese, and Korean children" be sent to the Oriental public school, and the school board responded by passing such a resolution. Out of some 25,000 San Francisco school children, only 93 were of Japanese extraction. Thus it was not a question of threatening numbers, but a manifestation of a broader anti-Japanese sentiment. An international incident was created that President Roosevelt alleviated through the "Gentleman's Agreement," an unofficial exchange of notes in which Japan promised to stop the emigration of laborers to Hawaii, from where many had continued on to the United States, in return for an end to the school segregation.

A. THE *SAN FRANCISCO CHRONICLE* SUPPORTS SCHOOL SEGREGATION, 1906[1]

[1]Editorial, *San Francisco Chronicle*, November 6, 1906.

JAPANESE IN SCHOOLS—REASONS WHY THEY ARE OBJECTIONABLE TO OUR PEOPLE

The most prominent objection to the presence of Japanese in our public schools is their habit of sending young men to the primary grades, where they sit side by side with very young children because in those grades only are the beginnings of English taught. That creates situations which often become painfully embarrassing. They are, in fact, unendurable.

There is also the objection to taking the time of the teachers to teach the English language to pupils, old or young, who do not understand it. It is a reasonable requirement that all students entering the schools shall be familiar with the language in which instruction is conducted. We deny either the legal or moral obligation to teach any foreigner to read or speak the English language. And if we choose to do that for one nationality, as a matter of grace, and not to do the same for another nationality, that is our privilege.

We do not know that the Japanese children are personally objectionable in grades composed of pupils of their own age. We do not know whether they are or not. There is, however, a deep and settled conviction among our people that the only hope of maintaining peace between Japan and the United States is to keep the two races apart. Whatever the status of the Japanese children while still young and uncontaminated, as they grow older they acquire the distinctive character, habits, and moral standards of their race, which are abhorrent to our people. We object to them in the familiar intercourse of common school life as we would object to any other moral poison.

While we deny any moral or legal obligation to give, at public expense, any education whatever to any alien, and consequently if we choose to give as a matter of grace to one and deny it to another, we have also as a matter of grace provided separate schools for the Japanese. In all the Southern States separate schools are provided for white and colored children. To say that we may exclude our own colored citizens from the schools attended by white children, but shall not exclude the children of aliens from such schools, is not only absurd but monstrous.

B. *HARPER'S WEEKLY* AND THE DIFFICULTIES OF ASSIMILATION, 1906

It was not only the West Coast that called for restrictive measures to be taken against the Japanese-Americans. George Harvey of Harper's

Weekly *drew the following Darwinian conclusions concerning the "Japanese problem."*[1]

It took a vast deal of time and no small pains to distribute the races of mankind where they ought to go. It was only partly a matter of distribution. It was chiefly a matter of development, since country and climate were the chief factors in making the differences in peoples. Redistribution can be accomplished nowadays at great speed, but it is a hazardous business; hazardous sometimes because the transplanted race does not do well, and hazardous at other times because it does too well. Imported rabbits overran Australia; imported gipsy-moths raised hob in Massachusetts; the phylloxera, imported from America, devastated the vineyards of France; imported water-hyacinths have choked the rivers of Louisiana and Florida; imported mongooses have become a pest in Jamaica; imported Africans are a problem in the United States and the West Indies, and imported Europeans have proved to be fatally disastrous to the aborigines of the Western Hemisphere. Self-preservation demands that a nation, whatever its traditions, shall have the power to exclude dangerous importations, whether bug, bird, beast, fish, seed, microbe, or human creature. The people of California have begun to call for the exclusion of the Japanese. There is no doubt that if the call is justified on grounds of self-preservation, it will prevail.

For the Japanese in the United States will always be Japanese. They will not become Americans. They will neither wish to merge with our people nor shall we wish to have them. Our capacious hospitalities are equal to the accommodation of a good many of them. They are clean, well mannered, and industrious; better folk by far in many particulars than a great many other newcomers. But they are not our kind, and will not merge. They belong to Asia. Their hearts are there; their interests are there. In this country we believe that they will always deserve good treatment, and that they will get it. But if there ever is danger that any part of the country will be overrun with them as Hawaii has been, there can be no doubt that proper and peaceable means will be taken to avert that danger.

C. STATE REPRESENTATIVE GROVE JOHNSON AND THE SEXUAL DANGERS OF SCHOOL INTEGRATION, 1909

The Gentleman's Agreement did not solve the school dilemma to the satisfaction of many Californians. Three years later, State Representative Grove L. Johnson spoke bitterly about the Government's interference

[1]George Harvey, "Comment," *Harper's Weekly*, December 1, 1906, p. 50.

with local schools. Grove L. Johnson was the father of Hiram, who, as a United States Senator, would lead the fight for Japanese exclusion in 1924.[1]

I have all respect for the intellect of James N. Gillett, Governor of California, and for his superior, President Roosevelt. But I am sent into this Chamber by my constituents and not by Governor James N. Gillett. I have been returned here again and again, and not because I bowed to the authority of James N. Gillett. I am here for the good of my people, the people who supported me, and who expect me to support them. I know more about the Japanese than Governor Gillett and President Roosevelt put together. I am not responsible to either of them. I am responsible to the mothers and fathers of Sacramento County who have their little daughters sitting side by side in the school rooms with matured Japs, with their base minds, their lascivious thoughts multiplied by their race and strengthened by their mode of life.

I am here to protect the children of these parents. To do all that I can to keep any Asiatic man from mingling in the same school with daughters of our people. You know the results of such a condition; you know how far it will go, and I have seen Japanese twenty-five years old sitting in the seats next to the pure maids of California. I shuddered then and I shudder now, the same as any other parent will shudder to think of such a condition.

[1]This speech was made in the California Assembly and quoted in Franklin Hichborn, *The Story of the Session of the California Legislature of 1909*, Press of the James H. Barry Co., San Francisco, 1909, p. 207.

3
The Japanese and American Law

In 1882, the Japanese avoided inclusion in a ban that prohibited Chinese from becoming citizens, largely because of the protests of the Japanese Government. But the anti-Japanese hysteria of the early 1900's caused the Bureau of Immigration and Naturalization in 1911 to order that declarations of intentions to file for citizenship could not be received from persons other than whites or Africans. Thereafter, courts refused naturalization to Japanese immigrants. In the early 1920's, Congress responded to national pressures and passed a series of immigration-restriction measures that culminated in the National Origins Act. The 1924 Act, enacted after considerable controversy, stated that "no alien ineligible to citizenship shall be admitted to the United States." This was aimed generally at all Orientals and specifically at the Japanese. Not until 1952 did Congress repeal this decision and allow an annual token Japanese quota of 185 immigrants.

A. REPRESENTATIVE EVERIS A. HAYES AND AN EARLY CALL FOR EXCLUSION, 1906

In 1906 Rep. Everis A. Hayes of California made the first Congressional speech devoted to Japanese exclusion. There would be many more before the Japanese Exclusion Act became law in 1924. Rep. Hayes made it quite clear that a lack of morality was endemic to the Japanese.[1]

What stamp of civilization will these people bring to us when they come to our shores? What elements of personal character have they that

[1]*Congressional Record*, 59th Cong., 1st Sess., March 13, 1906, pp. 3747–3753.

if stamped somewhat upon our already composite national character would add elements of strength not now possessed by us? What elements that would tend to weaken or corrupt the national life? Would their coming tend to threaten our institutions or destroy the civilization founded upon intelligence, morality, equality, and justice that we are trying with some success to build up here? I believe that these are some of the questions that we should ask and answer; these are the principal considerations that should determine our attitude toward this question.

The Japanese have made such strides and have been outwardly so transformed in the past fifty years that those of our fellow-citizens who only know them from a distance are apt to be filled with unmixed admiration. A personal contact close enough and long enough to pierce the outside veneer gives one an entirely different impression, however. A close acquaintance shows one that unblushed lying is so universal among the Japanese as to be one of the leading national traits; that commercial honor, even among her commercial classes, is so rare as to be only the exception that proves the reverse rule, and that the vast majority of the Japanese people do not understand the meaning of the word "morality," but are given up to the practice of licentiousness more generally than any nation in the world justly making any pretense to civilization. I am told by those who have lived in Japan and understand its language that there is no word in Japanese corresponding to "sin," because there is in the ordinary Japanese mind no conception of its meaning. There is no word corresponding to our word "home," because there is nothing in the Japanese domestic life corresponding to the home as we know it. The Japanese language has no term for "privacy." They lack the term and the clear idea because they lack the practice. . . .

All that has ever been said in Congress by the advocates of Chinese exclusion during the past forty years; all that has ever been written on the subject; all the information that has been collected and buried out of sight in Congressional committee reports as to the vileness and bestiality of Oriental vices, is as true of the Japanese in our midst as of the Chinese.

B. A PROFESSOR URGES A CHECK ON JAPANESE IMMIGRATION TO CALIFORNIA, 1921

The following article, written by a University of California professor after the passage of California's 1920 land exclusion bill, emphasized the dangers of the Japanese in America by playing to the usual fears and stereotypes.[1]

The most keenly contested issue of the recent election in California was over the action which should be taken on the initiative amendment prohibiting the selling or leasing of land to Japanese. Compared to this, interest as to who was to be president, or whether America would belong to the League of Nations was vague and remote. To many white farmers the vote on this amendment would determine whether they would continue to live on their farms or have to sell to an Oriental. The vote was therefore large. Public opinion was thoroughly aroused, and the majority of over three to one for the amendment showed clearly the trend of public opinion. . . .

For this action, and the feeling that lies back of it, the Japanese are responsible. The California farmer is easy-going and optimistic, not inclined to plan for the future. If during the last ten years the Japanese had gone into the farming districts as individuals and mingled with white farmers as individuals, there would today be no more prejudice against them as a race than there is against Swedes or Italians, which is none at all. The statement that they have not done so, but have sought to establish themselves as racial communities, is not made in the way of criticism but to help explain why Japanese land ownership is objected to.
. . .

The danger is that America will not understand what is taking place or realize the disaster which this migration is certain to bring if the movement is not stamped out at once. There is danger that this nation will be misled by catch phrases like "Race Equality," "Uplifting Asia" and "Personal Liberty."

In order to compete with the Japanese, the American farmer, who has to make his way by labor, must sacrifice rest, recreation and the giving of time to civic interests or the development of the higher life of a community. He must change his ideas of what is desirable in life and surrender inherited habit. Only by devoting all of the energy of himself, his wife and children to the hard task of making a living, can he pay the rents and do the other things necessary to withstand the rural competition of the Japanese. The thing which America ought to recognize is that requiring him to do this is not an advance but a backward step in our progress and it will not be made. The American subjected to this competition will go into the cities or to other countries and the Japanese

[1]Elwood Mead, "The Japanese Land Problem of California," *The Annals of the American Academy of Political and Social Sciences*, January 1921, pp. 51–55.

will continue to displace him as he has been displacing him during the last ten years.

C. THE SUPREME COURT AND JAPANESE CITIZENSHIP

When Earl G. Harrison resigned as United States Commissioner of Immigration and Naturalization in 1944, he said that the only country in the world, outside of the United States, that observed racial discrimination in matters relating to naturalization was Nazi Germany "and all will agree that this is not very desirable company."

In 1922, a decision made by the Bureau of Immigration and Naturalization 11 years earlier not to allow citizen applications from persons other than whites or Africans, was appealed to the Supreme Court. Takao Ozawa was born in Japan but had lived in the United States for 20 years, and it was admitted by the Court that he possessed all the legal qualifications—the only question was whether he was ineligible because of his race. Justice George Sutherland gave the unanimous decision that made it clear that America would have the anomalous situation of having in this country aliens legally resident yet ineligible for citizenship. After the Ozawa case, several naturalized Issei were taken to court and their papers declared null and void. The following is taken from Justice Sutherland's opinion.[1]

The appellant is a person of the Japanese race born in Japan. He applied on October 16, 1914, to the United States District Court for the Territory of Hawaii to be admitted as a citizen of the United States. His petition was opposed by the United States District Attorney for the District of Hawaii. Including the period of his residence in Hawaii appellant had continuously resided in the United States for twenty years. He was a graduate of the Berkeley, California, high school, had been nearly three years a student in the University of California, had educated his children in American schools, his family had attended American churches and he had maintained the use of the English language in his home. That he was well qualified by character and education for citizenship is conceded.

The District Court of Hawaii, however, held that, having been born in Japan and being of the Japanese race, he was not eligible to naturalization under section 2169 of the Revised Statutes, and denied the petition. . . .

[1]"Takao Ozawa v. United States," *U.S. Supreme Court Reports*, 260 U.S. 178, November 13, 1922, pp. 65–69.

In all of the naturalization acts from 1790 to 1906 the privilege of naturalization was confined to white persons (with the addition in 1870 of those of African nativity and descent), although the exact wording of the various statutes was not always the same. If Congress in 1906 desired to alter a rule so well and so long established it may be assumed that its purpose would have been definitely disclosed and its legislation to that end put in unmistakable terms. . . .

This brings us to inquire whether, under section 2169, the appellant is eligible to naturalization. The language of the naturalization laws from 1790 to 1870 had been uniformly such as to deny the privilege of naturalization to an alien unless he came within the description "free white person. . . . " It is true that in the first edition of the Revised Statutes of 1873 the words in brackets, "being free white persons, and to aliens" were omitted, but this was clearly an error of the compilers and was corrected by the subsequent legislation of 1875. Is appellant, therefore, a "free white person," within the meaning of that phrase as found in the statute?

On behalf of the appellant it is urged that we should give to this phrase the meaning which it had in the minds of its original framers in 1790 and that it was employed by them for the sole purpose of excluding the black or African race and the Indians then inhabiting this country. It may be true that those two races were alone thought of as being excluded, but to say that they were the only ones within the intent of the statute would be to ignore the affirmative form of the legislation. The provision is not that Negroes and Indians shall be excluded, but it is, in effect, that only free white persons shall be included. The intention was to confer the privilege of citizenship upon that class of persons whom the fathers knew as white, and to deny it to all who could not be so classified. It is not enough to say that the framers did not have in mind the brown or yellow races of Asia. It is necessary to go farther and be able to say that had these particular races been suggested the language of the act would have been so varied as to include them within its privileges. . . .

The briefs filed on behalf of appellant refer in complimentary terms to the culture and enlightenment of the Japanese people, and with this estimate we have no reason to disagree; but these are matters which cannot enter into our consideration of the questions here at issue. We have no function in the matter other than to ascertain the will of Congress and declare it. Of course there is not implied—either in the legislation or in our interpretation of it—any suggestion of individual unworthiness or racial inferiority. These considerations are in no manner involved.

D. FOUR INFLUENTIAL ORGANIZATIONS
SUPPORT EXCLUSION, 1924

It was, of course, California that brought the greatest pressure to bear on Congress to exclude Japanese. Four of its most powerful organizations joined together to send the Senate Committee on Immigration the following 1924 resolution urging quick passage of such a measure.[1]

Statement from California Department of American Legion, American Federation of Labor, the Grange, and Native Sons of the Golden West in Reply to Japan's Foreign Minister on the Subject of Japanese Immigration and American Immigration Laws

There is no discriminatory treatment of the Japanese in this country. They are accorded everywhere the rights and privileges to which all aliens, or aliens ineligible to citizenship under our laws, Federal and State, are entitled.

There is no Japanese exclusion bill now before Congress, and no such measure which mentions the Japanese. Minister Matsui probably refers to that provision in the general immigration bill which would exclude hereafter as immigrants or permanent residents all aliens ineligible to citizenship.

Far from singling out the Japanese, this provision applies to all the yellow and brown races, comprising about half the population of the globe, and includes Hindus, Malays, Chinese, Japanese, and Filipinos— of which the Japanese constitute only a small fraction.

The provision is in strict accord with the Federal law forbidding naturalization of certain aliens, passed in 1790, which law has not since been changed in this particular, nor was complaint in regard to this law or its effect on the Japanese people ever made by Japan at any time until within the past few decades, since she started her policy of colonization in the United States. The provision is certainly a fundamental step in the restriction of unassimilable immigration now demanded by the Nation. It has received unanimous indorsement in national conventions of the American Legion, the American Federation of Labor, and the Grange. . . .

We are friendly with Japan and wish to remain friendly; but, as President Roosevelt pointed out, that friendship can not continue if communities of unassimilable Japanese established in this country promote trouble through economic competition and racial friction.

[1]"Hearings before the Committee on Immigration," United States Senate, 68th Cong., 1st Sess., March 11, 1924, pp. 36–37.

4
The Relocation Camps

During the late spring months of 1942, 70,000 American citizens, as well as some 40,000 aliens, were uprooted from their West Coast homes and interned in several hastily erected relocation centers in the interior. No formal charges were made against these individuals; indeed, none could have been, since they had broken no laws. They were, however, all of Japanese ancestry.

On February 19, 1942, President Roosevelt issued Executive Order No. 9066, which allowed the military to prescribe certain critical areas from which any or all persons might be excluded. The President insisted that the danger of espionage and sabotage made such an order necessary. Less than a month later he established the War Relocation Board, which had the authority to "remove, relocate, maintain, and supervise" those persons detained under the previous order.

In the hysterical first days after Pearl Harbor, when it was even rumored that some of the Japanese pilots were still wearing their American college rings, and the William Randolph Hearst Marksmanship Teams pledged themselves to protect the Los Angeles area against parachutists and saboteurs, such fears for the West Coast could easily be understood; but by the spring of 1942 there had been no attempts at sabotage and no evidence of any fifth-column activity on the Coast. Nevertheless, the military commander for the area, General John L. DeWitt, ordered the complete evacuation of the Japanese-Americans from the West Coast as a security measure. Not included were 58,000 Italian and 23,000 German aliens. Nor had Hawaii seen fit to intern her 157,000 residents of Japanese extraction, although she was much closer to a possible invasion. It was not only the military that called for such a move; men of such varied backgrounds as human-rights crusaders Walter Lippmann and Earl Warren gave their approval, and in 1944 the United States Supreme Court upheld the decision.

A. A WEST COAST COLUMNIST CALLS FOR ACTION, 1942

Shortly after Pearl Harbor the Hearst press called for action to be taken against the Japanese-Americans in tones that were reminiscent of the preexclusion attacks. Henry McLemore was a columnist for Hearst's San Francisco Examiner. He had emerged out of sports-writing background, but there was little of the sportsman's proverbial fair play in his inflammatory prose.[1]

WHY TREAT THE JAPS WELL HERE?

Speaking strictly as an American, I think Americans are nuts. Twenty-four hours in Los Angeles have convinced me of this.

We are at war. California is our key State, not only because of its airplane industry, but because its shores offer the most logical invasion point.

So what does the Government do about the tens of thousands of Japanese in California? Nothing.

The only Japanese apprehended have been the ones the FBI actually had something on. The rest of them, so help me, are as free as birds. There isn't an airport in California that isn't flanked by Japanese farms. There is hardly an air field where the same situation doesn't exist. They run their stores. They clerk in stores. They clip lawns. They are here, there and everywhere.

You walk up and down the streets and you bump into Japanese in every block. They take the parking positions. They get ahead of you in the stamp line at the post office. They have their share of seats on the bus and streetcar lines.

This doesn't make sense, for half a dozen reasons. How many American workers do you suppose are free to roam and ramble in Tokio? Didn't the Japanese threaten to shoot on sight any white person who ventured out of doors in Manila? So, why are we so beautifully courteous?

I know this is the melting pot of the world and all men are created

[1]Reprinted by permission of United Press International from Henry McLemore, "Why Treat the Japs Well Here?" *San Francisco Examiner,* January 29, 1942.

equal and there must be no such thing as race or creed hatred, but do those things go when a country is fighting for its life? Not in my book. No country has ever won a war because of courtesy and I trust and pray we won't be the first one to lose one because of the lovely, gracious spirit.

Everywhere that the Japanese have attacked to date, the Japanese population has risen to aid the attackers. Pearl Harbor, Manila. What is there to make the Government believe that the same wouldn't be true in California? Does it feel that the lovely California climate has changed them and that the thousands of Japanese who live in the boundaries of this State are all staunch and true Americans?

I am for immediate removal of every Japanese on the West Coast to a point deep in the interior. I don't mean a nice part of the interior either. Herd 'em up, pack 'em off and give 'em the inside room in the badlands. Let 'em be pinched, hurt, hungry and dead up against it.

Sure, this would work an unjustified hardship on 80 percent or 90 per cent of the California Japanese. But the remaining 10 or 20 per cent have it in their power to do damage—great damage to the American people. They are a serious menace and you can't tell me that an individual's rights have any business being placed above a nation's safety.

If making one million innocent Japanese uncomfortable would prevent one scheming Japanese from costing the life of one American boy, then let the million innocents suffer.

In an earlier column I protested against American soldiers in Honolulu giving a military burial to a Japanese soldier. There were some readers who kicked me around in letters for such an attitude. There are sure to be some Americans who will howl and scream at the idea of inconveniencing America's Japanese population in order to prevent sabotage and espionage.

Okay, let them howl. Let them howl timber wolf type. Our Government has told us we face war. All out war. It has told us that we are up against the roughest days in our history. It has demanded of us sacrifice and sweat and toil and all of the other of Mr. Churchill's graphic words.

That's all right, we will answer. But let us have no patience with the enemy or with any one whose veins carry his blood.

Let us in this desperate time put first things first. And who is to say that to the men and women of this country there is anything that comes above America?

Personally, I hate the Japanese. And that goes for all of them. Let's quit worrying about hurting the enemy's feelings and start doing it.

B. EARL WARREN AND EVACUATION, 1942

Earl Warren's reputation for liberal causes is well known. In February, 1942, Earl Warren was Attorney General of California and laying the groundwork for a successful campaign for the governor's office. Unquestionably some of his remarks on the Japanese-Americans could be interpreted as political expediency, but Warren, then an active member of the American Legion and the Native Sons of the Golden West, both of which were strongly anti-Japanese, appeared convinced that Japanese-Americans, whether citizens or not, could not be an integral and loyal part of his America. The following testimony was given before the so-called Tolan Committee, a House committee that was charged with examining the problem of evacuation.[1]

ATTORNEY GENERAL WARREN. For some time I have been of the opinion that the solution of our alien enemy problem with all its ramifications, which include the descendants of aliens, is not only a Federal problem but is a military problem. We believe that all of the decisions in that regard must be made by the military command that is charged with the security of this area. I am convinced that the fifth-column activities of our enemy call for the participation of people who are in fact American citizens, and that if we are to deal realistically with the problem we must realize that we will be obliged in time of stress to deal with subversive elements of our own citizenry. . . .

A wave of organized sabotage in California accompanied by an actual air raid or even by a prolonged black-out could not only be more destructive to life and property but could result in retarding the entire war effort of this Nation far more than the treacherous bombing of Pearl Harbor.

I hesitate to think what the result would be of the destruction of any of our big airplane factories in this State. It will interest you to know that some of our airplane factories in this State are entirely surrounded by Japanese land ownership or occupancy. It is a situation that is fraught with the greatest danger and under no circumstances should it ever be permitted to exist. . . .

Unfortunately, however, many of our people and some of our authorities and, I am afraid, many of our people in other parts of the country

[1]*Hearings Before the Select Committee Investigating National Defense, Migration*, Part 29, "San Francisco Hearings," February 21 and 23, 1942, U.S. House of Representatives, 77th Cong., 2nd Sess., pp. 11009–11019.

are of the opinion that because we have had no sabotage and no fifth column activities in this State since the beginning of the war, that means that none have been planned for us. But I take the view that that is the most ominous sign in our whole situation. It convinces me more than perhaps any other factor that the sabotage that we are to get, the fifth column activities that we are to get, are timed just like Pearl Harbor was timed and just like the invasion of France, and of Denmark, and of Norway, and all of those other countries. . . .

I want to say that the consensus of opinion among the law-enforcement officers of this State is that there is more potential danger among the group of Japanese who are born in this country than from the alien Japanese who were born in Japan. That might seem an anomaly to some people, but the fact is that, in the first place, there are twice as many of them. There are 33,000 aliens and there are 66,000 born in this country.

In the second place, most of the Japanese who were born in Japan are over 55 years of age. There has been practically no migration to this country since 1924. But in some instances the children of those people have been sent to Japan for their education, either in whole or in part, and while they are over there they are indoctrinated with the idea of Japanese imperialism. They receive their religious instruction which ties up their religion with their Emperor, and they come back here imbued with the ideas and the policies of Imperial Japan. . . .

We believe that when we are dealing with the Caucasian race we have methods that will test the loyalty of them, and we believe that we can, in dealing with the Germans and the Italians, arrive at some fairly sound conclusions because of our knowledge of the way they live in the community and have lived for many years. But when we deal with the Japanese we are in an entirely different field and we cannot form any opinion that we believe to be sound. . . .

MR. SPARKMAN. I have noticed suggestions in newspaper stories. I noticed a telegram this morning with reference to the civil rights of these people. What do you have to say about that?

ATTORNEY GENERAL WARREN. I believe, sir, that in time of war every citizen must give up some of his normal rights.

C. GENERAL JOHN L. DEWITT EXPLAINS
THE NEED FOR EVACUATION, 1943

Lt. Gen. John L. DeWitt was Commanding General of the Western Defense Command and was thus charged with the responsibility of the evacuation. For those wishing to ignore the rights of Japanese-American

*citizens, Gen. DeWitt proved an able ally, for he not only called for
speedy and comprehensive measures but he also vigorously opposed the
releasing of any Japanese-Americans even if they could prove their loyalty. He made it clear, however, that he doubted that there was any way
to establish their loyalty, and he described them as "a large, unassimilated, tightly knit racial group, bound to an enemy nation by strong ties
of race, culture, custom and religion."*

*The following testimony was given on April 13, 1943, before a House
Subcommittee on Naval Affairs. Like the Tolan Committee, this subcommittee proved a sympathetic forum and provided the kind of testimony the anti-Japanese press could use to advantage. The day after the
first hearings the* Los Angeles Times *quoted the General as saying, "A
Jap's a Jap. . . . You can't change him by giving him a slip of paper."*[1]

MR. MAAS. General, is there anything that you would like to suggest in
connection with your problem? Have you any problem that you want
to leave with the Congressmen? We are probably in a position to assist
you.

GENERAL DE WITT. I haven't any except one—that is the development of
a false sentiment on the part of certain individuals and some organizations to get the Japanese back on the West Coast. I don't want any of
them here. They are a dangerous element. There is no way to determine
their loyalty. The West Coast contains too many vital installations essential to the defense of the country to allow any Japanese on this coast.
There is a feeling developing, I think, in certain sections of the country
that the Japanese should be allowed to return. I am opposing it with
every proper means at my disposal.

MR. ANDERSON. I wrote to the War Department when this policy was
announced asking how come. There was strong protest from my district.
I wrote the Secretary of War and inquired as to policy and they said it
was a new policy that they intended to follow. The attitude in my district is that if you send any Japanese back here we will bury them. I
think it is a mistake.

MR. MOTT. I received the same kind of an answer to my question but
I doubt if it is a War Department policy. I believe it is a policy imposed
upon the War Department by civilian agencies.

MR. BATES. I was going to ask—would you base your determined stand
on experience as a result of sabotage or racial history or what is it?

GENERAL DE WITT. I first of all base it on my responsibility. I have the
mission of defending this coast and securing vital installations. The

[1]*Investigation of Congested Areas, Hearings Before a Subcommittee of the Committee On Naval Affairs,* House of Representatives, 78th Cong., 1st Sess., April 13,
1943, pp. 739–740.

danger of the Japanese was, and is now—if they are permitted to come back—espionage and sabotage. It makes no difference whether he is an American citizen, he is still a Japanese. American citizenship does not necessarily determine loyalty.

MR. BATES. You draw a distinction then between Japanese and Italians and Germans? We have a great number of Italians and Germans and we think they are fine citizens. There may be exceptions.

GENERAL DE WITT. You needn't worry about the Italians at all except in certain cases. Also the same for the Germans except in individual cases. But we must worry about the Japanese all the time until he is wiped off the map. Sabotage and espionage will make problems as long as he is allowed in this area—problems which I don't want to have to worry about.

D. KOREMATSU V. UNITED STATES, 1944

Fred Toyosaburo Korematsu was born in Oakland, California in 1919. Educated in the Oakland public schools, he had never been out of the country and spoke no language except English. He had worked as a ship-yard welder until the attack on Pearl Harbor when he was expelled by the Boilermaker's Union because of his Japanese ancestry. He fell in love with a Caucasian girl, and, hoping that plastic surgery and a new name would prevent his detection, he attempted to evade the evacuation order. He was unsuccessful. After his arrest and conviction, he appealed the decision all the way to the Supreme Court, where he lost a split decision.

Korematsu and his lawyers tried to argue that (1) the military authorities had no power to order the detention of citizens; (2) the classification of citizens based solely on ancestry was a denial of due process and was forbidden by the fifth admendment; and (3) the exclusion order constituted a denial of due process because it made no provision for any hearing.

Justice Hugo Black delivered the majority opinion, to which was added a short concurring opinion by Justice Felix Frankfurter. Justices Frank Murphy, Robert Jackson, and Owen Roberts wrote dissenting opinions.[1]

Mr. Justice Hugo Black's Majority Opinion

The petitioner, an American citizen of Japanese descent, was convicted in a federal district court for remaining in San Leandro, California, a "Military Area," contrary to Civilian Exclusion Order No. 34 of the Com-

[1]"Korematsu v. United States," *U.S. Supreme Court Report*, U.S. 760, No. 22, December 18, 1944.

manding General of the Western Command, U.S. Army, which directed that after May 9, 1942, all persons of Japanese ancestry should be excluded from that area. No question was raised as to petitioner's loyalty to the United States. The Circuit Court of Appeals affirmed, and the importance of the constitutional question involved caused us to grant certiorari. . . .

Like curfew, exclusion of those of Japanese origin was deemed necessary because of the presence of an unascertained number of disloyal members of the group, most of whom we have no doubt were loyal to this country. It was because we could not reject the finding of the military authorities that it was impossible to bring about an immediate segregation of the disloyal from the loyal that we sustained the validity of the curfew order as applying to the whole group. In the instant case, temporary exclusion of the entire group was rested by the military on the ground. The judgment that exclusion of the whole group was for the same reason a military imperative answers the contention that the exclusion was in the nature of group punishment based on antagonism to those of Japanese origin. That there were members of the group who retained loyalties to Japan has been confirmed by investigations made subsequent to the exclusion. Approximately five thousand American citizens of Japanese ancestry refused to swear unqualified allegiance to the United States and to renounce allegiance to the Japanese Emperor, and several thousand evacuees requested repatriation to Japan. . . .

It is said that we are dealing here with the case of imprisonment of a citizen in a concentration camp solely because of his ancestry, without evidence or inquiry concerning his loyalty and good disposition towards the United States. Our task would be simple, our duty clear, were this a case involving the imprisonment of a loyal citizen in a concentration camp because of racial prejudice. Regardless of the true nature of the assembly and relocation centers—and we deem it unjustifiable to call them concentration camps with all the ugly connotations that term implies—we are dealing specifically with nothing but an exclusion order. To cast this case into outlines of racial prejudice, without reference to the real military dangers which were presented, merely confuses the issue. Korematsu was not excluded from the Military Area because of hostility to him or his race. He was excluded because we are at war with the Japanese Empire, because the properly constituted military authorities feared an invasion of our West Coast and felt constrained to take proper security measures, because they decided that the military urgency of the situation demanded that all citizens of Japanese ancestry be segregated from the West Coast temporarily, and finally, because Congress, reposing its confidence in this time of war in our military leaders—as inevitably it must—determined that they should have the power to do just this. There was some evidence of disloyalty on the part of some, the military authorities considered that the need for action was great, and time was short. We cannot—by availing ourselves of the calm perspective of hindsight—now say that at that time these actions were unjustified.

SELECTED READINGS

Daniels, Roger, *The Politics of Prejudice*, Atheneum, New York, 1968.
A valuable scholarly study of those who did the excluding rather than of those who were excluded; unfortunately, it stops in 1924.

Girdner, Audrie, and Lofts, Anne, *The Great Betrayal; the Evacuation of the Japanese-Americans During World War II*, Macmillan, New York, 1969.
A readable, well-researched history of the evacuation and resettlement.

Hosokawa, Bill, *Nisei; the Quiet Americans*, William Morrow & Co., New York, 1969.
Denver Post Editor Hosokawa, who himself went through the evacuation, not only ably describes the resettlement of the World War II Japanese-Americans, but also provides a comprehensive treatment of the historical background.

ten Broek, Jacobus, Barnhart, Edward, and Matson, Floyd, *Prejudices, War and the Constitution*, University of California Press, Berkeley, 1954.
This third volume of the University of California's series on the treatment of World War II Japanese-Americans concerns itself with the evacuation in terms of its historical origins, its political characteristics, the responsibility for it, and the legal implications arising from it.

Thomas, Dorothy, and Nishimoto, R. S., *The Spoilage; Japanese-American Evacuation and Resettlement*, University of California Press, Berkeley, 1946.
This opening volume in the University of California series concentrates on the experience of the Japanese-Americans in the relocation centers.

Thomas, Dorothy, *The Salvage*, University of California Press, Berkeley, 1952.
This middle volume of the University of California series follows the fortunes of those who left the relocation centers to resettle in American communities before the U.S. Army released the majority of the evacuees in December 1944.

VI
JEWISH-AMERICANS

Race is the controlling influence in the Jew, who, for two millenniums, under every climate, has preserved the same character and employments.

Ralph Waldo Emerson

INTRODUCTION

Anti-Semitism has long been equated with "crackpotism" in America. The German-American Bund, Gerald L. K. Smith, Father Charles Coughlin, and the Ku Klux Klan all have been scored for their overtly anti-Semitic behavior. Likewise, most Americans have been quick to criticize anti-Jewish pogroms abroad, whether in nineteenth-century Russia and Rumania or twentieth-century Germany. It has not been so easy, however, to recognize the dimensions of anti-Semitism in this country. Unlike the European form, American anti-Semitism has not been official government policy. It has been done in the private sector—in industry and trade, by banks and insurance companies, real estate boards and neighborhood associations, clubs and societies, and colleges and universities. Unofficially, the government too made its contribution when it refused to do more for the beleaguered Jews of Europe, both before and after World War II.

Unfortunately, by condemning the excesses of both domestic and foreign anti-Semitism, America overlooked the seriousness and depth of its own problem. For example, the excesses of Hitler paralleled a growing anti-Semitism in America. Social and economic restrictions in America greatly increased and college admission quotas were tightened—even after America went to war with Germany. It was not until the 1960's, when the various civil rights acts could be applied, that most of the overt examples of social, economic, and educational discrimination disappeared.

The first record of Jews in America dates back to 1654, when 27 Portuguese Jews obtained brief asylum in Manhattan; by the Revolution there

249

were perhaps 2000 Jews in the colonies; 125 years later there were almost a million Jews in New York alone. If the early Jews met with much prejudice, there is little public record of the fact until the Civil War, when Jews were charged with disloyal profiteering, and General Grant's infamous "Order No. 11" gave "the Jews as a class" twenty-four hours to leave his Department of Tennessee.

During the Gilded Age, some Jews were treated as a symbol of the parvenu spirit, and society began to exclude them; but they were not considered a national menace or an "unassimilable race." The fact that so many Americans were shocked when New York banker Joseph Seligman was excluded from a Saratoga Springs hotel in 1877 indicates that it was not a common practice.

Because of various pogroms in Russia, Rumania, and Austria, some 50,000 Jews a year came into this country between 1880 and 1910. Anti-Semitism grew in America along with the myth that these Jews were not as well educated or as skilled as older Jews who had largely Northern and Western European origins. Actually, anti-Semitism increased at a time when Jewish immigration was diminishing. Although as many as 1½ million Jews came in during this period, most of them were quickly swallowed up in the garment trade, where they had little contact with the outside world. It was not until their children became a threat to the established middle class by going to college and competing in the job market that anti-Semitism greatly increased. Historian John Higham suggests that "the Jews lost in reputation as they gained in social and economic status," and the increasing evidence of social and educational exclusion during the 1920's unquestionably supports his conclusion.

It was in 1922 that President A. Lawrence Lowell of Harvard openly called for the quota system at Harvard. Although his plan was defeated by the Board of Trustees, many other prominent universities did institute such a system.

The Ku Klux Klan, whose membership numbered several million in the early 1920's, also directed its attacks at the Jew, as did Henry Ford, whose *Dearborn Independent* reached a large national audience. It was Ford too who published an American edition of the "Protocols of the Elders of Zion," the document that purported to be the Jewish plan for world conquest. The classified advertisements of the 1920's show that anti-Jewish restrictions were greatly increasing in the resort trade and in some lines of employment.

Jacob Javits suggests that under the impact of Hitler and the Depression anti-Semitism reached a frightening peak in the United States during the 1930's. German propaganda had made Americans increasingly Jew-conscious, and anti-Semitic attacks by such popular figures as Father

Coughlin and Charles Lindbergh helped fan the fires of hate. The 1930's also witnessed the beginning of American insensitivity toward Jewish refugees. Although this country was appalled by Hitler's atrocities and roundly condemned him for them, America proved to be the most stubborn of nations when it came time to provide a sanctuary for his victims. This dismal story lasted until 1944, when the United States Government made a belated effort to save the few remaining Jews. But after the war, when thousands of Jewish displaced persons needed a home, America again made little effort to alleviate the situation.

It was not always clear why Americans discriminated against Jews. Some suggested that their poor manners and lack of social graces made them undesirable social companions or unwanted neighbors. But genteel manners had seldom explained most American success stories. Others maintained that Jews were too ambitious and unscrupulous in their business tactics, but such criticism had not prevented the Rockefellers and Vanderbilts from gaining their place in America. The old cry of clannishness and Old World commitments was also raised, but in reality it appeared to be the ability of the second-generation Jew to compete and succeed in an open society that made restrictions seem necessary.

1
Popular Images of the Jew

Anti-Jewish stereotypes certainly did not originate in America—yet Americans have often accepted them without serious challenge or final rejection. In both popular and scholarly sources the American Jew is usually indistinguishable from his European counterpart. The term "international Jew" itself spoke to a universality in both the character of the Jew and his conspiracy to control the financial empires of the world. Hence, the American Jew was characterized as a clannish, self-seeking lover of money who, shunning hard physical work, made his financial mark through the use of questionable, albeit shrewd, business practices. He was often overbearing in his manners and in his showy display of wealth, but he could also be overly generous and considerate if it suited his purpose. Finally, the very pervasiveness of his "Jewishness" prevented him from being accepted and assimilated into mainstream America.

The attention given Jews in the popular press corresponded roughly to the ebb and flow of national anti-Semitism. Around the turn of the twentieth century there were relatively few articles, but by the 1920's, when social, economic, and educational discrimination was more widespread and the threat of the New Immigrant was well defined, "the Jewish problem" received extensive coverage. Unlike most articles on other minorities, there was more balance in the kind of treatment provided. The Jews themselves were vocal in their defense, and liberal Gentiles often showed more sympathy for the Jews than they had for other threatened minorities. Nevertheless, many of the articles made it quite clear that the Jew was both racially and religiously different from the older immigrants.

The following selections cover the first four decades of the twentieth century and although each focuses on a different aspect of the Jew, they

253

all have in common the conviction that it was a "Jewish problem" rather than an American one.

A. *HARPER'S WEEKLY* AND THE JEWISH QUESTION, 1902

During the last years of the nineteenth century there were a scatter-ing of articles on the plight of the Russian Jews. While most Americans condemned the pogroms, there was little printed evidence that the country was ready to welcome the refugees. When Harper's Weekly printed the following article in 1902, Secretary of State John Hay had recently expressed his reservations concerning a new wave of Jewish refugees from Eastern Europe, this time from Rumania.[1]

Secretary Hay's note to the powers expressed a strong disrelish of Rou-manian Jewish immigrants forced to this country by religious persecu-tion. According to the census of 1900, there had then entered the United States 15,041 Roumanians, who, we may assume, were chiefly Jews. And the immigration was rapidly increasing. In 1890 it was only 517; in 1898 it had grown to be 900; the following year it was only 1606, but in 1900 it was 6459, and in 1901 it was 7155.

There would be, nevertheless, not so much occasion for alarm from this immigration were it not for the fact that, according to the *Statesman's Year-Book* for 1902, there are 269,015 Roumanian Jews, practically all of whom are inclined to seek refuge in this country from persecution at home, just as did the Russian Jews a few years ago. Our illustrations in-dicate the character of the population which so-called Christian nations in Europe have driven for shelter to the hospitable republic. To say the least of them, these immigrants make very undesirable additions to our heterogeneous population, and their race at home is being made still more so by the drastic, even savage, laws which the Roumanian government is enforcing despite the provisions of the Treaty of Berlin. Moreover, the undesirable immigration, as a whole, has enormously increased. Stated broadly, it constituted a little more than half of the immigration coming between 1890 and 1900, while the percentage of immigration from Can-ada, Germany, Great Britain, Ireland, and Scandinavian countries fell to 41.8 per cent. The significance of these figures may be the better judged when it is remembered that between 1880 and 1890 desirable immigra-tion constituted more than 75 per cent, and undesirable less than 18

[1] "Secretary Hay's Note and the Jewish Question," *Harper's Weekly*, October 11, 1902, p. 1447.

per cent of all coming here; from 1870 to 1880 the rates were 82.8 and 6.4 per cent respectively; from 1860 to 1870, 91.1 and 1.1; and that between 1820 and 1850 only three-tenths of one per cent of our immigrants were from these races.

These people when they arrive are herded at Ellis Island, and then moved out into the American world to shift for themselves. If they would take up unoccupied lands or settle in the West, they would make in time valued citizens, as do the Swedes, Germans, etc. But they do not. They settle largely in New York City, and make the Jewish quarter a strange foreign land. . . . They do not become Americanized. They do not learn English, and they preserve their own customs and ways, which are not in any sense American.

B.   WHY ANTI-SEMITISM? 1908

In 1908, the Independent *published an article by Sydney Reid on possible reasons for American anti-Semitism. The author first asked a rabbi whether anti-Semitism did indeed exist, and after receiving an affirmative reply, he proceeded to quiz various Gentiles on why this was true. The following represented some of their reasons, along with a bit of editorializing on the part of the author.*[1]

It was not easy to get frank testimony. Merchants, officials, hotel men, did not care to speak out. When they spoke at all they stipulated that their names should not be mentioned. It was only by putting many testimonies together that one was enabled to get the Gentile side of the case, which may be fairly presented in this manner:

"We have no prejudice against the Jews. We do dislike them but it is dislike based on knowledge and evidence which is so widespread and so general that it has resulted in an instinctive dislike. It is because of qualities which are manifested by Jews. The dishonest among them are out of all proportion to their numbers. No other people so persistently, shrewdly, cunningly, constantly, skim the very verge of crime, and many go over the verge."

"Police Commissioner Bingham was right in his idea about the large proportion of Jewish criminals, but wrong in the specific charge that he made. He did not mean misdemeanors, as his Hebrew assailants pretend. He meant felonies. In certain crimes where cunning is especially

[1]Sydney Reid, "Because You're a Jew," *Independent*, November 1908, pp. 1212–1217.

needed the Jews furnish most of the criminals, although they are only about one-quarter of the population of New York. Take arson, for instance, arson committed, not by a crazy firebug—some degenerate boy whose insane fancy is pleased by the sight of flames—but arson committed by a cunning shopkeeper who wants to collect insurance on the building and on stock that most likely he has secretly carried away and hidden on the premises of a fellow plotter. That is a typical Jew's crime, and so common among the people that quite recently a number of the insurance companies declared that they would no longer take risks on property owned by men whose names ended in 'ski' or 'sky.' But that was an easy problem for the would be criminals to solve—they simply took other names."

"Take fraudulent bankruptcies accompanied by all sorts of swindling and perjuries. That is another crime in which Jews are pre-eminent.

"Every railroad claim department has its pack of Jewish wolves following it up, with swindling claims put forth by Jewish lawyers for Jewish clients, and bolstered up by false affidavits of Jewish pretended witnesses. There are plenty of Gentile swindlers here, too, but they are not so numerous, so well organized, so clever, so unscrupulous, so well equipped with trained, perjured witnesses. . . ."

"There is another thing against the Jew. They are too prosperous. Where they contest they win. Five or six years ago, after the French Ball, there was a fight and the victor stood over the body of his antagonist and proudly proclaimed: 'The Jew is always on top.' The fact that the man whom he had defeated was also a Jew did not affect the truth he had uttered. The Jew is winning everywhere. By fair means or by foul means he wins. He has the commerce of the city in his hands now, and the signs on Broadway make one think of the main street in New Jerusalem and make Gentiles curse Titus and wish that he had never been born. Why couldn't he leave them alone in Judea? Perhaps he might have stayed there? As to the possibility of a great Zionist movement, it's too good to be true!

"One tentacle of the Hebrew octopus has caught our newspapers now, and we also see Jews running our theaters and giving us a drama that never before was so low. We see the Hebrew octopus seizing one enterprise after the other, and we can't stop it. They are beating us. . . ."

"Two or three Jews at a summer resort utterly spoil the place for the Gentiles. The first thing that the Jew does when he gets in a hotel is to bribe the head waiter. He must have the best steak, the best of everything, and be served first, and he is so persistent, so acute, so eager and so willing to resort to anything to get his way that he does get his way and makes every less strenuous person about him so uncomfortable that they'd sooner leave the place than contend. If he sits at a table near you and you have secured something especially good, his greedy eyes boring into you utterly spoil your repast. If you give your children new toys and send them out to play you will find in half an hour that the Jew children have the new toys while your youngsters are looking on. The young Jews are not violent, but they get what they want by reason of their greater appetite for it. They're insatiable and can only be repressed by force. . . ."

"How foolish, then, to associate with these people when there can by no means be any real assimilation."

That is the way the matter looks to intelligent Gentiles. As to the ignorant among them, the words of the poem put forth his feeling:

> "I do not like you, Dr. Fell,
> The reason why I cannot tell;
> But only this I know right well
> I do not like you, Dr. Fell."

C. THE NEED TO CONVERT JEWS, 1924

By the 1920's, religious voices too were warning of the dangers of un-assimilable outsiders. In the following article, the Missionary Review of the World *urged its readers to realize that their missionary efforts had to be carried to the Jewish immigrants if this country was to succeed in "making America a Christian nation."*[1]

The coming of 4,000,000 Jews to America has shifted the center of Jewish world influence and culture from Eastern Europe to this country. The eyes of the Jews everywhere are now turned to America as a new land of promise where the destiny of their people will be very largely determined. But their coming in such large numbers has created for America itself problems of the most perplexing kind—social, political, national, financial, humanitarian, and religious. With some of these the Christion Church may feel no immediate concern, but no one who knows the Jewish situation will deny that the task of making America a Christian nation will be harder and more protracted because of the multitude of Jews who are here, or that their coming has created a missionary problem of urgent importance. Whether we will or not, our program is bound

[1] John Stuart Conning, "Christian Approach to the Hebrews," *Missionary Review of the World*, October 1924, pp. 830–831.

up with the winning of the Jews. Until we find some way to break down their prejudices and turn the talents and energies of this most virile of peoples into Christian channels, the evangelization of America will proceed with faltering steps. . . .

The significance of these facts for the churches of America is very plain. There is a call of God to do something really worthwhile for this remarkable people. On the bare ground of self-defense far more effort must be put into the task of winning the Jews for Christ. May not the present time of change prove to be, if the Church is really awake, the most fruitful period in all history for their evangelization? From whatever angle we view the Jewish situation it constitutes a direct challenge to the Church.

The prevailing anti-semitism in many European countries, and the evidences of the same spirit here and there in America, make it incumbent upon the churches to oppose all propaganda directed against Jews as unAmerican and alien to the spirit of Christ. We are, moreover, called upon actively and sympathetically to inculcate the spirit of friendliness and good will, and thus redeem the name of "Christian" in the eyes of Jews from association with prejudice, injustice and oppression.

In establishing work in Jewish communities every effort should be made to prevent overlapping. No work should be undertaken in any field occupied by another denomination without direct consultation and in agreement with such denomination. Moreover, in Jewish work, Christian strategy suggests that two or more evangelical denominations could very profitably unite in the establishment and maintenance of centers of evangelism in the larger cities.

As the majority of Jews in America live in residential neighborhoods, and in proximity to Christian churches, an inescapable responsibility rests upon these churches to include Jewish neighbors in their ministry. This is a fruitful field that only recently has begun to be cultivated and which is already yielding rewarding results. Every church which has Jews in its community—even though it be but one family—should enlist in this enterprise and seek to bring the Jews into fellowship with the living Christ. The aggregate of such service would vastly exceed anything that has hitherto been attempted.

Much larger provision should be made for the publication and circulation of literature specially suited to Jewish people. The old literature prepared for orthodox Jews has ceased to be widely effective. A new type of literature of high quality prepared for American Jews is urgently needed. Some combined effort by the churches to meet this need would seem advisable.

Any adequate program of Christian approach to Jews will depend for its success upon the interest and support of the membership of the churches. Every effort should be put forth to have the need of a Christian ministry to the Jews presented in every church. Educational literature should be circulated, setting forth facts concerning the Jews and the obligation of Christians to seek their evangelization.

D. HENRY FORD AND THE INTERNATIONAL JEW

During the 1920's many Americans raised Henry Ford to a level of near deity. He seemed the epitome of the American success story, and his advice was sought and given on subjects far removed from the automobile industry. Ford dabbled rather seriously in politics and, assisted by John Cameron of the Dearborn Independent, *published several books on a variety of subjects. The threat of a Jewish conspiracy, both at home and abroad, held Ford's attention throughout most of the 1920's, particularly after he published his version of the "Protocols of the Elders of Zion," a forged document that insisted that the Jews were going to take over the world through the unlikely combination of capitalism and international communism. The* Dearborn Independent *published its first article on the Jewish threat in 1920 and its last in 1927, when Ford, under the threat of a pending lawsuit, publicly apologized. In the interim the articles had achieved sufficient popularity to warrant their publication in a four-volume work entitled* The International Jew. *The latter achieved the dubious distinction not only of gaining sizable sales at home but many of its passages also found their way into Hitler's* Mein Kampf. *The following passages are from* The International Jew.[1]

The motive of this work is simply a desire to make facts known to the people. Other motives have, of course, been ascribed to it. But the motive of prejudice or any form of antagonism is hardly strong enough to support such an investigation as this. Moreover, had an unworthy motive existed, some sign of it would inevitably appear in the work itself. We confidently call the reader to witness that the tone of these articles is all that it should be. The International Jew and his satellites, as the conscious enemies of all that Anglo-Saxons mean by civilization, are not spared, nor is that unthinking mass which defends anything that a Jew does, simply because it has been taught to believe that what Jewish lead-

---

[1] *The International Jew*, Vol. I, Preface (no author, publisher, or location of publication cited except in Spanish-language edition), pp. iii, 10, 17, 23, 39–40, 214; Vol. IV, pp. 50–51.

ers do is Jewish. Neither do these articles proceed upon a false emotion of brotherhood and apology, as if this stream of doubtful tendency in the world were only accidentally Jewish. We give the facts as we find them; that of itself is sufficient protection against prejudice or passion.

❀   ❀   ❀

The single description which will include a larger percentage of Jews than members of any other race is this: he is in business. It may be only gathering rags and selling them, but he is in business. From the sale of old clothes to the control of international trade and finance, the Jew is supremely gifted for business. More than any other race he exhibits a decided aversion to industrial employment, which he balances by an equally decided adaptability to trade. The Gentile boy works his way up, taking employment in the productive or technical departments; but the Jewish boy prefers to begin as messenger, salesman or clerk—anything—so long as it is connected with the commercial side of business.

❀   ❀   ❀

Unfortunately the element of race, which so easily lends itself to misinterpretation as racial prejudice, is injected into the question by the mere fact that the chain of international finance as it is traced around the world discloses at every link a Jewish capitalist, financial family, or a Jewish-controlled banking system.

❀   ❀   ❀

The main source of the sickness of the German national body is charged to be the influence of the Jews, and although this was apparent to acute minds years ago, it is not said to have gone so far as to be apparent to the least observing. The eruption has broken out on the surface of the body politic, and no further concealment of this fact is possible. It is the belief of all classes of the German people that the collapse which has come since the armistice, and the revolution from which they are being prevented a recovery, are the result of Jewish intrigue and purpose. . . .

Jewish hands were in almost exclusive control of the engines of publicity by which public opinion concerning the German people was molded. The sole winners of the war were Jews.

❀   ❀   ❀

The American Jew does not assimilate. This is stated, not to blame him, but merely as a fact. The Jew could merge with the people of America if he desired, but he doesn't. If there is any prejudice existing against him in America, aside from the sense of injury which his colossal success engenders, it is because of his aloofness. The Jew is not objectionable in his person, creed, or race. His spiritual ideals are shared by the world. But still he does not assimilate; he cultivates by his exclusiveness the feeling that he does not "belong." . . .

To make a list of the lines of business controlled by the Jews of the United States would be to touch most of the vital industries of the country—those which are really vital, and those which cultivated habit has made to seem vital. The theatrical business, of course, as everyone knows, is exclusively Jewish. Play-producing, booking, theater operation are all in the hands of Jews. This perhaps accounts for the fact that in almost every production today can be detected propaganda, sometimes glaringly commercial advertisement, which does not originate with playwrights, but with producers. The motion picture industry. The sugar industry. The tobacco industry. Fifty percent or more of the meat packing industry. Upward of 60 per cent of the shoemaking industry. Men and women's ready-made clothing. Most of the musical purveying done in the country. Jewelry. Grain. More recently, cotton. The Colorado smelting industry. Magazine authorship. News distribution. The liquor business. The loan business. These, only to name the industries with national and international sweep, are in control of the Jews of the United States, either alone or in association with Jews overseas.

                ❃   ❃   ❃

The most persistent denials have been offered to the statement that Bolshevism everywhere, in Russia or the United States, is Jewish. In these denials we have perhaps one of the most brazen examples of the double intent referred to above. The denial of the Jewish character of Bolshevism is made to the Gentile; but in the confidence and secrecy of Jewish communication, or buried in the Yiddish dialect, or obscurely hidden in the Jewish national press, we find the proud assertion made—to their own people!—that Bolshevism is Jewish.

                ❃   ❃   ❃

The only absolute antidote to the Jewish influence is to call college students back to a pride of race. We often speak of the Fathers as if they were the few who happened to affix their signatures to a great document which marked a new era of liberty. The Fathers were the men of the Anglo-Saxon-Celtic race. The men who came across Europe with civilization in their blood and in their destiny; the men who crossed the Atlantic and set up civilization on a bleak and rock-bound coast; the men who drove West to California and north to Alaska; the men who peopled Australia and seized the gates of the world at Suez, Gilbraltar and Panama; the men who opened the tropics and subdued the arctics—Anglo-Saxon men, who have given form to every government and a livelihood to every people and an ideal to every century. They got neither their God nor their religion from Judah, nor yet their speech nor their creative genius—they are the Ruling People, Chosen throughout the centuries to Master the world, by Building it ever better and better and not by breaking it down.

E. THE *CHRISTIAN CENTURY*, JEWS, AND DEMOCRACY, 1937

Although the Christian Century *has long been an organ of liberal opinion, it seemed to surprise the editors when a series of its articles on American Jews inspired a storm of protest from these Jews. The* Christian Century *condemned anti-Semitism in all forms, but it also insisted that the Jews themselves were in no small way guilty of producing this same anti-Semitism. This editorial was in answer to some of the criticism, and it reiterated the earlier views of the editors.*[1]

The situation in which the Jewish problem arises is in large measure Jewry's own creation. In other connections this paper has analyzed Christianity's cruel share of the total responsibility for the suffering that has been heaped upon Israel in Western Civilization. At the present moment the discussion is pointed in another direction. We hold that the Jew himself is responsible, in a high degree, and that no solution of his problem is possible until his own degree of responsibility is recognized. The first step toward its recognition is to discern that his determination to maintain a permanent racial status is incompatible with democracy. Only then can he confront the root cause of his trouble and deal with it.

And what is this root cause? The answer must be almost surgical in its sharpness. The root cause of the Jewish problem is the Jew's immemorial and pertinacious obsession with an illusion, the illusion that his race, his people, are the object of the special favor of God, who requires the maintenance of their racial integrity and separateness as the medium through which, soon or late, will be performed some mighty act involving human destiny. This is a highly generalized statement of the Jewish illusion. It purposely avoids specific details over which there is difference of opinion in Jewry itself. These details are irrelevant, for what concerns us is the attitude which this obsession induces in the Jewish community, and the inevitable human reaction on the part of any general community to this attitude.

From pre-Christian days the Jews belief in their divinely hallowed racial uniqueness provoked unfavorable reaction. And despite the unspeakable guilt of historic Christianity in this matter, the fact remains that the Jewish problem of today is rooted not chiefly in religious soil, but in the soil of common human psychology. Unregenerate human nature bluntly says, in effect: If this racial group feels that way about itself,

[1]Reprinted by permission of The Christian Century Foundation from "Jewry and Democracy," *Christian Century*, June 9, 1937, pp. 735–736.

and insists upon living apart in biological and cultural, as well as religious, aloofness, let it take the consequences! . . .

How can the vicious circle be broken by Jewish initiative? In only one way, as it seems to us, namely, for prophets to arise in Judaism who will begin to proclaim the terrible truth: that Judaism has been feeding its racial pride for millenniums on an illusion; that its martyrdom is in large measure self-invited; that its racial integrity is no more important in God's sight than any other race's integrity; that race is of so little importance in God's sight that he has not preserved the integrity of a single people now living, including the Jewish people; and that "God is able of these stones to raise up children unto Abraham."

Such prophets, if they shall arise in Jewry, will point out that it is just this obsession with the doctrine of a covenant race that now menaces the whole world, and that the Jews themselves are the chief sufferers from it. Their idea of an integral race, with its own exclusive culture, hallowed and kept unified by a racial religion, is itself the prototype of nazism. The Jewish position in American democracy may be visualized, in principle, by imagining five million Germans, held together in racial and cultural unity by the Hitler doctrine of the folkic soul, transported to America, established in our democratic land as the Jews now are, and determined to maintain their racial doctrine and their racial separateness.

F.   FATHER COUGHLIN AND THE INTERNATIONAL JEW, 1939

Like Henry Ford, Father Charles Coughlin saw Jews as synonymous with the international conspiracy that was trying to destroy his America. Although his Social Justice *probably did not exceed a circulation of about 300,000, his Sunday radio broadcasts were carried by more than forty stations and reached a listening audience that numbered in the millions. It was not until 1938 that Coughlin linked the Jew to the economic woes of the country, but thereafter until September, 1940, the Royal Oak (Mich.) priest found this an increasingly popular thing to do. The following radio speech was delivered on January 29, 1939 and was later published in a book entitled* Why Leave Our Own.[1]

For many months, unfortunately, the attention of Americans has been focused upon the European situation. To students of international affairs it was evident that a victory for the Spanish Communists would

[1]Father Charles Coughlin, *Why Leave Our Own*, Inland Press, Detroit, 1939, pp. 46–49.

have definite repercussions in France, England and in the United States. Had the Red forces in Spain been victorious, the Government of Daladier in France would have fallen and a leftist regime under the leadership of Leon Blum [a Jew] would have risen to power; the pacific Administration of Neville Chamberlain would have given way to one headed by Leslie Hore-Belisha [a Jew], the present Minister of War for Great Britain.

As for the United States, an open alliance by this time would have been declared with these two radical Administrations which have as their advertised objective the destruction of Naziism in Germany and the preservation of democracy. Informed persons are aware, however, that their ultimate aim is to establish a modified form of Communism. . . .

Let me outline for you the basic developments which almost catapulted us into the Spanish war—developments which, if not checked, will succeed in embroiling us in the impending world war.

Some months ago, when the persecution of the Jews in Germany was the chief topic of the day, I had occasion to invite the religious Jews of the United States to join with us in a crusade to end all persecution, both of Jews and Christians. In making my plea, I was careful to distinguish atheistic Jews from religious Jews. I regretted that callous silence in the press and on the radio has permitted the assassination of millions of Christians to go unnoticed. I rejoiced that extraordinary publicity was given to the persecuted Jews in Germany.

It was also pointed out that if Jews rightly challenged Christians for their sympathy against Nazi persecution, it was logical for Christians to challenge Jews for theirs against Communist persecution—particularly when so many atheistic Jews had played such a prominent part in the birth and organization of radicalism in Russia.

Following these broadcast statements I became the subject of discussion and the object of attack in every Jewish magazine and in many secular publications. The assertions which I made, namely, that Naziism was a defense mechanism set up again Communism, and that atheistic Jews were altogether too prominent in the promotion of Communism —these assertions were denied. But of most importance, the invitation which I extended to the Jews of America to join officially with the Christians in stamping out Communism has gone unheeded. . . .

It was November 20, 1938, when I broadcast the proposal to American Jews to take sides with American Christians in liquidating all persecution. It was only then that I observed that the atrocities committed by the Communists against Christians were exceedingly more serious than those suffered by the Jews at the hands of Nazis. At that time—less than three months ago—I also had occasion to observe that the well publicized persecution of Jews in Germany was remarkable in that not one Jew was put to death officially for his race or religion. In comparison with this, more than twenty million Christians had been done to death under the Trotskys and Bela Kuns of Communism, both of whom are Jews. . . .

On that date I was shocked to learn how far-reaching and international in scope the unsound Semitism of certain Jews extended. It was a Semitism which confused race and nationality. Because their co-racials in Germany were suffering from the persecutions of the Nazi Government —co-racials and co-religionists who were not co-nationals of the Jews in the United States—I was shocked when certain American Jews entertained the idea that the resources of this and other nations should be employed against the Hitler Government on the principle that the entire world should go to war on behalf of German Jews to settle an internal problem in Germany.

2

The Jews and
the Scientists

The Jew presented somewhat of a problem to the many scholars who stressed "racial" differences to the disadvantage of a particular minority. First they had to establish the Jews as a race rather than as a religious entity, and this was not always easy to do. Jews could be found in all parts of the world and they often looked more like the people with whom they lived than like a separate race. The fact too that many Jews insisted on only a religious designation rather than a cultural or racial one further complicated the problem. Finally there was the fact that most scholars found the Jew to be highly intelligent and not at all at a disadvantage when pitted against old-stock Americans in any kind of competitive situation. Thus, certain personality traits were attributed to Jews and used to differentiate them from other men. It was even suggested that these personality traits could affect their appearance and improve their intelligence.

A. A HARVARD DEAN AND "THE HEBREW PROBLEM," 1904

The question of Jewish characteristics has long perplexed Western man. In 1904, Nathaniel Southgate Shaler, the dean of Harvard University's Lawrence Scientific School, published The Neighbor, *a study in human relations. In a chapter entitled "The Hebrew Problem," he attempted to explain the Gentile's antipathy toward the Jew. He determined that the very way Jews first met strangers was likely to inspire an unfavorable response on the part of the latter. He also concluded that the Jew, unlike the "imitative Negro," was unable to change his customs and habits to fit those of the majority culture.*[1]

The greater number of the observers agree that there is a failure on the part of the Jews to respond in like temper to the greeting which they send them; they agree further that there is generally a sense of avidity, a sense of the presence of a seeking in the Jew for immediate profit, a desire to win at once some advantage from the situation such as is not immediately disclosed, however clear it might be in the mind of an interlocutor of his own race. Several have stated that the offense came from a feeling that the Jew neighbor was smarter than themselves, having keener wits and a mind more intent on gainful ends. Others state that the Israelitic spirit makes a much swifter response to the greeting the stranger gives them than the Aryan, and that the acquaintance is forced in such an irritating manner as to breed dislike.

This last noted feature in the contact phenomena of Israelites and Aryans appears to me a matter of much importance, especially as it accords with my own experience and with observations formed long before I began to devise and criticise theories on this subject. As one of the Deans of Harvard University I have been for ten years in a position where I have to meet from year to year a number of young Hebrews. It has been evident to me from the first that these youths normally respond much more swiftly to my greeting than those of my own race, and that they divine and act on my state of mind with far greater celerity. They are, in fact, so quick that they are often where I am in my slower way about to be before I am really there; this would make them at times seem irritating, indeed, presumptuous, were it not interesting to me from a racial point of view. To those who are in no wise concerned with such questions this alacrity is naturally exasperating, especially when the movement is not only of the wits but of the sympathies. We all know how disagreeable it is to have the neighbor call on us for some kind of affectionate response before we are ready to be moved, and how certain is such a summons to dry the springs which else might have yielded abundantly. In our slow Aryan way we demand an introductory process on the part of the fellow-man who would successfully appeal to our emotions. Our orators know this and provide ample exordiums for their moving passages; none ventures in the manner of the Hebrew prophet to assume that his hearers will awaken at a cry. . . .

It appears to me from my own observations, from those of the se-

[1]Nathaniel Southgate Shaler, *The Neighbor; The Natural History Of Human Contacts*, Houghton, Mifflin & Co., Boston, 1904, pp. 110–125.

lected persons who have aided me, as well as from the history of the Jews, that their minds work in a somewhat different manner from our own. Our habit is to separate the fields of action so that we have a limited field for preliminary intercourse with men, another for business relations, yet another wherein the sympathies may enter. With the Hebrew all the man's work is done in one field and all together; he is at the same time friend, trader, and citizen, all of his parts working simultaneously. There is a basis for much friction in this diversity of mental habit. We are naturally offended to find the business motive mingled with affections, for the excellent reason that it is not our way to do this; therefore it appears out of the natural order; were we to change nature with the Jew the offense would be none the less. . . .

It is instructive to contrast the lack of a tendency to imitation in the Jews with the excess of it among the American Africans. Although I have watched Jews closely for many years, I have never seen in them the least disposition to adapt themselves to their neighbors as a Negro quickly and instinctively does. The black man at once becomes the mirror of his superior whether the man above him is his master or not. He so naturally imitates the tones, gestures, and even the superficial aspects of thought of our race, that those alone who have taken pains to search behind the sympathetic mask perceive that he is not a white man in a black skin, but that his deeper nature in many and most important regards is profoundly different from all the other peoples with whom we have intimate relations. This spontaneous imitative humor has stood the Negroes in good stead. It has enabled them to win past the original antipathy which their physical peculiarities tend to arouse in vastly greater measure than those of the Hebrews, and to make the whites who are accustomed to them their friends. This curious identification, the most complete that has ever taken place between two widely parted stocks, is clearly due to the unpremeditated and singularly well-accomplished adoption by the Negroes of the white man's ways.

B.   A WELL-KNOWN ANATOMIST EXAMINES
THE JEWISH NOSE, 1913

For some three decades the University of Virginia's Robert Bennett Bean stood as one of this country's leading authorities on the identification of races through anatomy, and he felt the "Jewish nose" to be a distinguishing racial characteristic. Bean also accepted an accentuated Jewish facial expression. The idea of a uniquely Jewish facial appearance

did not originate with Professor Bean, but he alone attempted to use
the proverbial Jewish nose to explain the unique face.[1]

The peculiar position of the Jew for centuries may account for the origin of the Jewish nose. The shape of the nose depends upon inherent and extraneous influences. The latter do not concern us at present. Of the inherent influences, alterations in the bones of the head and face cause change in the shape of the nose; increased vascularization of the nasal mucus membrane and the erectile tissues of the nose, as in continued excessive sexual indulgence, may alter the shape of the nose; and the muscles attached to the nose may change its form.

The *quadratus labii superioris* muscle has four parts, all of which center around the alae of the nose and the base of the upper lip, and from there they radiate toward the eyes in the shape of an imperfect fan. . . . Assisted by the great zygomatic muscle and the caninus, the quadratus draws the tissues covering the chin upward and backward, pulls the corner of the mouth in the same direction and deepens the naso-labial groove. This sharpens the chin and makes it appear to tilt upward in the form of a beak. The depression of the point of the nose tilts this member downward and gives it the appearance of an inverted beak. The mouth is at the same time drawn back, and the double beak becomes more emphatic.

The quadratus muscle is said to produce expressions of the face that indicate a great variety of emotions, all of which may be grouped as related to indignation. It is essentially the muscle of disgust, contempt, and disdain, which lead to scorn, acknowledging guilt. Discontent follows, with a snarl, sneer, and defiance; after which come bitterness, and a menacing attitude, with pride. Indignation, anger, rage, and hatred rapidly succeed one another. This complex of emotions may be superseded by sadness, grief, or sorrow. That one small muscle group can express so many emotions is almost inconceivable, but an intimate analysis of the nineteen words used to enumerate the emotions expressed by the quadratus muscle are related, or proceed the one from the other in natural sequence.

The expression of the Jew is that which would result from very strong contraction of the quadratus muscle. The nose is depressed, and this is so marked that often an obtuse angle is made at the junction of the cartilage and nasal bones, which leaves the cartilage slanting very little and

[1]Robert Bennett Bean, "The Nose of the Jew and the Quadratus Labii Superioris Muscle," *American Anthropologist*, January, 1913, pp. 106–108.

at times vertical. The nose of the Jew is large, and the depression of the tip increases the prominence of the bridge and adds to its apparent size. The ala looks pulled upward and backward, a furrow is seen around the ala, and the naso-labial groove is deep. The upper lip and the corner of the mouth appear pulled upward and backward, and the tissues of the chin are drawn, giving the beaked look. This characteristic is not well marked on all Jews, being more emphatic on some than on others; it is also to be seen on those who are not Jews, but it is more pronounced on Jews than on other peoples, and that it is a Jewish feature cannot be doubted. Having become a recognizable characteristic, it was used in sexual selection. Those who showed it most strongly would be selected in marriage by the most orthodox, and would transmit a natural endowment to their offspring. Those who gave less evidence of it might marry outside the race. In this way the feature became fixed, and it is as much an inheritance as any other characteristic. The peculiar position of the Jew for centuries may account for the origin of the Jewish nose.

C.   AN ANTHROPOLOGICAL EXPLANATION OF THE FACIAL ASPECT OF THE JEW, 1916

Dean Shaler and others referred to the particular expression that seemed to characterize the Jewish face. Some scientists suggested that it was biological, while others insisted that it was acquired, but all agreed that it was peculiarly Jewish. The following article appeared in Current Opinion *magazine in 1916 and contributed to the growing fund of information that distinguished between Jew and non-Jew.[1]*

It is quite clear to Doctor Louis D. Covitt, of Clark University, that the facial expression of the Jew is a true character from the standpoint of heredity, and that therefore, the inner psychic personality of the race, of which it is only the outward manifestation, is likewise true and fundamental. What has caused the Jewish expression? Some think it is largely a result of long exile and social isolation, as one investigator, Jacobs, suggests. Ripley thinks it a matter of artificial selection. Fishberg thinks much of it is due to costume and the like. If we keep in mind that the race is the totality of all the elements that have played a part in history, we can easily see that the expression is a reflection of all the forces that have shaped the destiny of the Jewish people. . . .

The characteristic Jewish expression, which even Ripley, Fishberg and

[1]"Anthropological Explanation of the Facial Aspect of the Jew," *Current Opinion*, September, 1916, p. 178.

Weissenberg do not deny, is, as Fishberg thinks, "the expression of the Jewish soul"; but, unlike him, we maintain that it is the most potent determining factor for each and every race, that it is by far the best guide for distinguishing one race from the other; and while physical characters fail, being as they are subject to environment, physiological, and other changes, it persists in spite of all outward changes.

The persistence of the Jewish type is shown in Galton's composite photograph of a number of Jewish boys from a school for Jews in London. The typical Jewish expression is remarkably displayed. This typical Jewish expression, says Doctor Covitt, is not the result solely of Ghetto life, nor is it a result of artificial selection, nor can dress and social surroundings change it. These things may make it less accentuated, but the features cannot be demolished:

"In a word, it is not, in our mind, the result of any one thing, but it is a fusion of all the elements that made the Jew as we know him today. If we were asked to give those elements we would name them as follows: the sublimity and righteous indignation of the prophets and scribes; the pathos and tragedy of ages of persecution and martyrdom; the cunning and shrewdness that is characteristic of all people who have to live by their wits; a shade of anger or resentment. Finally, we see in the Jewish expression the calculation, coldness and scanning which so struck Galton and which we think is a result of long experience in financial operations. All these elements have by long use and repetition fused and become hereditary. The non-uniformity of expression among the different members of the race are [is] due to differences of individual experience."

Comparison of the ability of Jews with Gentiles confirms, apparently, the theory that the facial aspect of the Jewish is due to race, that it is an anthropological fact and not a mere accident. Thus statistics indicate a preponderance of Jewish excellence as actors, doctors, financiers, philosophers, musicians, philologists, poets; a slight excess as antiquarians, in natural science and in political economy. The Jews are below the highest standard in agriculture, novel writing, divinity, engraving, military and naval science, as sovereigns, statesmen and travelers. They are slightly below as painters, engineers and lawyers. They are about as good as Gentiles in the capacity of architects, scientists and sculptors.

D. PRINCETON'S CARL BRIGHAM AND JEWISH INTELLIGENCE

Although most psychologists either ignored or admitted the Jew's intellectual abilities, Princeton psychologist Carl Brigham found them to be inferior to old American stock. In 1923, Brigham published a book entitled American Intelligence, *which was based largely on the intelligence tests that the United States Army administered during World War I. Brigham reasoned that because the Russian-Americans scored lower on the intelligence tests than any other immigrants except those from Italy and Poland, and because over half of the Russian-Americans were Jewish, the popular belief of high Jewish intelligence was untrue.*[1]

It is unfortunate that our army data classify foreign born individuals only by country of origin, so that we have no separate intelligence distributions for the Jews. According to the 1910 census, about 50% of the foreign born population reporting Russia as their country of origin spoke Hebrew or Yiddish, about 25% spoke Polish, less than 3% spoke Russian, and the rest spoke Lithuanian, Lettish, German, Finnish, Ruthenian and other tongues. From the immigration statistics showing aliens admitted classified according to race or people, we find about 10% (arriving between 1900 and 1920) reported as Hebrew. It is fair to assume that our army sample of immigrants from Russia is at least one half Jewish, and that the sample we have selected as Alpine is from one fifth to one fourth Jewish.

Our figures, then, would rather tend to disprove the popular belief that the Jew is highly intelligent. Immigrants examined in the army, who report their birthplace as Russia, had an average intelligence below those from all other countries except Poland and Italy. It is perhaps significant to note, however, that the sample from Russia has a higher standard deviation (2.83) than that of any other immigrant group sampled, and that the Alpine group has a higher standard deviation than the Nordic or Mediterranean groups (2.60). If we assume that the Jewish immigrants have a low average intelligence, but a higher variability than other nativity groups, this would reconcile our figures with popular belief, and, at the same time, with the fact that investigators searching for talent in New York City and California schools find a frequent occurrence of talent among Jewish children. The able Jew is popularly recognized not only because of his ability, but because he is able and a Jew.

[1]Reprinted by permission of Princeton University Press from Carl C. Brigham, *A Study of American Intelligence*, Princeton University Press, Princeton. Copyright 1922 by Carl C. Brigham, pp. 189–190.

3
The Jew as
Literary Symbol

The Jew has long suffered from literary stereotyping. He was type-cast early in European letters, and this characterization later followed him to the New World. Most students are familiar with the greedy ma-nipulations of a Shylock or the peripatetic wanderings of the Jewish peddler. Greed and business adroitness were synonymous with tradi-tional Jewish types, but in the early twentieth century the Jew took on a different image for some American writers. He became the symbol of the social and moral disintegration that they felt marked the mechanistic age. Traditional values were disappearing before the onslaught of a ma-terialistic society that measured everything with a monetary yardstick, and symptomatic of the disease was the nouveau riche with his bad man-ners, crude business tactics, and social-climbing aspirations.

Authors like Henry Adams, Edith Wharten, Willa Cather, T. S. Eliot, Ezra Pound, and Thomas Wolfe used the Jew to symbolize this disinte-grating society. They found Jews everywhere—in the universities and art galleries, in private clubs and exclusive neighborhoods, but, above all, in control of the marketplace. To be sure, a Jewish character might have extremely negative qualities and still be honestly drawn, but when all Jews become a single character or a symbol for a diseased society, it rep-resents something less than literary integrity.

A. HENRY ADAMS AND THE UBIQUITOUS JEW

In the twilight of his life Henry Adams tried to return to a time when man had not vulgarized himself through shallow materialistic endeavors. Tradition was naturally strong in a man who represented the fourth gen-

eration of one of America's most illustrious families, and Adams proved painfully unwilling or incapable of accepting the social and economic changes that marked the late nineteenth century. Like other later writers he found a ready scapegoat in the ubiquitous Jew. In his travels Adams increasingly wrote of "a Jewish atmosphere" that seemed to mark the disintegration of a particular city or country. The following are excerpts taken from his travel letters during the last years of his life.[1]

(To Elizabeth Cameron, July 25, 1895)

. . . In London, I admit, it harmonizes well with the oceanic vulgarity which impresses me more and more every time I return to these haunts. The tide has now pretty well submerged everything. Between British taste and Jew taste, nothing survives untouched. The thing is stupendous. It awes me. It fascinates and scares me. I am going insane with it.

(To John Hay, May 5, 1898)

. . . Vienna is the most changed spot I have yet struck. I recognize nothing. It is practically all new since 1859 when I was last here. It bores me, of course, for it is wholly Americanised and Judaised [sic].

(To Charles Milnes Gaskell, June, 1899)

I can't find a tolerable piece of Chinese porcelain in Paris. I see none of the books I care for, or did care for, once. There are a thousand bric-a-brac dealers, and all have hopeless rubbish, except three or four Jews who force up prices by cornering fashions. Anything these Jews touch is in some strange way vulgarized. One does not want it any more. It has become a trade—the equivalent of a certificate for South African stock,— and one buys to sell again.

(To Elizabeth Cameron, Sept. 18, 1899)

But our interests require that the Boers should be brought into our system, and so we must kill them till they come; because all England and all America and all the Transvaal are a Jew interest,—that is, a great capitalist machine,—and we must run it, no matter whom it hurts. So we try to run the French army, in Jew interests, and we shall ultimately break it down, no doubt, as well as we shall break down the Boers.

[1]Reprinted by permission of Houghton Mifflin Company from Worthington Chauncey Ford, Ed., *Letters of Henry Adams*, 1892–1918, Vol. II, Houghton Mifflin Co., Boston, 1938, pp. 74, 175, 232, 241, 338, 620.

(To Elizabeth Cameron, Warsaw, August 14, 1901)

We had the pleasure of seeing at last the Polish Jew, and he was a startling revelation even to me, who have seen *pas mal de Jew*. The country is not bad; on the contrary, it is a good deal like our plains, more or less sandy, but well watered. It is the people that make one tired. . . . Warsaw is a big, bustling city, like all other cities, only mostly Jew, in which it is peculiar to Poland. I see little to remark in the streets; nothing in the shops. The people are uglier than on Pennsylvania Avenue which is otherwise my lowest standard. Like all other cities and places, it is evidently flattened out, and has lost most of its characteristics. The Jews and I are the only curious antiquities in it. My only merit as a curio is antiquity, but the Jew is also a curiosity. He makes me creep.

(To Charles Milnes Gaskell, Washington, Feb. 19, 1914)

The winter is nearly over, I am seventy-six years old, and nearly over too. As I go, my thoughts turn towards you and I want to know how you are. Of myself, I have almost nothing to tell. It is quite astonishing how the circle narrows. I think that in reality as many people pass by, and I hear as much as I ever did, but it is no longer a part of me. I am inclined to think it not wholly my fault. The atmosphere really has become a Jew atmosphere. It is curious and evidently good for some people, but it isolates me. I do not know the language, and my friends are as ignorant as I. We are still in power, after a fashion. Our sway over what we call society is undisputed. We keep Jews far away, and the anti-Jew feeling is quite rabid. We are anti-everything and we are wild uplifters; yet we somehow seem to be more Jewish every day. This is not my own diagnosis. I make none. I care not a straw what happens provided the fabric lasts a few months more; but will it do so?

B.   JOHN PEALE BISHOP'S "THIS IS THE MAN," 1933

John Peale Bishop was an American poet and essayist of the interwar period. In the 1920's he served as managing editor of Vanity Fair. *His poetry touched a wide variety of subjects and Jews did not make up a recurring theme in his work; nevertheless the following poem is noteworthy for its classic portrayal of the "eternal Jew."*[1]

[1]"This Is The Man" is reprinted by permission of Charles Scribner's Sons from *Now with His Love* by John Peale Bishop. Copyright 1933 Charles Scribner's Sons; renewal copyright © 1961 Margaret G. H. Bronson.

THIS IS THE MAN

This is the man who bore his shoulders hunched
And arched his backbone like an angry cat;
He also wore, derisively, a hat,
A low black Jewish hat, battered and punched
Out of all argument, with his ears conched
     Beneath it, small and strangely disparate;
     His lips skimmed back upon a smile that spat
Between his toothpick and a tooth. He scrunched

Along the pathway toward us and without
     Lifting his feet went past us with the smile
          Still pinned there by the toothpick and
Just at that moment turned. Semitic snout
     Returned and upturned eyes came back, and while
          I stared there speechless bent and kissed your hand.

C. THOMAS WOLFE AND THE JEW AS STUDENT
AND SENSUOUS WOMAN, 1935

Thomas Wolfe's Of Time and the River *rose to number three on the bestseller lists for 1935. The story is the autobiographical second volume in the continuing saga of Eugene Gant. The story is long and rambling but contains some interesting character sketches in the varied settings of Harvard, New York, and Europe. After completing his degree at Harvard, Eugene Gant took a teaching position at a predominantly Jewish college in New York. There the city became synonymous with "the struggle of man against the multitude," and its people were "the mindless and unwitting automatons of a gigantic and incomprehensible pattern." The young Gant had "the sense of drowning daily in the man-swarm," and his Jewish students became the very essence of the stifling oppression the city held for him. One of his students, Abe Jones, is a caricature of the whining, overly aggressive Jew who must at all costs succeed. His female students were also crudely assertive, but their aggressiveness was tied to their sensuality, a sensuality that engulfed and overwhelmed the young Gant.*[1]

[1]Reprinted by permission of Charles Scribner's Sons from *Of Time and the River* by Thomas Wolfe, pp. 419, 456–457, 468, 478–479. Copyright 1935 by Charles Scribner's Sons; renewal copyright © 1963 by Paul Gitlin, Administrator, C.T.A.

Already, when he had first met Abe Jones in the first class he taught, the process of mutation had carried so far that he was trying to rid himself of the accursed "Abraham," reducing it to an ambiguous initial, and signing his papers with a simple unrevealing "A. Jones," as whales are said to have lost through atrophy the use of legs with which they once walked across the land, but still to carry upon their bodies the rudimentary stump. How, in the last year, he had dared to make a final transformation, shocking, comical, pitifully clumsy in its effort at concealment and deception; when Eugene had tried to find his name and number in the telephone directory a month before, among the great gray regiment of Joneses, the familiar, quaint, and homely "Abe" had disappeared—at length he found him coyly sheltered under the gentlemanly obscurity of A. Alfred Jones. The transformation, thus, had been complete: he was now, in name, at any rate, a member of the great Gentile aristocracy of Jones; and just as "Jones" had been thrust by violence upon his father, so had Abe taken violently, by theft and rape, the "Alfred." There was something mad and appalling in the bravado, the effrontery, and the absurdity of the attempt: what did he hope to do with such a name? . . . That he should hope actually to palm himself off as a Gentile was unthinkable, because one look at him revealed instantly the whole story of his race and origin: if all the Polish-Russian Jews that ever swarmed along the ghettoes of the earth had been compacted in a single frame the physical result might have been something amazingly like Eugene's friend, Abraham Jones.

The whole flag and banner of his race was in the enormous putty-colored nose that bulged, flared and sprouted with the disproportionate extravagance of a caricature or a dill-pickle over his pale, slightly freckled and rather meagre face; he had a wide, thin, somewhat cruel-looking mouth, dull weak eyes that stared, blinked, and grew misty with a murky, somewhat slimily ropy feeling behind his spectacles, a low, dull, and slanting forehead, almost reptilian in its ugliness, that sloped painfully back an inch or two into the fringes of unpleasantly greasy curls and coils of dark, short, screwy hair. He was about the middle height, and neither thin nor fat: his figure was rather big-boned and angular, and yet it gave an impression of meagreness, spareness, and somewhat tallowy toughness which so many city people have, as if their ten thousand days and nights upon the rootless pavement had dried all juice and succulence out of them. . . .

Such a man was Abe Jones when Eugene first knew him: dreary, tortured, melancholy, dully intellectual and joylessly poetic, his spirit gloomily engulfed in a great cloud of Yiddish murk, a gray pavement cipher, an atom of the slums, a blind sea-crawl in the drowning tides of the man-swarm, and yet, pitifully, tremendously, with a million other dreary

Hebrew yearners, convinced that he was the messiah for which the earth was groaning.

* * *

At night, when he went to bed in his little cell at the cheap little hotel nearby where he lived, the thought of the class he had to meet the next day fed at his heart and bowels with cold poisonous mouths of fear, and as the hour for a class drew nigh he would begin to shake and tremble as if he had an ague; the successive stages of his journey from his room in the Leopold, to the class room at the university a few hundred yards away—from cell to elevator, from the tiled sterility of the hotel lobby to the dusty beaten light and violence of the street outside, thence to the brawling and ugly corridors of the university, which drowned one, body and soul, with their swarming, shrieking, shouting tides of dark amber Jewish flesh, and thence into the comparative sanctuary of the class room with its smaller horde of thirty or forty Jews and Jewesses, all laughing, shouting, screaming, thick with their hot and swarthy body-smells, their strong female odors of rut and crotch and arm-pit and cheap perfume, and their hard male smells that were rancid, stale, and sour. . . .

Their dark flesh had in it the quality of a merciless tide which not only overwhelmed and devoured but withdrew with a powerful sucking glut all rich deposits of the earth it fed upon; they had the absorptive quality of a sponge, the power of a magnet, the end of each class left him sapped, gutted, drained, and with a sense of sterility, loss, and defeat, and in addition to this exhaustion of the mind and spirit, there was added a terrible weariness and frustration of the flesh: the potent young Jewesses, thick, hot, and heavy with a female odor, swarmed around him in a sensual tide, they leaned above him as he sat there at his table, pressing deliberately the crisp nozzles of their melon-heavy breasts against his shoulder, slowly, erotically they moved their bellies in to him, or rubbed the heavy contours of their thighs against his legs; they looked at him with moist red lips through which their wet red tongues lolled wickedly, and they sat upon the front rows of the class in garments cut with too extreme a style of provocation and indecency, staring up at him with eyes of round lewd innocence, cocking their legs with a shameless and unwitting air, so that they exposed the banded silken ruffle of their garters and the ripe heavy flesh of their underlegs.

4
Social, Economic, and Educational Racism

Like most of our minorities, Jews have often faced social, economic, and educational discrimination. Already by the late nineteenth century, Jews were denied admittance to certain exclusive Eastern resorts and private clubs, and this kind of discrimination became worse in the twentieth century. In the economic sphere, not only did classified ads often exclude Jews, but employment agencies and the companies themselves regularly turned down applicants on the basis of their looks or the sound of their names. In education, it was the private schools and universities that discriminated against Jewish students—although admittedly not because they lacked ability. By the 1920's some of America's finest colleges had introduced a quota system that lasted until well into the 1960's.

A. THE RESORT TRADE

Although a prominent New York banker by the name of Joseph Seligman was refused accommodations at the Grand Union Hotel in Saratoga Springs in 1877, resort discrimination was much more a twentieth-century phenomenon. A casual sampling of the resort ads shows an increase in restrictions during the 1920's. A reading of the New York Times' *resort ads on a given Sunday in 1928 shows that about 15% of them openly discriminated against Jews. Twenty years later such overt ads had disappeared from the* Times, *although such phrases as "American table," "American cuisine," "distinguished clientele," "congenial clientele," and "Protestant and Catholic churches nearby" made the point almost as well.*

In the Midwest, discriminatory ads came somewhat later, but a 1940

279

reading of the Chicago Tribune *resort ads for Michigan and Wisconsin shows that more than one third of them openly excluded Jews. Two years later, in the midst of America's war against Hitler's racism, more than one third of the Michigan ads still listed restricted clientele.*

1. *The following ads are from the* New York Times, *July 15, 1928.*[1]

BLODGETT LODGE
LAKE SUNAPEE
Featuring every indoor and outdoor sport. College Orchestra. Elevation 1100 feet. All rooms with hot and cold running water. Rates, including meals, $21 to $30 per week. Christian ownership.

MONMOUTH BEACH HOTEL
Monmouth Beach, N.J.
OPENS JUNE 21, 1928
Commuting distance from New York, rail or water. A high-class hotel catering exclusively to refined, restricted clientele. Acceptable season guests enjoy privilege of membership in Monmouth Beach Club, the special centre of this splendid Summer colony. Christian house.

BEAR ISLAND HOUSE
LAKE WINNIPESAUKEE,
NEW HAMPSHIRE
Famous for years; bathing, fishing, boating, tennis; own farm produce; $3.50 day; $17.50 up wkly; Gentile house.

AVON INN
Avon-by-the-Sea, N.J.
NOW OPEN
Every Room Has Hot And
Cold Running Water
ENTIRE BLOCK ON
THE OCEAN FRONT
Five miles of Continuous Boardwalk, Dancing, Tennis, Boating, Golf. Bathing directly from your room. Catering to a carefully selected clientele.

THE
LAFAYETTE
ASBURY PARK, N.J.
A HOTEL OF DISTINCTION
Ocean and Lake View; Select Clientels; Capacity 300; White Service; Orchestra, Elevator. Tel. 1434.

---

2. *The following advertisements are from the* Chicago Tribune, *July 7, 1940.*

FOR RENT—AT LAKESIDE, MICH.
Modern cottages—2 on Lake—6 for rent for season. Gentiles only.

WILLOW BROOK FARM
Ideal farm resort. Mod. Plumb; good beds; exc. eats: milk, eggs, vegetables, etc. Gentiles. $12 week.

RIVER BLUFF FARM
Coolest spot in South Haven. Modern resort, all comforts, amusements. Large, beautiful grounds. Home cooking, baking. $14 wk. Gentiles.

SABLE INN—Hamlin Lake
Ludington, Mich.
FAMOUS FOR ITS WONDERFUL
MEALS
Exceptionally good beds. Fine fishing and bathing. Modern conveniences, Golf, Horseback riding, Dancing, Water Skiing, Tennis, Boats, Archery, etc.
Rates, $22, $25, $30 per week. Racial restrictions.

FERN PARK—Upper Scott Lake,
Pullman
Housekeeping cottages, boats, sandy beach. Good fishing. Private ground. Gentiles.

VOSS' BIRCHWOOD RESORT
One of Wisconsin's leading resorts. Modern hotel. 18 cottages. Am. plan. Excellent food, fishing, golf, horses, sandy beach. $35.— to $45 per week. Restricted clientele.

TABOR FARM. SODUS, MICH.
Private golf, pool. Showers, heat, etc. in cottages. $30 wk. Gentiles.

BELVEDERE BEACH—South Haven
Badminton, Tennis Court, Shuffle Board, near Golf. Gentiles.

SHADY SHORES RESORT—Dewey LAKE, DOWAGIAC, MICH.
Mod. hotel cabins. Am. plan, $4 daily. All sports. Restricted clientele.

CAMP MORRISON—Bass Lake,
Pentwater, Mich.
Cabin with meals $15.00 wk. Marvelous Beach on Lake Mich. Many guests first here 20 years ago. Restricted clientele.

B. HELP WANTED AND UNWANTED

Advertisements for office girls contained much the same kind of restrictions as did the resort ads. Ten out of 20 ads for office girls in the July 6, 1941, Chicago Tribune *included obvious restrictions. Some simply insisted on Gentiles, while others asked for the applicant's nationality or religion.*

TYPIST
Order dept. Hektowriter exp. desirable but not essential. Mfg. concern located Northwest side. State age, exp., ed., nationality, previous earnings, and references.

OFFICE GIRL
Neat, energetic; 18 to 20; Southwest side mfg'er. Handle mail desk and miscellaneous office duties. Good future. State age, ed., nationality, and religion.

SOCIAL SECRETARY
Protestant. 35 to 40. Take full charge Protestant home; Milwaukee suburb; no housework involved; small family; all adults; good educational, cultural, and social background essential; good salary.

STENO. and gen. off. girl (Gentile) for small adv. agency. Must be fast and accurate. Will consider bright beginner who wants to develop in creative writing or art work. State exp. or schooling and sal.

STENOGRAPHER—At least 10 years' experience office building management office. State fully age, experience, education, references. Gentile. Substantial salary.

STENO-SECRETARY—For work in Crawford area of Central mfg. dist. Gentile. 5 d. wk. Good sal. Call for appoint.

STENOGRAPHER — Expd., intell., alert; perm. position; Gentile. Write full details of exp. and sal. des.

STENO-GEN. OFC.; some knowledge payroll. S.S.A. work; state age, educ., nat., refs., exper.

TYPIST-FILE CLERK—Also bookkeeper and typist; chance for advancement; state qualifications, salary expected, full particulars; Gentiles.

TYPIST—Young. h.s. grad; good phone voice; quick at figures. State age, nationality, details.

C. THE UNIVERSITIES AND THE QUOTA SYSTEM

Already by the turn of the century some universities were excluding Jews from honorary societies, social fraternities, and other campus activities. Shortly before World War I, a clergyman at Yale, hoping to preserve his school's homogeneity, warned that "compulsory chapel is the only way by which you can keep the Catholic and Jew out of Yale." But it was not until the 1920's, when second-generation Jews were seeking an exit from the ghettos through education, that the quota system was widely used at many Eastern and Midwestern colleges for the express purpose of restricting the number of Jewish students. Most colleges denied that such a system existed, but various governmental and private investigations made after World War II showed that not only did such a system exist but also that it had become more restrictive, especially in the professional schools. In spite of various investigations, it was not until the civil rights legislation of the 1960's that the quota system disappeared.

1. President Lowell of Harvard Defends the Quota System, 1922

In 1922, President A. Lawrence Lowell of Harvard openly admitted that Harvard was introducing a quota system for Jewish students. In language reminiscent of President Wilson's rationale for segregating blacks in Federal agencies, Lowell explained that this was the best way to head off a rising anti-Semitism. Thirty-two years later, after the German gas chambers had been exposed, the President of Dartmouth, Dr. Ernest M. Hopkins, explained that his university's quota was also set up to protect the Jews from anti-Semitism. President Hopkins insisted that his study of Germany made it clear that the presence of too many Jews in the professions only resulted in anti-Semitism.

President Lowell's comments were carried on the front page of the New York Times *under the headline: "LOWELL TELLS JEWS LIMIT AT COLLEGES MIGHT HELP THEM.*[1]

There is perhaps no body of men in the United States, mostly Gentiles, with so little anti-Semitic feeling as the instructing staff of Harvard University. But the problem that confronts this country and its educational institutions is a difficult one, and one about which I should very much like to talk with you. It is one that involves the best interests both of

[1]*New York Times*, June 17, 1922; © 1922 by The New York Times Company. Reprinted by permission.

the college and of the Jews, for I should feel very badly to think that these did not coincide.

There is, most unfortunately, a rapidly growing anti-Semitic feeling in this country, causing—and no doubt in part caused by—a strong race feeling on the part of the Jews themselves. In many cities of the country Gentile Clubs are excluding Jews altogether, who are forming separate clubs of their own. Private schools are excluding Jews, I believe, and so, we know, are hotels. All this seems to me fraught with very great evils for the Jews, and very great perils for the community. The question did not originate here, but has been brought over from Europe—especially from those countries where it has existed for centuries.

The question for those of us who deplore such a state of things is how it can be combated, and especially for those of us who are connected with colleges, how it can be combated there—how we can cause the Jews to feel and be regarded as an integral part of the student body. The anti-Semitic feeling among the students is increasing, and it grows in proportion to the increase in the number of Jews.

If their number should become forty per cent of the student body, the race feeling would become intense. When, on the other hand, the number of Jews was small, the race antagonism was small also. Any such race feeling among the students tends to prevent the personal intimacies on which we must rely to soften anti-Semitic feeling.

If every college in the country would take a limited proportion of Jews, I suspect we should go a long way toward eliminating race feeling among the students, and, as those students passed out into the world, eliminating it in the community.

This question is with us. We cannot solve it by forgetting or ignoring it. If we do nothing about the matter the prejudice is likely to increase. Some colleges appear to have met the question by indirect methods which we do not want to adopt. It cannot be solved except by a cooperation between the college authorities and the Jews themselves. Would not the Jews be willing to help us in finding the steps best adapted for preventing the growth of race feeling among our students, and hence in the world?

The first thing to recognize is that there is a problem—a new problem, which we have never had to face before, but which has come over with the immigration from the Old World. After the nature of that problem is fairly understood, the next question is how to solve it in the interest of the Jews, as well as of every one else.

2. Some Student Views on Harvard's Quota System, 1922

President Lowell was not without student support for his quota system. A few weeks after his declaration, the Nation *carried an article en-*

titled "Harvard Student Opinion on the Jewish Question." The students quizzed were from a class in social ethics that for the past year had been studying societal relationships.[1]

What are the facts? Opportunity to get at them offered itself at the end of the college year, when, in a class in the department of Social Ethics, Dr. Richard C. Cabot gave the following as a part of the examination:

> Discuss as fairly as you can this question For the good of *all* persons concerned, is a college ever ethically justified in limiting to a certain percentage the number of any particular race who are admitted to the freshman class each year?

The students concerned were from the three upper classes. For a year they had been considering the ethics of human relationships, of property, of veracity, of freedom and restraint, confidence and suspicion. . . .

The bald facts of the lineup are these: of the eighty-three men examined, forty-one believed in the justice of a policy of race-limitation under certain circumstances. Thirty-four held that such a policy was never justified. Eight stayed on the fence. Of this last group one name was Jewish. Seven of those who opposed restriction had Jewish names. Those who favored it were all Gentiles.

All the proponents of limitation made the assumption that the number of Jews in Harvard College was increasing out of all proportion to the increase in the number of other races, and argued that this boded ill for the future of the institution. "Harvard is an American college, devoted to American ideals, maintained for the good of the greatest number. If it becomes top-heavy from an over-supply of some one race, it serves neither that race nor America." "Harvard must maintain a cosmopolitan balance. Restriction, not to preserve a mere aristocratic tradition, but to keep the proportions on which fruitful educational contact depends, is justifiable and democratic."

Not all the restrictionists took this ground. Three maintained that "a college is a private institution and can sell its goods or not, as it sees fit, to whomever it pleases." One asserted that the overseers of a college have no more to do with the public weal than the directors of a bank. One even went so far as to compare Harvard College to an automobile "which I am obliged to lend to all comers simply because they would like to ride in it." For the most part, however, the restrictionists agreed

[1]William T. Ham, "Harvard Student Opinion on the Jewish Question," *Nation* September 6, 1922, pp. 225–227.

that "while the endowed college is a private corporation, it has a public function, recognized by the state."

The founding fathers, of course, came in for a deal of attention. They, it seems, "wanted certain traditions maintained, and it is a duty to maintain them because they align the college with the church for noble and light-giving qualities." Moreover, this inheritance is quite Anglo-Saxon. In fact, "Harvard should be the natural segregating place of the Anglo-Saxons," for they "founded this country and this college." "The Jews tend to overrun the college, to spoil it for the native-born Anglo-Saxon young persons for whom it was built and whom it really wants."

In various ways would Harvard College be injured by predominance of the Jews? Those who favor limitation shudder when they think of what would happen to her prestige. "Imagine having an alumni so strongly Jewish that they could elect their own president and officers! God forbid!" Eleven papers express great concern over the prospects for endowments in the future, and fear that the alumni will cease to feel interest in the college if Harvard fellowship becomes Semitic. But misgiving as to the future product of the college is more potent still and the reasoning is this: The aim of the college is to graduate men who will take high positions in the affairs of the country. The college cannot graduate such men without finding such material among the freshmen. The presence of this material depends upon the reputation of the institution, which, in turn, rests upon a cosmopolitan balance of races in its student body. . . .

Now why is it that the presence of the Jew is so inimical to this highly desirable "atmosphere" that is the cynosure of endowment-givers and their sons? The restrictionists agree that it is because of the objectionable personal character of the Hebrew. They bristle with accusations, the general effect of which is to make him seem as hard to live with as a porcupine. A few say that he is in this condition irredeemably; the rest imply that if he would only improve his manners and get new ancestors, his chances would be better. "The Jewish race makes 'Take away' its motto, rather than 'Give and take.' They are governed by selfishness. They care nothing for the friends they make save as future business acquaintances; to them the social side of college life is only so much twaddle." "They want property for power rather than for use. Even in the gymnasium they take possession of the apparatus, not by using it, but by sitting on it." "Expediency is their standard of action; traditions mean nothing to them"—this of the Chosen People! "They go through college as cheaply as possible, and, having acquired their education, depart to be heard from no more, not even at the most urgent solicitations of Loan Fund collectors."

One accusation has to do with scholarship. "'In harmony with their policy of getting all they can for as little as possible, Jews incidentally take a majority of the scholarships. Thus they deprive many worthy men of other races of a chance."

3. New York City Medical Schools and Jewish Exclusion, 1947

Although one might expect the shock of Hitler's racism to have discouraged the growing anti-Semitism in the universities of postwar America, the record indicates that this certainly was not the case. In 1947, a Presidential Commission of Higher Education published a report that indicated that between 1935 and 1946 the proportion of Jewish students in professional schools had been drastically cut—sometimes by more than 50 percent. Increasingly, applicants had to answer questions that had no bearing on their actual qualifications for graduate school. Some schools not only asked for religious preferences, but also for the applicant's mother's maiden name and the country where his parents were born. The University of Southern California and the University of Virginia Medical Schools asked applicants whether they were Anglo-Saxon, French, Germanic, Italian, Negro, Oriental, Scandinavian, Slavonic, or Spanish.

In 1946, The Council of the City of New York authorized an investigation of admission practices and policies of "nonsectarian institutions" in New York City. The committee hoped to compare the application forms and credentials of the students who were accepted with those who were rejected, but unfortunately the schools under investigation had destroyed such records—although one school admitted that in the past such records had been preserved. The following is part of the committee's report as it was written by the chairman, Walter R. Hart.[1]

One of the purposes of the examination was to ascertain the number of graduates from city colleges admitted to the college or professional school each year. With this information available, the Committee was enabled to draw up exhibits showing whether or not the number of students accepted from the city colleges increased or decreased during the period from 1920 to 1946. The result of this examination revealed that in each of the medical schools in New York City, there was a significant decrease in the number of graduates of city colleges admitted in the forties as compared with the number admitted in 1920.

In six of the past ten years, not a single graduate of the College of

[1]Walter R. Hart, "Anti-Semitism in New York Medical Schools," *American Mercury,* July 1947, pp. 53–63.

the City of New York was admitted to Cornell University, School of Medicine and, in the remaining four years, a total of nine were admitted. From 1942 to 1946, inclusive, 218 graduates of City College applied for admission to Cornell Medical School. Only five were admitted. Forty-eight of these applicants had an average of A-minus or better.

Not a single graduate of Hunter College has been admitted to Cornell University, School of Medicine since 1924. Not a single graduate of Brooklyn College was admitted to Cornell University, School of Medicine prior to 1946, in which year one was admitted.

During the past ten years, Cornell University, School of Medicine accepted 801 students, of whom only 11 were from city colleges, an average of 1.4 percent. It is significant to note that in 1920, out of 44 acceptances, 22 or 50 percent, were graduates of city colleges.

In 1920, the College of Physicians and Surgeons, Columbia University, admitted 98 students, 14 of whom were graduates of city colleges, or 14.3 percent. In 1928, 1932, 1933, 1937, 1939 and 1940, not a single graduate of any of the city colleges was among those accepted. In 1929, 1930, 1931, 1935 and 1938, only one graduate of a city college was accepted out of approximately 110 students admitted in each of these years or an average of less than 1 percent. . . .

It has been shown that the number of acceptances of graduates of the city colleges decreased from approximately 50 percent in 1920 to the extent that, in some years, none of the graduates of the city colleges succeeded in obtaining admission to some of the medical schools. It is also revealed that even graduates of the College of the City of New York with averages of A-minus or better were unsuccessful in their efforts to be admitted to city medical schools. . . .

Prior to 1920, an applicant for admission to a professional school was required merely to set forth in the application prepared by the school the following information: "Name, address, age, place of birth, name of college, years in college, scholastic record and recommendations." Subsequent thereto, the information required of the applicant included a statement concerning his "religion" and "place of birth of father and mother." Thereafter, there was added the requirement that he furnish a photograph. Some of the schools, apparently because of criticism concerning the requirement that the applicant state his religion, substituted a question concerning the "racial origin" of the applicant. Thereafter, this question was dropped and applicants were required to state their "mother's maiden name."

Every witness questioned by the Committee stated that the answers to these questions concerning religion, racial origin or mother's maiden name were of no value in determining the qualifications of the applicant.

Each of the witnesses likewise admitted that by looking at a photograph, he could not determine the qualifications, or even the personality of an applicant. One of the witnesses, who testified that he was prejudiced against "Irish-Catholic" applicants and "mildly" prejudiced against applicants of the Jewish faith, stated that he and other members of the Committe would use this information for the purpose of making a "guess" as to the religion or racial origin of the applicant. . . .

Dr. Charles O. Warren [Cornell University] testified that the members of the Admissions Committee would discuss the racial origin and religion of an applicant. At a private hearing, held on October 7th, 1946, when asked how he determined the religion of an applicant, he replied, "We make a guess."

Q. And you are aided in that guess by his name, the photograph; is that correct?

A. That's right.

Q. Sometimes by the birthplace?

A. Probably.

Q. All right. And having made that guess, now, just exactly what factors enter into your consideration in determining how his religion or his racial origin affects his personality?

A. I would rather not answer that.

Q. You know the answer, don't you, Doctor?

A. I know an answer.

           ❁   ❁   ❁

Q. Did you look at the applicant's picture and his name for the purpose of determining, among other things, what his religious background was?

A. Why don't we just assume that and let it go off the record?

Q. Is that a fair assumption?

A. Yes.

Q. Well, now, Doctor, in determining questions of personality based upon religious persuasion and background, you were affected either favorably or unfavorably; weren't you, in your opinion?

A. Well, naturally. . . .

Q. And when you say you make as honest an effort as possible to deal with it, just exactly how do you make that effort? Just what do you do?

A. Not to be unduly influenced by prejudices that we all have.

Q. What prejudices do you have?

A. I would rather not answer that. We all have prejudices one way or the other about these matters. It is foolish to deny it, and I think we have made as honest an effort as we can to override these.

Q. Override these what?

A. To consider the admission of candidates.

Q. Do you mean religious prejudices, when you say, "We all have prejudices"?

A. Yes.

Q. Do you have them?

A. Now, Fellow, look, I am trying to be on the up and up with you.

Q. Against what particular group are you prejudiced, however strongly or however weakly?

A. I am not prejudiced against any racial group. I am prejudiced against the personality that appears in certain racial groups.

Q. Do you mean Hebrews?

A. I would rather not answer it.

Q. Can you answer this, then: You don't mean Catholics, do you?

A. That is another thing. I happen not to like the Irish.

Q. And being human, that does sometimes affect your attitude with respect to applicants who are Irish or Irish Catholics?

A. That's right, exactly. I don't like also certain Americans.

Q. Certain Americans?

A. In certain situations.

Q. Do you like the Hebrews?

A. Some of my very best friends are among them. . . .

5
The Jewish
Refugee Problem

One of the saddest and most shameful chapters in this country's history is still unknown to most Americans. Although two monographs have recently been published on the subject, America's refusal to play a more prominent role in the saving of Hitler's Jewish refugees has largely been ignored by most recent historians. How many Jews could have been saved from the gas chambers by the United States is, of course, conjecture, but the number certainly would have exceeded a million. Added to this is the intangible value of the fine example it would have served for other countries that had also proved unwilling to save many of Europe's Jews.

From the inception of the Third Reich, Americans were appalled by Hitler's treatment of the Jews, but they were equally appalled by the thought of thousands of Jewish refugees pouring into this country. While one 1939 poll found that 94% of the American people disapproved of Germany's treatment of the Jews, another poll also showed that fully 83% of our people felt that there should be no easing of American immigration quotas to aid the Jews. Nor did the President differ from his people. Roosevelt openly condemned Hitler's atrocities, but he refused to exercise the kind of executive leadership that might have produced Congressional action. Eleanor Roosevelt later wrote that although the President was greatly affected by the plight of the Jews, he could not risk the wrath of isolationist-minded Congressmen by pushing an unpopular refugee-relief bill.

By September, 1939, when war shut off immigration, England had taken in 9000 young refugees without permits; Holland, 2000; France, 600; Sweden, 250; and the United States, 240. The fact that the United States had some 1¼ million unfilled places on its immigration quotas between 1933 and 1943 inspired some Jewish Congressmen to suggest that some of these places be used for Jewish refugees. Nor was Germany herself taking her full quota. But as late as 1943, when Hitler's "final solution" was already known, the United States could only admit 4705 Jews—this in a year when the annual quota was undersubscribed by some 125,000.

Who was to blame for America's rejection of the refugees? Foremost blame must go to the State Department, which, until the problem was taken out of its hands in 1944, placed almost insurmountable barriers in the way of the refugees. President Roosevelt, who until 1944 felt that political expedience precluded executive action, also must share in the blame. Then, too, Congress proved most recalcitrant toward any bill that might have brought more of the refugees into this country. But above all it was the change that had taken over the entire country in the twentieth century. Americans no longer thought of this nation as a sanctuary for the oppressed. The immigration laws passed during the 1920's and official footdragging on the displaced-persons problem after World War II made this painfully clear. To be sure, many individual Americans wanted to do something, but the country generally did not. It was left for a German newspaper to sum up American policy: "We see that one likes to pity the Jews as long as one can use this pity for a wicked agitation against Germany," editorialized the *Danziger Vorposten*, "but we also see that no state is prepared to fight the cultural disgrace of central Europe by accepting a few thousand Jews."

A. THE REFUGEE CHILDREN'S BILL, 1939

In 1939 there was a move to rescue 20,000 Jewish children from Germany. Their entry was to be in addition to the regular German quota and was to be supervised by the Quakers. Within a day after the plan was announced, 4000 American families of all faiths had offered to adopt the children. Congress, however, had 60 anti-alien bills before it and was scarcely in the mood to save anyone—not even 20,000 children, all of whom were under 14 years of age. Congressional hearings were held on the Wagner-Rogers Bill, which would have brought in a maximum of 10,000 children in 1939 and another 10,000 in 1940, but the bill was so amended and weakened that its original sponsors dropped it and the children were left to their German fate. Nor was there any encouragement from the White House; in fact, the President summarized a great deal of our inaction with his response to a note from Representative Caroline O'Day of New York, which requested his views on the Wagner-

Rogers bill. The President put aside her memo with the terse comment: "File, No Action, FDR."

1. Secretary of State Cordell Hull and the Refugee Children's Bill, 1939

When Congressional hearings opened on the Wagner-Rogers Bill, Secretary of State Hull sent a letter to Chairman Richard Russell warning that such a bill would create great difficulties for his Department and might produce harmful consequences for the country itself. Most insensitive was his comment that such a measure would necessitate his department's hiring extra help and seeking additional space.[1]

DEAR SENATOR RUSSELL: I refer again to your communication of February 10, 1939, requesting the views of this Department with respect to Senate Joint Resolution 64, a joint resolution to authorize the admission into the United States of a limited number of German refugee children.

While I am very mindful of the plight of many German children today and am in sympathy with the laudable objective of Joint Resolution 64 to relieve the suffering of these children, there are features of this proposed resolution of which, I am sure, your committee will wish to give particular attention. These features relate both to technical and administrative aspects of the resolution. . . .

The children whose admission is proposed by Senate Joint Resolution 64 are to be admitted in addition to existing quotas, but they are required to be otherwise eligible. In this connection you will recall that section 3 of the Immigration Act of Feburary 5, 1917, excludes, among other classes of aliens, "all children under 16 years of age unaccompanied by or not coming to one or both parents, except that any such children may, in the discretion of the Secretary of Labor, be admitted if in his opinion they are not likely to become a public charge and are otherwise admissable." Presumably many of the children will neither be accompanying their parents nor proceeding to join them in the United States. Section 3 of the Immigration Act of February 5, 1917, also excludes from admission "persons whose ticket or passage is paid for by any corporation, association, society, municipality, or foreign government, either directly or indirectly." Many of the children undoubtedly will be financially assisted in obtaining transportation or passage to the United States.

Children 14 years of age or under, who reside, or at any time since January 1, 1933, have resided in any territory now incorporated in Ger-

[1]"Admission of German Refugee Children," *Joint Hearings before a Sub-Committee on Immigration, U.S. Senate and a Subcommittee of the Committee on Immigration and Naturalization, House of Representatives,* April 20, 1939, pp. 2–3.

many, subject to certain conditions, are entitled to the benefits of the resolution. It will be remembered that country of birth and not country of residence is a basic feature of the quota system in the act of 1924. While a departure from this basic principle for a period of two years and for the humanitarian purpose of relieving suffering might not be regarded as a precedent, your committee, I am sure, will give consideration to this feature of the resolution because of the possibility of its opening the door to similar or more radical departures from the quota system established by the existing law. . . .

While I can assure you and your committee of the wholehearted support of our consular officers and of this Department in complying with the provisions of the resolution, if it should become law, the issuance of 10,000 immigration visas in addition to an estimated 30,000 immigration visas now being issued annually in that country will inevitably necessitate increased clerical personnel, unfamiliar with the law and regulations, as well as additional office accommodations.

Section 11 (f) of the Immigration Act of 1924 limits the monthly issuance of immigration visas in quotas of 300 and over to 10 percent of the annual immigration quotas. This statutory provision regulates the rate at which visas are issued as well as the flow of immigrants arriving at ports of entry. Assuming that added personnel and office accommodations were to be made available, a monthly limitation on the issuance of visas to the refugee children would be essential as a measure of control to insure proper administrative action with respect to the applications of these children as well as to those provided by the present quota law.

2. The American Coalition Opposes the Refugee Children's Bill, 1939

As in the hearings on immigration restriction during the 1920's, the patriotic organizations added vocal support for continued restriction. The argument put forth was often couched in economic terms, but antiSemitic feelings were thinly disguised. Many of the economic arguments used against the Jewish children were dropped when the U.S. Government agreed to take in many English children whose lives were endangered by the blitz. The following comments are from John B. Trevor, a Columbia University lawyer who served as Trustee for both the American Museum of Natural History and New York University, and who now purported to represent 115 patriotic, civil, and fraternal societies.[1]

My name is John B. Trevor. I represent the American Coalition, a patriotic and fraternal society, whose board of directors is composed of

[1]"Admission of German Refugee Children," *Joint Hearings*, April 24, 1939, pp. 215–224.

delegates representing 115 patriotic, civil, and fraternal societies of this country. . . .

I think I am safe in saying that the delegates to the convention clearly expressed the popular viewpoint in regard to the admission of refugees, because *Fortune* magazine made a survey of this question which is published in the April issue. That survey showed that today only 8.7 percent of the people favor the admission of refugees, 83 percent are opposed to the admission of refugees, and 8.3 percent do not know what they think. These figures have particular importance, in our opinion, Mr. Chairman, because they show that the opposition to the admission of refugees has risen from 67.4 percent, as shown by the *Fortune* survey last July. *Fortune* says:

> Here is an American tradition put to the popular test, and here it is repudiated by a majority of nearly 10 to 1. There is about this answer a finality that seems to mean that the doors of this country should be virtually closed to refugees, and should stay closed to them, no matter what their need or condition. The answer is the more decisive because it was made at a time when public sympathy for victims of European events was presumably at its highest. . . .

Now, Mr. Chairman and members of the committee, let me say that every argument advanced in favor of this resolution is equally valid for the admission of thousands of refugee Spanish children whose parents were associated with the defense of the Communist and anarchist regime in control of the so-called Loyalist Government in Spain. The arguments are equally valid for the admission of millions of Chinese children who have been driven from their homes, or whose parents have been slain in the war now going on in the Far East.

In my opinion this resolution is going to be the prelude for legislation to provide for the reunion on American soil of the parents of these children and their brothers and sisters. I say this because as a social measure this bill is an iniquity insofar as it would separate children from their parents. The proponents of this resolution, I understand, have raised large sums of mony to put its provisions into effect. If the money which they have raised were used to transfer these children, with their parents, to some country where they could be admitted they would be doing a humane and constructive act.

The Wagner resolution strikes at the vitals of the whole principle upon which numerical restriction of immigration is based. These children, if admitted, will presumably grow up and as youths they will become competitors with American citizens for American jobs.

I know of an honest, hard-working man in New York City with five of as nice children as you could find in this country. The eldest girl wants to work, but, Mr. Chairman, those who have raised the charge that restriction upon immigration was based on race prejudice, practice it. The American-born child in many places must yield to the foreign-born refugee because of race affinity. The Congress of the United States enacted the national-origins quota system to abolish national and racial discrimination among immigrants eligible for citizenship. The Wagner resolution would enact a special privilege for alien children who have resided in Germany. That is straight out discrimination without qualification or reservation. . . .

In conclusion, may I say, Mr. Chairman and gentlemen of the committee, that the Government of the United States was created to protect and promote the interests of the American people. The *Fortune* poll . . . proves conclusively, that the overwhelming majority of our fellow citizens has neither the intention nor the desire to turn this country into an orphan asylum for the indigent children and refugees of all the world, and that poll, Mr. Chairman and gentlemen, was taken with a full knowledge of conditions now existing in Europe.

Our contention is—charity begins at home!

B.   CONGRESSIONAL VOICES ON THE REFUGEE PROBLEM

That President Roosevelt would have had problems promoting a refugee program in Congress can be seen by the 60-odd antirefugee bills that were introduced in the 1939–1940 session. Most of the Congressmen stressed that the country's economic problems precluded any possibility of admitting refugees. This was an effective argument for a country that still had millions unemployed and hungry, but some of these same Congressmen had opposed any extension of Roosevelt's domestic relief measures, and it became increasingly apparent that the economic argument was often a subterfuge for more fundamental objections.

1.   Representative Thomas Jenkins Opposes the Refugees, 1938

Ohio's Thomas Jenkins was one of the Congressional leaders who argued for immigration restriction. Jenkins carefully utilized the economic argument, but he also appealed for support to those who had only recently become immigrants themselves.[1]

When this great crowd of refugees is brought here it must be remembered that they come for permanent residence. We will never be able to deport them. Why? For the simple reason that there will be no

---

[1]*Congressional Record*, 75th Cong., 3rd Sess., March 28, 1938, pp. 4227–4228.

place to which they can be deported. Nobody will take them back.

Neither our financial nor our economic structure, strained to the limit as it is, can stand this additional strain. The man looking for a job should not be put into further competition with this additional group. The family on relief should not be expected to divide its already meager allotment with another family, especially one from a foreign country. . . .

With actual death-dealing red warfare being carried on between two great nations off to the west of us, and with rumors of wars coming to us every day from Europe—a veritable powder keg—why should we project ourselves into this danger?

Without regard to party affiliation, without regard to sectionalism, but with full regard to the safety and best interests of our country, all of us must agree that we are confronted with great social, economic, and financial problems that have to date defied solution. Our own people are despairing. Our own people are suffering. Why add to our troubles and threaten our very existence? . . .

When we finance the importation of thousands of persons into our midst that are practically drawn from foreign lands, we will in effect demoralize our whole immigration system. Our country has been the model of all other countries in immigration matters; we have been pioneers; we founded our selective system fairly and scientifically. Millions of our people have gone through our immigration and naturalization processes proudly and are proud of their citizenship. They now are full-fledged citizens. They feel that they have in a way earned their citizenship. How will they feel when they see these thousands practically paid to become citizens?

2. Representative Jacob Thorkelson Explains the Jewish Problem, 1939

Montana's Jacob Thorkelson's dislike of Jews went well beyond the refugee problem. In language reminiscent of Ford's The International Jew, *Thorkelson found the Jews to be an un-American element in society. In private life, Thorkelson was an M.D. who had graduated from the University of Maryland.*[1]

It was Germany that discovered the insidious wiles of these internationalists, first, when they brought about inflation and second, when they attempted to take charge of the German Government by the control of gold and credit. It was only natural for Germany, understanding the socialism of Marx and Engels better than any other country, to call their hand. But when Germany said to the money changers, "You are dis-

[1]*Congressional Record, Appendix,* 76th Cong., 1st Sess., August 1, 1939, p. 3694.

covered. You are destroying the morale of our people, and you are undermining our nation," the Communist, in dismay at having been caught redhanded, exclaimed, "Germany is anti-Semitic, and the Nazi is our enemy."

In the United States, the same crowd, filled with hatreds, has organized over a thousand anti-Nazi leagues, the sole purpose of which is to boycott Germany. Nazi is a word coined by the international Communists. They want it to be known that Germany is an enemy to civilization, and they advocate, "Do not trade with the enemy." It is indeed strange that this particular group of people should take it upon themselves to designate a friendly nation as an enemy to the United States because such nation set its own house in order. They do not seem to consider that 120,000,000 Gentiles or Christian Americans may not agree with them. They assume instead that because Germany is selected by them as their enemy, that in itself is sufficient grounds for the whole Nation to rally to their support. This, if nothing else, is extraordinary reasoning. As a matter of fact, it borders on the ridiculous. Let us suppose that other nationals in the United States presumed to pursue the same course. We would then have thousands of leagues advocating that those who discover their attempted destruction of our Government be declared anti-English, anti-Irish, anti-Scandinavian, and so forth. And if they pursued this course further, as is now done by the Jews, then we would have the slogan, "Do not trade with any foreign nation, for they are enemies to civilization." . . .

It should now be clear that when we follow such faulty reasoning, all patriotic organizations, papers, and periodicals, that stand in defense of constitutional government and for the American ideals of our founding fathers are called anti-Semitic, Nazi, Fascist, reactionary—by whom? By the Jew-Communist and the international fanatics; and, believe it or not, these words were coined by them.

C. ASSISTANT SECRETARY OF STATE BRECKINRIDGE LONG AND THE REFUGEE PROBLEM

On January 23, 1940, Breckinridge Long became Assistant Secretary of State and took over virtually all aspects of the refugee problem. Long's inordinate fear that Germany would place spies among the refugees and his insistence that all prospective immigrants be carefully screened made his office the chief bottleneck for those who were trying to expedite the refugee problem. At times Long appeared simply to be a woefully inept administrator, but on other occasions his opposition was clearly tied to a distaste for the people he was supposedly trying to save. The following are selections from his war diary.[1]

(June 27, 1940)

Proposed to the Secretary and Welles in regard to the tri-partite conference the strengthening of our border controls and exercising additional authority over both non-immigrant and immigrant visas, such as visitors permits, reentry permits and transit permits as well as regular immigration control. After explaining the needs for it and going into the matter thoroughly they both agreed as to principle and subsequently in conference with Berle, Warren and the head of the Immigration Service we decided upon very drastic orders and the appropriate telegrams are being prepared.

(September 18, 1940)

A number of developments in our procedure in granting visas in excess of the quota have troubled me recently. It was brought to a head by the visit of a vessel named the *Quanza* to Norfolk. It has eighty-odd persons aboard who left Portugal on the ninth of August in an effort to get to some country in the Americas. They were all Jewish. They all had money. The vessel got to Vera Cruz, Mexico, and the Mexican Government refused to permit them to land. Nicaragua refused them permission. Their travel documents were repudiated by the Governments there. It seems there is a prevailing habit for the Consuls and other officers of some South American and Central American countries to accept from $100 to $500 for the privilege of granting visas and other papers. These people all had visas to go to some third country, but they are repudiated by the Governments in Central America. Unable to land there they proceeded ostensibly for Portugal and then conveniently discovered that they would have to put into Norfolk for coal. As soon as it became known that they were to arrive at Norfolk I was flooded with pressure groups and telegrams and telephones and personal visits to permit the landing of persons off of the boat. I consistently declined to deviate from the procedure which we had adopted and said that the fact that the people were on the boat and were nearing the American shores did not constitute an emergency of any kind.

Mrs. Roosevelt called me up and expressed her interest in the children and a few other categories. She talked to the President, and the President asked me to call him the next day. They were then in Hyde

<hr/>

[1]Reprinted from *The War Diary of Breckinridge Long*, edited by Fred L. Israel, by permission of University of Nebraska Press, pp. 114–115, 130–131, 161, 225. Copyright 1966 by the University of Nebraska Press.

Park, and he was about to return to Washington. I called the next day, but it was apparent that he did not want to talk to me on the subject, and I inferred—and it now seems correctly so—that he would leave the matter entirely in my hands. . . .

(December 12, 1940)

As regards refugees, which is a continuing and complicated problem, Rabbi Wise and Rabbi Teitelbaum headed a delegation and asked me to accept 3,800 additional names from Lithuania and that part of the present Russian jurisdiction. After a long conversation I was noncommittal as to what the Department would do but feel it is just a part of the movement to place me and the Department in general in an embarrassing position.

The attacks against the Department continue. *PM* this afternoon reprints an editorial from the [Louisville] *Courier Journal* in which it condemns the whole Department underneath Hull and suggests we all ought to be kicked out and even damns Hull himself with faint praise. The Secretary is considerably worried about the entire business and spoke to me again about the memorandum which I have in preparation. The continuing attacks on the Department are unpleasant and indicative of a determined effort on the part of some groups to undermine the work of the Department and to interfere with the continuation of its general policies.

(November 28, 1941)

Steinhardt is an able man and has decisiveness and courage. He took a definite stand on the immigration and refugee question and opposed the immigration in large numbers from Russia and Poland of the Eastern Europeans whom he characterizes as entirely unfit to become citizens of this country. He says they are lawless, scheming, defiant—and in many ways unassimilable. He said the general type of intending immigrant was just the same as the criminal Jews who crowd our police court dockets in New York and with whom he is acquainted and whom he feels are never to become moderately decent American citizens.

I think he is right. . . .

SELECTED READINGS

American Jewish Yearbook, 71 volumes, The Jewish Publication Society of America, New York, 1899–1970.

First published in 1899, this comprehensive fact book includes many instances of American anti-Semitic behavior.

McWilliams, Carey, *A Mask for Privilege; Anti-Semitism in America*, Little, Brown and Company, Boston, 1947.
A good survey of anti-Semitism in America. McWilliams views much of the anti-Jewish feeling in terms of majority fears of social and economic competition with Jews.

Morse, Arthur, *While Six Million Died; A Chronicle of American Apathy*, Random House, New York, 1968.
An emotional, well-told story of our refusal to play a more prominent role in the saving of European Jews before and during World War II.

Rose, Peter, Ed., *The Ghetto and Beyond: Essays on Jewish Life in America*, Random House, New York, 1969.
A series of scholarly essays, some of which describe and analyze anti-Semitism in the United States.

Weintraub, Ruth G., *How Secure these Rights? Anti-Semitism in the United States in 1948*, Doubleday & Company, Garden City, New York, 1949.
An Anti-Defamation League Survey that gives the reader an in-depth study of anti-Semitism in postwar America.

Wyman, David S., *Paper Walls; America and the Refugee Crisis, 1938–1941*, University of Massachusetts Press, Amherst, 1968.
An excellent, scholarly treatment of the refugee problem. A second volume will complete the story.

VII

THE ANGLO-SAXON
AND THE
NEW IMMIGRANT

We must remember that we have not only the Present but the Future to safeguard; our obligations extend even to generations yet unborn. The unassimilated alien child menaces our children, as the alien industrial worker, who has destruction rather than production in mind, menaces our industry.

Calvin Coolidge, 1921

INTRODUCTION

In the four decades between the 1880's and the restrictive immigration legislation of the 1920's, several minorities discovered that they were no longer welcome in the American melting pot. What most of these immigrants had in common was not only their Southern and Eastern European origin, but also the fact that in the New World they came to be equated with radical movements, cultural and religious decadence, and biological inferiority. They also came to a country that increasingly defined itself in Anglo-Saxon or Nordic terms. Prominent immigration historian Oscar Handlin once noted that the hyphenate designation so gratuitously applied to so many Americans never seemed to apply to the Anglo-American. Handling was correct, and most Americans concluded that not only was their past characterized by a unified racial héritage, but, also, their future would be endangered if anything threatened this homogeneity.

Although Americans were to lump the New Immigrants together as a common threat, they were scarcely a homogeneous people. Coming from many different countries in Southern and Eastern Europe, they were alike neither in culture, tradition, nor religion. They were for the most

301

part unskilled and uneducated but certainly no more so than the early English settlers, and their industriousness was readily admitted. They did, however, enter the country at a time when various developments would make them a ready scapegoat for America's internal fears and conflicts.

The "danger" of these immigrants was not immediately recognized. Historian John Higham suggests that nativism as a significant source dated from the Haymarket Square incident in 1886. The deadly bombing, the shootings by the police, and the subsequent hangings of several radical leaders signified the country's growing fear of a radical labor movement—a movement that many equated with the unwanted immigrants. The economic booms and busts and the accompanying labor problems produced the kind of tense situation in which both management and labor could point an accusing finger at the New Immigrant.

In 1887, the American Protective Association started its restrictionist work, and within ten years it claimed over 500,000 members. Other nativist societies sprang up to match the increased activity of such traditional groups as the D.A.R. and the G.A.R. Although originally centered primarily in the East, with the Panic of 1893 nativism spread into the West and South. The decade of the 1890's also saw this country embark on a variety of imperialistic adventures that contributed to a growing nationalism and "race pride." The concept of the "white man's burden" might mean that America was willing to uplift these unfortunates abroad, but Americans certainly had little desire to bring them home.

Paralleling the popular feeling of national pride in the 1890's was the development of scholarly race theories. The intellectuals had not been particularly comfortable with the excesses of earlier nativist thought—anti-Catholicism and antiradicalism—but the concept of race and its impact on national destinies was more appealing. Scientists had been trying to classify people well before this period, but the advent of social Darwinian thought gave a new dimension to race thinking. "Survival of the fittist" and "natural selection" became terms that were easily applied to nations and their inhabitants—nature picked the strong, and the weak fell by the wayside. This led naturally into eugenics and the preoccupation with good breeding. Social as well as biological traits were inherited, concluded the eugenicists, and one could predict the behavior of the offspring by examining the parents. Anthropologists cataloged specified traits for the various races, and the sociologists explained the results. Finally, the historians could take these theories and apply them to the past. Many found that there was a lineal development to American history that could be traced to the primeval forests of northern Germany. These intellectual currents quickly found their way into popular literature, with the scholars themselves doing much of the writing.

Prior to the 1890's America scorned the New Immigrant for his habits and customs, but now he became a threat to the American way of life. In the past, the country had confidence in its ability to assimilate immigrants, but now assimilation meant a lowering of standards and the adulteration of bloodlines. The conviction of the Progressive reformers that they could order the future by improving the present also brought a kind of reform fervor to the restrictionist movement. If you could improve the environment through intelligent, rational thought, certainly you could improve people in the same way; in fact, to improve the basic stock seemed more appealing, and between 1910 and 1914 there were more articles printed on racial genetics and heredity than on the three questions of slums, tenements, and living standards combined. Yet in the classrooms of America today the emphasis remains on the reform legislation of the Progressive era, not on the racial theories that concerned so many of the contemporaries.

World War I and the subsequent Red Scare of 1919 added another emotional dimension to the move for restriction. The Federal demands for conformity were matched throughout the country by a growing hostility toward anything that appeared radical or "un-American." During the war, for example, Iowa banned any language except English in all schools, church services, conversations in public places, and on the telephone. The Palmer raids and the resultant mass deportations of 1919 and 1920, as well as the more than 70 alien-sedition acts introduced by the Federal and state legislatures, exemplified how serious America considered this threat to be.

During the 1920's this nation's insistence on total "Americanism" did not lessen. The entire experience of the war and Wilson's relentless crusade for international involvement resulted in an aversion toward anything European, and this boded ill for the immigrants. The newly created American Legion now added its strong voice to those of other patriotic organizations, and with little opposition Congress acted to restrict or eliminate the undesirable immigrants. Several plans were suggested and tried, and all meant the exclusion of the Oriental and the sharp curtailment of the immigrants from Southern and Eastern Europe. The National Origins Act finally went into effect on July 1, 1929, and of the 150,000 annual openings only 23,000 were granted to the countries of Southern and Eastern Europe. This put the question to rest, until the displaced-persons controversy after World War II resurrected many of the old arguments against opening the door to undesirable immigrants.

1
Popular Images

"We may well ask . . . whether this in-sweeping immigration is to foreignize us, or we are to Americanize it," wrote Josiah Strong, the Congregationalist minister whose writings achieved great popularity in the late nineteenth century. The outcome of this clash between American civilization and foreign customs and ideologies became of paramount importance for an increasing number of Americans who were frightened by the economic polarization, labor disputes, urban corruption, and rapid spread of slums that seemed everywhere in evidence in the late nineteenth century. The immigrant provided a ready explanation of these ills, and the fact that his numbers were rapidly swelling from Southern and Eastern Europe was brought to public attention by the popular press of the day. Government officials, novelists, labor representatives, businessmen, and folk heroes, as well as the professional journalists, began to urge the closing of the immigration door; and although the economic argument was often mentioned, it was the "inferior" stock of these New Immigrants that gained increased attention. For example, Charles Lindbergh warned in a 1939 *Reader's Digest* article that Americans must "guard our heritage from Mongol, Persian, and Moor, before we become engulfed in a limitless foreign sea." It was also an era of increasing literacy, and with the immigration controversy the publishers had the kind of emotional issue that sold magazines. Even after the new immigrant was effectively barred, some writers continued to remind Americans that the door must be kept closed.

A. JOSIAH STRONG AND THE THREAT TO OUR MORALS AND INSTITUTIONS, 1885

When the Rev. Josiah Strong's Our Country *was published in 1885, it found a ready audience. The urban-dwelling, literate American was*

305

acutely aware of the social problems facing the nation, and Strong provided him with an easily recognizable culprit. Although he thoroughly discussed the crisis, Strong remained confident that the world's future would still be shaped by the Anglo-Saxons, with the American-type predominating. Within a few years, his book had sold almost 200,000 copies, and the Rev. Strong had suddenly become an influential figure of national proportions.[1]

Consider briefly the moral and political influence of immigration.

(1) Influence on morals. Let me hasten to recognize the high worth of many of our citizens of foreign birth, not a few of whom are eminent in the pulpit and in all the learned professions. Many come to us in full sympathy with our free institutions, and desiring to aid us in promoting a Christian civilization. But no one knows better than these same intelligent and Christian foreigners that they do not represent the mass of immigrants. The typical immigrant is a European peasant, whose horizon has been narrow, whose moral and religious training has been meager or false, and whose ideas of life are low. Not a few belong to the pauper and criminal classes. From a late report of the Howard Society of London, it appears that "seventy-four per cent of the Irish discharged convicts have found their way to the United States." Every detective in New York knows that there is scarcely a ship landing immigrants that does not bring English, French, German, or Italian "crooks." Moreover, immigration is demoralizing. No man is held upright simply by the strength of his own roots; his branches interlock with those of other men, and thus society is formed, with all its laws and customs and force of public opinion. Few men appreciate the extent to which they are indebted to their surroundings for the strength with which they resist, or do, or suffer. All this strength the emigrant leaves behind him. He is isolated in a strange land, perhaps doubly so by reason of a strange speech. He is transplanted from a forest to an open prairie, where, before he is rooted, he is smitten with the blasts of temptation.

We have a good deal of piety in our churches that will not bear transportation. It cannot endure even the slight change of climate involved in spending a few summer weeks at a watering place, and is commonly left at home. American travelers in Europe often grant themselves license, on which, if at home, they would frown. Very many church-members, when they go west, seem to think they have left their

---

[1]Josiah Strong, *Our Country*, 1891 revised edition, Baker & Taylor Co. for the American Home Missionary Society, New York, pp. 55–59.

Christian obligations with their church-membership in the East. And a considerable element of our American-born population are apparently under the impression that the Ten Commandments are not binding west of the Missouri. Is it strange, then, that those who come from other lands, whose old associations are all broken and whose reputations are left behind, should sink to a lower moral level? Across the sea they suffered many restraints which are here removed. Better wages afford larger means of self-indulgence; often the back is not strong enough to bear prosperity, and liberty too often lapses into license. Our population of foreign extraction is sadly conspicuous in our criminal records. This element constituted in 1870 twenty per cent of the population of New England, and furnished seventy-five per cent of the crime. That is, it was twelve times as much disposed to crime as the native stock. The hoodlums and roughs of our cities are, most of them, American-born of foreign parentage. Of the 680 discharged convicts who applied to the Prison Association of New York for aid, during the year ending June 30, 1882, 442 were born in the United States, against 238 foreign-born; while only 144 reported native parentage against 536 who reported foreign parentage. . . .

Moreover, immigration not only furnishes the greater portion of our criminals, it is also seriously affecting the morals of the native population. It is disease and not health which is contagious. Most foreigners bring with them continental ideas of the Sabbath, and the result is sadly manifest in all our cities, where it is being transformed from a holy day into a holiday. But by far the most effective instrumentality for debauching popular morals is the liquor traffic, and this is chiefly carried on by foreigners. In 1880, of the "Traders and dealers in liquors and wines," sixty-three per cent, were foreign-born, and of the brewers and maltsters seventy-five per cent while a large proportion of the remainder were of foreign parentage. Of saloon-keepers about sixty per cent of these corrupters of youth, these western Arabs, whose hand is against every man, were of foreign extraction.

(2) We can only glance at the political aspects of immigration. As we have already seen, it is immigration which has fed fat the liquor power; and there is a liquor vote. Immigration furnishes most of the victims of Mormonism; and there is a Mormon vote. Immigration is the strength of the Catholic church; and there is a Catholic vote. Immigration is the mother and nurse of American socialism; and there is to be a socialist vote. Immigration tends strongly to the cities, and gives to them their political complexion. And there is no more serious menace to our civilization than our rabble-ruled cities.

B. DECLINING AMERICAN BIRTHRATE BLAMED
ON IMMIGRANT'S PRESENCE, 1896

The startling thesis that the United States had not needed the immigrant to populate the land in the half-century between 1830 and 1880 was advanced in the early 1890's by General Francis A. Walker, Chief of the U.S. Bureau of Statistics and Superintendent of the Census. Walker, who was also a professor of political economy and history at Yale and, later, president of M. I. T., claimed that "Americans shrank alike from the social and economic competition" with immigrants, and thus became "increasingly unwilling" to have children. Without the presence of these degraded foreigners, claimed Walker, America's birthrate would have produced a population at least equal to what it actually was in the 1880's.

The following article appeared in 1896 in the Atlantic Monthly, *and was similar to several he published during that decade on the subject of the declining American birth rate.*[1]

But it may be asked, is the proposition that the arrival of foreigners brought a check to the native increase a reasonable one? Is the cause thus suggested one which has elsewhere appeared as competent to produce such an effect? I answer, Yes. All human history shows that the principle of population is intensely sensitive to social and economic changes. Let social and economic conditions remain as they were, and population will go on increasing from year to year, and from decade to decade, with a regularity little short of the marvelous. Let social and economic conditions change, and population instantly responds. The arrival in the United States, between 1830 and 1840, and thereafter increasingly, of large numbers of degraded peasantry created for the first time in this country distinct social classes, and produced an alteration of economic relations which could not fail powerfully to affect population. The appearance of vast numbers of men, foreign in birth and often in language, with a poorer standard of living, with habits repellent to our native people, of an industrial grade suited only to the lowest kind of manual labor, was exactly such a cause as by any student of population would be expected to affect profoundly the growth of the native population. Americans shrank alike from the social contact and the economic com-

[1]Francis A. Walker, "Restriction of Immigration," *Atlantic Monthly*, June 1896, pp. 822–829.

petition thus created. They became increasingly unwilling to bring forth
sons and daughters who should be obliged to compete in the market for
labor and in the walks of life with those ·whom they did not recognize
as of their own grade and condition. . . .

Did the foreigner come because the native American refused longer
to perform any kind of manual labor? No; the American refused because
the foreigner came. Through all our early history, Americans, from Governor Winthrop, through Jonathan Edwards, to Ralph Waldo Emerson,
had done every sort of work which was required for the comfort of their
families and for the upbuilding of the state, and had not been ashamed.
They called nothing common or unclear which needed to be done for
their own good or for the good of all. But when the country was flooded
with ignorant and unskilled foreigners, who could do nothing but the lowest kind of labor, Americans instinctively shrank from the contact and the
competition thus offered to them. So long as manual labor, in whatever
field, was to be done by all, each in his place, there was no revolt at
it; but when working on railroads and canals became the sign of a want
of education and of a low social condition, our own people gave it up,
and left it to those who were able to do that, and nothing better. . . .
The entrance into our political, social, and industrial life of such vast
masses of peasantry, degraded below our utmost conceptions, is a matter
which no intelligent patriot can look upon without the gravest apprehension and alarm. These people have no history behind them which is
of a nature to give encouragement. They have none of the inherited instincts and tendencies which made it comparatively easy to deal with
the immigration of the olden time. They are beaten men from beaten
races; representing the worst failures in the struggle for existence. Centuries are against them, as centuries were on the side of those who formerly came to us. They have none of the ideas and aptitudes which fit
men to take up readily and easily the problem of self-care and self-
government, such as belong to those who are descended from the tribes
that met under the oak trees of old Germany to make laws and choose
chieftains. . . .

C. WILLIAM ALLEN WHITE AND THE SUPERIORITY OF THE TEUTONIC ARYAN, 1910

*For almost a half century after his 1895 editorial, "What's the Matter
with Kansas," catapulted him into national prominence, William Allen
White was the voice of "Middle America." Witty, perceptive, and widely
quoted, White lived all his life in his hometown of Emporia, Kansas,*

*where he published his newspaper and wrote countless articles and
books on the national scene. The following selection from* The Old
Order Changeth *(1910) illustrates his belief that the vitality of American institutions stemmed from the superiority of the people who reside
in this country.*[1]

In these closing years of the first decade of the twentieth century,
there are in the United States ninety millions of us—mostly Aryans. Some
of us are Latin Aryans from the south of Europe; a few of us are Slavic
Aryans from the north of Europe; a distinguishable strain of our blood
is Norseman Aryan, from the west of Europe, and many of us are Celtic
Aryans, cropping out of any of half a dozen other Aryan breeds; but
the dominant blood is the Teutonic blood of the Angles and the Jute
and the Saxons—the blood that absorbed the Latins, and the Celts, and
the Normans, who came to the British Isle as conquerors in battle, and
lost in the struggle of the blood. For here in the United States we have
two things which have made the Teuton strong in this earth: the home
with the mother never out of caste, and the rule of the folk by "the
most ancient ways"—the supremacy of the majority. Other branches of
the Aryan race have come into this continent, have established half-caste
homes with native wives, and the outlawed woman has dragged these
races down to her level. Other Aryans have come to the land under the
rule of a king or a priest and tyranny has inbred and destroyed them.
But the Teutonic Aryan brought his home, kept his Teutonic women
full caste; the blood has never degenerated, and tyranny has never undermined our institutions. So here we are, ninety millions of us, if not
all of one blood, at least all of one mind. The free woman in the home
has made the free school; the free school has preserved the free man;
and the free man, still abiding by the most ancient ways—the rule of
the majority—is working out free institutions.

Now this freedom of ours is of its own kind. There is said to be in
the harbor of Havana a most remarkable statue of liberty. A woman
stands, with ecstasy in her face, with a shout of joy all but on her lips,
with almost delirious eyes turned upward toward her wide-stretched
arms, whereon the broken manacles are dangling useless. That is the
Latin idea of liberty. But our freedom is another thing. It is not so
new-born. If it might be symbolized by a woman, the figure could be
represented as a mother who never felt a shackle, toiling wearily yet
happily for her family. For this freedom of ours is little more than the

[1]William Allen White, *The Old Order Changeth*, Macmillan Co., New York, 1910,
pp. 197–199.

right of a human being to be useful; and to be useful one must sacrifice, must give, must deny, and be happy only in the joy of others. Our freedom, that comes from a free mother in a free home, partakes of her self-abnegation. And so we alone of the Aryans that have no bondwoman's blood in our veins, we who have no half-caste mothers, have been able to rear the children of democracy, men to whom freedom means sacrifice. And as the Aryans of Greece tried democracy with their bondwomen and failed, and the Aryan of Rome tried a Republic with slaves and failed, so they who came to America from Latin countries failed in this new world because their new world homes were half-caste and not free, and the liberty they sought was license and not sacrifice. And by this token we must know that so long as our democracy is altruistic, so long as it is based on self-sacrifice and self-restraint, it will endure.

D. KENNETH L. ROBERTS AND THE THREAT OF "MONGRELIZATION" IN AMERICA, 1922

By the early 1920's large numbers of Americans had been convinced that continued acceptance of the melting-pot theory seriously threatened their American way of life. No writer was more active in describing this threat than Kenneth L. Roberts, a Cornell graduate, who gained fame first as a journalist before turning to historical novels. Between 1919 and 1928, Roberts served as both a European and a Washington correspondent for the Saturday Evening Post, *turning out numerous articles on the immigration question. The following selection is from* Why Europe Leaves Home, *a book based on Roberts' observations in Europe following the close of World War I.*[1]

Assimilation hadn't been any too good in the United States for the twenty years prior to the war. If more and more immigrants continue to pour in, and assimilation continues bad, one of two things will inevitably happen: either the United States will develop large numbers of separate racial groups, as distinct as those which exist in Czecho-Slovakia, or America will be populated by a mongrel race entirely different from the present American people as we know them today. Our climate may, as some claim, change the stature of immigrants, but nothing can alter the

[1]Pp. 21–22, 113–114 from *Why Europe Leaves Home,* by Kenneth L. Roberts. Copyright 1922 by The Bobbs-Merrill Company, Inc., renewed 1949 by Kenneth L. Roberts. Reprinted by permission of the publisher.

shape of their skulls or the distinct racial traits that have characterized them throughout the centuries.

Races can not be cross-bred without mongrelization, any more than breeds of dogs can be cross-bred without mongrelization. The American nation was founded and developed by the Nordic race, but if a few more million members of the Alpine, Mediterranean and Semitic races are poured among us, the result must inevitably be a hybrid race of people as worthless and futile as the good-for-nothing mongrels of Central America and Southeastern Europe. . . .

It is not particularly pleasant to continue to harp on the necessity of keeping the United States a nation of Nordics; for there are always a large number of sentimentally inclined readers, whose belief in the whimsical fairytale of the melting pot is stronger than their common sense, who write hectic and vitriolic replies to any remarks on the respective merits of a continued Nordic strain of people and a mixed strain. So far as I have been able to gather from the letters that frequently reach me on this subject, no mention should be made of racial differences because all people are equal in the eyes of St. Peter. This is probably true; and everybody will unquestionably be delighted if it is. Here on earth, however, there are certain biological laws which govern the crossing of different breeds, whether the breeds be dogs or horses or men. If an otter hound is crossed with a Welsh terrier, the result is a mongrel. But if other otter hounds are crossed with other Welsh terriers, and the results of these crossings are mated in turn, the result is an Airedale, which is a very excellent dog. Excellent results can usually be obtained from cross-breeding followed by inbreeding. But the only results that can ever be obtained from promiscuous and continued cross-breeding is mongrelization; and a mongrel—in spite of the excellence of the stock from which he may have sprung—is a total loss. The same thing is true of humans. A mongrelized race of people is incapable of producing great artists or authors or statesmen or poets or architects or sculptors, or explorers or warriors. A mongrelized race sinks to the dead level of mediocrity. Its government becomes corrupt, its art and its literature become degenerate and silly, its judiciary becomes venal, its public and its private morals become depraved. Nothing is left to it but the sharpness, the trickiness and the cunning of its unscrupulous traders and an exalted opinion of its own importance, based on the records of the pure but vanished race which it supplanted. These facts should be of considerable interest to a great many citizens of the United States; for so many millions of non-Nordic aliens have poured into this country since 1880 that in several of America's largest cities the foreign-born and the children of foreign-born far outnumber the native Americans. The inevitable result of such a state of affairs, unless it is checked at once and forever, is mongrelization; and many of America's large cities are already displaying all the ear-marks of mongrelization. There are still many millions of good Americans who hold, in the innocence of their mistaken belief in the equality of mankind, that the person who believes in race purity is a snob; but before many years have gone by, he will be a benighted American who doesn't know that race purity is the prime essential for the well-being of his children and the continued existence of the things that made his country great.

E. THE BUSINESS WORLD AGREES: "UNCONTAMINATED" AMERICA IS BEST, 1930

Throughout most of the nineteenth century, the business world generally agreed that an "open-door" immigration policy best served their interests. The growing strength of the nativist movement in the twentieth century, however, caused business to agree to limited restrictions for patriotic reasons. In addition, some businessmen felt that anarchy was a real threat. A spokesman for the business world in this period was John E. Edgerton, a Tennessee woolen manufacturer who served as president of the National Association of Manufacturers from 1921 to 1931. In the following selection, Edgerton claimed that "the economic prosperity of the Country cannot be divorced from sound morals, social progress, and political stability."[1]

By the millions they have come to our shores through the last half century, and while the sturdier elements have made contributions to our progress, an infinitely larger number have been a continuous national liability. . . .

If that which I have suggested is shocking or requires proof, I ask you to call the roll of the armies of gunmen in our cities, of the worst criminals in our jails and penitentiaries, of the anarchists, communists, foreign-language newspapers, and other lists of disturbers containing unpronounceable or exchanged names. Then go back to the time when the foreign tides began to sweep into our country and measure the distance that we have retreated in those years from the moral and political standards which we then commonly recognized and accepted. . . .

[1]Reprinted by permission of D. G. Brinton Thompson from John E. Edgerton, "The Effect of Recent Immigration upon the Future of this Country," from Madison Grant and Charles Stewart Davidson, Eds., *The Alien in Our Midst, or Selling Our Birthright for a Mess of Pottage*, Galton Publishing Co., New York, 1930, pp. 4–8.

Because Americans at large and manufacturers in particular, and the real producers of our country in general are for the most part native, loyal, Godfearing citizens, I am daring to bring to your attention these matters which seem to me to be of primary importance. By no intemperate word or incautious act would I encourage snobbishness or any intolerance of such invidious nature as would deny to any citizen all of the rights and opportunities promised by our Constitution and written indelibly into every truly American institution. But I am one of those who believe that these rights and opportunities and all of the liberties established by our forefathers are safest while kept under the guardianship and control of the most competent of their descendants. We can serve best the ends of civilization and all the peoples of the earth by retaining at all cost the uncontaminated identity of that nationally distinctive political, social, moral and spiritual character by the power of which we have become one of the greatest nations on earth. As fast as we fall under the spell of any seductive idea or catch-word, coined and put into circulation by alien minds, and, at the behest of expediency, compromise the principles underlying our tower of national greatness, it will surely crumble as did others which have preceded it. It should, therefore, be matter of first concern to every worthy citizen to so conduct himself and so order his individual conduct as to conserve these certain essentials to assured progress.

As a manufacturer I feel the primary importance to the entire manufacturing interests of this country of the views which I have expressed. The economic prosperity of the country cannot be divorced from sound morals, social progress, and political stability. Due primarily to the operation of uncontrolled alien influences our national integrity is threatened at these points. I have indicated the cure which should be applied. Both the obligation and the right of leadership in all corrective or forward movements involving interpretations of American ideals belong inseparably to those natives of our country having no divided allegiance or attachments and having in their very blood an appreciative understanding of our institutions.

2
The Anglo-Saxon
and Literature

The importance of literary stereotypes must not be underestimated. Before the advent of radio and television, most people were likely to base their fantasies and aspirations on literary experiences. Their fictional heroes and heroines were made of the stuff that could conquer the trials of everyday living, and they fervently hoped to find these qualities in their offspring as well as themselves. These noble figures could fill Americans with a sense of accomplishment, and their successes became personal ones. Weak and distasteful characters, however, also had their influence on Americans. They were easily equated with the nation's own fears and dislikes. If the hero could explain the positive, the "underman" could explain the negative, and if America's children should emulate the qualities of the former, they must at all costs avoid contact with the latter.

Although various images of Anglo-Saxon heroes and their unwholesome adversaries appeared early in American literature, by the twentieth century race thinking had reached the point where the character and behavior of many literary types could be entirely explained by their racial heritage. The positive types were easily recognizable by their blonde hair, blue or grey eyes, rosy cheeks, firm noses and lips, and unblemished skin. In addition, in times of crisis they seemed always able to call on an inner strength that they had inherited from some lusty Nordic ancestor. Unfortunately, racial inheritance also explained the appearance and behavior of less appealing characters. They were not always cast in the role of villains, but they invariably were easily recognized by their displeasing countenances and their inability to face critical situations with the same determination and courage as could their Anglo-Saxon counterparts.

315

A. THE "WILD MOTLEY THRONG," 1892

In the following poem Thomas Bailey Aldrich contrasts the beauty, integrity, and homogeneity of his America and its inhabitants with the negative qualities of the newly arriving unassimilable hordes. This poem appeared in the Atlantic Monthly *in 1892, and it marks one of the first literary attempts to warn Americans of the peril of the nation's newest immigrants.*[1]

UNGUARDED GATES

Thomas Bailey Aldrich

Wide open and unguarded stand our gates,
Named of the four winds, North, South, East and West;
Portals that lead to an enchanted land
Of cities, forests, fields of living gold,
Vast prairies, lordly summits touched with snow,
Majestic rivers sweeping proudly past
The Arab's date-palm and the Norseman's pine—
A realm wherein are fruits of every zone,
Airs of all climes, for lo! throughout the year
The red rose blossoms somewhere—a rich land,
A later Eden planted in the wilds,
With not an inch of earth within its bound
But if a slave's foot press it sets him free!
Here, it is written, Toil shall have its wage,
And Honor honor, and the humblest man
Stand level with the highest in the law.
Of such a land have men in dungeons dreamed,
And with the vision brightening in their eyes
Gone smiling to the fagot and the sword.

Wide open and unguarded stand our gates,
And through them presses a wild motley throng—
Men from the Volga and the Tartar steppes,
Featureless figures of the Hoang-Ho,

[1]Thomas Bailey Aldrich, "Unguarded Gates," *Atlantic Monthly*, July 1892, p. 57.

Malayan, Scythian, Teuton, Kelt, and Slav,
Flying the Old World's poverty and scorn;
These bringing with them unknown gods and rites,
Those, tiger passions, here to stretch their claws.
In street and alley what strange tongues are these,
Accents of menace alien to our air,
Voices that once the Tower of Babel knew!
O Liberty, white Goddess! is it well
To leave the gates unguarded? On thy breast
Fold Sorrow's children, soothe the hurts of fate,
Lift the down-trodden, but with hand of steel
Stay those who to thy sacred portals come
To waste the gifts of freedom. Have a care
Lest from the brow the clustered stars be torn
And trampled in the dust. For so of old
The thronging Goth and Vandal trampled Rome,
And where the temples of the Caesars stood
The lean wolf unmolested made her lair.

B. "THE SUICIDE OF THE ANGLO-AMERICAN," 1912

The increasing literacy of Americans made possible the growth of mass-circulation magazines. In the early decades of the twentieth century magazines like Collier's *and the* Saturday Evening Post *were as important in educating Americans as television is today. In addition to the essays on important issues, the short stories would sometimes leave their romantic settings to reflect on the problems of the day. The following 1914 story from* Collier's *embraced all the fears that Americans entertained concerning the new immigrant. In contrast to the older stock, this new arrival was dirty, unintelligent, prolific, more inclined toward crime and immorality, and ignorant of American institutions. More important was the fact that his very presence was forcing down Anglo-American birthrates to a point of near extinction.*[1]

What Is An American?

The Suicide of the Anglo-American

Up in a stone quarry in Massachusetts, a few years ago, two men got jobs on the same day. The American of one man's name was Masso. He

[1]Honoré Willsie, "What Is An American?" *Collier's*, November 9, 1912, pp. 13–14. 42.

was a south European, short of body and long of arm. Masso had been in this country five years and spoke English fairly well.

The other man's name was Ezra. He was tall and lean and nervous. Ezra's forefathers once had held in grant from England the land on which the quarry lay, but Ezra's father had given it up. Farm labor was hard to get. The land thereabouts was being bought up by Poles and south Italian hucksters, who lived on what they could not sell and whose wives and children were their farm hands. Ezra's father could not compete with this condition. Ezra had drifted back from the city with the hope of buying, somehow, some time, the old farm.

The two men were put at like work, at the same wage—two dollars a day. The quarry was one of a great string owned by a combination of companies. It was poorly equipped. Not a cent more of the profits was put back into the quarry than was absolutely essential for turning out stone. The result was crude methods, many accidents, and a constant inflow of raw hands.

Masso found a house near the quarry. It was a shack, containing one room and a kitchen lean-to. Into this moved Masso with his wife and five children. The house looked good to them. In the old country their house had one room and a dirt floor.

Ezra found a little four-room cottage, a good distance from the noise of the quarry. There was a porch and a bathroom. Into this moved Ezra with his wife and one child, a boy about twelve years old.

Masso's wife seemed to be at her housework all the time, but the house was always dirty, and so were the children. But they were healthy, and Mrs. Masso had a laugh that was good to hear.

Ezra's wife was nervous and energetic and wore the half-worried, half-wistful look of so many New England women. Her house and her one child were immaculate.

Masso managed to lay aside part of his wages each week toward the farm he was going to buy in the old country. But after the newspaper and little Ezra's magazine, by way of luxuries, had been paid for not a cent of Ezra's wages was left.

Ezra and Masso, working shoulder to shoulder, day by day, developed a sort of liking for each other, in spite of the fact that Ezra held immigrants in utter contempt. At noon, when they sat in the shade of a stone block, eating their lunch, Ezra would try to get at Masso's ideas.

"What did you come to this country for, Masso?" he asked one hot July noon.

Masso gnawed his onion and bread thoughtfully. "Make money easy here," he answered, "then go back to old country rich."

"Well, what else?" urged Ezra.

Masso looked blank.

"I mean," said Ezra, "did you like this Government better'n yours? Did you like our ways better'n yours? Understand?"

Masso shrugged his shoulders. "Don't care 'bout gov'ment if I made the money. What did you come to this country for?"

Ezra flamed, "I was born here, you Wop you! This very dirt here made the food that made me! Understand? I'm a part of this country same as the trees are! My folks left comfort and friends behind 'em and came to this country when it was full of Indians, to be free, free; can you get that? And what good did it do them? They larded the soil with their good sweat to make a place for fellows like you. And what do you care?"

"I work," said Masso stolidly. "I work all the time and I make the money. That's enough." . . .

Ezra considered this for a few minutes. Then as he lighted his pipe he said: "I don't know anything about it except what I see and what I read in the papers. I ain't got anything personal against you. You're a human being like me, doing your best according to your light. But I'd like to bet that if they'd shut the doors after the Civil War and let those that was in the country have their chance, this country would be a whole lot farther along than it is now. I'll bet if they had fifty men in this quarry like me, instead of a hundred like you, it would turn out twice the work it does now." . . .

The blocks of stone were loaded on to flat cars by means of old-fashioned wooden-arm derricks that always were breaking and endangering the lives of the men. One day the guide rope of one of the biggest derricks broke and the great block of stone swept across the flat car, breaking the leg of a Polak and all but mashing the life out of a little Italian water boy.

Ezra was enraged. He went to the boss and demanded new equipment all around. The boss laughed.

"The equipment is good enough for a lot of Wops and Bohunks."

"I'm not a Wop or a Bohunk!" retorted Ezra. "I won't work where you don't take any better care of your men than you do here."

The boss hesitated. The American workman was valuable in the intelligence he brought to his work.

"Well, I'll write to the company," he said, evasively.

Ezra's lips tightened. "You gotta get us some decent equipment," he growled. . . .

Early in November, when the work was getting slack but bitter hard in the raw weather, there came a ten per cent cut in wages. Ezra, with the panicky feeling closing in on his heart, talked it over with his wife.

It was of no use to quit and look for work that time of year, they decided.

Yet the twenty cents a day loss must be met. At first they thought of discontinuing the boy's magazine. But at last they decided that by Ezra giving up tobacco and by giving up cream for coffee and cereal, by getting no new clothes for themselves, they still could pay the rent for the pretty cottage with the bathroom, still keep little Ezra well dressed and in school, and tide through the winter somehow—if there was no sickness.

The next morning Masso appeared on the job with a dirty-faced small boy.

Said Masso to Ezra: "I take him out of school soon's I hear of the cut. Boss, he give him job as tool boy. He work cheaper than that American boy they got there."

"He's too small to work," said Ezra. "You'd ought to keep him in school. Give him a chance."

"Chance for what?" asked Masso.

"Chance to grow into a decent citizen," snarled Ezra with the old feeling of having his back to the wall while the pack worried him in front.

"Oh, he goes back to the old country with me in a few years!" said Masso. "He find books no good over there."

The boy looked up quickly. "I ain't going back. Me, I'm an American!" he said. "I'll be rich some day."

The father gave him a push, and the boy went off to his work. John looked after him proudly. "That's right," he said. "He won't go back. He's a good American now. My six children, they all Americans."

"Good, Americans!" sneered Ezra. "What do you mean by good American?"

"Oh, he learn how to make much money quick!" answered Masso, nodding he head knowingly.

"That's not being an American!" shouted Ezra. "He'll never make an American, that kid!"

Masso scowled, "Why not?" he growled.

Ezra straightened his tired shoulders and looked out over the dreary waste of November fields beyond the quarry. It was the land that his father held in grant from an English king. The fields that had made Ezra's flesh and blood were dotted with Italian huts. The lane where Ezra's mother had met his father when he returned crippled from Antietam was blocked by a Polak road house.

Ezra looked from the fields back to the alien eyes of his hearer. He started to speak, then stopped. . . .

Ezra had the one child. Every year of the three that Masso and Ezra worked together in the quarry Masso had a baby. As his wages went down and his birth rate went up, Masso merely moved into cheaper quarters, bought cheaper food, went dirtier and poorer clothed, and took another child out of school and put him or her to work. . . .

The thing that differentiated Masso from Ezra was the thing that kept Ezra from having more children. Ezra had an ideal. The ideal of progress, of breeding better than he had been bred, the idea that demanded a certain standard of living. And rather than forego the ideal, Ezra committed race suicide. . . .

Little Ezra had small chance of maintaining Ezra's line. A man, by the law of averages, must have at least four children to stand a good chance of his line continuing.

But to industry the cheapest portion of its equipment has been its inexhaustible human labor supply. It was Ezra who had pleaded for the new derricks. It was Ezra who managed the derrick's machinery most deftly. And so it was Ezra who was sent to the danger spots, he having the keenest wits, the best knowledge of the danger spots. And so it was Ezra, and Masso, his helper, who were caught under the giant block when the derrick broke from its moorings and dropped clean across the quarry.

It was too common a tragedy for even the local papers to give more than a passing column to it. And outside of the human pitifulness of the waste of it and the suffering to the mothers and the babies, one is not prepared to urge that the tragedy had special significance.

Had Masso known enough, before his broken chest choked him, he might have said: "it doesn't matter! After all, I have done a man's part. I have worked to the limit of my strength and I shall survive through my fertility. What I have done to America no one knows." But Masso was ignorant, and all that he said was some futile word to the priest who knelt in the sleet beside him. Masso never had gotten very far from the thought of his Maker.

Ezra, lifted to the edge of the quarry to lie on the border of the fields where his fathers had dreamed and hoped and sweated and fought, thought of the small Ezra and the losing fight ahead of the little fellow, and for the last time the sense of having his back to the wall, the pack suffocating him, closed in on him, blinded him and merged into the darkness into which none of us has seen. Ezra and his line were dead.

C. JACK LONDON AND THE ANGLO-SAXON

In several of his stories Jack London drew lusty portrayals of Anglo-Saxon characters, They could easily be recognized by their pleasing ex-

teriors and the depths of their inner strength. Invariably their love of battle, gritty determination, and ability to lead made them stand in sharp contrast to their lesser adversaries. London had to reconcile his race theories with his professed socialism, but as he himself once put it at a Socialist Party meeting in San Francisco, "I am first of all a white man, and only then a socialist."

Mutiny on the Elsinore (1914) is a tale of an American coal-carrying ship sailing around the Horn in 1913. It is captained by a domineering tyrant, officered by mates of the old, hard-driving, man-killing breed, and manned by a crew of insane, crippled, and criminal seamen. Observing the entire scene is a most perceptive Anglo-Saxon individual who strongly feels his racial affinity for the leaders on board, and he concludes that the ship and its crew are symbolic of the whole struggle of superior and inferior beings in the face of insurmountable odds.[1]

Every one of us who sits aft in the high place is a blond Aryan. For'ard, leavened with a ten per cent of degenerate blonds, the remaining ninety per cent of the slaves that toil for us are brunettes. They will not perish. According to Woodruff, they will inherit the earth, not because of their capacity for mastery and government, but because of their skin-pigmentation which enables their tissues to resist the ravages of the sun.

And I look at the four of us at table—Captain West, his daughter, Mr. Pike, and myself—all fair-skinned, blue-eyed, and perishing, yet mastering and commanding, like our fathers before us, to the end of our type on the earth. Ah, well, ours is a lordly history, and though we may be doomed to pass, in our time we shall have trod on the faces of all peoples, disciplined them to obedience, taught them government, and dwelt in the palaces we have compelled them by the weight of our right arms to build for us.

The *Elsinore* depicts this in miniature. The best of the food and all spacious and beautiful accommodation is ours. For'ard is a pigsty and a slave pen. As a king, Captain West sits above all. As a captain of soldiers, Mr. Pike enforces his king's will. Miss West is a princess of the royal house. And I? Am I not an honorable, noble-lineaged pensioner on the deeds and achievements of my father, who, in his day, compelled thousands of the lesser types to the building of the fortune I enjoy? . . .

[Later, during a storm at sea] I have repeatedly said that the sea

---

[1]Jack London, *Mutiny of the Elsinore*, Macmillan Co., New York, 1914, pp. 148–149, 195–198.

makes one hard. I now realized how hard I had become as I stood there at the break of the poop in my wind-whipped, spray-soaked pajamas. I felt no solicitude for the forecastle humans who struggled in peril of their lives beneath me. They did not count. Ay—I was even curious to see what might happen, did they get caught by those crashing avalanches of sea ere they could gain the safety of the fife-rail.

And I saw. Mr. Pike, in the lead, of course, up to his waist in rushing water, dashed in, caught the flying wreckage with a turn of rope, and fetched it up short with a turn around one of the port mizzen-shrouds. The *Elsinore* flung down to port, and a solid wall of down-toppling green upreared a dozen feet above the rail. The men fled to the fife-rail. But Mr. Pike, holding his turn, held on, looked squarely into the wall of the wave, and received the downfall. He emerged, still holding by the turn the captured bridge. . . .

The *Elsinore* rolled to port and dipped her deck full from rail to rail. Next, she plunged down by the head, and all this mass of water surged forward. Through the creaming, foaming surface, now and then emerged an arm, or a head, or a back, while cruel edges of jagged plank and twisted steel rods advertised that the bridge was turning over and over. I wondered what men were beneath it and what mauling they were receiving.

And yet these men did not count. I was aware of anxiety only for Mr. Pike. He, in a way, socially, was of my caste and class. He and I belonged aft in the high place; ate at the same table. I was acutely desirous that he should not be hurt or killed. The rest did not matter. They were not of my world. I imagine the old-time skippers, on the middle passage, felt much the same toward their slave-cargoes in the fetid 'tween-decks.

The *Elsinore*'s bow tilted skyward while her stern fell into a foaming valley. Not a man had gained his feet. Bridge and men swept back toward me and fetched up at the mizzen-shrouds. And then that prodigious, incredible old man appeared out of the water, on his two legs, upright, dragging with him, a man in each hand, the helpless forms of Nancy and the Faun. My heart leapt at beholding this mighty figure of a man—killer and slave-driver, it is true, but who sprang first into the teeth of danger so that his slaves might follow, and who emerged with a half-drowned slave in either hand.

I knew augustness and pride as I gazed—pride that my eyes were blue, like his; that my skin was blond, like his; that my place was aft with him, and with the Samurai, in the high place of government and command. I nearly wept with the chill of pride that was akin to awe and that tingled and bristled along my spinal column and in my brain. As for the rest—the weaklings and the rejected, and the dark-pigmented things, the half-castes, the mongrel-bloods, and the dregs of long-conquered races—how could they count? My heels were iron as I gazed on them in their peril and weakness. Lord! Lord! For ten thousand generations and centuries we had stamped upon their faces and enslaved them to the toil of our will.

3
The Scholars
Analyze The
Anglo-Saxon's Enemies

The immigration restriction acts of the 1920's were the culmination of many factors, not the least of which were the race theories popularized by various intellectuals during the first decades of the twentieth century. Prominent historians, economists, political theorists, and scientists began in the late nineteenth century to attribute the superior nature of American institutions to the common history of a people whose undiluted blood had been inherited from Anglo-Saxon ancestors. In particular, it was the scientists, writing for both their students and the general public, who were most influential in giving scholarly legitimacy to race thinking.

The translation of scientific racial theories into a popular creed was effectively carried out in a very short time. Greatly influenced by their contemporaries in Europe, the resurrection of Mendel's work on heredity, and their own version of Social Darwinism, the American scientists claimed that the quality of human society could be radically improved by selective breeding. During the Progressive era, eugenicists calling for race improvement had no trouble capturing the ear of a public already well attuned to reform slogans of a different kind. The immigration problem, it appeared, could be reduced to its lowest biological denominator, and the possibility of race suicide was held up to those who thought they could ignore these realities. At the same time, scientists neatly classified the nationalities of Europe into Nordic, Alpine, and Mediterranean groupings, thereby making it that much easier for those emphasizing the racial nature of our ancestors.

Such groupings became even more significant because many scientists insisted that not only were biological deficiencies passed on to the offspring but social and psychological behavior as well. By claiming that the immigrants included an extraordinarily high percentage of lunatics and criminals, and by pointing to their low intelligence test scores, the scientists made it clear that here was a new kind of immigrant, who, if crossed with the native stock, would produce a new, inferior-type American.

A. THE CALL FOR A NATIONAL EUGENICS POLICY, 1910

The eugenics movement was launched in England in the mid-nineteenth century by Sir Francis Galton, and by the end of the century it had won many followers among American scholars. The eugenicists focused on improving the basic stock through careful breeding, and they warned that feeblemindedness, criminality, and pauperism were also strongly influenced by hereditary factors. The movement was appealing to those patrician intellectuals who felt their traditional world threatened by various social and economic changes and who in the New Immigrant found an example of what happens when a society loses its respect for good breeding. Many of the eugenicists were located in prominent Eastern universities, as was Robert DeCourcey Ward, a Boston-born Harvard graduate who returned to teach climatology at his alma mater and who in 1894 helped found the Immigration Restriction League. His following article succinctly sets forth the basic contentions of the eugenicists of that period.[1]

There are those who believe that the Anglo-Saxon American will disappear as the American Indian and the American buffalo have disappered, and they have some basis for their belief.

What kind of a race will this new one be, made up of such diverse elements that, as Professor William Z. Ripley says, "the most complex populations of Europe seem ethnically pure by contrast"? Truly, this is a "melting-pot" for all the nations and peoples of the world. Into it we have allowed Europe, and even Asia and Africa, to throw every sort of material, while we ourselves have been blissfully—shall we not rather say criminally?—careless as to what the final product is to be. Will the new American type be a superior or an inferior one? Who can say? Evi-

[1]Robert De Courcey Ward, "National Eugenics in Relation to Immigration," *North American Review*, July 1910, pp. 56–67.

dence is available on both sides of the question, and opposite views upon it are held by those authorities who have studied it. In the midst of disagreement among the scholars, what shall the layman do? One thing is clear: the results of biological study go to show that the crossing of types should not be carried too far, or be too extreme. In the light of the evidence which is available, it seems to the writer that the burden of proof is distinctly upon those who hold that the new American race will be a better, stronger, more intelligent race, and not a weak and possibly degenerate mongrel. . . .

This falling birth-rate in the United States is no peculiarity of our own people. A low and falling birth-rate is a world-wide phenomenon. In Great Britain, for example, the birth-rate fell from thirty-six per thousand in 1876 to twenty-seven per thousand in 1907. But the most serious thing is that the fall is not the same in all classes. If the lowest stratum of society in England had been affected equally with the higher the twenty-seven per thousand would have been still further reduced. Society is recruiting itself from below. The eugenically less valuable portion of the community is furnishing a disproportionately large share of the next generation. A selective birth-rate has been established which is tending towards a degeneration of the stock. But clearly, if the race is to progress, the fitter part of the population should be the most fertile. Small wonder that the eugenists cry out: "The choice for Western civilization will ere long be the final one between eugenics or extinction. . . . " Advancing civilization has brought about a more and more artificial death-rate by prolonging the life of thousands of unfit persons who in old days would have died without reproducing their kind. Today many of these not only live, but marry and have children. It has, therefore, become of the highest importance to have a selective birth-rate, selective according to eugenic standards, if the race is to progress. . . .

We in the United States have an opportunity which is unique in history for the practice of eugenic principles. Our country was founded and developed by picked men and women. And today, by selecting our immigrants through proper immigration legislation, we have the power to pick out the best specimens of each race to be the parents of our future citizens. But we have left the choice almost altogether to the selfish interests which do not care whether we want the immigrants they bring, or whether the immigrants will be the better for coming. Steamship agents and brokers all over Europe and western Asia are today deciding for us the character of the American race of the future. . . .

Professor Karl Pearson has well said: "You cannot change the leopard's spots, and you cannot change bad stock to good; you may dilute it, possibly spread it over a wide area, spoiling good stock, but until it ceases to multiply it will not cease to be."

B.   THE UNIVERSITY OF WISCONSIN'S EDWARD A. ROSS
AND THE "DISCARDED MOLDS OF THE CREATOR," 1914

Edward A. Ross was a prominent sociologist at the University of Wisconsin during the first decades of the twentieth century. He considered himself one of the nation's immigration watchdogs, and he promised that he was "not one of those who consider humanity and forget the nation." The following passage is taken from his The Old World and the New.[1]

To the practiced eye, the physiognomy of certain groups unmistakably proclaims inferiority of type. I have seen gatherings of the foreign born in which narrow and sloping foreheads were the rule. The shortness and smallness of the crania were very noticeable. There was much facial asymmetry. Among the women, beauty, aside from the fleeting, epidermal bloom of girlhood, was quite lacking. In every face there was something wrong—lips thick, mouth coarse, upper lip too long, cheekbones too high, chin poorly formed, the bridge of the nose hollowed, the base of the nose tilted, or else the whole face prognathous. There were so many sugar-loaf heads, moon-faces, slit mouths, lantern-jaws, and goosebill noses that one might imagine a malicious jinn had amused himself by casting human beings in a set of skew-molds discarded by the Creator. . . .

That the Mediterranean peoples are morally below the races of northern Europe is as certain as any social fact. Even when they were dirty, ferocious barbarians, these blonds were truthtellers. Be it pride or awkwardness or lack of imagination or fair-play sense, something has held them back from the nimble lying of the southern races. Immigration officials find that the different peoples are as day and night in point of veracity, and report vast trouble in extracting the truth from certain brunet nationalities. . . .

When a more-developed element is obliged to compete on the same economic plane with a less developed element, the standards of cleanliness or decency or education cherished by the advanced element act on it like a slow poison. William does not leave as many children as

[1]Edward A. Ross, *The Old World And The New*, The Century Co., New York, 1914, pp. 286, 293, 303.

'Tonio, because he will not huddle his family into one room, eat maca-roni off a bare board, work his wife barefoot in the field, and keep his children weeding onions instead of at school.

C.   COLUMBIA'S HENRY FAIRFIELD OSBORN AND THE NORDIC AS SOLDIER, 1917

Because of the country's overriding concern with war in 1917, pale-ontologist Henry Fairfield Osborn emphasized the role of America's Nordic youths in his preface to the second edition of Madison Grant's The Passing of the Great Race. *For Osborn, the kind of response of the "blue-eyed, fair-haired" boys was further evidence of the Anglo-Saxon's superiority. Osborn, a Princeton graduate, taught for a number of years at his alma mater before serving as a Columbia University dean from 1890 to 1910. As president of the American Museum of Natural History after the war, he continued to stimulate interest in the eugenics move-ment.*[1]

History is repeating itself in America at the present time and inci-dentally is giving a convincing demonstration of the central thought in this volume, namely, that heredity and racial predisposition are stronger and more stable than environment and education.

Whatever may be its intellectual, its literary, its artistic or its musical aptitudes, as compared with other races, the Anglo-Saxon branch of the Nordic race is again showing itself to be that upon which the nation must chiefly depend for leadership, for courage, for loyalty, for unity and harmony of action, for self-sacrifice and devotion to an ideal. Not that members of other races are not doing their part, many of them are, but in no other human stock which has come to this country is there displayed the unanimity of heart, mind and action which is now being displayed by the descendants of the blue-eyed, fair-haired peoples of the north of Europe. In a recent journey in northern California and Oregon I noted that, in the faces of the regiments which were first to leave for the city of New York and later that, in the wonderful array of young men at Plattsburg, the Anglo-Saxon type was clearly dominant over every other and the purest members of this type largely outnumber

---

[1]Reprinted by permission of D. G. Brinton Thompson from Henry Fairfield Osborn, "Preface," in Madison Grant, *The Passing of the Great Race*, 2nd edition, Charles Scribner's Sons, New York, 1917, pp. xi–xiii.

the others. In nothern California I saw a great regiment detrain and with one or two exceptions they were all native Americans, descendants of the English, Scotch and north of Ireland men who founded the State of Oregon in the first half of the nineteenth century. At Plattsburg fair hair and blue eyes were very noticeable, much more so than in any ordinary crowds of American collegians as seen assembled in our universities.

It should be remembered also that many of the dark-haired, dark-eyed youths of Plattsburg and other volunteer training camps are often three-fourths or seven-eighths Nordic, because it only requires a single dark-eyed ancestor to lend the dark hair and eye color to an otherwise pure Nordic strain. There is a clear differentiation between the original Nordic, the Alpine and the Mediterranean strains; but where physical characters and characteristics are partly combined in a mosaic, and to a less degree are blended, it requires long experience to judge which strain dominates.

With a race having these predispositions, extending back to the very beginnings of European history, there is no hesitation or even waiting for conscription and the sad thought was continually in my mind in California, in Oregon and in Plattsburg that again this race was passing, that this war will take a very heavy toll of this strain of Anglo-Saxon life which has played so large a part in American history.

War is in the highest sense dysgenic rather than eugenic. It is destructive of the best strains, spiritually, morally and physically. For the world's future the destruction of wealth is a small matter compared with the destruction of the best human strains, for wealth can be renewed while these strains of the real human aristocracy once lost are lost forever. In the new world that we are working and fighting for, the world of liberty, of justice and of humanity, we shall save democracy only when democracy discovers its own aristocracy as in the days when our Republic was founded.

D.   MADISON GRANT AND RACE SUICIDE, 1921

The haunting fears of extinction by the patrician intellectuals were neatly summarized in Madison Grant's The Passing of the Great Race. *First published in 1916, by 1921 it had gone through four editions. Grant, a lawyer and founder of the New York Zoological Society, did much to synthesize earlier race theories, but it was particularly his conclusion that America was committing racial suicide through unscientific mixing that had appeal for the restrictionists. In this introduction to the book's fourth edition in 1921, Grant, an officer of the Immigration Restriction League, writes frankly of his personal beliefs and the book's great purpose.*[1]

To admit the unchangeable differentiation of race in its modern scientific meaning is to admit inevitably the existence of superiority in one race and of inferiority in another. Such an admission we can hardly expect from those of inferior races. These inferior races and classes are prompt to recognize in such an admission the very real danger to themselves of being relegated again to their former obscurity and subordinate position in society. The favorite defense of these inferior classes is an unqualified denial of the existence of fixed inherited qualities, either physical or spiritual, which cannot be obliterated or greatly modified by a change of environment. Failing in this, as they must necessarily fail, they point out the presence of mixed or intermediate types, and claim that in these mixtures, or blends as they choose to call them, the higher type tends to predominate. In fact, of course, the exact opposite is the case and it is scarcely necessary to cite the universal distrust, often contempt, that the half-breed between two sharply contrasted races inspires the world over. Belonging physically and spiritually to the lower race, the unfortunate mongrel, in addition to a disharmonic physique, often inherits from one parent an unstable brain which is stimulated and at times overexcited by flashes of brilliancy from the other. The result is a total lack of continuity of purpose, an intermittent intellect goaded into spasmodic outbursts of energy. Where the parent races are not so widely separated, as in case of crosses between Negroes, Indians and whites, we may have a generation which gives us individuals occupying the border land between genius and insanity.

The essential character of all these racial mixtures is a lack of harmony—both physical and mental—in the first few generations. Then, if the strain survives, it is by the slow reversion to one of the parent types —almost inevitably the lower.

The temporary advantage of mere numbers enjoyed by the inferior classes in modern democracies can only be made permanent by the destruction of superior types—by massacre, as in Russia, or by taxation, as in England. In the latter country the financial burdens of the war

---

[1]Reprinted by permission of D. G. Brinton Thompson from Madison Grant, *The Passing of the Great Race*, 4th edition, Charles Scribner's Sons, New York, 1921, pp. xxviii–xxxiii.

and the selfish interests of labor have imposed such a load of taxation upon the upper and middle classes that marriage and children are becoming increasingly burdensome.

The best example of complete elimination of a dominant class is in Santa Domingo. The horrors of the black revolt were followed by the slow death of the culture of the white man. This history should be studied carefully because it gives in prophetic form the sequence of events that we may expect to find in Mexico and in parts of South America where the replacement of the higher type by the resurgent native is taking place. . . .

The danger is from within and not from without. Neither the black, nor the brown, nor the yellow, nor the red will conquer the white in battle. But if the valuable elements in the Nordic race mix with inferior strains or die out through race suicide, then the citadel of civilization will fall for mere lack of defenders. . . .

The rapidly growing appreciation of the importance of race during the last few years, the study of the influence of race on nationality as shown by the after-war disputes over boundaries, the increasing complexity of our own problems between the whites and blacks, between the Americans and Japs, and between the native Americans and the hyphenated aliens in our midst upon whom we have carelessly urged citizenship, and, above all, the recognition that the leaders of labor and their more zealous followers are almost all foreigners, have served to arouse Americans to a realization of the menace of the impending Migration of Peoples through unrestrained freedom of entry here. The days of the Civil War and the provincial sentimentalism which governed or misgoverned our public opinion are past, and this generation must completely repudiate the proud boast of our fathers that they acknowledged no distinction in "race, creed, or color," or else the native American must turn the page of history and write: "FINIS AMERICÆ"

E.   THE U. S. ARMY INTELLIGENCE TESTS AND
NORDIC SUPERIORITY, 1923

The intelligence tests given to army recruits during World War I provided the eugenicists with the evidence they needed to illustrate the inborn mental abilities of the various races. Robert M. Yerkes, a Harvard Ph.D. and president of the American Psychological Association, headed a team of distinguished psychologists that gathered data on the intellectual abilities of blacks, native whites, and foreign-born American soldiers. Their findings were popularized by nativist writers after the

*war, prompting Yerkes to speak out against the more extravagant state-
ments. In this selection, however, Yerkes made no attempt to downplay
the data that manifested the "tragically poor showing" of the Mediterranean races.[1]*

Nor can we safely overlook the effect of men of foreign birth on the
intellectual status of the army. Altogether they are markedly inferior
in mental alertness to the native-born American. In the group of soldiers
especially studied by the psychologists, about 18 per cent were foreign-
born. The United States Census reports for the total population about
14 per cent of foreign birth; so the draft was somewhat more heavily
weighted than is the total population. Whereas the mental age of the
American-born soldier is between thirteen and fourteen years, according
to army statistics, that of the soldier of foreign birth serving in our army
is less than twelve years. To claim, then, that the inclusion of foreigners
lowers the average mental age of the group by one half-year is conservative. . . .

What of the intelligence of different races? Some years ago I read a
book whose thesis was "Mind is fundamentally one and the same for
mankind." If this is true, so also is the thesis that body—including such
traits as hair-color and texture, complexion, height, cranial capacity—is
essentially the same for all mankind. I have marveled that the learned
gentleman found it in his heart to write so much with the hope of establishing what, obviously, is false! If we may safely judge by the army
measurements of intelligence, races are quite as significantly different as
individuals. . . . [and] almost as great as the intellectual difference between negro [sic] and white in the army are the differences between
white racial groups.

Of natives of England serving in the United States Army only 8.7 per
cent graded D or lower in intelligence; of natives of Poland, 69.9 per
cent. In the English group, 19.7 per cent graded A or B, and in the
Polish group, one half of one per cent. . . .

The measurements of intelligence for different races are appreciably
influenced by familiarity with English and facility in its use, as well as
by amount of schooling. However, there is no reason to suppose that
the English or Scotch have marked advantage over the Irish in their
familiarity with the English language. Nevertheless, the English and
Scotch groups show few intellectual inferiors and many superiors;
whereas for the Irish group the reverse is the case. More than 39 per

[1]Reprinted by permission of the *Atlantic Monthly* from Robert M. Yerkes, "Testing
the Human Mind," March 1923, pp. 358–365.

cent of the Irish graded D or lower, and only 4 per cent graded A or B.

The tragically poor showing, in the racial statistics, of the Italian and Polish groups is worthy of particular note, because these races at present figure so conspicuously among our immigrants.

Dr. Carl C. Brigham of Princeton University has recently reexamined and carefully analyzed the army data bearing on nativity and length of residence in the United States. His results have not yet been published, but I am permitted to say that, in the main, they confirm the statements of this article. He has studied with care the intelligence of immigrants for different periods of the history of our country, and has discovered rather marked diminution of intelligence, which seemingly is due to change in the proportions of immigrants from Northern and Southern Europe.

For the past ten years or so the intellectual status of immigrants has been disquietingly low. Perhaps this is because of the dominance of the Mediterranean races, as contrasted with the Nordic and Alpine.

By some people meagre intelligence in immigrants has been considered an industrial necessity and blessing; but when all the available facts are faced squarely, it looks more like a burden. Certainly the results of psychological examining in the United States Army establish the relation of inferior intelligence to delinquency and crime, and justify the belief that a country which encourages, or even permits, the immigration of simple-minded, uneducated, defective, diseased, or criminalistic persons, because it needs cheap labor, seeks trouble in the shape of public expense.

It might almost be said that whoever desires high taxes, full almshouses, a constantly increasing number of schools for defectives, of correctional institutions, penitentiaries, hospitals, and special classes in our public schools, should by all means work for unrestricted and nonselective immigration.

4
Closing the Door

Prior to the 1880's, the United States had no clearly defined immigration policy; in fact, the Federal Government only concerned itself with counting the number of entrants for statistical purposes and with establishing certain minimum conditions aboard ships bound for this country. But under pressure from New York and California, the two states that processed the great majority of immigrants, Congress in 1882 denied admission to all lunatics, idiots, and persons likely to become a public charge, and halted the entry of Chinese laborers. These were the first acts that indicated a loss of faith in the melting pot, and the first steps toward closing the door to undesirable newcomers.

Stimulated by new race theories, labor disorder, and the growing number of urban poor, the agitation for immigration restriction began to take hold in the last decade of the nineteenth century. Congress became involved when statistical evidence began to show that immigrants from Northwestern Europe were being outnumbered by those from the Southeast. In 1896, both houses of Congress passed an immigrant literacy test. Although President Cleveland vetoed it, similar legislation was reintroduced three times in the next 20 years until finally passed in 1917 over Wilson's veto.

Restrictionists were hopeful that immigration could be reduced by 25 percent through use of the literacy test, and particularly it was thought that the immigrants from Southeastern Europe would be affected. In 1921, however, Congress responded to new cries for restriction by establishing a quota system that limited immigration to three percent of the number of foreign born residing in the United States in 1910. Although Wilson ignored the bill, Harding signed it, thus establishing, in effect, a system that reduced immigration from Southeastern Europe to 20 percent of its 1914 total. A limit of 355,000 was placed on all immigration.

The new system was designed only as a stop-gap measure until a permanent system could be worked out. By 1924, legislation was ready that embodied the concept of racial and cultural homogeneity. It utilized the 1890 census and effectively eliminated the possibility of Southeastern Europeans coming into this country in large numbers. The law, which passed both houses with overwhelming majorities, cut immigration to 150,000 a year and called for a "national origins" quota system to be implemented in 1927.

The national-origins section of the 1924 law stated that future immigration quotas would be based on the composition of racial groups living in the United States in 1920. Restrictionists gave little thought to the concept until 1927 when the special Quota Board made known the new figures. Suffering drastic reductions under the system were Ireland, Germany, and the Scandinavian countries, while England was allocated 50 percent of the total European immigration figure. The intense debate that followed was among Nordics themselves fighting over the preferential quotas they had already won in 1924. Finally, after two postponements because of the pressure from the nationality groups hardest hit by the new quotas, Congress allowed a slightly revised national-origins system to become operative on July 1, 1929.

After World War II the spectre of "undesirable immigrants" flooding American shores was again raised by Congress when President Truman called for America to take its share of the war's refugees. Many of these displaced persons were Jews and Catholics from the same countries classified as undesirable in 1924, and the arguments sounded exceedingly familiar.

A.   HENRY CABOT LODGE CALLS FOR
IMMIGRATION RESTRICTION, 1891

As both student and professor at Harvard, Henry Cabot Lodge displayed strong racial prejudices, and like so many other Eastern patrician intellectuals, he was horrified by the immigration statistics of the 1880's, which showed the sharp increase in immigrants from Southern and Eastern Europe. As a Congressman, he became the leading advocate of immigration restriction and the spearhead of the drive to establish a literacy test for arriving immigrants. The following article, which appeared in the January 1891 issue of the North American Review, *illustrates not only Lodge's own racial antipathies but also those of American officials abroad. A few months later in the same magazine Lodge ex-*

plained how this lax immigration policy was in no small way responsible for the lynching of eleven Italians in New Orleans.[1]

During this century and until very recent years these same nations, with the addition of Ireland and the Scandinavian countries, have continued to furnish the chief component parts of the immigration which has helped to populate so rapidly the territory of the United States. Among all these people, with few exceptions, community of race or language, or both, has facilitated the work of assimilation. In the last ten years, however, as appears from the figures just given, new and wholly different elements have been introduced into our immigration, and—what is more important still—the rate of immigration of these new elements has risen with much greater rapidity than that of those which previously had furnished the bulk of the population of the country. The mass of immigration, absolutely speaking, continues, of course, to come from the United Kingdom and from Germany, but relatively the immigration from these two sources is declining rapidly in comparison with the immigration from Italy and from the Slavic countries of Russia, Poland, Hungary, and Bohemia, the last of which appears under the head of Austria. Of the generally good character of the immigration from the United Kingdom, Germany, and the Scandinavian countries it is hardly necessary to speak; but I will quote a single sentence from the State Department report already referred to, in regard to the immigration from the United Kingdom and Germany:

> The diagrams show the remarkable predominance of the United Kingdom and Germany in supplying the United States with skilled labor, and also the fact that the Germans represent those industries that depend upon hand labor or the requirements of everyday life, while the English supply the mechanical element. While Germany sends blacksmiths, butchers, carpenters, coopers, saddlers, shoemakers, and tailors, the United Kingdom supplies miners, engineers, iron- and steel-workers, mechanics and artisans, weavers and spinners. This distinction is clearly marked and is certainly important.

Now as to the immigration from the other countries, which has been increasing so much faster than that to which we have been accustomed, and which we know from experience to be in the main valuable. Consul-General Jussen says in his report (1886) in regard to the Austrian immigration:

[1]Henry Cabot Lodge, "The Restriction of Immigration," *North American Review*, January 1891, pp. 30–32.

The young men who want to escape military service, the ultra-socialist, the anarchist, the men who have lost all social and business footing here, the bankrupt, embezzler, and swindler, stop not to obtain permission of the government, and naturally the authorities have no sort of record here either as to the number or the place of destination of this class of emigrants. . . . The government would, as a matter of course, prohibit, if it could do so, the emigration of all young men subject to military duty, but it is quite natural that it feels no regret to get rid of the ultra-socialists and anarchists, and that it is quite willing the bankrupt and swindler should depart for foreign countries and that the paupers should find support away from home.

He also speaks as follows in regard to the Bohemian emigration, which forms a large part of that which is classed under the head of Austria:

The labor and agricultural classes of Bohemia probably supply the greatest number of emigrants to the United States, and among the Bohemian industrial laborers some of the most violent ultra-socialists are to be found. The great majority of these Bohemian laborers, both of the industrial and agricultural class, are illiterate and ignorant in the extreme. They stand in great awe of the police authorities at home.

In regard to Hungarian emigration, Mr. Sterne, consul at Budapest, speaks (1886) as follows:

I am of the opinion that with the present condition of the labor market in the United States there is no room there at present for this class of people. I even believe that under more favorable conditions in the United States these Slovaks are not a desirable acquisition for us to make, since they appear to have so many items in common with the Chinese. Like these, they are extremely frugal, the love of whiskey of the former being balanced by the opium habit of the latter. Their ambition lacks both in quality and quantity. Thus they will work similarly cheap as the Chinese, and will interfere with a civilized laborer's earning a 'white' laborer's wages.

The emigration from Italy comes largely from the southern provinces —from Naples and Sicily; a smaller proportion being drawn from the finer population of northern Italy. In regard to the Italian emigration, Mr. Alden, consul-general at Rome, says (1886):

As to the habits and morals of the emigrants to the United States from the northern and central portions of Italy, both men and women are sober and industrious, and as a rule trustworthy and moral. They are generally strong, powerful workers, and capable of enduring great fatigue. A less favorable view may be taken of the emigrants from the southern districts and Sicily. These are the most illiterate parts of Italy, and in these districts brigandage was for many years extremely prevalent.

In regard to the emigration from Russia, Mr. Young, the consul-general, says (1886):

> The government of Russia does not encourage emigration. On the contrary, it prohibits all Russian subjects from leaving the empire of Russia, except Poles and Jews. . . . The Mennonites have emigrated perhaps more extensively than any other class of Russian subjects. . . . The lowest classes generally form the greater part of emigration.

Thus it is proved, first, that immigration to this country is increasing, and, second, that it is making its greatest relative increase from races most alien to the body of the American people and from the lowest and most illiterate classes among those races. In other words, it is apparent that, while our immigration is increasing, it is showing at the same time a marked tendency to deteriorate in character.

B.   WOODROW WILSON AND THE HYPHENATES, 1901

Woodrow Wilson was a paradoxical figure in the quest for exclusion. As a historian he had belittled the qualities of the immigrants from Southern and Eastern Europe. In his 1912 campaign for the presidency, however, he appealed openly for their vote and insisted that the Democratic Party would be proud to open its gates to everyone who loved liberty. Four years later, while campaigning against Charles Evans Hughes, Wilson capitalized on isolationist sentiment as he returned to attacking the hyphenates. In 1917 he vetoed a literacy act for the second time in two years, and in the following year his concept of self-determination for the defeated powers of Europe brought a kind of cosmopolitan nationalism to the immigrant question; yet when his Versailles Treaty faced increased opposition, he insisted that the "Hyphens are the knives that are being stuck into this document." During his last bedridden months in the White House he proved incapable or unwilling to halt Attorney General A. Mitchell Palmer's "Red Scare" attacks on the various immigrants.

The following passage is from Wilson's 1901 History of the American People.[1]

[1]Woodrow Wilson, *History of the American People*, Vol. V, Harper's, New York, 1901, pp. 212–214.

The census of 1890 showed the population of the country increased to 62,622,250, an addition of 12,466,467 within the decade. Immigrants poured steadily in as before, but with an alteration of stock which students of affairs marked with uneasiness. Throughout the century men of the sturdy stocks of the north of Europe had made up the main strain of foreign blood which was every year added to the vital working force of the country, or else men of the Latin-Gallic stocks of France and northern Italy; but now there came multitudes of men of the lowest class from the south of Italy and men of the meaner sort out of Hungary and Poland, men out of the ranks where there was neither skill nor energy nor any initiative of quick intelligence; and they came in numbers which increased from year to year, as if the countries of the south of Europe were disburdening themselves of the more sordid and hapless elements of their population, the men whose standards of life and of work were such as American workmen had never dreamed of hitherto. The people of the Pacific coast had clamored these many years against the admission of immigrants out of China, and in May, 1892, got at last what they wanted, a federal statute which practically excluded from the United States all Chinese who had not already acquired the right of residence; and yet the Chinese were more to be desired, as workmen if not as citizens, than most of the coarse crew that came crowding in every year at the eastern ports. They had, no doubt, many an unsavory habit, bred unwholesome squalor in the crowded quarters where they most abounded in the western seaports, and seemed separated by their very nature from the people among whom they had come to live; but it was their skill, their intelligence, their hardy power of labor, their knack at succeeding and driving duller rivals out, rather than their alien habits, that made them feared and hated and led to their exclusion at the prayer of the men they were likely to displace should they multiply. The unlikely fellows who came in at the eastern ports were tolerated because they usurped no place but the very lowest in the scale of labor.

C. WARREN G. HARDING CALLS FOR RESTRICTION, 1920

As a newspaper editor in Marion, Ohio, Warren G. Harding had first warned of the perils of unchecked immigration in 1886. More than three decades later, during his 1920 presidential campaign, he had not changed his mind. Given the repercussions of the recent Red Scare and the popular clamor for restriction, it would have taken a candidate of considerable courage to come out in opposition, and courage was not a Harding characteristic.[1]

[1]*New York Times*, September 15, 1920. © 1920 by The New York Times Company. Reprinted by permission.

The problem incident to racial differences must be accepted as one existing in fact and must be adequately met for the future security and tranquillity of our people. We have learned during the anxieties of the World War the necessity of making the citizenship of this Republic not only American in heart and soul but American in every sympathy and every aspiration.

No one can tranquilly contemplate the future of this Republic without an anxiety for abundant provision for admission to our shores of only the immigrant who can be assimilated and thoroughly imbued with the American spirit.

From the beginning of the Republic America has been a haven to the oppressed and the aspiring from all the nations of the earth. We have opened our doors freely and have given to the peoples of the world who came to us the fullness of American opportunity and political liberty. We have come to that stage of our development where we have learned that the obligations of citizenship of necessity must be assumed by those who accept the grant of American opportunity. From this time on we are more concerned with the making of citizens than we are with adding to the man-power of industry or the additional human units in our varied activities.

As a people and a nation . . . we do have the moral, the natural, and the legal international rights to determine who shall or shall not enter into our country and participate in our activities. With a new realization of the necessity of developing a soul distinctly American in this Republic we favor such modification of our immigration laws and such changes in our international understandings, and such a policy relating to those who come among us as will guarantee to the citizens of this Republic not only assimilability of alien born but the adoption by all who come of American standards, economic and otherwise, and a full consecration to American practices and ideals.

D. CALVIN COOLIDGE AND THE FEAR OF THE "CHEAP MAN," 1921

When the Immigration Restriction Act of 1924 passed Congress, it was a foregone conclusion that President Coolidge would lose little time in signing it. In 1921, Vice-President Coolidge had written an article for Good Housekeeping *magazine entitled "Whose Country Is This?" and it was quite apparent that the new immigrant was not one of the owners.*[1]

[1]Calvin Coolidge, "Whose Country Is This?" *Good Housekeeping*, February 1921, pp. 13–14, 106, 108.

We want no such additions to our population as those who prey upon our institutions or our property. America has, in the popular mind, been an asylum for those who have been driven from their homes in foreign countries because of various forms of political and religious oppression. But America cannot afford to remain an asylum after such people have passed the portals and begun to share the privileges of our institutions.

These institutions have flourished by reason of a common background of experience; they have been perpetuated by a common faith in the righteousness of their purpose; they have been handed down undiminished in effectiveness from our forefathers who conceived their spirit and prepared the foundations. We have put into operation our faith in equal opportunity before the law in exchange for equal obligation of citizenship.

All native-born Americans, directly or indirectly, have the advantage of our schools, our colleges, and our religious bodies. It is our belief that America could not otherwise exist. Faith in mankind is in no wise inconsistent with a requirement for trained citizenship, both for men and women. No civilization can exist without a background—an active community of interest, a common aspiration—spiritual, social, and economic. It is a duty our country owes itself to require of all those aliens who come here that they have a background not inconsistent with American institutions.

Such a background might consist either of a racial tradition or a national experience. But in its lowest terms it must be characterized by a capacity for assimilation. . . . It would not be unjust to ask of every alien: What will you contribute to the common good, once you are admitted through the gates of liberty? Our history is full of answers of which we might be justly proud. But of late, the answers have not been so readily or so eloquently given. Our country must cease to be regarded as a dumping ground. Which does not mean that it must deny the value of rich accretions drawn from the right kind of immigration.

Any such restriction, except as a necessary and momentary expediency, would assuredly paralyze our national vitality. But measured practically, it would be suicidal for us to let down the bars for the inflowing of cheap manhood, just as, commercially, it would be unsound for this country to allow her markets to be overflooded with cheap goods, the product of cheap labor. There is no room either for the cheap man or the cheap goods. . . .

If we believe, as we do, in our political theory that the people are the guardians of government, we should not subject our government to the bitterness and hatred of those who have not been born of our tradition and are not willing to yield an increase to the strength inherent in our institutions. American liberty is dependent on quality in citizenship. Our obligation is to maintain that citizenship at its best. We must have nothing to do with those who would undermine it. The retroactive immigrant is a danger in our midst. His discontent gives him no time to seize a healthy opportunity to improve himself. His purpose is to tear down. There is no room for him here. He needs to be deported, not as a substitute for, but as a part of his punishment.

We might avoid this danger were we insistent that the immigrant, before he leaves foreign soil, is temperamentally keyed for our national background. There are racial considerations too grave to be brushed aside for any sentimental reasons. Biological laws tell us that certain divergent people will not mix or blend. The Nordics propagate themselves successfully. With other races, the outcome shows deterioration on both sides. Quality of mind and body suggests that observance of ethnic law is as great a necessity to a nation as immigration law. . . .

We must remember that we have not only the present but the future to safeguard; our obligations extend even to generations yet unborn. The unassimilated alien child menaces our children, as the alien industrial worker, who has destruction rather than production in mind, menaces our industry. It is only when the alien adds vigor to our stock that he is wanted. The dead weight of an alien accretion stifles national progress. But we have a hope that cannot be crushed; we have a background that we will not allow to be obliterated. The only acceptable immigrant is the one who can justify our faith in man by a constant revelation of the divine purpose of the Creator.

E. A BRUTAL CRIME IS BLAMED ON IMMIGRATION POLICY, 1924

Although Congress in 1924 was almost as one in favor of further restriction on immigration from Southern and Eastern Europe, America's representatives in Washington used vastly different styles in developing verbal cases against a continuation of the existing system. In this selection, Senator James Thomas Heflin of Alabama dramatically describes a brutal murder and then plays on the sympathy of his audience while promoting an end to the "stupid and dangerous immigration policy." As Senator Heflin desired, the new law passed, and the chances of a boy with a name like Paul Rapkowskie entering the country were greatly reduced. The law cut immigration from Southern and Eastern Europe from 155,585 in 1921 to approximately 20,000 in 1924.[1]

[1]*Congressional Record*, 68th Cong., 1st Sess., April 15, 1924, pp. 6376–6377.

Less than 10 days ago in New York City, the metropolis of America, an American boy bearing an honored American name—William Clifford, Jr., a name as old as the Government itself—while walking with his father along the streets of his home city, in his native land, was attacked without a moment's warning, stabbed in the back, and murdered before his father could realize what had happened. His assailant was a 12-year-old boy not long in our country. He is the poisoned product of a stupid and dangerous immigration policy. His name was Paul Rapkowskie. He had just robbed a store, had committed the double crime of burglary and larceny, and among other things that he had stolen was a dirk knife, and when asked why he had murdered young Clifford he replied: "I just wanted to see how deep I could drive the dirk into his back."

Mr. President: I am thinking of that brutal and barbarous crime against this American boy, of the crime against his father and mother, and of the crime against the institutions that the dead boy's forebears have loved and supported for 100 years and more.

They were soldiers in the War of the Revolution. A distinguished American by his name, Nathan Clifford, was once a Member of Congress, later Attorney General under President Polk, and for 20 years a Justice of the Supreme Court, of the United States. But William Clifford, Jr., descended from a long line of American patriots, is dead as the result of our unsound and dangerous immigration policy. No more his welcome footfall is heard in the doorway of the Clifford home. Hushed is the music of his merry laughter in the American home place now so sad and sorrowful. There a grief-stricken American father and a heart-broken American mother "long for the touch of a vanished hand and the sound of a voice that is still." As they looked upon the quiet face . . . what must have been their thoughts? I wonder if in the pain and darkness of that awful hour they ever thought that Members of Congress, the President and our immigration officers, those trusted with the care and conduct of their Government, through carelessness and indifference to the duty and necessity of protecting the American people from an influx of criminal foreigners, were responsible for the death of their boy?

What are the facts? The young criminal from a foreign country, he who sneaked up behind this American boy in an American city and without a moment's warning, murdered him, came into our country under an immigration law passed by Congress and approved by the President, or some unfaithful and corrupt immigration officer in violation of the law accepted a bribe and permitted him to come in, and in so doing he admitted into the sacred precincts of our dearest inheritances a moral degenerate and a dangerous enemy. The passport thus bartered to this young European criminal was not paid for alone in money. It cost an American boy his life, struck down and destroyed one of the indispensable forces in the national defense and left in the heart of an American father and mother an aching void that the world can never fill. . . .

There is nothing more interesting, more fascinating and promising than a plain, sincere, and upstanding American boy. His intelligent judgment in the years of our country and his courage and patriotism must be relied upon to defend it in the hour of its peril. He will be the Nation's first and last reliance when man power is required for the preservation of our rights and liberties. . . .

Mr. President, in behalf of the American boy and his sister, I appeal to the Senate to close our immigration doors. If I have my way about it, no immigrant shall come into the United States in the next 12 months. I would close the doors for a period of two years at least and wait until we assimilate these who are here. I would wait until we taught them to speak English and taught them American ideals. I would work to the end of making of them law-abiding American citizens. I would want by the principles of right and the laws of justice to educate out of them the spirit of the Bolshevik. I would want to crush the spirit of the communist, which is the deadly enemy of the American home and the Christian civilization. I would try to get those who are criminals out of the ranks of the peaceful, law-abiding people, and into the penitentiaries so that boys like young Clifford, who sleeps in a grave not yet 10 days old, may be safe as they walk the public roads and the streets of the towns and cities of their homeland. This boy has not died in vain. In his name and in the name of the father and mother who weep for him I ask the Senate to wake up on this question and take the American view of it and close the doors for the good of our American country.

In the name of William Clifford, this dead American boy who cannot speak for himself, and in the interest of millions of American boys and girls, and in behalf of all loyal Americans, I appeal to this American Senate to do that whch will redound to the highest and best interest of the American people.

F. THIRTY-FOUR AMERICAN SCHOLARS URGE APPROVAL OF THE NATIONAL ORIGINS ACT, 1927

On July 1, 1927, the vital "national origins" clause of the 1924 immigration act was scheduled to go into effect. Exerting great pressure to nullify or postpone implementation of this clause were those Northern European immigrant groups who had seen their quota figures drastically reduced under the new system. Among those defending the concept were the same scholars who had played such an important role in the restrictionist debates of previous years. They had successfully argued that the Southern and Eastern Europeans were biologically and culturally inferior and hence impossible to assimilate. Now, with their cherished national-origins legislation in trouble, they sent the following resolution to Congress urging that the national-origins concept be applied not only to Europe but also to the countries of the Western Hemisphere. Representative L. Bacon of New York introduced the resolution into the Congressional Record, *and it was signed by many of the country's leading scholars.*[1]

MR. BACON. In accordance with permission given to me, I insert herewith in the *Record* a statement signed by 34 distinguished and learned Americans in favor of upholding our present immigration policy. I am glad to call it to the attention of Members of Congress. The statement is as follows:

We, the undersigned, all citizens of the United States, impressed with the vital importance to the country of maintaining and perfecting the present system of immigration restriction, respectfully submit to the President of the United States, to the Senate, and to the House of Representatives, the following expression of our views with respect to specific aspects of this question.

1. We urge the extension of the quota system to all countries of North and South America from which we have substantial immigration and in which the population is not predominantly of the white race. We believe that without such extension the present restriction of immigration is already inadequate and will become increasingly so in the near future. During each of the last two fiscal years we have been admitting upwards of 75,000 immigrants from Mexico, the West Indies, Brazil, and elsewhere, who are for the most part not of the white race and who because of their lower standards of living, are able to compete at an advantage with American workers engaged in various forms of agricultural and unskilled labor.

2. We further urge the prompt putting into effect of that provision of the immigration act of 1924, whereby the quotas, after July 1, 1927 at present determined by the number of foreign born of each nationality here in the year 1890, are to be adjusted so as to conform to the officially estimated number of persons now in the country of each national origin, either by birth or descent. We believe that this permanent basis for fixing the quotas, already provided for by law, is bound in principle and fair to all elements in the population. Only by this method can that large proportion of our population which is descended from the colonists and other early settlers, as well as the members of the newer immigration, have their proper racial representation in the

---

[1]*Congressional Record*, 69th Cong., 2nd Sess., January 18, 1927, p. 1904.

quotas. We believe that Congress wisely concluded that only by such a system of proportional representation in our future immigration could the racial status quo of the country be maintained or a reasonable degree of homogeneity secured. Without much basic homogeneity, we firmly believe, no civilization can have its best development.

E. G. Conklin, professor of biology, Princeton University; Ulric Dahlgreen, professor of biology, Princeton University; L. R. Cary, assistant professor of biology, Princeton University; E. G. Butler, Instructor of biology, Princeton University; Walter M. Rankin, professor of biology, Princeton University; C. F. W. McClure, professor of comparative anatomy, Princeton University; E. Newton Harvey, professor of physiology, Princeton University; William Starr Myers, professor of politics, Princeton University; Phillip M. Brown, professor of international law, Princeton University; Edwin S. Corwin, professor of politics, Princeton University; Robert de C. Ward, professor of climatology, Harvard University; E. M. East, professor of biology, Harvard University; J. N. Carver, professor of economics, Harvard University; Joseph Lee, social worker, author; Richard M. Bradley; Edward A. Ross, professor of sociology, University of Wisconsin; J. E. Irelin, professor of sociology, University of Wisconsin; William H. Kickhofer, professor of economics, University of Wisconsin; John R. Commons, professor of economics, University of Wisconsin; Henry R. Trumbower, professor of economics, University of Wisconsin; Madison Grant, president, New York Zoological Society; Henry Fairfield Osborn, president, American Museum of Natural History; Robert M. Yerkes, professor of psychology, Yale University; Ellsworth Huntington, professor of geography, Yale University; Irving Fisher, professor of political economy, Yale University; H. P. Fairchild, professor of sociology, New York University; John Johnston, professor of chemistry, Yale University; Eugene N. Foss, president, B. F. Sturtevant Co., ex-Governor of Massachusetts; Leon F. Whitney, field secretary American Eugenics Society; C. C. Little, president, University of Michigan; Charles B. Davenport; Roswell H. Johnson, president, American Eugenics Society; H. H. Laughlin, biological experiment station, Cold Spring Harbor, N.Y.

G. THE DISPLACED-PERSONS' CONTROVERSY REVIVES OLD FEARS, 1948

Shortly after the end of World War II, President Truman directed that in applying immigration quotas, preference should be given to displaced persons. Unfortunately, most of those needing new homes came from countries that had been granted very small quotas under the national-origins system, and by June 1948 America had taken in only

36,996 of the more than 600,000 refugees who still needed to relocate. In that same year a Displaced Persons' Act was introduced that was supposed to allow America to take its share of the refugees. Slightly over 200,000 were to come in without regard to the quota restrictions, but as the amended bill finally passed on June 2, 1948, it indirectly discriminated against many of the people who most needed the help. The provision to restrict eligibility to the DP's who entered Germany, Austria, or Italy on or before December 22, 1945, effectively excluded large numbers of Jews and Catholics who fled from Eastern Europe after this cutoff date. Furthermore, the act required that at least 40 percent of those admitted had to come from areas that had been annexed by a foreign power. These areas included the Baltic States and the former East Poland, whose population was largely Protestant or Greek Orthodox. Finally, 20 percent had to have been engaged in agriculture before the war, and this too worked against most of the Jews, who made up approximately one-fourth of the displaced persons in 1948. These were thinly disguised attempts to restrict the kind of refugees this country would admit, and until America finally eliminated these discriminatory provisions in 1950, only 129,000 refugees entered—a figure far below that accepted by England and Israel.

Although many of the arguments used against the DP's were reminiscent of the 1920's, they did not have the same broad support behind them. Both Dewey and Truman agreed that the 1948 act was anti-Catholic and anti-Jewish, and they called for liberalizing amendments. Likewise, the popular magazines and various religious and educational organizations campaigned for the generous admittance of the DP's. As expected, the patriotic organizations remained adamant in their opposition, but it was primarily Congress that proved to be the barrier. Influential senators like Pat McCarran, James Eastland, and Richard Russell resurrected the fears and arguments that had so effectively eliminated the New Immigrant in the 1920's.

1.   Senators Russell and Eastland Oppose the DP Act, 1948

For Senators Russell and Eastland, even the 1948 Act with its restrictive provisions was too liberal. In the following Congressional debate these two Senate powers spoke of the dangers of such a bill for their America.[1]

MR. EASTLAND. When the present immigration law was written in 1924, many great Americans said that was a turning point in the history of our

[1]*Congressional Record*, 80th Cong., 2nd Sess., June 2, 1948, pp. 6900–6905.

country. But I am sorry to say that program is being destroyed. It is being destroyed piecemeal, and this bill is the opening wedge in the movement to destroy it.

Mr. President, of the aliens who have entered our country in the past few years—the same kinds and same types as the persons who will be admitted to the United States under the provisions of the pending bill—of course many of them are good people, but the very opposite is true as to a majority of them.

Furthermore, with a tremendous housing shortage in the metropolitan areas of the United States, it should be pointed out that 95 percent of those aliens have located in the city of New York and in other metropolitan areas, where they fill up the slums, whereas only one percent have gone on the farms of the United States, where they are needed. . . .

MR. RUSSELL. I do not know whether the distinguished Senator from Mississippi proposes to go any further into his argument about the danger of the precedent which this proposed legislation will establish. That is the point which frightens me about the enactment of this legislation. No one can go to Europe without feeling great compassion for millions of people in and out of the displaced persons camps; but I have also had occasion in times past to visit in India and in China. The numbers of displaced persons in Europe today are a mere bagatelle as compared with the numbers of displaced persons in India . . .

I am quite sure that if we inaugurate this movement on the theory that we owe it to the persons who are displaced and have no home to which they may move, it can be said with equal truth, and with greater reason, that we should accept tens of thousands of Indians and Moslems from India; and of course there are millions of displaced persons in China . . . [and] we have already started the process of whittling away our immigration laws. Within the past few years we have changed them to grant a quota to immigrants from China. We have passed legislation granting a quota to immigrants from India. We have enacted legislation which permits a quota, I think, from Korea, and there is legislation now pending to allow to Siam a quota of immigrants. Of course all other countries will come along.

MR. EASTLAND. Mr. President, I thank the distinguished Senator from Georgia. I certainly agree with him that we are dealing here with dynamite. In my judgment we shall come back next year to face other bills of this character, designed to destroy our immigration system. When we do that, we change the whole form of American life and the ideals of the people of this country. We also change the viewpoint of the men who come to the Congress of the United States. . . .

The claim that immigration has strengthened the United States in the past and would strengthen it now is refuted by the fact that the immigrants we secure now settle usually in the metropolitan centers, and that they will not help America because of their alien philosophies, and their biological incompatibility with America's parent stocks.

Mr. President, recently I read a very learned discussion on immigration. The author, a very prominent American, traced radicalism, socialism, communism, our labor troubles, the subversive elements we have in the United States today to the immigrants we took from eastern Europe. We are intensifying that very situation now.

I have never in my life seen such a demonstration as that made by the thousands who came to Washington today to lobby against the Mundt-Nixon bill. Looking at those people, I should say that nine-tenths of the white persons in the group were from eastern Europe. There can be no doubt what their political philosophy is. If I correctly understand, they were here boldly and brazenly under the banner of the Communist Party. We are opening the floodgates. We are further intensifying our problem. We are taking America away from the people who built it and made it great. . . . Biological conquest is far more serious than military conquest. Biological conquest is final. There is no appeal from it. It is a condition which cannot be remedied. It is as irrevocable as death.

2. The American Legion and the DP's, 1949

For two years after its passage, Senator Pat McCarran's Subcommitttee on Amendments to the Displaced Persons Act held intermittent hearings on whether the 1948 Act should be liberalized. Much of the testimony was reminiscent of the Twenties and Thirties, since the same organizations came forth in opposition. In addition to Nevada's McCarran, Senators James Eastland of Mississippi, Herbert O'Conor of Maryland, Forrest C. Donnell of Missouri, and William Jenner of Indiana served on the Subcommittee. Not too surprisingly, they and Staff Director Richard Arens, who was later to do the same kind of work for the House Un-American Activities Committee, were sometimes guilty of leading the witnesses. The following testimony is from General John Thomas Taylor, the National Legislative Director of the American Legion. Like Eastland before him, General Taylor could effectively connect America's growing fear of Communists to the possibility of thousands of subversives using a modified Displaced Persons Act to infiltrate the country.[1]

GENERAL TAYLOR. The question of immigration is not a new one to the American Legion. We have been appearing before Congress now for over 25

---

[1]"Displaced Persons," *Hearings Before the Subcommittee on Amendments to the Displaced Persons Act of the Committee on the Judiciary,* United States Senate, 81st Cong., 1st Sess., September 30, 1949, pp. 460–466.

years on this very subject matter. We appeared and favored the National Origins Act. And in my opinion, the sole purpose now of enlarging on Public Law 774, the so-called Displaced Persons Act, is to totally destroy our immigration laws and immigration policies. It is to wreck it. The same people, I say that, although they may be under entirely new and different group names, but certainly the same individuals are the ones who favored the Displaced Persons Act, and who are now favoring an extension of it. As to why on the extension, I don't know, because the very language of the bill itself, instead of increasing the possible immigration some 100,000 or more, in my opinion, as a matter of fact, it opens up the doors for literally millions of displaced persons, and I suspect personally that is the intent, to destroy our present existing immigration laws. . . .

Particularly I am glad to see the way in which your committee and your subcommittee has considered this whole matter objectively. Certainly there has been no rancor or bias injected into the discussion or the hearings, and this committee has been looking upon this matter, as have we of the American Legion and other patriotic organizations, as to what is best for this country. . . .

In the beginning the idea was that so far as the displaced persons were concerned, they were to be people who had gathered or had gotten into camps who were the effects and the results of the war. But in these past years, thousands of people have taken advantage of that situation, not the real displaced person during the war at all. They have gotten in there because they want to come to America, and you know that, Mr. Chairman, just as well as I do. And it is not a question of a hundred thousand. We said at the hearings at that time that this would not be satisfactory, that this would lay the ground work and that they would come back, these organizations would come back to demand that this law be extended. If you start in extending it, it will be extended and extended. What we ought to do, what the American Legion says we should do, we should insist that the immigration laws themselves absolutely and positively be observed. . . .

We are pouring billions of dollars into the rehabilitation of all of these countries; must we also take all of the individuals who live in those countries that do not want to live there anymore, but want to come over here to America? Is it to cover every possible phase of human life and human existence? Are we to be motivated strictly by our hearts or are we to pay some attention to the present and the future of America? . . .

MR. ARENS. Do you have information respecting the number of refugees or displaced persons who were admitted into the United States during the war years or immediately after the Hitler regime started in Europe?

GENERAL TAYLOR. No, I have not; but the figures that I have heard are so shocking, because they run into the millions, I don't have the exact figures. I know this, that the FBI are asking or did ask for funds to investigate over

500,000 who are illegally in this country. Just think of that. Just think of it, the avenue that this opens admitting into this country the very people that are causing all of our trouble in this country at the present time. These subversive elements that this committee is investigating. I tell you it is a serious situation.

MR. ARENS. Do you or does the Legion have views to express respecting the information which has been revealed by this committee on the infiltration of subversives in the United States?

GENERAL TAYLOR. It is what we are fearful about, that very thing; that is just what I said. They are coming in and they have come in. The number that are under arrest for deportation now answers that question, and this is the avenue by which they come. You know it and I know it. That testimony certainly has been brought before this committee by expert witnesses. That is the position of the Legion. It should not be done. We should get back to the basic immigration laws, and if possible, strengthen them.

SENATOR O'CONOR. I might say, just in observation on your last comment, as to what has been brought before the attention of the committee with regard to subversives, I attempted to make that known.

GENERAL TAYLOR. You made a very fine speech on it. I congratuate you upon it. Splendid. That is our position. Thanks ever so much.

SELECTED READINGS

Dinnerstein, Leonard, and Jaher, Frederic Cople, *The Aliens*, Appleton-Century-Crofts, New York, 1970.
  This work contains a series of helpful essays on the various minorities and ethnic groups discussed in this reader.

Divine, Robert A., *American Immigration Policy*, 1924–1952, Yale University Press, New Haven, 1957.
  In this excellent treatment of our immigration legislation, Divine covers the movements to restrict immigrants from Europe, Asia, and Latin America.

Gossett, Thomas F., *Race; the History of an Idea in America*, Schocken Books, New York, 1965.
  A comprehensive introduction to the race thinkers of America.

Handlin, Oscar, *The Uprooted*, Little, Brown and Company, Boston, 1951.
  Using a sociological approach, this prominent immigration historian describes the impact of America on the immigrant.

Higham, John, *Strangers in the Land; Patterns of American Nativism, 1860–1925*, Rutgers University Press, New Brunswick, New Jersey, 1955.
   The definitive study of the American nativist developments that culminated in the immigration restriction legislation of the 1920's.

Hofstadter, Richard, *The Paranoid Style in American Politics*, Alfred A. Knopf, New York, 1965.
   An excellent examination of the conspiratorial mind that so often has seen disaster lurking in the "un-American" elements of society.

Steinfield, Melvin, *Cracks in the Melting Pot*, Glencoe Press, Beverly Hills, 1970.
   A series of largely secondary sources that effectively comment on racism and discrimination in American history.